BARRIERS TO RECONCILIATION

Case Studies on Iraq and the Palestine-Israel Conflict

Edited by

Jacqueline S. Ismael
William W. Haddad

University Press of America,® Inc.
Lanham · Boulder · New York · Toronto · Oxford

Copyright © 2007 by
University Press of America,® Inc.
4501 Forbes Boulevard
Suite 200
Lanham, Maryland 20706
UPA Acquisitions Department (301) 459-3366

PO Box 317
Oxford
OX2 9RU, UK

Library of Congress Control Number: 2006929009
ISBN-13: 978-0-7618-3554-7 (paperback : alk. paper)
ISBN-10: 0-7618-3554-7 (paperback : alk. paper)

CONTENTS

ACKNOWLEDGEMENTS

The Editors would like to thank the International Centre for Contemporary Middle Eastern Studies of the Eastern Mediterranean University in Northern Cyprus for hosting the conference on conflict settlement in the Middle East, 29 April-1May 2004. The majority of the articles in this collection were presented there and subsequently revised and updated for publication. Two of the chapters, by Haifa Zangana and Dahr Jamail, were presented as scholarly papers at the Conference of the International Association of Contemporary Iraqi Studies, held at the East London University, 1 and 2 September 2005.

The Editors, also, would like to thank Maria Hernandez-Figueroa, Robert D. Miller and Jill D. Call for their valuable editorial assistance in the preparation of this manuscript.

INTRODUCTION

෨෬

Jacqueline S. Ismael

The project on *Barriers to Reconciliation* emanated out of a conference in April 2004 on patterns of conflict settlement and political
reconstruction in the Middle East organized by the International Centre for
Contemporary Middle Eastern Studies and held at the Eastern Mediterranean University, Cyprus. It became painfully apparent during the conference proceedings that Palestine looms like a dark cloud over the prolific
discourse on conflict resolution and settlement; and that the seedbed for
another intractable conflict was being laid in Iraq. The case studies
presented here represent the individual efforts of scholars to address issues
underlying conflict in Iraq and Palestine. These issues constitute structural
barriers to peace building and relate fundamentally to issues of social
justice. However, social justice issues have largely been set aside in Iraq
and Palestine.

Reconciliation is focused on because it relates directly to problems of
social justice, an issue generally passed over or trivialized as sentimentalist
and idealist in mainstream discourse on conflict resolution. However, social
justice was placed on the agenda of reconciliation discourse by the
prominence of South Africa's Truth and Reconciliation Commission, and
is reflected in a burgeoning scholarly literature on it. To clarify the distinct
nature of reconciliation from conflict resolution and settlement, Nadim
Rouhana has provided a useful taxonomy:

Table 1:   Conflict Settlement, Conflict Resolution, and Reconciliation:
            Similarities and Differences

	Conflict Settlement	Conflict Resolution	Reconciliation
Goals	Formal agreement	Principled compromise	Historic reconciliation
Parties	Governments	Elites	Societies
Nature of peace	Irrelevant	Sustainable	Genuine; no further claims
Future relations desired	Abiding by agreements	Working relations	Good relations
Important of mutual acceptance	Not important	Important	Essential
Terms of reference	Power relations	Basic human needs	Justice
Truth about wrongdoing	Ignored	Not central	Should be commonly acknowledged
Historical responsibility	Ignored	Not central	Should be acknowledged and faced
Social and political restructuring	Not required	Substantial restructuring	Major restructuring

Source: Nadim N. Rouhana, "Group Identity and Power Asymmetry in Reconciliation Processes: The Israeli-Palestinian Case," *Peace and Conflict: Journal of Peace Psychology*, 10(1) 2004, 34.

As the table suggests, peace-making may be conceived of in terms of three distinct categories of process: conflict settlement, conflict resolution and reconciliation. Conflict settlement is the most uncomplicated of these in that its goal is simply termination of conflict based on imposition of a peace agreement that usually favors the interests of the stronger party to the conflict. Based on a realist conception of power politics, conflict settlement appears more reflective of international relations throughout most of the twentieth century and the interstate conflicts that dominated global politics.

The process of conflict resolution is both more complex and more indicative of peacemaking processes in the era of globalization, and the intrastate conflicts that are its primary focus—peace processes that Ronnie Lipschutz has characterized as neo-liberal because their "primary purpose is to foster economic liberalization and growth in the hope that private profits generated through low wages and social costs, as well as international competition, will also result in growth in the public national product and a range of earning opportunities for those with little else to offer but their labour."[1] Thus, conflict resolution encompasses conflict management processes that move beyond conflict settlement to seek a sustainable peace based on viable working relations between the elites of conflicting parties. Charles-Philippe David's representation of the realist approach to peace building effectively captures the nature of conflict resolution in the era of globalization:

> Conflict management does not mean reconstruction; it means negotiation with a view to suspending or putting an end to hostilities rather than resolving conflicts. Peace is achieved not by bringing the parties responsible for the war to justice, but rather by negotiating security compromises with them that let them keep their grip on power.[2]

Reconciliation is by far the more complex and multi-faceted of the three categories of peace-making for it seeks to construct "a kind of relationship between the parties that is founded on mutual legitimacy."[3] Synthesizing the literature on reconciliation, Rouhana proposed that reconciliation could be defined "as a process that brings about a genuine end to the existential conflict between the parties and transforms the nature of the relationship between the societies through a course of action that is intertwined with psychological, social, and political changes."[4] As represented in the taxonomy proposed by Rouhana, it moves beyond conflict resolution in three major respects—the parties are not only elites but entire societies; mutual legitimacy is not only political but also social; justice is not only political (in terms of democratization) and economic (in terms of distributive) but also social (in terms of openly confronting issues of wrongdoing and historical responsibility).

In the aftermath of the twentieth century, when the dark side of civilization merged with technological progress to culminate in history's bloodiest century, violence may well seem like the normal state within and between societies, and reconciliation idealistic and utopian. However, if we consider society in terms of the exciting scientific developments around self-organizing systems and the philosophical debates these developments entail, we should consider peace as the equilibrium state, punctuated by periods of violent disequilibrium, with reconciliation as the process that facilitates transition to equilibrium.[5]

While systems theory is not new to social science and was a dominant paradigm for a few decades in the last half of the twentieth century, it was seriously compromised by the positivist trappings in which it was wrapped. However, emerging perspectives on the dynamics of complex systems, and a new mathematical understanding of self-organization, provide an analytic framework for transcending the biological and historical determinism of twentieth century paradigms by taking a design perspective on social dynamics and by treating human agency as conscious and purposeful, with the potential for independent impact on the dynamics of change that define the architecture of a complex system.[6] Human beings are primarily (though perhaps not exclusively) social animals, and reconciliation is an inherent characteristic of sociability. In other words, the evolution of the human being from primitive cave dweller to modern individual has been coterminous with the evolution of human society from simple self-organizing units of kith and kin to complex self-governing units of civilization, and with the complexification of patterns of reconciliation. If reconciliation is a normal process in evolutionary development, it should emerge spontaneously in communities fraught with sustained violence—perhaps first in localized niches (as evidenced by localized peace groups) that grow more robust as violence weakens the social fabric of society, unless structural barriers to reconciliation prevent this. If this is right, the best thing to do is allow the process to emerge, removing all externally imposed systems of control and putting in place mechanisms that facilitate communication and interaction.

Barriers to reconciliation in Iraq and Palestine are examined in this context. Part I focuses on Iraq, where the U.S. military occupation is laying the groundwork for intractable social divisions. The groundwork itself, in other words, presents the major barrier to reconciliation. The first chapter, "Democratization by Occupation" by Tareq Ismael, introduces this by examining U.S. policy in Iraq in terms of principles, plans and actions. The logic of the policy is found in American militarism. Ismael argues that the neo-conservatives in control of the While House and Pentagon were driven by ideology and jingoistic myths of America's Manifest Destiny, which is a popular nineteenth-century doctrine propagating American expansionism. From the outset, their aim was the de-institutionalization of Iraqi society in order to build a "utopian free market" for American transnationals that would operate securely according to the laws introduced by the occupation, and protected by the American armed forces stationed in military bases in Iraq. The objectives of U.S. policy de-institutionalization of Iraqi society and institutionalization of a satellite economy proceeded through plans and actions from occupation through pseudo-democratization. True to the traditional colonial policy of divide and conquer in pursuing its policies, the U.S. created winners and losers among Iraq's different ethno-cultural and sectarian groups, thus laying the groundwork in the framework of a democratic façade and in effect institutionalizing the basis for intractable social conflict.

The military occupation of Iraq is the tip of the colonization iceberg. The civil corollary to military occupation is reflected in the next two chapters. "Colonial Feminists from Washington to Baghdad: "Women for a Free Iraq" as a Case Study" by Haifa Zangana examines the role of U.S.-funded Non-Governmental Organizations (NGOs) in the American occupation of Iraq. In the few months preceding and following the occupation, several U.S.-funded Iraqi women's NGOs were established in Washington. Their hastily staged birth was deemed necessary to engage "important voices which were missing from the debate—those of Iraqi women with personal experience of Saddam Hussein's oppression."[7] It was a last minute rush to provide the much needed moral legitimacy to the immoral invasion. Zangana argues that these NGOs are an important part of the U.S. military occupation and an arm of the U.S. government in Iraq representing its colonial policy rather than the interests of the Iraqi people, women in particular. They were instrumental in rallying support for the invasion and occupation of Iraq, and continue to do so. Furthermore, they have played a damaging role affecting the much needed work by genuine independent women's organizations. Like the occupiers, they underestimated the Iraqi people's feelings against occupation. They confused the need to get rid of a tyrannical regime with imposing a new colonial order. Their "women's rights" claims are often seen by Iraqi women as the second supply-line of U.S. colonial policy in Iraq. At its best it is considered "cosmetic" as it fails to address the priorities of Iraqi women under occupation. Through its substantial financial support for occupation friendly NGOs, the U.S. is laying the groundwork for the polarization of the women's movement in Iraq into politically influential and economically well healed pro-occupation NGOs and politically marginalized financially starved grassroots NGOs.

The brutal nature of the military occupation is dramatically revealed in Dahr Jamail's chapter, "Iraqi Hospitals Ailing under Occupation." Prior to the 1991 Gulf War, Iraq's health care delivery system ranked among the most advanced in the Middle East, providing comprehensive publicly-funded health care to all citizens. The 1991 war and twelve years of sanctions severely diminished its functioning. The occupation appears to be systematically dismantling what is left. Early in 2004, before the study reported here, Geert Van Moorter, a Belgian M.D., conducted a fact-finding mission to Iraq where he surveyed hospitals, clinics, and pharmacies. Van Moorter concluded: "Nowhere had any new medical material arrived since the end of the war. The medical material, already outdated, broken down or malfunctioning after twelve years of embargo, had further deteriorated over the past year."[8] The findings reported in Dahr Jamail's chapter suggest that Van Moorter's findings have been compounded with the continued deterioration of equipment, supplies, and staffing, further complicated by an astronomical increase in patients due to the violent nature of the occupation of Iraq.

His chapter documents the desperate supply shortages facing hospitals, the disastrous effect that the lack of basic services like water and electricity have on hospitals and the disruption of medical services at Iraqi hospitals by U.S. military forces. This report further provides an overview of the situation afflicting the hospitals in Iraq in order to highlight the destruction of Iraq's publicly funded universal healthcare system. Reconstruction efforts by U.S. firms have patently failed, while Iraqi contractors are not allowed to do the work.

The destruction of Iraq's publicly-funded system may well presage the development of a U.S. model of a "free trade globalized system" in health care.

"Reconstructing Civil Society and Citizenship in Iraq" by Jacqueline Ismael takes a broad historical and theoretical perspective on the role and nature of civil society to examine the relationship between state and civil society in modern Iraq. The term "civil society" has origins in both liberal and Marxist theory. It is a corollary concept to the notion of the democratic state as an entity that exercises a monopoly of force and is viewed as legitimate. This is contrasted with the notion of an uncivil state as an entity that has a monopoly on the use of force but not the authority to legitimately exercise that power. The impact of the uncivil state on civil society, reflected in Baathist rule in Iraq, relates to the deconstruction of a democratic political culture. By the time of the Anglo-American invasion of Iraq in March 2003, Iraqis had already endured the ruthless brutality of the Saddam regime for thirty five years and the callous brutality of sanctions for thirteen years. Rather than invading a society in disarray, what the occupying forces found was a population with nothing to lose and well organized in underground civil society formations—that is, associations driven from the public sector under the Saddam regime and entrenched in the private sector under sanctions as a buffer against both the regime and sanctions in the struggle of everyday life. Their resistance to the U.S. effort to reconstruct citizenship and civil society on an American model has been met with the unleashing of an army of American funded NGOs in Iraq as missionaries of the American model, as reflected in Haifa Zangana's chapter, and with the effort to delegitimize indigenous Iraqi political culture in the framing of the constitution.

The U.S. role as chief architect in the construction of barriers to reconciliation in Iraq has been addressed in the first four chapters in this part. The final chapter, "Nation Building or Culture War? America's Credentials as an Honest Broker in the Middle East" by Fuad Shaban, focuses attention on the question of why the U.S. has assumed such a role. America's involvement inthe affairs of theArab World has intensified during the past fifty years. However, while the initial U. S. policy towards the Middle East was mainly concerned with support for Israel and maintaining America's strategic and economicinterests,it has become fashionable in the official and public corridors of power in the U.S. during the last two decades to talk of 'nation building' and 'regime change'. These tasks are now associated with America's mission to spread democracy and freedom in the 'Larger Middle East'. Forty million dollars have been allocated as an initial amount for this noble undertaking.This program of spreading democracy and freedom throughout the Middle East has also been presented especially after 11 September as a clash between two opposing ideologies. And with the rise to power in the U. S. of a self-confessed right-wing religiously-inclined administration, this culture war takes on new dimensions. The open alliance between the administration and the Neo-Conservative camp has also added fuel toa conflict already set along cultural lines. One more important factor which has come onto play in the making of America's policy in the Middle East is the support given to Bush's election campaigns by the Christian Right. Christian Right quarters, with their open pronouncements against Islam and Muslims, are now expecting payback in the form of a stronger stand against a perceived collective Islamic enemy. Officials in the present administration have been quoted as stating that the conflict is with the 'Medrassa' and the 'clerics' in the Islamic World. A 'culture war' or 'war of ideas' has been declared. In the context of this war of ideas, for example, scores of missionaries have been dispatched to Iraq and Afghanistan to help in the process of the rebuilding of minds.

While the previous chapters in this section all focus on U.S. policy under the presidency of the second Bush in the construction of barriers to reconciliation, this administration's policy by no means represents an anomaly in U.S. policy toward Iraq. To the contrary, it represents a logical extension of past practice, as suggested in the final article in this section, "Iraq, the United States, and International Law: Beyond the Sanctions" by Richard Falk. Addressing the rhetorical question of "what accounts for the obsessiveness of American policy toward Iraq over the course of more than a decade?", Falk places the policy of Bush (II) in the context of U.S. policy under previous administrations. Since the 1991 ceasefire that ended the Gulf war, Falk maintains, U.S. policy toward Iraq has violated the most basic precepts of international law, including the UN Charter, and the fundamental economic and social rights of the Iraqi people. Arguing that the criminality of a head of state or of official policies pursued does not impair the sovereignty of that state, nor provide grounds for suspending the application of international law, Falk examines the central role the U.S. played in perpetuating the maintenance of punitive sanctions on Iraq, especially in the face of mounting evidence of their humanitarian toll on the Iraqi population and their failure to weaken the Saddam Hussein regime. This is compared to the central role of U.S. policy in the post-WWII Germany and Japan. In contrast to its role in fostering post-war reconstruction in Germany and Japan, the U.S. role in the Security Council has consistently served as a barrier to the reconciliation of the Iraqi state with the international community.

Part II focuses on Palestine where conflict between Arabs and Israelis, sustained for more than seven decades, seems innate and intractable. To the contrary, the perspective on barriers to reconciliation advanced here suggests that structural barriers have prevented the advancement of reconciliation niches that spontaneously emerge in the face of violent conflict as people struggle to make sense of their lives and get on with them in the face of continued violence. From this perspective, the papers in Part II examine the nature of the barriers as they are manifested in the twenty-fist century. The first chapter in this section, "The Israeli Alliance with Christian Zionists" by Norton Mezvinsky, picks up the same theme Part I closed on, arguing that it is not without cause that Prime Minister Sharon, others in the Israeli government, and numerous Israeli political commentators have termed Christian Zionists Israel's best friends and allies.

From the late 1970s on, evangelical Christian Zionism has increasingly affected the Arab-Israeli conflict and has been a barrier to peaceful resolution. Although evangelical Christian Zionists exist in many countries, they are most prominent in the United States and have impeded the possibility that the United States would move toward a more even-handed approach to the Palestinian-Israeli problem. Demonstrating that they are skillful in manipulating opinion, evangelical Christian Zionist leaders have significantly influenced United States presidents, administration officials, and members of Congress to back and support almost blindly Israeli governmental positions and policies. Indeed, a goodly number of members of Congress, administration officials, and President George W. Bush believe in the theological formulations and ideology of evangelical Christian Zionism.

Evangelical Christian Zionism postulates that prior to the Second Coming of Jesus Christ and the Messianic Age, Jews must be in total control of the "Holy Land," i.e. present day Israel or historic Palestine. (Some Christian Zionist spokespeople maintain that the actual boundaries of the biblically promised "Holy Land" far exceed the present area of the state of Israel and incorporate all of some and major parts of other current Arab nation-states.) Christian Zionism also postulates that prior to the Second Coming of Jesus Christ the great majority of Jews and others will follow the Anti-Christ and ultimately be destroyed in an Armageddon situation, which will become the "mother of all Holocausts." A remnant of the world's population composed of the true followers of Jesus Christ, including 144,000 Jews, will be raptured in the air during the seven-year Armageddon period and will return with Jesus to the new kingdom thereafter. All other Jews will be killed. (A minimum of Christian Zionist leaders believe that more than 144,000 Jews will be saved from destruction.) Christian Zionists and Israeli Jews, in other words, are strange bedfellows, and their alliance constitutes a major barrier to reconciliation.

The next two chapters (seven and eight) focus on two diametrically opposite approaches to the solution of the Palestinian-Israeli conflict—the two-state strategy versus a one-state proposal. Taking the two-state solution as the point of departure, "On the Trail of the Palestine State" by John Strawson examines what is meant by the creation of a Palestinian state. Taking its starting point from the Oslo agreements it plots the manner in which apparently recognized Palestinian legal rights were whittled away during the negotiations. Despite the condemnation of Israeli settlements as illegal by the United Nations Security Council and the International Court of Justice, it became a given through Oslo's last days after the Camp David talks that most would in fact become permanent. When Ariel Sharon and George Bush announced the disengagement plan four years later, settlements had become "major Israeli civilian population centers." This forms an essential background to understanding the trajectory of a roadmap which aimed at creating a Palestinian state through three phases by the end of 2005. The plan, however, is based on re-modeling Palestinian institutions and testing their behavior rather than on any recognition of the right to self-determination. The projected Palestinian state is thus conditional. Not only will the security needs to Israel dictate its shrinking borders, but the powers of institutions will be subject to severe limits including having no control of those borders. What is offered, it appears, is a weak state in about fifteen to twenty percent of historic Palestine. International law which appears formally to support Palestinian claims is revealed as a system of indeterminate norms and doctrines that is malleable in the hands of the powerful negotiating position of Israel, backed by the United States. The international community seems intent on creating a state in name only in an attempt to end the Palestinian-Israeli conflict. However, the idea of a state as representing the sovereignty of a people seems about to be emptied of its content in the Palestinian case. Reconciliation, however, is unlikely to be lasting if is based on injustice.

In sharp contrast to the two-state solution, "Greater Israel as an Undemocratic State" by Glenn E. Perry proposes a one-state approach. The essence of the Palestinian cause has always been a struggle against violations of democratic principles, even if the community violating Palestinian rights has governed itself democratically. Such was the establishment of a Jewish state in Palestine in 1948 in disregard of the rights of the majority of the population. Perry argues further that since 1967, the Jewish state has in fact incorporated the rest of the country (the West Bank and Gaza Strip) into its territory, the absence of any official declaration of annexation (aside from Jerusalem) notwithstanding. The proper approach to solving the problem is not to call for a Bantustan for the

Palestinians in fifteen to twenty percent of their country (which would in fact have to be under an authoritarian client regime acting as Israel's "enforcer") but rather to start a process of demanding democratic rights, that is the transformation of Greater Israel from a *Herrenvolk* democracy into a true democracy in which both peoples can share the whole country. The establishment of Jewish settlements in the territories and the unwillingness to give up all the territory acquired in 1967 makes the achievement of minimal Palestinian demands through partition unrealistic (now hard-line Israelis are calling for a truncated Palestinian state as a solution to their "demographic problem"), and thus the Israelis unwittingly have set the stage for the emergence of a movement of Palestinians and moderate Jews for a one-state democratic solution as in South Africa.

Perry maintains that not only is the democratization of Greater Israel the best solution but that it also is a viable one. Admittedly, the absence of a common identity and the recent heritage of conflict between the two peoples will pose problems for a democratic state. But the situation in some important ways is more favorable that it was in South Africa, where the democratic solution has so far succeeded, for this would emerge slowly in Greater Israel. And unlike in the South African case, the present dominant ethnic group in Greater Israel would not constitute a small minority, while the Palestinian majority, when or if it emerges, would not be monolithic. Perry draws on various theorists to show that this situation is particularly suitable for democratization. Greater Israel provides a good example of what Robert Dahl calls a favorable "path to polyarchy" in that contestation (as in South Africa) within one group has preceded inclusiveness (that is, the extension of the of rights to the whole population). The Israeli system of proportional representation and the resulting multiparty system can facilitate democratization, as it will guarantee that the present dominant group will not face the kind of exaggerated majorities that single-member elections tend to produce.

Various guarantees to the different communities (what Arendt Lijphart calls "consociational democracy") that deviate from the principle of majoritarian rule and thus to some extent from classical concepts of democracy can facilitate the transition in this case. Such arrangements can be expected to emerge as what may by then be a Jewish minority demand them as protection from the perceived specter of the tyranny of a Palestinian majority. Consociational devices, as Lijphart tells us, include the establishment of grand coalitions, mutual vetoes, proportionality, and some sort of segmental autonomy and federalism. But Perry suggests some possibilities, the exact nature of these arrangements will have to be left for a time when it becomes generally obvious that the partition of Greater Israel is unviable and undesirable and when the move for democratization gains momentum.

Whatever their merits and shortcomings, alternative approaches to peace have been side-lined by the construction of a physical barrier to reconciliation. The implications of this are examined by Barry Collins in "Locating Sovereignty in International Law: Reflections on the Construction of a Wall in Palestine." Every legal decision involves an exploration of the relation between law and politics. However, the Advisory Opinion issued by the International Court of Justice (ICJ) on the "Legal Consequences of the Construction of a Wall in Occupied Palestinian Territory" of 9 July 2004 is notable for its explicit examination of this terrain. The decision of the ICJ was a significant intervention into the politics of the Middle East; one which delivered a powerful indictment of Israel's policies in the West Bank into the field of international law. The Advisory Opinion, although not a 'binding' judgment of the ICJ, confirmed the illegality of the construction of the Israeli wall in international law by a majority of fourteen votes to one. It further declared that Israel was under an obligation to cease construction of the wall, to dismantle those parts of the wall already constructed, to make reparation for all damage caused by its construction and (by a majority of thirteen votes to two) advised that states not recognize the "illegal situation" resulting from the wall's construction.

Collins's chapter does not focus on the legality or political consequences of the construction of the wall itself, nor does it seek to assess the issues of international humanitarian law or self determination discussed in the Advisory Opinion. Instead, the intention is to articulate some of the questions concerning the relationship between the legal and the political that are thrown together by the case. In particular, the chapter examines the way in which much of the 'international community', in particular most Western states, while expressing opposition to the construction of the wall, also opposed the intervention of the ICJ in such a 'political' matter. In their written submissions to the ICJ, many states argued that the political nature of the question before the ICJ meant either that the Court could not or should not issue an Advisory Opinion. In doing so, these written submissions insisted on a rigid distinction between law and politics that is at odds both with the experience of international law and with the settled jurisprudence of the Court. This chapter will explore some of the theoretical assumptions that underlie such claims, and ask: What can the insistence on the distinctness of international law from the field of politics tell us about notions of sovereignty in an international legal order?

"Enemies of Peace—the Tripartite American Alliance to Prevent a Resolution to the Palestine-Israel Conflict" by William W. Haddad provides an overview of the barriers to reconciliation in the Palestinian-Israeli conflict, arguing that the movement to stop a negotiated settlement between Israelis and Palestinians has three major prongs—American imperialists, Christian fundamentalists, and Neoconservative ideologues. While these themes were scrutinized individually in earlier chapters in both Parts I and II, Haddad's chapter relates them to each other to demonstrate how they came together in the framework of U.S. policy to sideline efforts at peace in the Middle East in the twenty-first century. The Project for a New American Century (PNAC) is focused on to examine the first prong, American imperialism. American imperialists emerge from the alliance of big business with the military establishment to form the military-industrial alliance President Eisenhower cautioned Americans about in his 1960 farewell address. American imperialists favor the pacification, by force if necessary, of any challenge to American imperial dominance in world affairs in general, and the imposition of a pax Americana in the Middle East in particular. They believe in the efficacy of American military power, covet control of Middle East oil, and view Israel as a bastion of capitalist democracy in the Middle East.

The second leg of the troika is the Christian Zionists. They argue that a close relationship between Israel, the world's Jews, and Christian Zionists is necessary for the fulfillment of biblical prophecy, and have joined forces with right-wing Israeli Zionists to oppose any fetters on Israeli expansion. With the Likud Party in power in Israel and the Bush administration in the White House, fundamentalist Christian and Jewish versions of right-wing Zionism have in effect seized the reigns of power to pursue their common objective of Israeli expansion.

The third leg of the troika, neoconservative ideologues, represents an extreme right-wing component of the American imperialist camp. They can be distinguished from them by their overzealous promotion of Israeli expansion and invasion/occupation of Iraq. Their effective control of foreign policy in the Bush administration renders them a distinct force in the obstruction of peace in the Middle East.

The closing chapter, "Imagining Peace in the Middle East" by Kamel Abu Jaber, closes the volume with an essay by one of the region's most respected elder statesman and scholar. The battle for the heart and soul of the Middle East has been raging since the dawn of history. Its strategic geographic location between Asia, Africa, and Europe first caused it to be coveted by conquerors and empire builders. Now, with the discovery of oil which has become the life line of modern societies, particularly the most industrialized, its control has become a matter of life and death for the powerful. The confrontation between East and West or rather Islam and the West, continues to deepen and widen and became more violent with the West's espousal of Zionism as a humanitarian and biblical fig leaf for its continued intrusion and penetration. Globalization, while contributing much to modernization, nevertheless rages on, trying to impose Western values on the traditional "God-centered" Middle Eastern societies. While external challenges and manipulation are not the only factors fuelling underdevelopment, the question should be raised as to whether the West truly wants the Middle East area to stabilize. If it does, why has it not happened over the past two centuries since the last Western incursion that commenced with the Napoleonic invasion?

In fact, internal factors including the persistence of tyrannical authoritarian regimes; fatalism; the inability of the various rigid mosaic millets to compromise; and the traditional "God centered," other directedness of Middle Eastern societies are perhaps as important as barriers to reconciliation as the external factors. The combination of internal and external factors also explains the fierce resistance to change giving the traditional groups the needed ammunition to equate modernity with the feared Westernization. This combination no doubt explains, at least in part, the continued economic stagnation, the uneven development and the inability to escape the web of the politics and economics of despair.

Notes

1.   Ronnie D. Lipschutz, "Beyond the Neoliberal Peace: From Conflict Resolution to Social Reconciliation." *Social Justice* (Winter 1998), V. 25, No. 4, p. 4 of 12.
2.   Charles-Philippe David, "Alice in Wonderland Meets Frankenstein: Constructivism, Realism and Peacebuilding in Bosnia," *Contemporary Security Policy*, Vol. 22, No. 1 (April 2001), p. 4.
3.   Rouhana, p. 35.
4.   Rouhana, p. 35.
5.   For example, Steven Johnson, *Emergence: The Connected Lives of Ants, Brains, Cities, and Software* (New York: Simon and Schuster, 2001); Steven Strogatz, *Sync: How Order Emerges from Chaos in the Universe, Nature,*

and Daily Life (New York: TheiaBooks, 2003); Philip Ball, *Critical Mass: How One Thing Leads to Another* (New York: Farrar, Straus and Giroux, 2004).

6. Jenann Ismael, *The Situated Self* (Oxford University Press, 2006).
7. http://www.defenddemocracy.org/about_FDD/about_FDD_show.htm?doc_id=257042&attrib_id=7615
8. Dr. Greet Van Moorter, M.D., "One Year After the Fall of Baghdad: How Healthy is Iraq?," *Medical Aid for the Third World*, 28 April 2004.

PART I

Iraq

1

DEMOCRATIZATION BY OCCUPATION: THE IRAQI QUANDARY

℘ℭ℞

Tareq Y. Ismael

E ven those who once believed that the invasion of Iraq was a lesser evil carried out in pursuit of a greater good are increasingly identifying the American invasion and occupation of Iraq as a colonial exercise to seize its oil wealth within a larger agenda. A cursory scan of Iraq's newspapers reflects that most Iraqis believe that an army capable of launching a "shock and awe" invasion also possesses the capacity to prevent widespread looting and the destruction of civilization's irreplaceable archeological and historical treasures. In January 2003, an American delegation of scholars, museum directors, art collectors, and antiquities dealers met with officials at the Pentagon to specifically warn that Baghdad's National Museum was the single most important site in the country. McGuire Gibson, from the Oriental Institute of the University of Chicago, said that he thought he was given assurances that sites and museums would be protected. Gibson and his colleagues sent several e-mail reminders to military officers in the weeks before the war began. On 24 January 2003, about sixty collectors and dealers from New York organized themselves into a new group called the American Council for Cultural

Policy, and met with the Bush Administration and Pentagon officials to argue for opening up private trade in Iraqi artifacts. Moreover, on 26 March 2003, the Pentagon's Office of Reconstruction and Humanitarian Assistance (ORHA), headed by retired Lieutenant General, Jay Garner sent a five-page memo on sixteen institutions that merited security to prevent further damage, destruction or pilferage of records and assets to all senior U.S. commanders. First on the list was the Iraqi Central Bank, which is now a ruin; second was the Museum of Antiquities which was wasted; sixteenth was the Oil Ministry, the only place that U.S. forces actually defended. John Curtis, the British Museum authority on many Iraqi archaeological sites, reported in December 2004 that he saw "cracks and gaps where somebody had tried to gouge out the decorated bricks forming the famous dragons of the 'Ishtar Gate' and a 2,600-year-old brick pavement crushed by military vehicles." Other observers say that the dust stirred up by U.S. helicopters had sandblasted the fragile brick façade of the palace of Nebuchadnezzar II, king of Babylon from 605 to 562 BC. Archaeologist Zainab Bahrani reports, that "Between May and August 2004, the wall of the Temple of Nabu and the roof of the Temple of Ninmah, both of the sixth century B.C., collapsed as a result of the movement of helicopters. Heavy machines and vehicles were parked nearby, on the remains of a Greek theater that had survived since the era of Alexander of Macedon." At a conference on art crimes held in London, a year after the looting disaster in 3-4 April 2003, Curtis reported that at least half of the forty most important stolen objects had not been retrieved. Of the 15,000 looted articles from the Antiquity Museum, 8000 had yet to be traced. Its entire collection of 5,800 cylinder seals and clay tablets, many containing cuneiform writing and other inscriptions, some of which go back to the earliest discoveries of writing itself, was stolen. As a result of an amnesty for looters, about 4,000 of the artifacts have been recovered, and over a thousand have been confiscated in the United States. Curtis noted that random checks of Western soldiers leaving Iraq had led to the discovery of some illegally acquired ancient objects. Customs agents in the U.S. reported that they found some precious artifacts. Officials in Jordan have impounded about 2,000 pieces smuggled from Iraq; in France, 500 pieces have been recovered; in Italy, 300; in Syria, 300; and in Switzerland, 250 have been seized. Lesser numbers have been seized in Kuwait, Saudi Arabia, Iran, and Turkey. But none of these objects has as yet been sent back to Baghdad. In the months before the invasion, when talking about Iraqi oil was taboo, George Bush and his senior officials spoke of preserving Iraq's "patrimony." At that time, and now, patrimony for Mr. Bush apparently meant Iraqi oil.[1]

The argument of this article, simply put, is that institutionalized American militarism, combined with a sinister Manichaen vision of the neo-conservative faction has pursued an agenda of world dominance and support of Israel by the dual instruments of unrivaled military power, and the physical control of oil as a geostrategic asset to subdue or contain the emerging economic challengers, particularly China, whose energy needs are accelerating. Militarism needs war for its self-preservation. The discourse of the neo-conservative group places the U.S. on the side of "good," being in a state of war against "evil," which constitutes a necessary condition for pre-eminence. Pre-eminence, in turn, can be maintained globally if, particularly economic challenges are permanently controlled. Hence, physical control of the access to oil transforms the situation of simple preeminence, to global dominance. Iraq comes into the equation by having the second largest oil reserves in the world after Saudi Arabia, which is already a satellite in U.S. policy orbits.

Institutionalized Militarism and the
Neo-Conservatives

The roots of American militarism may arguably be traced back to the mine-explosion that sank the American battleship, U.S.S. Maine, in Havana in 1898. The Assistant Secretary of the Navy, Theodore Roosevelt exploited the event for war propaganda against Spain, and the news media began a series of bellicose articles that seized the American people.[2] By February 1909, the sixteen first-class battleships that constituted the U.S. navy returned home after the longest cruise in naval history, covering forty-five thousand miles around the world in an ostentatious display of power.[3] While Elihu Root is known to have forced the Platt Agreement on Cuba, and took it for granted that strong states are bound to exercise some rights over weak states he, also, re-organized the War Department, and created the "general staff" of senior officers of the standing army, derived from the European militaristic vision of imperialism.[4] In parallel, Woodrow Wilson, who strongly believed that the U.S. had an obligation to spread its principles and way of democracy to the rest of the world, laid the intellectual foundation for today's American "global mission" to democratize the world. Wilson, also, provided the grounding for the rhetoric of humanitarian military intervention and supplied the articles for contemporary ideologists who rationalize American imperial power in terms of the exporting of human rights and democracy,[5] which, on many occasions, has been the basis of the millenarian rhetoric of Mr. Bush.

Although the military is a historically important institution of the modern nation-state, it is different from militarism, as a policy, which places the institutional preservation of the armed forces ahead of national security or commitment to the integrity of governmental structure.[6] One indicator of militarism is the emergence of a professional army class that glorifies its ideals, a phenomenon that gained visibility after the defeat in the Vietnam War. On the political front, the leaders of a newly ascendant far-right (Reagan and Bush Senior in the 1980s) concluded that the main lesson from Vietnam was to relocate foreign policy to the realm of national security management, which could then operate without media prying, the oversight of Congress or the involvement of the public. This ultimately bred a class of professional militarists; both uniformed and civilian that visibly filled the senior level of the Executive, and operated in secrecy. Civilian militarists tend to be ideology-prone and display a ruthless warrior-culture, perhaps in compensation for their lack of genuine combat experience. This was particularly conspicuous in the invasion of Iraq in 2003.[7]

The second hallmark of militarism is the preponderance of arms representatives and military officers in high positions in the government, and the consequent devotion to military preparedness rather than to policies that would prevent military confrontations. The Bush Administration exemplifies this phenomenon.[8] While no nation, or even group of nations has the capacity to confront the U.S. militarily, George Bush, nonetheless, in his inaugural address in 2001 said that he would build U.S. defenses beyond challenge lest weakness invite challenge. As he spoke, the U.S. expenditure on the military let alone its existing overkill of nuclear and advanced conventional arms arsenal, already accounted for thirty-seven percent of the total amount of $798 billion expended globally in 2000.[9]

An intricate confluence of constitutive mechanisms ensures the survival of the institution of militarism within the American social fabric. These mechanisms are mutually reinforcing, and include, inter alia, a pervasive military recruiting apparatus that attracts the young (age range of recruits lies between adolescence and twenty-four years) into enlisting in the army, in most cases for reasons other than patriotism or a sense of national duty.[10] A second survival mechanism is the Pentagon-Hollywood nexus that goes back to 1927, whereby the film industry produces pro-war films that glorify the American armed forces. The third device is the mass media-military symbiosis, in which the former cultivates pro-military public sentiment thwarting, in the process, potential public scrutiny in return for the latter's provision of hot news that increases circulation which increases profits from commercial advertising. The fourth is the "Special Access Program," devoted to secret arms development, whose budget is beyond any public oversight, and is estimated in the neighborhood of $30-35 billion annually. The fifth bolster is comprised of the regional commanders in the four central command structures that gird Planet Earth, and are commonly known as CENCOM, in the Middle East; PACOM, in the Pacific; EUCOM, in Europe and SOUTHCOM, in Latin America. These commanders not only exert more influence in their regions of operation than ambassadors and diplomatic missions; they also shape the key ingredients of foreign policy, draw military strategy, oversee intelligence and supervise arms sales. The enormity of their power is easily adducible from the most recent military coup d'etat in Pakistan. In 1999, President Clinton contacted Pervez Musharraf, who had led the military coup in Pakistan, and requested that Musharrf call him back. Instead, Musharraf called the head of CENCOM, General Anthony Zinni who most strongly supported Musharraf and ignored the Congressional ban on aid to governments founded on coups.[11]

However, the institution of militarism cannot reproduce itself without the conditions conducive to continual war which, not only legitimizes its existence in principle, but also as war depletes equipment and munitions such that they require immediate replenishments that continuously inject funds into the arms industry and augment the industrial-military complex. Domination-motivated war is the obverse of militarism, which, as an institution, can concoct and stage world-wide conditions for war, as were the cases of the Cold War, the war on drugs, humanitarian wars, the war on terrorism and most recently, in 2003, the democratization invasion of Iraq. Thus, imperialism can not survive without the support of a strong military machine that subdues resistance and an enabling finance of an economic structure that can sustain an expensive, expansive and unproductive military.

Toward the end of the Vietnam War, and the subsequent defeat, all economic indicators pointed to a worrisome decline of the American economy, which ultimately culminated in turning the U.S. into the largest debtor nation in the world. The U.S. government responded by a gigantic repackaging of two centuries old notions of liberal economics, re-labeling them neo-liberalism, which eventually ushered in what is called Globalism. The main thrust of neo-liberal thought is the encouraging of an all-encompassing privatization and support for the global role of multinational corporations, MNC. As early as 1981, the U.S.'s main strategy was to maintain its world prominence by employing international institutions, like the GATT, IMF and the World Bank to weaken countries with state-assisted enterprises, and exploit the Third World countries to the advantages of its MNC.[12] During the 1980s, proponents of American imperial projects mutated into two groups: one, which the Clinton Administration represents, labeled its imperialist ventures as "humanitarian intervention," and camouflaged domination and exploitation under international economic institutions, multilateral military structures and support for the notion of Globalization. The Clinton Administration was as militarist as that of Bush in the sense that its defence spending averaged $278 billion, which was the Cold War standard.[13] The second group, which George W. Bush represents, and is usually referred to as "neo-conservatives," advocates unilateral domination by employment of the U.S.'s unmatched military capability. While militarism-based domination was camouflaged under the Clinton Administration, it gained further impetus and overtness from self-righteousness notions propounded by neo-conservative circles.

Understanding the term "neo-conservatives" or "neo-cons" helps chart the trajectory of their policies and predict the implications of their worldview. Although some prominent Catholics are neo-conservatives, the movement remains predominantly Jewish, and derives its worldview from self-consciously drawn inferential lessons form the Holocaust, which was all evil. Their worldview, therefore, tends to be Manichaen, of good and evil, which accords well with both the thinking of the Christian Right, and Bush himself, since he stands with the forces of good. Policies of appeasement must be discarded because war is a natural state, and peace, therefore, is a dream that ought to be distrusted. It follows that a policy of multiplying American power bases bodes well for the U.S., and negotiation with enemies can be seen as taboo. The moral correctness, and indeed goodness of the United States is beyond question, and requires a unilateralist policy lest, by subjecting its will to the wishes or agreements of other countries, or global institutions, the United States would actually prevent itself from fulfilling its moral mission.

While there may be some nuances in the neo-cons' application of these tenets, the security of Israel, and the platform of its right wing is fundamental to all of them.[14] The policy of the neo-cons, in essence, reveals the same ideas of nineteenth Century America of "Manifest Destiny" and of its "Good Mission," and domination of the other, but with a further Israeli component. Amy Goodman, in an interview with Osama Siblani, in *Democracy Now*, reported that Mr. Bush told Osama, who is editor-in-chief of *The Arab-American Weekly* in Michigan, that he intended to take Saddam out. The interview took place during the election campaign in about mid May 2000 when Mr. Bush was not even a Republican nominee. Professor Juan Cole, of the University of Michigan, reaffirmed the credibility of the report.[15] The former U.S. Secretary of the Treasury, Paul O'Neill, whom Bush fired in December 2002 because he opposed expanding tax-cuts for corporate dividends, also revealed an insider's knowledge of the President and the cabinet in his book *The Price of Loyalty*.[16] The book reveals that as early as the first three months of 2001 the Bush administration was already examining military options for removing Saddam Hussein, and investigating contractors for Iraqi oil fields.[17] O'Neill quotes the President as saying, "God find me a way to do this." It was all about finding a way to invade Iraq,[18] and capture its oil.

On 13 January 2004 ABC news, quoted another official in the Bush Administration, who confirmed O'Neill's revelations, and added that he had attended the same National Security Council meeting as O'Neill, when Mr. Bush, long before the attacks of 11 September, had told Pentagon officials to explore military options for Iraq, including the use of ground forces. The official, speaking on the basis of anonymity, told ABC news that the plan "went beyond the Clinton administration's halfhearted attempts to overthrow Hussein without force."[19]

On 1 May 2005, the *London Times* divulged a secret memo prepared by Mathew Rycroft, who was a Downing Street foreign policy aide, summarizing the Anglo-American political and military position versus Saddam Hussein. The memo, which was dated 23 July 2002, coded S 195\02 and circulated among very few top British ministers, emphasized that there was a perceptible shift in American attitude towards military action, and Bush wanted to remove Saddam through military action, justified by the conjunction of terrorism and WMD. Hence the intelligence and facts were being fixed around the policy. However, there was little discussion in Washington of the aftermath after military action. Nevertheless, the case was thin because Saddam was not then threatening his neighbors, and his WMD capability was less than that of Libya, North Korea, or Iran. The memo further, explained that the Anglo-American concerted efforts should work up a plan for an ultimatum to Saddam to allow back in the UN weapons inspectors as this would help with the legal justification for the use of force.[20]

On 1 June 2002, President Bush, at West Point, said that the U.S. must be prepared to "wage war on terror against as many as sixty countries,...taking the battle to the enemy,...confront the worst threats before they emerge...through pre-emptive action to defend our liberty..."[21] Preventive war, the hallmark of the American National Strategy is, therefore, not necessarily the outcome of the events of 11 September as the Bush Administration would like people to believe. Rather, it was in all likelihood the manifestation of an already forged militarist mindset, and that 11 September was merely the catalyst for its revelation.

From the twentieth century until the present, the main character of the international relation system has been the inability of the rich, established powers, like Britain and the U.S. to accept peacefully the emergence of new power centers. The result has been wars of various degrees of gravity, including wars of national liberation against the arrogance and racism of imperialism. The U.S., as the only superpower in the beginning of the twenty-first century appears to be unable to adjust to the emergence of China as a modern economic power, let alone as a military power. China is the fastest growing economy in the world, with an average rate of 9.5 percent per annum for over two decades, whereas both the U.S. and Japan suffer huge and mounting debts and, in the case of Japan, stagnant growth rates. China is the second-largest economy on Earth measured on a purchasing power parity basis in terms of what China actually produces rather than prices and exchange rates. The CIA calculates the gross domestic product (GDP) of the United States, that is the total value of all goods and services produced within a country, for 2003 at $10.4 trillion, and China's $5.7 trillion. In 2004, the European Union was the largest trading partner with China whose trade volume for the same year was $1.2 trillion, third world rank, after the U.S. and Germany, and well ahead of Japan's $1.07 trillion. During the same year, China's trade with the U.S. increased thirty-four percent, and grew to $169.6 billion; with Europe at $177.2 billion; and with Japan at $167.8 billion. While China's growing economic weight in the world is widely recognized the U.S. fears China's growth rates. The National Intelligence Council of the CIA forecasts that China's GDP will equal Britain's in 2005, Germany's in 2009, Japan's in 2017, and that of the U.S. in 2042. But Shahid Javed Burki, former vice president of the World Bank-China Department, and a former finance minister of Pakistan, predicts that, based on a conservative prediction of a six percent Chinese growth rate sustained over the next two decades, China by 2025 will probably have a GDP of $25 trillion in terms of purchasing power parity, and will have become the world's largest economy followed by the United States at $20 trillion and India at about $13 trillion.[22] Nations with strong economies tend to have a strong say in international affairs, hence the U.S. worries about economic challengers.

Long before the invasion of Iraq, China had its eyes on Iraq as the source for satisfying its ever-increasing needs for energy to meet its phenomenal economic growth rates. In 1997, China negotiated a $1.3 billion contract with Saddam Hussein to develop the Ahdab oil field in central Iraq. By 2001, they were negotiating for rights to develop the much larger Halfayah field. Between them, the two fields might have accounted for almost 400,000 barrels per day, or thirteen percent of China's oil consumption in 2003. However, under the UN Oil- for-Food Program, China was prevented from activating these deals. Ironically, China and other potential oil customers had a great stake in the renewed UN inspections that could lead to lifting the sanctions if inspectors should issue a report finding no evidence of weapons of mass destruction in order to activate the lucrative oil deals. Thus, an American invasion would virtually ensure the end of China's hope for Iraq's oil.[23]

For the neo-cons, Iraq was a geostrategic asset to be used against any global contenders for U.S. pre-eminence, as well as being an open field to establish a "utopian free market" for American transnationals that would operate securely according to laws introduced by the occupation, endorsed by a puppet government and protected by American armed forces stationed in military bases in Iraq. In pursuit of their policy, the neo-cons cared less to plan sufficiently for a post-war Iraq, alienated the professional military, marginalized the Middle Eastern expertise at the State Department, disregarded the American public, undermined the good faith of American allies, and damaged their credibility in the international community.

Militarism and Politics in the Bush Administration

The blueprint for America's global quest for domination was drawn up for the incoming Bush administration and its principal advisors (Vice-President Dick Cheney, Secretary of Defense Donald Rumsfeld, Deputy

Secretary of Defense Paul Wolfowitz, Secretary of State [former National Security Advisor] Condoleezza Rice, and Vice-President Dick Cheney's Chief of Staff Lewis 'Scooter' Libby) by the think tank Project for the New American Century (PNAC). The report, entitled "Rebuilding America's Defenses: Strategies, Forces and Resources" (RAD), strongly underlined the importance of U.S. global dominance and set about a strategy to increase and maintain it. Furthermore, the document strongly argued the case for maintaining a global U.S. pre-eminence that precluded the rise of any rival power, and for shaping the international order in line with American principles and interests as far into the future as possible, essentially calling for the creation of a global *Pax Americana*. It maintained that one of the primary short-term objectives for the American military was the "fighting and winning [of] multiple large-scale wars."[24] The RAD document argued that the United States has sought to play a permanent and unchallenged role in Gulf regional security for decades.

The logic of the plan to conquer Iraq is embedded in the U.S. geopolitical strategy that sees Iraq as central not only to control of the Gulf's vast oil resources but also to world dominance. By taking over Iraq first, the U.S. would theoretically be able to isolate major pockets of opposition to Israel and to American hegemony in the Middle East, especially in Syria, and also subvert Iran to achieve a regime change as Iran is seen to be a potential regional hegemon, rich in oil and gas, and opposes the policies of the U.S. and Israel in the region. The U.S. would enjoy strategic control of more than half of the world's energy resources—the Caspian Sea, the Gulf, Iraq, and Iran, thereby aiding U.S.-Israeli hegemony in the region; and undercutting the challenge of the economic power of China and the EU.

The roots of the plan go back more than a decade. "During the 1990s the notion of toppling Saddam's regime was championed by a circle of neo-conservative thinkers, led by Richard Perle, a former assistant secretary of defense for international security policy under President Reagan...."[25] The neo-conservative framework for U.S. foreign policy was cast in 1990 by a team set up by then Secretary of Defense Dick Cheney after the fall of the Berlin Wall to re-cast American foreign policy in a unipolar world. Membership in this group included Paul Wolfowitz, Lewis Libby, and Eric Edelman. Wolfowitz presented a proposal for "Defense Planning Guid- ance" that impressed Cheney so much that he "briefed President Bush, using material mostly from Wolfowitz, from which George H. W. Bush prepared a major foreign-policy address. But he delivered it on...the day that Iraq invaded Kuwait, so nobody noticed."[26] However, when a draft version of the Wolfowitz document itself was leaked to the *New York Times* in 1992, it was met with outrage for its bellicose language and unilateral position. In it, Wolfowitz declared a robust and aggressive U.S. military posture for the post-Cold War era, proposing:

> ... that with the demise of the Soviet Union, the United States doctrine should be to assure that no new superpower arose to rival America's benign domination of the globe. The U.S. would defend its unique status both by being militarily powerful beyond challenge and by being such a constructive force that no one would want to challenge us. We would participate in coalitions, but they would be "ad hoc." The U.S. would be "postured to act independently when collective action cannot be orchestrated." The guidance envisioned pre-emptive attacks against states bent on acquiring nuclear, biological or chemical weapons. It was accompanied by illustrative scenarios of hypothetical wars for which the military should be prepared. One of them was another war against Iraq, where Saddam had already rebounded from his Gulf-war defeat and was busily crushing domestic unrest.[27]

Prior to joining the Bush administration, Wolfowitz published an article in *The National Interest* arguing that U.S. power needed to be flexed, "by demonstrating that your friends will be protected and taken care of, that your enemies will be punished and that those who refuse to support you will live to regret having done so."[28]

When Dick Cheney became vice president in 2001, his team, much like him, was predominantly neo-conservative. In addition to Wolfowtiz, Libby and Perle, the Cheney team included William Luti, who served under Newt Gingrich, and held the position of the Chief of Middle Eastern policy in the Pentagon; Stephen J. Hadley, a former member of the first President Bush administration; Douglas Feith, former special counsel to Richard Perle when he was Assistant Secretary of Defense under Ronald Reagan, and then Under Secretary of Defense for policy at the Pentagon; and David Wurmser, another Perle associate.[29]

Richard Clarke, who served under seven presidents as a counter-terrorism expert and was the National Coordinator for Security and Counter-terrorism for both Presidents Clinton and George W. Bush, is reported to have said that right after 9/11 Rumsfeld talked about bombing Iraq, and Bush dragged him into a room and instructed him to find out whether Iraq was responsible for 9/11. The gist of the conversation, according to Clarke, was to report back that Iraq had done this.[30] Clarke, in early 2004, published his book, *Against All Enemies,* in which he confirmed allegations that a section of the Bush administration, probably much like Bush himself, had placed Iraq on the agenda long before assuming power and compromised American national security in order to pursue their objectives. He further argued that Paul Wolfowitz had been pushing for an invasion of Iraq in spite of contradictory evidence from the CIA and other intelligence agencies and that such a link between the Iraqi regime and al-Qaida was unwarranted. Moreover, Wolfowitz insisted publicly that al-Qaida was incapable of pulling off a major operation on American soil by itself.[31] Clarke pointed out that Wolfowitz maintained the position that Al Qaida had been sponsored by Iraq, a stance he had held since the 1993 attack on the World Trade Center (WTC), despite the lack of any available evidence.[32] Immediately following 9/11 attacks on the WTC in 2001, both Rumsfeld and Wolfowitz, along with a handful of supporters, utilized the opportunity to transform the event into momentum for their longstanding objectives in Iraq. Clarke wrote:

> The administration of the second George Bush did begin with Iraq on its agenda... Paul Wolfowitz had urged a focus on Iraqi-sponsored terrorism against the U.S. even though there was no such thing. In 2001 more and more the talk was of Iraq, of CENTCOM [Central Command] being asked to plan to invade.[33]

In December 2001, Bush instructed Tommy Franks that CENCOM should start war plans against Iraq, which should include lines of attack, targets for missiles and the composition of a highly mechanized ground force. In late 2001, while Bush was receiving aid workers from Afghanistan he remarked, "Fuck Saddam, we're taking him out."[34]

Much to the consternation of the Joint Chiefs of Staff, Secretary of Defense Donald Rumsfeld initially suggested an invasion force that comprised only 60,000 troops, even though the officers charged with planning the invasion had recommended a presence of no less than 300,000 soldiers.[35] According to Pentagon advisor Daniel Goure,

> ... When Mr. Rumsfeld took over the Pentagon, he was determined to wrest it back from military control, primarily because during the Clinton administration, senior officers became used to having a free hand due to the inexperience and weakness of many of the civilian leaders. Additionally, many senior military officers have come to believe that civilian

Pentagon officials don't understand the reality of conflict because they have never served in uniform. Supporters of Mr. Rumsfeld ...were infuriated by such claims and hit back by denigrating some generals as being almost pathologically cautious and reluctant to commit troops.[36]

The *Daily Telegraph* reported that on 13 March 2003, Mr. Rumsfeld, Chairman of the Joint Chiefs of Staff General Richard Myers, and Myers' deputy, Peter Pace, outlined the administration's thinking on a potential war against Iraq: a "lightning drive" to Baghdad, by a highly mechanized and mobile ground force, bypassing possible confrontations in Iraq's southern cities. The race for the capital would be combined with an intensive bombing campaign, generating what was termed a "shock and awe" assault.[37] A compromise was reached for a total of almost 250,000 combat troops, and an intensive, protracted aerial bombardment, which consequently destroyed what was left of Iraqi civilian infrastructures after more than a decade of British and U.S. bombings. This plan, highly dependent upon aerial bombardment, resulted in 40,414 sorties by the U.S. military, which saw 84,991 guided bombs fired, and 1,529 fireballs—or "dumb" bombs, utilizing incendiaries dropped against no particular target, which scorched extensive areas indiscriminately.[38]

The Anglo-American Orchestration for War

Despite the military conquest and occupation of Afghanistan, purportedly carried out to destroy al-Qaida, its leaders, Osama Bin Laden and Mullah Omar and their lieutenants have at the end of 2005 eluded capture. Many Taliban fighters simply "evaporated" upon the arrival of the American troops, only to "re-emerge," in hit-and-run raids on the American forces and their allies, casting more doubt on the self-declared success of the U.S. in combating terrorism. Additionally, al-Qaida subsequently claimed responsibility for massive terror attacks in Spain on 11 March 2004, which killed 191 and injured over 1,800 just prior to the national elections.[39] Furthermore, the failure of the U.S. to even contain terrorism is made ever more transparent with the irony that the American occupation of Iraq has engendered acts of mass-terror from which Iraq was free under Saddam.

In spite of the continuing volatility of the Afghan situation, the targeting of Iraq gained momentum in late 2001. There was a concerted campaign to manufacture consent for an American military intervention in Iraq. The key ingredient in this campaign was linking Iraq to the "war on terror" by presenting Iraq as a serious threat to U.S. security and as a source of terrorism. From January 2002, Afghanistan and Bin Laden were replaced by the "threat" posed by Iraq and Saddam Hussein, which were now packaged as the embodiment of "terror." When President Bush then listed Iraq amongst his "Axis of Evil" in the 29 January 2002 State of the Union Address, the media fix on Iraq solidified in an unprecedented wave of uncritical reporting.

The Administration began an orchestrated propaganda campaign as early as September 2002, arguing that Iraq posed a threat to "Western civilization." Tom Goodrich from the U.S. Air Force, reported on 26 July 2005, that he was deployed from Afghanistan to Saudi Arabia in August-October 2002, when the U.S. Air Force deliberately flew over 100 war planes over the no-fly zone, bombing massive areas in Iraq with the goal of luring Saddam into confrontation or weakening his air defences in preparation for the planned invasion.[40] When the U.S. failed to drag Saddam into a military confrontation by such massive bombardment, the American propaganda machine began playing the keynote that Saddam Hussein was in possession of weapons of mass destruction (WMD), and that these weapons could fall into the hands of terrorists,[41] thus, laying the grounds for the invasion. Furthermore, this claim rested on the assumption that weapons of mass destruction (WMD) were in the hands of a madman whose *raison d'être* was to destroy America, a supposition that was established in the propaganda preceding the 1991 Gulf war. The argument that the American government put forth regarding WMD focused on Iraq's alleged possession of a massive stockpile of biological and chemical weapons, and its alleged attempts to acquire nuclear weapons. The Office of Special Plans (OSP), established in the Pentagon to 'vet' intelligence related to Iraq, claimed it had ascertained reliable intelligence suggesting that Iraq was in possession of WMD.[42] As the Administration moved toward war, it solidified its leadership in the Pentagon, and members of the OSP, such as William Luti, took on increasingly important responsibilities. The operation of the OSP, at least as Paul Wolfowitz conceived it, was to gather intelligence to support claims about Iraqi possession of WMD and Iraqi connections to Al-Qaida. It was essentially an intelligence agency that relied on data gathered by the other intelligence agencies, foreign governments, and Iraqi exiles such as Ahmad Chalabi and his Iraqi National Congress (INC) to provide the administration with intelligence supporting its policies. The OSP reported directly to Paul Wolfowitz and Donald Rumsfeld, and undermined the influence of the various U.S. intelligence agencies, as well as that of the uniformed officials. Patrick Lang, the former chief of Middle East Intelligence at the Defense Intelligence Agency (DIA), said, "The Pentagon has banded together to dominate the government's foreign policy, and they've pulled it off. They're running Chalabi. The DIA has been intimidated and beaten to a pulp. And there's no guts at all in the CIA."[43]

Under the pretext of an Iraqi threat, the U.S. secured UN Security Council Resolution 1441 on 8 November 2002, calling for the return of United Nations weapons inspectors to Iraq to ensure the elimination of WMD. This was a calculated gambit in preparing the legal grounds for military action against Iraq, which accords well with the text of the Downing Street Memo. UN Security Council Resolution 1441 warned of "serious consequences" in case of Iraqi non-cooperation or non-compliance. The notion was that the Iraqi possession of WMD posed a grave threat to the security of the U.S., and created a sufficiently powerful moral mandate to wage a war against Iraq. American political calculations appear to have assumed that Iraq would not allow the return of inspectors, and that a direct Iraqi refusal to participate would have established a legal and moral case for war, which the UN would then be forced to authorize after they had failed in drawing Saddam into a confrontation in Autumn 2002. However, Iraq approved the return of the inspection team headed by Hans Blix, and went further than ever before in providing open access for the inspection of sites throughout the country, including presidential palaces, a cause for a long controversy between the UNSCOM inspectors and the Ba'athist regime. On 12 December 2002, Iraq, as required under Resolution 1441, submitted to the Security Council three copies of an 11,000 page report on the status of its WMD program, along with copies of the documents and invoices from the firms that provided materials and equipment for the purpose of manufacturing biological and chemical weapons. Minutes later, a CIA team arrived, and forced the office of the UN Security Council to hand over all three copies, which were only returned the next day, with thousands of pages missing. The names of all the firms that were involved in supplying the materials and building the manufacturing facilities had been removed.[44] It is quite reasonable to assume that removing the names of the firms from the report was a politically calculated move. The publication of any such information would have allowed the UN to request information regarding the exact extent and location of WMD facilities and equipment through the governments of countries with any firms named in the Iraqi documentation. The weapons, or evidence of their destruction, would then be verifiably located, allowing for either the immediate destruction of prohibited weapons or conclusive evidence of compliance with the Security Council without wasting time in inspections and speculation.[45] Such a diplomatic riposte would have nullified the urgent call for war, and probably triggered enough world pressure to lift the sanctions and nipped in the bud the U.S. agenda.

American propaganda about WMD was so deafening that expert opinions were often never heard. It is not common public knowledge that biological and chemical weapons, like consumer commodities, have an expiration date or potency period. Chemical weapons tend to have little more than a five-year potency, and most biological weapons have a shelf life of approximately three years, after which they must be destroyed or re-grown in specialized facilities. Bio-weapons, in particular, pose a lethal danger to the environment because they tend to leak after they have expired. UN inspection teams—UNSCOM—had already verified destruction of all such Iraqi facilities between 1992 and 1995. *The Boston Globe*, on 20 July 2002, reported that the chief weapons inspector between 1991 and 1998, Scott Ritter, gave testimony to the hollowness of the Bush administration's claims regarding Iraq. He stated,

> We did ascertain a 90-95 percent level of verified disarmament. This figure takes into account the destruction of every factory associated with prohibited weapons manufacture and all significant items of production.
>
> With the exception of mustard agent, all chemical agents produced by Iraq prior to 1990 would have degraded within five years.... Effective monitoring inspections, fully implemented from 1994-1998 without any significant obstruction from Iraq, never once detected any evidence of retained proscribed activity or effort by Iraq to reconstitute that capability...[46]

However, Ritter's testimony was ignored in the thunderous propaganda that exploited the fear of the American people and galvanized public opinion behind the American government's position. The anti-sanctions/anti-war British MP, George Galloway, for example, later wrote: "Even I, the archest of skeptics when it came to western fables about Iraq, had fallen for the biggest hoax in modern history. For as it has turned out, the dictator was telling the truth [about not possessing WMD] and the self-appointed leaders of the free world were guilty of mendacity."[47] In May 2005, Mr. Galloway requested to meet with the American Senate, which cast aspersion on his integrity by insinuating that he had a financial involvement with Saddam. Galloway, publicly undercut the ground from under the Senate, and called the U.S. war "a pack of lies" which left the Senate speechless.[48]

UNMOVIC's reports, provided to the Security Council in 2002, pointed to increasing Iraqi cooperation with inspectors, although still falling short of expectations in the time frame allowed. Claims that Iraq was importing aluminum tubing to enrich uranium, and had tried to buy yellowcake uranium from Niger, had been shown to be false before U.S. forces launched their invasion. Dr. Hans Blix, chief weapons inspector, exhaustively detailed to the United Nations Security Council in February and again in March 2003, how UNMOVIC inspectors had visited nearly seventy sites in the country without locating any substantial evidence of Iraqi non-compliance that could justify an invasion. While much documentation remained unaccounted for, Blix argued that more inspections would clearly have helped answer the remaining questions. Blix repeatedly asserted that UNMOVIC had found nothing to substantiate U.S. claims and implored U.S. authorities to provide the intelligence for independent verification. Prior to the invasion Blix clearly articulated his belief that by expanding the time frame called for in Resolution 1441 by a few additional months, the inspectors would be able to ensure that Iraq was free of prohibited WMD. The U.S. and its ally, Britain, rejected the provision of any further time beyond the three months prescribed in Resolution 1441. This rejection decisively laid bare the rift between the Anglo-American political alliance and the rest of the international community. Moreover, opposition to the Anglo-American position expressed itself through the protests of millions of people in street demonstrations all over the world, including Britain and the United States itself, on 15 February 2003, the world's largest simultaneous protest ever. The rejection of the extension of the inspection timeframe is extremely understandable within the U.S. geo-strategy of taking Iraq as a strategic asset for controlling economic challenges, and eventually toppling the Iranian regime. Extending the time for more inspection would have proven Iraqi compliance with the UN Resolutions regarding WMD, and hence the potential for lifting the sanctions and the subsequent implementing of Iraqi oil deals with China.

As the Iraqi regime saw the potentially devastating consequences of the American military build up in the Gulf and Kuwait, it attempted in early

February 2003 to avert the war and retain its power. It sent a message to the Pentagon through a mutually known and trusted Lebanese businessman, Imad Hage, who straddles two cultural milieus and enjoys effective top-level relationships in many countries, including Syria, Iraq and the U.S..[49] The chief of the Iraqi Foreign Intelligence Services, Hassan al-Obeidi, with Saddam's approval, asked Hage to relay to the U.S. Administration that the Iraqi regime maintained its position that it no longer possessed weapons of mass destruction, and offered to allow American troops and experts to conduct unfettered searches. At one point, the Iraqis even pledged to hold legitimate elections.[50]

According to the article in the *New York Times*, Mr. Obeidi explained that the Iraqis wanted to cooperate with the Americans and could not understand why the U.S. government was so focused on Iraq when countries like Iran had a long history of publicly opposing the U.S., and supporting radical movements.[51] Obeidi said, "If this is about oil, we will talk about U.S. oil concessions. If it is about the peace process, then we can talk. If this is about weapons of mass destruction, let the Americans send over their people. There are no weapons of mass destruction." Mr. Obeidi added that the "Americans could send 2,000 FBI agents to look wherever they wanted." Mr. Hage made sure that Richard Perle received the Iraqi message, and heard from Mr. Perle that the answer from the Pentagon was "Tell them that we will see them in Baghdad."[52]

At this stage, the U.S. sought a new UN Resolution in a last ditch attempt to bestow the necessary legitimizing cover for the invasion in the eyes of the American soldiers, American public and the international community. However, the world did not "buy" the notion that Iraqi WMD existed, or that they constituted a legitimate threat. The international community and an overwhelming portion of international public opinion favored "more time to [be given] to the Inspection Committee." When Hans Blix dismissed Powell's case for war, based on U.S. satellite 'evidence', as a fraud, international opinion sided with the inspectors.[53]

The failure of Powell's UN venture testified not so much to the ineptness of the ex-General, but rather to the ever-increasing gap in perspective between the international community and the U.S. Administration. Hindsight, buttressed by mounting evidence that the rationale of the WMD was disingenuous, suggests that the ideologues of the Bush administration entertained the fantasy that once the world witnessed the destruction of Saddam and his brutal regime, the "righteousness" of the mission would become apparent and the questions of moral legitimacy would dissolve into the annals of history. Moreover, the architects of this strategy seem to have placed an unquestionable faith in the notion that overwhelming military force creates new facts on the ground, compelling countries that had opposed the U.S. war in Iraq, or that remained hesitant to support the occupation, to concede to the new reality. This is quite likely the thinking behind the RAD report's advocacy for fighting and winning decisive wars. Coinciding with this, there was a volley of derogatory remarks towards 'old Europe' by Donald Rumsfeld, and threats to bar all those who opposed the war from participating in lucrative reconstruction contracts. The administration updated the list of the *casus belli* for the attack to include liberating Iraq from a bloodthirsty tyrant, and introducing to Iraq the decidedly American model of 'democracy' and 'freedom'[54] that would force the rest of region to follow suit. The new focus of liberation and democratization of Iraq in the American propaganda is reminiscent of its British counterpart when General Satanley Maude, on capturing Baghdad in the pursuit of expanding and consolidating *Pax Britanica*, issued a proclamation in March 1917 declaring to the Iraqis that:

> Our armies have not come into your cities and lands as conquerors or enemies but as liberators. Since the time of Hulaku your citizens...have groaned in bondage. It is the wish not only of my King but it is also the wish of the great nations with whom he is in alliance that you should prosper... It is not the wish of the British Government to impose upon you alien institutions.[55]

Ignoring warnings about the imminent dangers of invasion and occupation, the Bush Administration pursued channels that confirmed their agenda. According to a report by Robert Dreyfuss in December 2002, the administration actually preferred analysis provided by the Iraqi National Congress to that of long-standing members of the CIA.[56]

The Combined Roles of the INC and OSP

The Iraqi National Congress (INC) was formed in June 1992. It brought together the two Kurdish militias—the Kurdistan Democratic Party (KDP) headed by Masud Barzani, and the Patriotic Union of Kurdistan (PUK) headed by Jalal Talabani, along with nearly 200 delegates from dozens of other opposition groups who met in Vienna. In October 1992, a handful of Shiite groups joined the coalition, and the INC established a three-person

Leadership Council, as well as a twenty-six-member Executive Council. The three members of the Leadership Council were the moderate Shiite Muslim cleric Muhammad Bahr al-Ulum, ex-Iraqi General Hasan Naqib and the head of the KDP, Masud Barzani. The chair of the Executive Council was Ahmad Chalabi, who is a secular Iraqi Shiite Muslim, educated as a mathematician in the United States.[57] Before taking up business in Britain, he had been the chairman of the Petra Bank International in Washington D.C. and Petra Bank in Jordan from which he fled facing charges of fraud, embezzlement and currency-trading irregularities, for which he was convicted in *absentia* by Jordanian authorities. Members of the Bush administration had come to know Chalabi through his work in the early 1990s with the CIA, where he had made contact with Richard Perle.[58]

In spite of declining relations with the CIA, which apparently had found Chalabi and the INC unreliable sources of intelligence, those associated with advocating regime change in Iraq found the contacts invaluable. Iraqi defectors presented by the INC became the primary source for numerous stories that received wide media attention in the mainstream print and electronic media. They purported to provide evidence of expansive Iraqi WMD development and rampant United Nations delinquency in the conduct of inspections. Almost immediately after 9/11, the INC began to publicize stories of defectors who claimed that they had information connecting Iraq to al-Qaida.[59] A supporting source of Chalabi was the Jewish Institute for National Security Affairs (JINSA), which saw in him the leader that would pressure the Arab countries towards peace with Israel. Chalabi's leanings for Israel brought him valuable friends in the American Enterprise Institute and in key newspapers, like Jim Hoagland of the *Washington Post*, Judith Miller of the *New York Times*, and Claudia Rosset of the *Wall Street Journal*.[60]

The rising influence of the Office of Special Plans (OSP) was accompanied by a decline in the influence of traditional intelligence agencies including the CIA and the DIA. A former CIA task-force leader said that many analysts in the CIA were convinced the Chalabi group's defector-reports were of little value. He added,

> ... even the DIA could not find any value in it. The people of the OSP and the civilian leadership of the Pentagon have convinced themselves that they were on the side of angels, and everybody else in the government was a fool. The Pentagon and the Office of the Vice-President wrote their own

pieces, based on their own ideology. We collected so much stuff that you could find anything you wanted.[61]

The Pentagon, however, denied that there had been disputes between the CIA and the Office of Special Plans over the validity of intelligence.[62]

As if resurrecting the British Imperial policy with regards to Baghdad in 1917, Feith, Rumsfeld and Wolfowitz schemed as early as Autumn 2002 to ensure that the future politics of Iraq would fall under the supervision of the Pentagon's civilian militarists, and would exclude the international community, the United Nations and the U.S. State Department. On 29 March 1917, the British War Cabinet, through its Mesopotamia Administration Committee concluded that "Baghdad [was] to be an Arab state with a local ruler or Government, but a British protectorate in everything but name; and behind the Arab facade, an administrative council presided over by a British High Commissioner would be an effective solution."[63] The maneuvering of the Pentagon's neo-cons excluded many of the most knowledgeable U.S. and international experts on both Iraq and post-conflict reconstruction development. The Pentagon dismissed "The Future of Iraq" project headed by Tom Warrick, which focused on rebuilding Iraq. Judith Yaphe, a former CIA analyst, and an expert on Iraq at the National Defence University complained,

The Office of the Secretary of Defense has no interest in what I do. They've brought in their own stable of people from [the] American Enterprise Institute (AEI), and the people at the State Department who worked with the Iraqi exiles are being kept out. The Pentagon military do not have a clue as to what's going on. The Pentagon politicians do not have plans in place for the transition in Iraq, they don't know where the money is going to come from, they do not have any organization and they just don't know anything about Iraq.[64]

Many State Department officials and outside experts on Iraq acknowledged that the INC should have some role in a new regime, though they preferred it to be a marginal one. Bathsheba Crocker of the Center for Strategic and International Studies, a think tank based in Washington, argued that, "It's very important to make sure we don't try to make Ahmed Chalabi the Iraqi Karzai."[65] However, Danielle Pletka, vice-president of the American Enterprise Institute, declared,

The Defense Department is running post-Saddam Iraq. The people at the State Department don't know what they are talking about! Who the hell are they? Who gives a good goddamn what they think? They need to remember that the president of the United States needs to be boss, and the simple fact is that the president is comfortable with people who are comfortable with the INC.[66]

According to the first American Administrator of Iraq, retired General Jay Garner, relations between the Pentagon civilian militarists and State Department personnel were both tense and sour because of inter-agency rivalry. Garner was known for his successful and lucrative relationships with military industrialists and strong support for Israel through his cordial public relationship with the Jewish Institute for National Security Affairs (JINSA). To assuage Iraqi concerns over his ties with Israel, Garner sought Iraqi input into his administration. This brought him into conflict with the neo-cons that staffed the ranks of the Pentagon, and he was removed from office within two months of his appointment and replaced by Paul Bremer. At this juncture, the main concern was to keep Iraqi oil underground where American military boots could control it.

In fact, Garner reported that he learned of a detailed study by Secretary of State Colin Powell for postwar Iraq only a few weeks before the war began in March 2003. When he suggested utilizing it, Rumsfeld forbade him.[67] Paul Bremer, however, enjoyed the unqualified support of President Bush and his neo-con administration. Under the administration of Bremer the UN was neither been able to assume the financial auditing role in Iraq, which the Security Council Resolution 1483 assigned to it, nor has the U.S. fulfilled its responsibilities under the Geneva convention as an occupying power to relieve the dire misery of the population resulting from the absence of basic needs such as electricity, gasoline, potable water and a sewage system due to the war-damaged civil infrastructure.

American Credibility:
Occupation Versus Liberation

On 2 June 2003, the Coalition Provisional Authority (CPA) hosted a meeting of nearly 300 tribal leaders and representative of all major Iraqi religious and ethnic groups. Hume Horan, former U.S. ambassador to Saudi Arabia and fluent in Arabic, served as a political advisor to Paul Bremer and addressed the audience in Arabic about the efforts the coalition would be making, and the need for Iraqi support. After Horan finished speaking, Sheikh Munthr Abood, from Amarra, thanked President Bush for removing the Ba'ath regime and said that he had seen the mass graves of Shi'ites in the south and that he had been firmly opposed to Saddam Hussein. He then asked Horan if the coalition forces in Iraq were liberators or occupiers. Horan responded that they were "somewhere between occupier and liberator." This did not sit well with the Iraqi audience. Sheikh Abood stated that if America was a liberator, then the coalition forces were welcome indefinitely as guests, but if the U.S. military were occupiers, then he and his descendants would "die resisting" the occupiers.[68]

The militarists, however, projected the invasion to the American public in the Hollywood style in which the American military was cast as heroes defending the homeland from a dangerous and ruthless enemy. In the American version, the Anglo-American war on Iraq began on 19 March 2003, and officially ended on 1 May 2003 when President Bush boldly declared, "mission accomplished." The reality of the invasion, however, was considerably different. For example, the commander of the First Marine Expeditionary Force in Iraq, Lt. Gen. James Conway, remarked that he was surprised that he had not encountered any chemical weapons when his forces invaded Iraq. Army Chief of Staff, General Eric Shinseki, resigned his position following a public disagreement with Rumsfeld and Wolfowitz over the size and composition of U.S. forces needed to invade and occupy Iraq. In addition, the sudden retirement of General Franks was followed by the retirement of Army Secretary General Tom White after a number of clashes with Rumsfeld and the neo-cons of the Pentagon.[69] According to CNN, Rumsfeld had already chosen his successor, Air Force Secretary Jim Roche, a trusted friend who shared Rumsfeld's vision for the military.[70]

In October 2003, David Kay, who led a 1,400-man team into Iraq to search for Iraqi WMD, and was a staunch believer in their existence, presented an interim report that stated bluntly that there was no evidence of any WMD manufactured after 1991. His only finding was one vial of live C botulinum Okra B from which a biological agent could be produced. Mr. Bush seized on this single finding, equating it with evidence of WMD. However, Dr Glen Rangwala of Cambridge, U.K., in analyzing Kay's report, said,

> The vial held not the super deadly type A but the less lethal type B and there was no evidence found by Kay's group of any preparations for the extensive process required for weaponization.[71]

Further, Botulinum strain B is used for vaccinating livestock and removing wrinkles in cosmetic surgery. It is also used as an antidote to common Botulinum poisoning.[72] In January 2004, David Kay also resigned his post and made it clear that he did not believe that there were any WMD to be found in Iraq. Following Kay's report, the neo-conservative self-justified imperial project focused on "the principles of the Wilsonian export of democracy," which President Bush reiterated in his trip to Europe, in February 2005, but it fell on deaf ears as regards to the leaders of the European Union.

The invasion of Iraq also left Colin Powell's credibility seriously compromised. In early January 2004, he was forced to acknowledge that there was no "smoking gun" linking Saddam's regime to al-Qaida, much less to the 11 September attacks. He added that it was prudent to have considered the possibility of such connections prior to the war,[73] and left the Administration in its second term. In late August 2005, Lawrence Wilkerson, Powell's chief of staff since 2002 said, in an interview with CNN, that what Powell presented at the UN Security Council, in February 2003 were the intelligence papers according to the White House, which turned out to include fabrications that the CIA never vetted.[74]

A comprehensive 107-page report that the Washington-based Carnegie Endowment for International Peace (CEIP) released on 8 January 2004 concluded that the Bush Administration "systematically misrepresented" the threat posed by Iraq's weapons of mass destruction. The Carnegie analysts found "no solid evidence" of a cooperative relationship between Saddam and al-Qaida, nor any evidence to support the claim that Iraq would have transferred WMD to al-Qaida. Moreover, it reasoned that, "the notion that any government would give its principal security assets to people it could not control in order to achieve its own political aims is highly dubious."[75] The report called for the creation of an independent commission to fully investigate what the U.S. intelligence community knew, or believed to know, about Iraq's WMD program from 1991 to 2003, and to determine whether intelligence was tainted by foreign intelligence agencies or political pressure. The report's co-author, Joseph Cirincione, told reporters that "It is very likely that intelligence officials were pressured by senior administration officials to conform their threat assessments to pre-existing policies."[76] The influence of CEIP comes from the fact that it is the publisher of the journal *Foreign Policy*, and that it has long been non-partisan, as indicated by the presence of right-wing figures such as neo-conservative writer Robert Kagan amongst its staff. In a brief reaction to the report, Powell stressed that what he had presented at the UN were the views of the intelligence community. "I was representing them," he said. "It was information they had presented publicly, and they stand behind it."[77]

Another supporter of regime change in Iraq, Kenneth Pollack, who had been a Clinton-era National Security Council member, scathed the Bush Administration for its justification of the war as at "best faulty, at worst, deliberately misleading."[78] In early January 2004, the Strategic Studies Institute of The U.S. Army War College published a paper entitled "Bounding the global war on terrorism," which found that the administration's doctrinaire view of the war on terror, which lumped together Saddam's regime and al-Qaida as a single undifferentiated threat, led the U.S. on a dangerous "detour" into an unnecessary war. The author, Jeffrey Record, a visiting scholar at the Strategic Studies Institute and a former staff member of the Senate Armed Services Committee, claimed that "the global war on terrorism as presently defined and conducted is strategically unfocused, promises much more than it can deliver, and threatens to dissipate U.S. military and other resources in an endless and hopeless search for absolute security."[79]

The American Neo-Liberalization of Iraq

Three weeks after declaring "mission accomplished," on 22 May 2003, the Bush administration succeeded in securing UN Resolution 1843, which rubber-stamped the U.S. occupation and essentially made Iraq a U.S. mandate. The UNSC Resolution minimized the role of the UN, confining it to an advisory financial auditing position, overseeing only the Iraqi Development Fund and other various humanitarian functions. Furthermore, it excluded Russia and the European states that had opposed the war, particularly France and Germany, which might have hoped for a portion of the re-construction contracts, estimated at more than $50 billion.

Bremer acted as a neo-con enforcing neo-liberal policies. Although Resolution 1843 called for the establishment of an interim Iraqi government, Bremer's first impulse was to ignore it, along with the requirement to establish a UN Advisory Financial Auditing Body to oversee the Iraqi Development Fund (into which Iraq's oil revenues were deposited). Bremer, then, cancelled all oil contracts drawn under Saddam, thus, wiping out China's stakes. The war and its aftermath have reshaped China's basic conception of the geopolitics of oil and added urgency to its mission to lessen dependence on Middle East supplies. It has reinforced China's fears that it is locked in a zero-sum contest for energy with the world's lone superpower, prompting Beijing to intensify its search for new sources.[80] China responded by strenuously seeking to develop renewable sources of energy, like wind, solar and nuclear, and pursuing oil and economic projects with Iran, and Latin American countries, which the U.S. regard as its own backyard. In March 2004, China signed a twenty-five-year deal to import 110 million tons of liquefied natural gas from Iran. In addition, in October 2004, China and Iran signed a gas-and-oil deal worth about $100 billion.[81]

Bremer then disbanded the Iraqi army and police forces, banned the Ba'ath Party and purged its members from government employment. This resulted in not only the spiraling of the unemployment rate to sixty to seventy percent but in the actual collapse of the Iraqi state. The state was founded on the army, which was itself controlled by the Ba'ath Party, and the party had monopolized the political, social and economic life of Iraq for thirty-five years. Thus, once the party's institutions ceased to function, the Iraqi state collapsed, and only the pre-Ba'ath primordial social institutions—tribal, religious, communal—re-emerged in the vacuum, precipitating Bremer's loss of order and control. Additionally, disbanding the standing army of 300,000 men, along with its civilian support of 100,000 people, amplified and spread public dissatisfaction, and provided an endless reservoir of potential recruits for the emerging resistance to occupation.[82]

In an investigative report from Iraq by Naomi Klein, published in *Harper's Magazine*, Klein wrote that the massive destruction brought about by the American invasion was a neo-conservative policy in practice.[83] She argued that by applying a pervasive "shock therapy," that is expunging Iraqi existence, the neo-conservatives firmly believed that a new stage would be set to establish a free market "utopian" economy dominated by the American transnationals or the MNC. This is the American model of market democracy propounded by the captains at the helm of neoliberalism.

It was assumed that the Iraqis would be too shocked by the travails of war, the collapse of the old regime and the struggle to make ends meet, to be actively preoccupied with the kind of legislation the occupiers were setting in place. According to Klein, two months before the invasion U.S.AID drafted a work order to KPMG, which is a business consulting firm, and an offshoot of Bearing Point Incorporation, to oversee Iraq's transition to a sustainable market-driven economic system, and to take appropriate advantage of the unique opportunity for rapid progress in this area presented by the current configuration of political circumstances.[84] Bearing Point Incorporation was founded 100 years ago, and specializes in security issues and re-construction projects

Paul Bremer was in charge of the task of re-configuration. He followed through by arranging the largest state liquidation sale of economic enterprises since the collapse of the U.S.SR.[85] While he opened the borders to unrestricted imports, he introduced a set of laws in September 2003 to bring in transnational corporations. Order 37 lowered corporate tax from almost forty to fifteen percent; Order thirty-nine permitted foreign companies to own 100% of Iraqi assets, and allowed investors to transfer 100% of the profits made in Iraq without any stipulation for re-investment or taxation. The same order entitled the foreign companies to leases or contracts that could remain in effect for forty years. Order forty was designed for foreign banks with the same favorable terms. What remained of Saddam's economic policies and laws were the rules that restricted collective bargaining and trade unions.

Bremer's architectural design for Iraq was a large factor in the escalation of the armed resistance that followed. In the first four months after his arrival 109 U.S. soldiers were killed, and 570 wounded. When Bremer's shock therapy took effect in the following four months, the number of American casualties almost doubled.[86] Bremer's policies that created half a million jobless people overnight afforded them only "resistance" as an alternative to unemployment. Further, his design for the future of Iraq threatened small business owners who, therefore, invested in financing the armed resistance for self-protection. With sixty-seven unemployment, the import of foreign products and workers has added more fuel for the resistance as such imports aggravate the suffering that is part of daily Iraqi life.[87]

The neo-conservative project of a utopian free market for Iraq was arrested, however, by international law, which stipulates that occupation forces can not dispose of the assets of the occupied country in any shape or form. Bremer's belated realization of this block was further compounded by the escalating resistance that rendered the issue of the security vacuum tangible and concrete, and which, in turn, scared away many transnationals. Bremer responded by hastily forming the Iraqi Governing Council (IGC) which consisted of twenty-five hand-picked members, and forced it to agree to the Interim Constitution, alternatively named the Transitional Administrative Law (TAL). In the TAL, Bremer inserted Article 126, stating that "for the duration of the interim government the laws, regulations, orders and directives issued by the Coalition Provisional Authority...shall remain in force" and could only be changed after general elections were held in January 2005. Many Iraqis have dubbed the IGC as "collaborators," primarily because the IGC has no legitimate authority, and does not represent any constituencies within Iraq. Until January 2005, according to Bremer's plan, investors could buy Iraqi assets and sign contracts for forty years. Should future Iraqi governments decide to change the laws, investors could sue for compensation.[88]

Bremer, before his departure on 28 June 2004, hastened to put together an interim Iraqi government that would do his bidding, after the so called "transfer of sovereignty to the Iraqis," which commenced in July 2004, and thus, could avoid the stipulations of international law. The hand-picked Prime Minister, Iyad Allawi, a Ba'athist who fell out of favor with Saddam, and collaborated with the CIA largely subscribes to Bremer's privatization program for Iraq.[89]

Herbert Docena, at the Iraq International Occupation Watch Center, on a visit to Iraq in December 2003, reported from Baghdad that most of Iraq was suffering from power interruptions that would last, on average, sixteen hours per day. In addition, the access that Iraqis had to scant gasoline supplies had created three kilometer line-ups of cars at pumping stations. Iraq possesses the second largest petroleum reserves in the Middle East, hence, suspicions about the reasons behind the shortage of gasoline were widespread. The scarcity of gasoline illustrates the problem. Not only do the refineries need repair, but also the oil infrastructure itself requires rehabilitation, for which the U.S. Government has contracted Kellogg, Brown & Root, (KBR), a Halliburton subsidiary. Workers from the Southern Oil Company in Basra are not aware of any repairs that KBR has actually undertaken. KBR is also employed, under a cost-plus contract, to import gasoline into Iraq from Kuwait and Turkey. In early December 2003, it was discovered that KBR was charging approximately twice the market price for imported gasoline, while repairs at the refineries were progressing remarkably slowly.[90]

Docena also reported that "Iraqis suffer not only from insufficient power supplies, uninstalled and destroyed phone lines, shoddily repaired schools, clogged roads, uncollected garbage, defective sewerage, and a nonexistent social infrastructure, but also mass unemployment, reaching upwards of twelve million people, and widespread poverty."[91] This situation has astonishingly persisted long since Bush declared "Mission Accomplished" in May 2003. At the Najibiya power station in Basra, Iraq's second largest city, the general director has pleaded with the U.S. contractor, Bechtel,[92] since May 2003 to deliver urgently needed spare parts for their antiquated turbines. The reason for the apparent incompetence of this giant corporation is that Iraqi power turbines were mostly manufactured in Russia, France and Germany. Due to the U.S. administration's ban on the participation of these countries in post-Iraq reconstruction, as a result of their opposition to the war, Bechtel had to go through a lengthy and costly process to procure the components. Bechtel is currently being paid, using Iraqi funds and American taxpayers' money, to determine what the Iraqis will "need" to buy in the future. In determining the future power needs of Iraq, Bechtel never consulted Iraqi power stations and utility managers.[93]

In this environment—collapsed state, large-scale unemployment, the American grand design of Iraqi privatization, and the continuing humanitarian crisis due to impaired civil services (water, electricity, health, education, etc)—the Iraqi resistance grew, improved its organization and spread all over Iraq, causing a progressively rising death toll among the U.S. soldiers. It takes only a fraction of the population to be actively involved in resisting an occupation, combined with extensive popular sympathy, to form a successful guerrilla insurgency. The performance of the already existing American corporations, Halliburton and Bechtel, raises not only questions about their competence but it also tends to increase popular sympathy for the resistance.

The American Democratization of a Satellite Iraq

The U.S. Agency for International Development has appointed the private Research Triangle Institute (RTI) as one of a battalion of private contractors attempting to fashion Iraq's legal, economic, political and social institutions so that they will be conducive to U.S. interests. Most of the contracts are funded by U.S.AID as foreign aid. In Iraq, RTI is recruiting and mobilizing Iraqis, who, it hopes will push for and defend preferred U.S. policies—both within the state and in civil society—in a sovereign Iraq.[94] The employees of RTI have roamed the country in search of "the most appropriate, 'legitimate'[95] and functional leaders," according to their contract with U.S.AID. The definition of "legitimate," according to Fritz Weden of the U.S.AID Office of Transition Initiatives, is to "identify those groups, those leaders that you can work with."[96] The task of the RTI is to ensure that only the "legitimate" leaders prevail in order to create a base that will support the continued U.S.-led occupation. Thomas Carothers, director of the Democracy Project at the Carnegie Endowment for International Peace, said, "beneath the new interest of the United States in bringing democracy to the Middle East is the central dilemma that the most powerful, popular movements in Iraq are the ones that we are deeply uncomfortable with."[97]

While RTI recruits people at the grassroots, The National Endowment for Democracy (NED) and its affiliates developed the machinery for scores of political formations that contested the national elections in January 2005. Various American affiliates set up shops to teach an American concept of democracy. Larry Diamond, a senior advisor to the CPA and former co-director of NED, offered a preview of this project in a lecture at Hilla University in January 2004. According to the CPA press release, Diamond told his audience that a basic element of "democracy" is a "market economy" and among the most fundamental rights is the right to own property—a view affirmed by U.S.AID. This, in turn, calls for a kind of democracy in which social equality is not a necessary aim and in which inequalities may in fact be necessary.[98]

In Iraq, invasion was the "entry point" for NED, U.S.AID and their instruments. The "national opening" for the work of the instruments was the collapsed state that Bremer accomplished. Without any existing institutions to work through, the U.S. is attempting to create them from the ground up. The "legitimate leaders" are not to be identified and co-opted, as in Latin America; they have to be groomed and primed. In other countries, U.S.AID operators have to cajole or effectively coerce governments to submit to its "reforms." In Iraq, they were the government. Despite the "transfer of sovereignty" on 28 June 2004, they have continued to exercise considerable power over the interim government, especially since Allawi's power was negligible at best and he was totally dependent upon U.S. protection. There was no need to tinker with Iraq's laws because they would be written on a blank slate by the first elected government. All this is possible because of the rare opportunity offered by the war. In Iraq, the first step was not "legitimation" or "constituency building." It was dropping bombs.[99] Despite the appearance of enormous latitude for action, the intensity of the Iraqi resistance has left the socio-political projects of U.S.AID and NED very uncertain.

Iraqi Elections and the Draft Constitution

The Iraqi election of 30 January 2005 took place amidst the strangest of circumstances that bring into question the very legitimacy of the election. It was conducted under a state of martial law and foreign occupation, boycotted by twenty percent of the population in the so-called Sunni triangle, and lacked the promised international election monitors. There was virtually no political campaigning by the 7500 candidates, scattered among 257 lists, and at least 6000 of them were too fearful to declare their names until Election Day.[100] Despite the Sunni boycott of the election the voter turn out on Election Day was reported to be about fifty-eight percent. The voting pattern had two hallmarks: one was the expressed wish of voters that the incoming Iraqi government would insist on the withdrawal of the foreign forces;[101] the second was the segmented character of voting which applies with equal weight to the non-voting of the Sunni community. It was not the normal national voting pattern. The Shi'ites received a religious edict from Ayatollah Ali al-Sistani as to the imperative of voting for the United Iraqi Alliance; the Kurds voted for the Kurdish list; the Sunnis obeyed the boycott call of the Muslim Association of Scholars. Others, like the Communists or Allawi's list that tried to reach for the votes of Iraqis beyond community barriers, received minimal support at best. Iraqi voting reflected not a nation-state, but segmented communities in an uneasy co-existence.[102]

With Sunni political parties boycotting the election, the election was dominated by Shi'ite and Kurdish parties. The Shi'te United Iraqi Alliance, which is the list put together by al-Sistani, won fifty-one percent of the votes and captured 140 seats out of 275. The Kurdish list came second, capturing about twenty-six percent of the votes and about seventy-five seats. The loss of the list of Iyad Allawi was a surprise because Allawi had all the advantages of incumbency. According to Juan Cole, professor of history at the University of Michigan, Allawi dominated the airwaves in December and January. In addition, he went to Baghdad University and made a variety of promises to the students there, and it was dutifully broadcast. Allawi's list also spent an enormous amount on campaign advertising. The source of these millions is unknown, since Paul Bremer passed a law making disclosure of campaign contributions unnecessary. Despite these enormous advantages, clear American backing, money, etc., Allawi's list won only about 14% of the votes, 40 seats and even with outside support Allawi failed to become the future Prime Minister, a defeat for the American Administration. According to the Interim Constitution, the formation of a government requires a "supermajority" of two-thirds. This stipulation forces the Shi'ites to seek an expedient alliance with the Kurds who insist on resolving the problematic demography of the City of Kirkuk and its oil in the Kurdish favour even prior to negotiations. These Kurdish demands have been a subject of intense negotiations behind closed doors.

The Shi'ite-Kurdish committee, charged with drafting the Iraqi Constitution, attempted to engage the Sunni input in order to lend legitimacy to the draft by presenting it as a national formula, and simultaneously undercut the potential of Sunni support to the resistance. However, the Western mainstream media has focused on issues of confederation, oil sharing, and Kirkuk as the problems that have plagued the process of drawing the draft. Neither the context nor the power agents involved have been discussed, nor has the substance of the draft constitution been analyzed. The Sunni representatives withdrew from the process, and disavowed the draft as not representing the aspirations of the Iraqi people, and vowed to turn it down in the referendum. The inter-factional struggle delayed the completion of the draft beyond the deadline of 15 August 2005. Further, the draft was not signed by the Iraqi Parliament, and was only passed as ready for a public referendum in December 2005.

The concrete context in which the constitutional proceedings took place was tainted with so much illegality that this alone could render the constitution illegal under international law. Ziad Al-Ali, a legal expert who oversaw the constitutional process, reported that the U.S. intervened in three basic ways. First, the occupation forces selected the commission that was charged with drafting the permanent constitution. Second, the occupation set up the limits and parameters within which the constitution was to be drafted. Third, the American forces intervened directly in order to safeguard U.S. interests in the context of the constitutional negotiations. An example of such significant American interference was dropping a clause in an earlier draft that forbade foreign military bases in Iraq. Justin Alexander, legal affairs officer for the office of constitutional support with the United Nations Assistance Mission to Iraq (UNAMI), who oversaw the drafting process reported that " The U.S. ambassador, Zalmay Khalilzad, took an extremely hands-on role," to the point of "Even going so far as to circulate at least one U.S. draft." Dr. Marinos Diamantides, senior lecturer in law at the University of London, said that one could argue that the entire process was a contravention of international law. He explained that "according to the 1907 Convention (the convention for the pacific settlement of disputes), the occupying power has a duty to maintain the legal system of the country it occupies. This is the first time ever that an occupying power has dismantled the internal law system of the country it occupies."[103]

In every step, from the invasion to drafting the Iraqi Constitution, the U.S. has endeavored to lock up its economic and political interests in Iraq in such a way as to become non-eradicable. The U.S. selected the Iraqi Governing Council, which approved Bremer's 100 laws that opened the country to a "fire-sale" of the nation's economic enterprises to foreign corporations, thus paving the way to de facto privatization. The U.S. sent its instruments of democratization to bring on a "market democracy," not equality and social justice, and identify collaborators that could serve American interests in Iraq. The election of January 2005, whose legitimacy is legally doubtful, brought in an American-approved cabinet of Shi'ite-Kurdish power agents that have their own agenda that coincides with that of the U.S.. In preparation for drawing the draft constitution, the Iraqi Parliament conducted a massive information campaign that included questionnaires and focus group discussions across the country in order to identify the wish list of the Iraqi people. The wish list emphasized a Scandinavian-type welfare system, with Iraq's wealth spent on upholding every Iraqi's right to education, health care, housing, and other social services. And Iraq's natural resources would be owned collectively by the Iraqi people, and only Iraqis could operate businesses, and when foreign partnership was allowed, it should not exceed forty-nine percent.[104] It was, however, the American wish list, not the Iraqis' that the draft constitution incorporated.

The Kurdish and Shi'ite parties, under the ubiquitous presence of Zalmay Khalilzad and the British diplomats, have agreed to a document that not only sanctions the privatization of the state-owned oil industry and the free market restructuring of the economy but also preserves Bremer's laws.[105] Article twenty-five declares "the state shall guarantee the reforming of the Iraqi economy, according to modern economic bases, in a way that ensures complete investment of its resources, diversifying its sources and encouraging and developing the private sector." Article 110, clause two, of the constitution declares Iraq's energy resources will be developed "relying on the most modern techniques of market principles and encouraging investment."[106] By "reforming" the framers of the constitution could only have meant the usual stock of neo-liberal economic policies that include privatizing state-owned enterprises, liberalizing trade, deregulating the market, and opening it up to foreign investors. "Modern techniques of market principles," in Article 110, most likely refers to current plans to privatize the Iraqi National Oil Company and to open up Iraq's oil reserves to the big oil companies. Adil Abdel Mahdi, Iraq's vice president, referred to such plans when he said in Washington just before the election of January that, "This is very promising to the American investors and to American enterprises, certainly to oil companies."[107] By embodying Bremer's laws in the Iraqi Constitution, the framers have allowed foreigners to have as much right as Iraqis to ownership of Iraq's national resources, real estate and capital, and paved the way to foreign ownership of Iraqi oil. Providing social services to Iraqis are vaguely mentioned, and the delivery conduit was named the private sector, which opens the way to complete privatization of the social welfare system.[108]

In exchange for a constitution that allows the U.S. to plunder the Iraqi economy, the U.S. supported the Shi'ite-Kurdish agenda for a federal system. Within federalism, the oil-rich region of both the Shi'i in the south, and the Kurdish in the north becomes autonomous, with full authority over oil operations and revenues drawn therefrom. The U.S. support stems from the assured record that the main power players in the Shi'ite and Kurdish camps are staunch privatizers. The central government in Baghdad will have the power to administer only the "oil and gas extracted from current fields," in cooperation with the regions. Future oil fields are subject to 100 percent control by the region in which they are located. In other words, the central government is empowered only to maintain a common market within Iraq while the power to regulate the market is relegated to autonomous regions whose ruling elite groups are American clients.[109] Powerful regions clearly undermine the authority of the central state in power sharing contrary to the strong federal model of the United States itself. This is the Iraqi federalist recipe supported by the Bush Administration.

The second article of the constitution declares Islam the official state religion and a source of law, and that "no law can be passed that contradicts the undisputed rules of Islam." The constitution, further, declares Iraq as a part of the "Islamic World," thus divorcing the Iraqi people from an Arab identification. The Supreme Court, which will interpret the constitution, will have to include clerics as individuals with the necessary expertise in Islamic law.[110] The Bush Administration does not care about what religion or God is in Iraq so long as it has in place powerful groups that do its bidding for economic and political dominance. Nor does the U.S. heed the widespread popular opposition to federalism, even among the Shi'tes. The International Republican Institute, which is a U.S. government-funded entity, tasked to build support for free market Iraqi political parties, conducted a survey in July 2005 for the purpose of identifying popular trends. The survey reported that sixty-nine percent of Iraqis from across the country wanted the constitution to establish "a strong central government," and only twenty-two percent wanted it to give "significant powers to regional governments." In the Shi'ite-majority areas in the south, only twenty-five percent want federalism while sixty-six percent reject it.[111] Mahmoud Othman, a Kurdish member of the constitutional committee who was involved in the caucuses reported that, "The Americans say they don't intervene, but they have intervened deeply. They gave us a detailed proposal, almost a full version of a constitution. They try to compromise the different opinions of all the political blocs. The Anglo-American officials were not acting as neutral mediators, but were being governed by their domestic agenda." Nechirvan Barzani, the Prime Minister of the Kurdistan regional government in Arbil, and a close ally of the U.S., confirmed Othman's charges, and added that "The U.S. and the U.K. are working behind the scenes, dealing with all the groups, saying it should be like this and like that."[112]

American Military Bases

In tandem with the American re-configuring of the dynamics of Iraqi socio-economic formations, the U.S. Administration has persevered in building new military bases, in addition to expanding and improving the already existing ones. Military bases have been the American instrument of not only a projection of power, but also an actual exercise of authority over alien communities. At one enormous military base, which the Americans erected at Baghdad International Airport, waiters in white shirts, black pants, and black bow ties serve dinner to the officers of the eighty-second Airborne Division in their heavily guarded compound. One-third of the funds appropriated for the war in Iraq (about $30 billion) went into private American hands to make the daily existence of the military seem like a Hollywood version of life at home. Some of these bases are so gigantic that they require as many as nine internal bus routes for soldiers and civilian contractors to get around inside the earthen berms and concertina wire. Camp Anaconda, headquarters of the Third Brigade, Fourth Infantry Division, has the job of policing some 1,500 square miles of Iraq north of Baghdad, from Samarra to Taji. Anaconda occupies twenty-five square kilometers and will ultimately house as many as 20,000 troops.[113]

It is estimated that four to six permanent bases will exist to house the American military: at the Baghdad International Airport and the Tallil air base near Nasariyah; in the western desert near the Syrian border, and at the Bashur air field in the Kurdish region of the north. This count excludes Anaconda, which is currently being called an "operating base," though it may very well become permanent over time.

According to the Defense Department's annual Base Status Report for the fiscal year of 2003, which itemizes foreign and domestic U.S. military real estate, the Pentagon currently owns or rents 702 overseas bases in about 130 countries and has another 6,000 bases in the United States.[114] The 2003 Base Status Report fails to mention any garrisons in Kosovo even though it is the site of the huge Camp, Bondsteel, which was built in 1999, has been maintained ever since by Kellogg, Brown & Root. The Report similarly omits bases in Afghanistan, Iraq, Israel, Kuwait, Kyrgyzstan, Qatar, and Uzbekistan, although the U.S. military has established colossal base structures throughout the so-called arc of instability in the four years since 9/11. For Okinawa, which has been an American military colony for the past fifty-eight years, the report deceptively lists only one Marine base, Camp Butler, when in fact Okinawa "hosts" ten Marine Corps bases, including Marine Corps Air Station Futenma occupying 1,186 acres in the center of that modest-sized island. Marine Brigadier General, Mastin Robeson, who commands 1,800 troops that occupy the old French Foreign Legion base at Camp Lemonier in Djibouti at the entrance to the Red Sea, asserted that *Pax Americana* which he calls "preventive war" requires a "global presence," by which he means gaining hegemony over any place that is not already under the "American thumb."[115]

According to the right-wing American Enterprise Institute, the idea is to create "a global cavalry" that can ride in from "frontier stockades" and shoot up the "bad guys" as soon as we get some intelligence on them.[116]

Conclusion

The mainstream media have not only consistently avoided reporting the realities of the insupportable living conditions of the Iraqi people but have also seemed to deliberately focus on minor issues of ethnicity and national identity as problems in framing the draft constitution. They have avoided any concrete reference to the U.S. pressure on the formulation of a constitution that guarantees the American economic and political interests in Iraq as a springboard to the larger Middle East. Furthermore, the media never mention the present efforts at re-construction, from which Iraqi firms are excluded despite their expertise. It was one of Bremer's orders that denied the Iraqi government the ability to give preference to Iraqis in the re-construction plans, and instead, more than 150 U.S. companies have been awarded contracts totaling more than $50 billion, more than twice the GDP of Iraq. These contractors answer only to the U.S. government, not to a "Sovereign Iraq." Despite the billions earmarked for Iraq, the American companies have yet to provide accessible water, sanitation and electricity at pre-war levels, more than three years after the official cessation of hostilities.[117]

Proclaiming Islam as the main source of law in the constitution will enhance the religious authority of Al-Sistani as the ultimate reference in religious matters. This may explain his tacit endorsement of the American economic agenda for Iraq. Further, enshrining "fighting terrorism" in the document can be seen as justifying the American military presence in Iraq, and the continuance of American military bases. Stripping Iraq of its Arab identity, coupled with a weakened central state in the proposed federalism will also ensure that Iraq cannot play any significant political or economic role in the Arab world, thus, leaving Israel as the only hegemonic power in the Arab area. With the vote for the draft constitution turning out to be "yes, the Bush Administration realized its goal of controlling enough oil to deter economic challenges, while providing American corporations with unparalleled economic freedom in Iraq. The Bush Administration pushed forcefully to finalize the draft in August to be placed for public referendum in October 2005. The underlying tactic is to create the impression among the American voters that the invasion has brought democracy to Iraq, and the Administration has delivered on its promises, whereby the carte blanche given to the Executive remains intact, and theoretically allows the administration to launch further campaigns against the two opposition states: Iran and Syria.

Democratization under occupation has unleashed sectarian and nationalist political forces in Iraq that will have far-reaching repercussions on the region: sectarian tendencies and Kurdish nationalism. While the occupation destabilized Iraq and threw the country into social chaos, the democratization process imposed by the occupation has done virtually nothing to address these problems. Ironically, American-created lawlessness and the spiraling of resistance have thwarted, for the moment, U.S. designs on Iran, as the American military has become stretched to its limit. The U.S. invasion has supplied Iran with a self-interested friend in the UN Security Council, China, which can veto proposed American sanctions on the Iranian nuclear program. The chaos and the persistence of the absence of basic human needs under the Anglo-American occupation have led the newly elected Shi'ite government to sign economic deals, and mutual security understandings with Iran, the nemesis of the U.S. and Israel in the region. As the terrorist bombing of the World Trade towers marked a watershed in U.S. politics and unleashed the forces of American imperialism, the occupation of Iraq has unleashed political forces the nature of which may well be beyond the control potential of the technologically based military superiority on which American hegemony is founded. The U.S. has been willing to ignore, if not break outright, international law to achieve its foreign policy objectives. But perhaps even more importantly, by its tardiness in reconstructing the social infrastructure of Iraq has frittered away the broadly based popular acceptance it may have had for removing Saddam Hussein that would have undercut support for the resistance that has now been directed into the social, sectarian and humanitarian chaos that is engulfing Iraq. For the Iraqis, the failure of the world's only superpower to provide basic services has revealed the true imperialistic intent of the invasion, and made laughable the American rhetoric of democratization.

Notes

1. Chalmers Johnson, "the Smash of Civilization," 7 July 2005, URL: http://www.tomdispatch.com/index.mhtml?pid=4710
2. Chalmers Johnson, *The Sorrows of Empire*, New York, Metropolitan Books, 2004, p. 40.
3. Warren Zimmermann, *First Great Triumph*, New York, Farrar, Straus and Giroux, 2002, p. 3.
4. Ibid. PP. 472-473. See also Chalmers Johnson, pp. 40, 45.

5. Chalmers Johnson, Op cit. Pp. 47-48, 51.
6. Ibid. Pp. 23-24.
7. Ibid. Pp. 60-61.
8. Examples of military officers are Colin Powell and Richard Arimatage. Representatives of arms industry include Peter Teets, former president of Lockheed Martin Corporation; Gordon England, vice president of General Dynamics and James Roche, an executive in Northrop Grumman. For further details on the background and the representatives of the military \ industrial nexus that prevails over the Bush Administration see Michael Moore, *Stupid White Men*, New York Harper Collins Publishers INC. 2001, pp. 16-24.
9. Chalmers Johnson, Op Cit. Pp. 62-64.
10. Ibid. Pp. 97-99, 103, 106, 110-112.
11. Ibid. Pp. 112-115, 117-118, 124-126.
12. Ibid. Pp. 259-260, 264, 266, 268-269.
13. Ibid. Pp. 56, 67, 255, 268-269.
14. Jim Lobe, "What Is a Neo-Conservative Anyway?," 12 August 2003, URL:http://www.ipsnews.net/interna.asp?idnews=19618
15. Amy Goodman, "Juan Cole and Osama Siblani on Middle East Politics," 11March 2005 URL:http://www.democracynow.org/article.pl?sid= 05/03/11/ 1449249
16. Ron Suskind. *The Price of Loyalty*, (New York: Simon & Schuster Inc., 2004).
17. "Bush Planned Iraqi Invasion Before Sept. 11" Reuters (11 January 2004) http://www.globalresearch.ca/articles/REU401A.html.
18. Neil Mackay, "Former Bush aide: U.S. plotted Iraq invasion long before 9/11" *Sunday Herald*, (11 January 2004). http://www.sundayherald.com/39221.
19. http://abcnews.go.com/sections/wnt/U.S./oneill_charges_040113.html
20. David Manning, "The Secret Downing Street memo," 1 May 2005, *London Times*, URL: http://www.timesonline.co.uk/article/0,,19809-1593637,00.html.
21. Chalmers Johnson, Op. Cit. pp. 5-6.
22. Chalmers Johnson, "No Longer the Lone Superpower: Coming to terms with China," 15 March 2005; URL: http://www.tomdispatch.com/index.mhtml? pid=2259.
23. Michael Schwartz, "The Ironies of Conquest: The Bush Administration's Iranian nightmare," 9 August 2005; URL: http://www.tomdispatch.com/ index.mhtml?pid=11233.
24. "Rebuilding America's Defenses: Strategy, Forces and Resources for a New Century." Project for a New American Century, (September 2000) http:// www.newamericancentury.org/RebuildingAmericasDefenses.pdf.
25. "The Path to War," *Vanity Fair* (May 2004), p. 232.

26. Nicholas Lemann, "The Next World Order," *The New Yorker* (1 April 2002), p. 43.
27. Bill Keller, "The Sunshine Warrior," *New York Times Magazine* (22 September 2002), http://www.nytimes.com/2002/09/22/magazine/22 WOLFO WITZ.html?8hpist
28. Paul Wolfowitz. "Remembering the Future," *The National Interest* (Spring, 2000); for analysis see Keller, Op. Cit
29. For an incisive report on the ideological web behind the Bush administration, see "The Path to War," *Vanity Fair* (May 2004), pp. 100-116, 169-174.
30. David Phillips, *Losing Iraq*, Westview Press, 2005; p. 17.
31. Richard A. Clarke. *Against All Enemies: Inside America's War on Terror*, (New York, London, Toronto, Sydney: Free Press, 2004), pp. 231-32
32. Ibid. pp. 30, 231-232. For an alternative perspective on the Iraq-al-Qaida link see Laurie Mylroie. *The War Against America: Saddam Hussein and the World Trade Center Attacks: A Study of Revenge.* 2nd edition (New York Harper Collins, 2001). However, the theory put forth by Mylroie is largely unsubstantiated and specious.
33. Ibid. p. 264
34. David Phillips, op. cit. pp. 18-19, 256
35. Eric Schmitt, "Pentagon Contradicts General on Iraq Occupation Force's Size," *New York Times*. (28 February 2003).
36. Toby Harnden, "Ex-generals fall out with Rumsfeld," *The Daily Telegraph*, (26 March 2003). http://www.telegraph.co.uk/news/main.jhtml?xml=/news/2003/03/26/wrums26.xml.
37. Julain Coman, "Dissent rounds on Rumsfeld: The U.S. Defence Secretary is emerging as the fall guy amid accusations of ignored intelligence and poor tactics." *The Daily Telegraph*, (30 March 2003). http://www.telegraph.co.uk/news/main.jhtml?xml=/news/2003/03/30/wus30.xml&secureRefresh=true&_requestid=4660.
38. Mohamed H. Heikal, "Al-kuwat al-Musal'laha fi al-Siyasa al-Amrikiyaa [The Armed Forces in American Policy] October 2003 in http://www.aljazeera.net/wejhat/article.asp?aid=78&ft=1.
39. "Al-Qaida 'Claims Madrid Bombings'" *BBC News* (14 March 2004) http://news.bbc.co.uk/2/hi/europe/3509426.stm.
40. Tom Goodrich, from "Iraq Veterans against the War," founded in July 2004; URL: http://www.truthout.org/multimedia.htm.
41. Henry A. Waxman, "Iraq on the Record: The Bush Administration's Public Statements on Iraq" (16 March 2004), p. 5 http://www.house.gov/reform/min/features/iraq_on_the_record/.
42. The Office of Special Plans (OSP) was established following the attacks of September 11. Abram Shulsky, the OSP's founding director, had worked on intelligence and foreign-policy issues for three decades, and served in the

Pentagon under Assistant Secretary of Defense Richard Pearle during the Reagan Administration, after which he joined the Rand Corporation. William Luti, the Under-Secretary of Defense, oversees the Office of Special Plans. He is a retired Navy captain, and an early and longstanding advocate of military action against Iraq.

43. Seymour M. Hersh, "Selective Intelligence: Donald Rumsfeld has his own special sources. Are they reliable?" (5 May 2003) http://www.abc.com/islam/english/jewishp/usa/herchcabal.htm.
44. Mohamed H. Heikal, op. cit. Also, Chalmers Johnson, op. cit. p. 224.
45. Ibid.
46. Scott Ritter, "Is Iraq a True Threat to the U.S.?," *The Boston Globe*, (20 July 2002). http://www.commondreams.org/views02/0721-02.htm.
47. George Galloway, "Corruption and Mendacity Won't Rescue Iraq's Occupiers," *The Guardian*, 24 April 2004.
48. "Galloway Versus the Senate," 17 May 2005; URL: http://www.common dreams.org/views05/0517-35.htm
49. James Risen, "Iraq Said to Have Tried to Reach Last-Minute Deal to Avert War," *New York Times*, (6 November 2003) in http://www.nytimes.com/2003/11/06/politics/06INTE.html
50. Ibid.
51. Ibid.
52. Ibid.
53. Toby Harnden, "Change of tone as Powell takes it personally," *The Daily Telegraph*, (15 February 2003). http://www.telegraph.co.uk/news/main.jhtml?xml=/news/2003/02/15/wblix215.xml.
54. When used in this context, both of the terms "freedom" and "democracy" also assume the primacy of the free market. This can be seen in the repeated adjoining of these terms in the National Security Strategy of the United States of America, September 2002.
55. Ghassan R. Attiyah, *Iraq: 1908-1921, A Socio-Political Study*, The Arab Institute for Research and Publication, (Beirut, 1973) p. 151.
56. "Ahmed Chalabi," Disinfopedia. http://www.disinfopedia.org/wiki.phtml?title=Ahmed_Chalabi
57. http://www.fas.org/irp/world/para/inc.htm
58. Robert Dreyfuss, "Tinker, Banker, NeoCon, Spy: Ahmed Chalabi's long and winding road from (and to?) Baghdad" *The American Prospect Online*. http://www.prospect.org/print/V13/21/dreyfuss-r.html.
59. Seymour M. Hersh, Op. Cit.
60. David Phillips, Op. Cit. Pp. 71-72
61. Seymour Hersh, Op. Cit.
62. Ibid.
63. Ghassan R. Attiyah; Op. Cit. Pp. 153-154.

64. Robert Dreyfuss, "Humpty Dumpty in Baghdad: How the Pentagon plans to dominate postwar Iraq." http://www.prospect.org/print/V14/5/dreyfuss-r.html
65. Ibid.
66. Ibid.
67. Jay Garner, "U.S. made major mistakes in Iraqi occupation," *Associated Press*, (27 November 2003) http://www.mytelus.com/news/article.do?pageID=world_home&articleID=1468723; see also: *PBS Frontline* "Truth, War and Consequences," (October 2003) http://www.pbs.org/wgbh/pages/frontline/shows/truth/view/. The Frontline documentary contains lengthy interviews with Garner on pre-War planning.
68. Nir Rosen, "When the liberator is an occupier," *Asia Times*, 4 December 2003 in http://www.atimes.com/stimes/Middle_East/EL04AK04.html
69. Wayne Madsen, "Weaponsgate: The Coming Downfall of the Lying Regimes?" *Counterpunch*, (10 June 2003) http://www.globalpolicy.org/security/issues/iraq/unmovic/2003/0610weaponsgate.htm
70. "General Tommy Franks to Retire," CNN.com (22 May 2003) http://www.cnn.com/2003/U.S./05/22/franks.retires/.
71. Alexander Cockburn, "Bush, Straw, Seize Broken Reed: Kay's Misleading Report," *Counterpunch Diary*, (11-13 October 2003). http://www.counterpunch.org/cockburn10112003.html.
72. Dilip Hiro, *Secrets and Lies*, (New York: Nation books, 2004), p. 434.
73. "Damaged Credibility," *St. Petersburg Times*, (13 January 2004). http://www.sptimes.com/2004/01/13/Opinion/Damaged_credibility.shtml.
74. CNN Documentary, "Dead wrong: inside Intelligence meltdown" URL: http://www.cnn.com/2005/WORLD/meast/08/19/powell.un/.
75. Jim Lobe, "Iraqi WMD: Myths and more myths," *Asia Times*, (10 January 2004). http://www.atimes.com/atimes/Middle_East/FA10Ak01.html.
76. Ibid.
77. Ibid.
78. Tom Regan, "White House's rush to war was reckless," *Christian Science Monitor*, (14 January 2004). http://www.csmonitor.com/2004/0114/dailyUpdate.html?s=mets
79. Ibid. Italics are mine.
80. Robert Dreyfuss, "Oil-Control Formula," 18 July 2005, URL: http://www.tompaine.com/articles/20050718/oilcontrol_formula.php.
81. Jephraim P. Gundzik, "The Ties that bind China, Russia and Iran," *Asia Times*, 4 June 2005, URL: http://www.atimes.com/atimes/China/GF04Ad07.html.
82. On 15 December 2004, Bush presented the Presidential Medal of Freedom to Paul Bremer. See David Phillips, op. cit. p. 221.

83. Naomi Klein, "Baghdad Year Zero: pillaging Iraq in pursuit of neocon utopia," *Harper magazine*, Vol. 309 number 1852, September 2004, p. 44

84. Ibid.

85. Ibid.

86. Ibid. Pp. 44, 48.

87. Ibid. Pp.48- 49.

88. Ibid. P. 48.

89. Ibid. P. 45.

90. Herbert Docena, "Iraq re-construction's bottom-line," *Asia Times*, (25 December 2003). http://www.atimes.com/atimes/Middle_East/EL25Ak05.html

91. Ibid.

92. Keep in mind that Bechtel's record as a harbinger of goodwill is seriously disputed. The company has a track record of what many consider 'profiteering' or even 'piracy.' It is the company that was given the contract for water distribution in Cochabamba after the Bolivian water system was privatized in ordinance with WTO regulations. Bechtel hiked water prices to an unmanageable level and was driven out by major uprisings in 2000. The company subsequently sued Bolivia for recovery of 'projected' profits, which could cause even more financial problems on a country already riddled with endemic poverty. For more information see *The Democracy Center* http://www.democracyctr.org/bechtel/bechtellegalaction.htm.

93. Herbert Docena. (25 December 2003) Op. Cit.

94. Herbert Docena, "Silent Battalions of Democracy" (3 September 2004), in http://www.zmag.org/content/showarticle.cfm?SectionID=15&ItemID=6159.

95. Quotation marks around "legitimate" appear in the original contract

96. Herbert Docena, (3 September 2004), Op. cit.

97. Ibid.

98. Ibid.

99. Ibid.

100. Iraqis Respond to the Election: Commentary from Imad Khadduri, Tahrir Swift, and Munir Chalabi," 1 February 2005, URL: http://www.occupation watch.org/article.php?id=9106.

101. Beth Potter, "Now that they voted, Iraqis want U.S. out," *Washington Times*, 17 February 2005. URL: http://www.washingtontimes.com/upi-breaking/2005 0217-094301-1888r.htm.

102. Juan Cole, "Informed Comment," 13 February 2005, URL: http://www.juancole.com. See also Al-Jazeera News,URL: http://www.aljazeera.net/NR/exeres/A44036F0-5090-4EF8-A8DC-DCA76418260A.htm.

103. Dahr Jamail, "UN Official Says U.S. Interfering in Iraq Constitution Process," 6 September 2005. URL: http://www.antiwar.com/jamail/?articleid=7164.

104. Herbet Docena, "How the U.S. got its neo-liberal way in Iraq," *Asia Times*, 1 September 2005; URL: http://www.atimes.com/atimes/Middle_East/GI01 Ak01.html.
105. Ibid.
106. James Cogan, "Iraq's draft constitution: a recipe for neo-colonial rule," 31 August 2005, URL: http://www.globalresearch.ca/index.php?context=view Article&code=20050831&articleId=893.
107. Herbert Docena, "How the U.S. got its neo-liberal way in Iraq," Op. cit.
108. Ibid.
109. Ibid. See also James Cogan, Op. cit.
110. James Cogan. Op. cit.
111. Herbert Docena, "How the U.S. got its neo-liberal way in Iraq," Op. cit.
112. Ibid.
113. Chalmers Johnson, "America's Empire of Bases" January 2004, in http://www.nationinstitute.org/tomdispatch/index.mhtml?emx=x&pid=1181
114. Ibid.
115. Ibid.
116. Ibid.
117. Antonia Juhasz, "Bush's economic invasion of Iraq," *Los Angeles Times*, 14 August 2005, URL: http://www.latimes.com/news/opinion/commen tary/la-oe-juhasz14aug14,0,11886.story?coll=la-news-comment-opinions.

2

COLONIAL FEMINISTS FROM WASHINGTON TO BAGHDAD:
Women for a Free Iraq:
A Case Study

ഈറ

Haifa Zangana

Introduction

In the months preceding and following the occupation of Iraq, several United States (U.S.)-funded Iraqi women's Non-Governmental Organizations (NGOs) were established in Washington. Their hastily staged birth was deemed necessary to engage "important voices which were missing from the debate—those of Iraqi women with personal experience of Saddam Hussein's oppression."[1] It was a last minute rush to provide the much needed moral legitimacy to the immoral invasion.

I will argue that these U.S.-Iraqi women's NGOs are an important part of the U.S. combat team and an arm of the U.S. government in Iraq representing its colonial policy rather than the Iraqi people's interests, in particular women. They were instrumental in rallying support for the invasion and occupation of Iraq. They continue to do so. Furthermore, they have played a damaging role affecting the much needed work of genuine independent women's organizations. Like the occupiers, these colonial

NGOs underestimated the feelings of the Iraqi people against occupation. They confused the need of the Iraqi people to get rid of a tyrannical regime with their objective of imposing a new colonial order. Their "women's rights" claims are often seen by Iraqi women as the second supply-line of U.S. colonial policy in Iraq. At its best it is seen as "cosmetic," for it fails to address the priorities of Iraqi women under occupation.

Background for Iraqi women's NGOs

U.S. policy towards NGOs was reformulated in the aftermath of September 11. Bush's words, "You are either with us or against us" became the 'Holy Grail' that governs all aspects of U.S. policy, including that toward non-governmental organizations. They have not been spared the transformation of world politics that ensued from 'war on terror.' Former U.S. Secretary of State Colin Powell outlined the new vision when addressing NGOs in 2001, arguing that:

> Just as surely as our diplomats and military, American NGOs are out there serving and sacrificing on the front lines of freedom. NGOs are such a force multiplier for us, such an important part of our combat team.[2]

Andrew Natsios, the Administrator for the U.S. Agency for International Development (U.S.AID), bluntly spelled out the same vision. He told international humanitarian leaders that "NGOs and contractors are an arm of the U.S. government."[3] Women's organizations are obviously included. That explains why in April 2003, the State Department magazine featured a signed message from the Under Secretary of State for Global Affairs entitled "Women's Issues Are Integral to Our Foreign Policy."[4]

How does this redefinition of policy reflect on U.S.-Iraqi women's organizations working in Iraq, a country the U.S. government deems vital to its national interests?

Establishment of an Iraqi Women's NGO

Several U.S.-funded Iraqi women's organizations were established either immediately before and after the invasion of Iraq. They all described themselves as NGOs and began working in Iraq immediately after 'mission accomplished.' They claimed to represent the Iraqi people, women in particular. A typical example and the most prominent of these women's NGOs is Women for a Free Iraq (WFFI).

WFFI was established in Washington D.C in February 2003, a month before the invasion of Iraq. Two U.S. institutions spawned WFFI: the Foundation for the Defense of Democracies (FDD) and the Committee for the Liberation of Iraq (CLI). But the call to establish WFFI came from FDD which is "a non-partisan, non-profit policy institute based in Washington D.C dedicated to winning the war of ideas."[5] Its board of directors includes Steve Forbes, Jack Kemp, and Jeane Kirkpatrick. Prominently listed as Distinguished Advisors are Newt Gingrich and James Woolsey. Its Board of Advisors includes Bill Kristol, Richard Perle, and "members of Congress from both parties, as well as leading political figures from opposite sides of the political spectrum." They are all united in "recognizing the dangers facing the United States."[6]

Among the FDD's most celebrated achievements was sending its representatives in February 2004 to the International Court of Justice at The Hague "to defend Israel's right to build a security fence to protect its citizens from terrorist attacks. FDD was the only non-partisan, non-religious, non-governmental organization at The Hague standing up for Israel's right to self-defense."[7]

FDD also "provided the inspiration and support for the resurrection of the Committee on the Present Danger (CPD), twice in 1950 and 1976, for the robust prosecution of the Cold War." CPD has been resurrected recently to "oppose the new present danger: the danger posed by Jihadists—radical Islamists and Islamo-fascists—assisted by rogue regimes."[8]

It is worth emphasizing that FDD did not show any interest in Iraqi women's suffering before the build up for the invasion of Iraq by the Bush administration. In fact, their suffering was totally ignored by the U.S. administration and FDD alike over several decades. Their timely interest in the suffering of Iraqi women conveniently blossomed for reasons best explained by themselves:

> When President George W. Bush was considering intervention in Iraq, FDD recognized that important voices were missing from the debate—those of Iraqis with personal experience of Saddam Hussein's oppression, brutality and genocide. FDD brought together a group of Iraqi women who could help Americans understand what had been taking place in Iraq—and what was at stake there. [9]

FDD brought together fifty Iraqi women (most of them U.S. citizens) to establish WFFI. Its birth was embraced by the Bush administration in an unprecedented way. It was launched at the Foreign Press Center in Washington D.C. on 6 March 2003, by Paula J. Dobriansky under Secretary of State for Global Affairs; attended by prominent members of WFFI- Tanya Gilly, Zainab Al-Suwaij, Maha Alattar and Esra Naama, who were received earlier in the day by White House officials.

Ms. Gilly, the FDD Director of Democracy Programs, read the WFFI statement which made no mention of America's systematic silence towards the Iraqi people's plight for many decades, its support for Saddam's regime especially during the Iran-Iraq war, and the impact of economic sanctions on the Iraqi people. Rather, she stated that:

> We are women who fled from Iraq to escape persecution by Saddam Hussein's regime. We have come together to speak up about the suffering of the Iraqi people under his regime and their yearning to be liberated.[10]

She went on:

> We were honored to have the opportunity today to share with Vice President Cheney, Congresswoman Price, Dr. Condoleezza Rice, Dr. Wolfowitz, and Dr. Khalilzad the message that we expressed to President Bush in a letter last week.

In their statement, the WFFI sang homilies to the U.S. administration, offered their support "to President Bush for his principled leadership," and applauded "the determination of the American Government to disarm Saddam, and its commitment to help liberate the people of Iraq."[11]

Thus "Being grateful to the Americans for liberating us" has become the *Bismallah* of their speeches, media interviews, press conferences and photo opportunities with U.S. officials.

Financially, WFFI was also supported by the Committee for the Liberation of Iraq (CLI) which was set up in late 2002 by Bruce Jackson, a director of the Project for the New American Century and dominated by neo-cons and foreign policy hawks like Jeane Kirkpatrick, Robert Kagan, Newt Gingrich, Richard Perle, William Kristol, and James Woolsey.[12]

In an interview with the *American Prospect's* John Judis, Jackson said that acquaintances in the Bush administration asked him if he could replicate the success he had had pushing for NATO expansion through his

U.S. Committee for NATO by establishing an outfit aimed at supporting the administration's campaign to convince Congress and the public to go along with a war. He said, "People in the White House said, 'We need you to do for Iraq what you did for NATO.'"[13]

Speaking for Iraqi People

The WFFI claims that it speaks for the Iraqi people with the aim of putting an end to their suffering. What have members of WFFI done to justify this claim before and after the invasion of Iraq?

Since its establishment, WFFI has worked relentlessly to echo the U.S. call for war on Iraq. It claimed that the war on Iraq was the only means to liberate the Iraqi people and put an end to their suffering. This was in no way a reflection of the Iraqi people's needs and aspirations. In fact it was exactly the opposite of what the majority of Iraqis, Arabs, Muslims, and the international community were demanding and struggling to achieve. Furthermore, the WFFI chose to maintain a blind eye to the fact that it is women and children who bear the brunt of the absence of law and order, the lack of security and the availability of weapons in the aftermath of war. To understand how misleading the claims of WFFI are, it is worth listening to a few other Iraqi and non-Iraqi voices who campaigned against the war.

Act Together: Women's Action for Iraq (previously Women Against Sanctions and War on Iraq) warned In February 2003 that, "If a new military assault takes place it is highly likely that much of Iraq's infrastructure will again be destroyed, with devastating effects for ordinary Iraqis."[14] Calling for no more bombs on Iraq, it reminded war pundits that, "In the Gulf War, Western bombs transformed Iraq from a modern, urban society into a pre-industrial one."

Iraqis in Exile Against War, a group of professionals, writers, teachers, and other responsible and concerned citizens, many of whom have personally experienced the persecution of the dictatorship in Iraq, argued in an open letter:

> We are told a war on Iraq is needed to pre-empt a threat to the region and to free the Iraqi people from Saddam Hussein tyranny. We as Iraqis already free from that tyranny, living outside Iraq and in the western democracies, say that both these claims are false. We say: no to war; not in our name, not in the name of the suffering Iraqi people.[15]

Like women members of Act Together they believe "that Saddam Hussein's regime is responsible for leading Iraq from a situation of great promise into one of unmitigated catastrophe, and this regime must be held to account for its abject failure and for the crimes it has committed against Iraqi people" but unlike WFFI and other organizations funded by the U.S. administration, they warned that "the remedy must not cause greater damage to the innocent and to society at large."

> To build a new, democratic Iraq, Iraqis in exile are convinced that: Real change can only be brought about by the Iraqi people themselves within an environment of peace and justice for all the peoples of the Middle East. A change of this kind, combining truth and reconciliation with legal processes of punishing offenders is being espoused all over the world. Why shouldn't that be the case for Iraq?

As an alternative to the war they called on the United Nations (UN):

> To put together a timetable for the lifting of the economic sanctions and do all it can to halt the drive for war that will only plunge the region into the abyss. We also call on everyone to challenge the dangerous and irresponsible war plans of the U.S. administration.[16]

In the wider Arab and Muslim world similar calls were made. Nine women's organizations signed a statement against the war, stating: "We, Arab women say 'No to the war against Iraq' because we are certain that when armies invade, only destruction will prevail."[17]

At the international level, a joint statement by British aid agencies working either in Iraq or in the wider region, was issued to convey their belief that "Military action could cause a humanitarian catastrophe." The agencies included Action Aid, Cafod, Christian Aid, Oxfam GB, and Save the Children.[18]

Oxfam expressed its sentiment on 18 February 2003: "The people of Iraq are still suffering the effects of bombing during the 1991 Gulf War. Twelve years of economic sanctions, and their own government's policies, have made things worse." The statement went on to emphasize that, "Those who propose war have not yet shown that any threat from Iraq is so imminent that it justifies the risk of so much human suffering."[19] Human Rights Watch warned on 13 February 2003 that Iraqi civilians could face tremendous hardship if war disrupted their access to food and water.

The World Alliance of Reformed Churches stated that "The war urged by Mr. Bush and Mr. Blair will undoubtedly increase the suffering of the people of Iraq and violence in the world rather than achieve a desirable democratic outcome for the people of Iraq or increase world peace and security. Any war on Iraq will affect the lives of common people gravely.The children, young people, women and men of Iraq have suffered enough, without being subjected to yet another devastation."[20]

Peace movements, U.S. historians,[21] law experts, and internationally recognized archeologists concurred. Millions of people in scores of countries took to the streets to protest against the preemptive war on Iraq, none of them defending Saddam's regime or dismissing his crimes but concerned about the safety of the Iraqi people, women and children in particular, the long term devastating effect on human life, and on the country's cultural heritage. All were proved to be right.

On 20 March 2003, at around 0230 GMT, the U.S. launched its first series of air strikes on Baghdad. Iraqis had to live through war and death again. On 23 March, bombs and missiles began to strike Baghdad, in a massive scaling-up of air strikes that were designed to "shock and awe" the Iraqi people into submission.[22] On 31 March, American B-52 bombers continued their heavy raids on Baghdad. Iraq says that night's raids killed 106 civilians. The Red Cross warned of a humanitarian emergency as water supplies began to run out in Basra.[23] U.S. troops killed seven women and children at a checkpoint in Najaf, southern Iraq. On 5 April, American tanks blasted their way into the city. "I saw houses totally destroyed, with pieces of children flying in the air," an eye witness said. Jamal Abd Hassan, the director of al-Yarmouk, the city's biggest casualty center, said: "Last night it was carnage…too many dead, and too many wounded."[24] U.S. - led troops used in their assault thousands of tons of D.U, MK77 (Napalm), and cluster bombs. They also managed to destroy much of the infrastructure rebuilt after its destruction in the 1991 war.

At the same time, members of WFFI made more than 200 media appearances, including an interview with Barbara Walters to "offer their support to President Bush for his principled leadership."[25] With FDDs help, they twice visited the White House for meetings and photo opportunities with the President, the Vice President and the National Security Advisor. While Iraqi women were mourning the death of their loved ones and the destruction of their country, WFFI women were "instrumental in rallying support for the 'liberation' of Iraq." WFFI's spokesperson, Esra Naama, put it to the press accordingly: "We want to thank President Bush and the troops that are there in the desert. Thank you for helping my people and for going to liberate my country." [26]

Brands Multiplying

On 21 April, a few days after Bush declared "mission accomplished," nineteen members of WFFI attended a meeting to form The Women's Alliance for a Democratic Iraq (WAFDI) in order to be eligible for international aid. WAFDI is described as "an international non-partisan and not-for-profit women's rights organization, dedicated to a free and democratic Iraq with full and equal individual rights for women."[27] Basma Fakri was chosen as President; Susan Dakak, Vice President; Zakia Hakki, Administration Director; and Tanya Gilly, steering committee. Some of the WAFDI members moved with U.S. troops into Iraq to develop "projects in advancing women's participation in rebuilding Iraqi civil society," examples of which I will highlight later.

WAFDI claims to be "The voice of our sisters by providing other venues of activities such as lobbying elected government officials, media appearances, and fostering awareness through letter writing campaigns. WAFDI will participate in fundraising, project proposals, and lobbying public agencies, funds, and symposiums."[28] Most of their letters were addressed to U.S. officials with a mantra like "we must all continue to fight evil," and headed with the phrase "the mission of the mothers and the daughters of the new Iraq."[29]

In August 2004, WAFDI helped to select women leaders from inside Iraq for a visit to the U.S., the highlight of which was a photo opportunity with George Bush. "The Iraqi women were joined in the Oval Office by American soldiers that had just returned from Iraq. They were eager to thank the soldiers for their freedom and for their personal sacrifice on behalf of the Iraqi people. Raz Rasool, the Executive Director of WAFDI, characterized her meeting with the President saying, "We have met the brave soldiers, American soldiers...WAFDI worked closely with Deputy Secretary of Defense, Paul Wolfowitz, to create a bi-partisan agenda that would showcase the political process from the local level up to the White House."[30]

Another organization closely linked to WFFI is The American Islamic Congress (AIC). AIC was created after 11 September 2001 by an Iraqi-American woman named Zainab Al-Suwaij, herself later a founding member of WFFI. AIC describes itself as "an organization dedicated to building interfaith and interethnic understanding, in the belief that American Muslims should take the lead in fostering tolerance, respect for human rights, and social justice."[31] Zainab moved to Iraq with the U.S. forces to be "actively engaged in reconstruction projects in Iraq."

The parent organization of the WFFI, the FDD further established an umbrella body for all U.S.-funded Iraqi NGOs, called the Iraq-America Freedom Alliance (IAFA).[32] This includes all members of WFFI in addition to WAFDI, the American Islamic Congress, and the Iraq Foundation which was established in 1991 by Kanaan Makia and Mrs. Rand Francke.

According to the FDD, this development was crucial for two reasons. First:

> When the major U.S. news outlets did not adequately cover the progress in Iraq following liberation, FDD established a grassroots organization, the Iraq-America Freedom Alliance (IAFA), to tell the untold story of Iraq's fight to build a peaceful democracy. The alliance established a web site, to highlight the good news coming from Iraq. It also invited Iraqis to tour America and tell their stories of oppression under Saddam Hussein's regime, of gratitude for their liberation and of hope for a future as part of the Free World. These courageous Iraqis spoke to audiences and local media in cities across the country, and appeared in print and broadcast media more than 400 times.

The second reason is:

> To win the war of ideas, FDD has launched a number of allied organizations. They operate under different "brands," but they all adhere to a consistent set of principles. In particular, all believe in defeating terrorism and defending freedom. It is critical that these many voices speak out to a multitude of audiences. [33]

IAFA was exceptionally active in August 2004, before the U.S. general election, organizing speaking tours for Iraqi women to visit military camps in the U.S.. They thanked the U.S. soldiers for their sacrifices in Iraq and painted a rosy picture of Bush's mission in Iraq.

Although these organizations, and some others based in the UK, are registered under a variety of names, and claim varying objectives and programs, they have, in fact, been established and run by the same handful of Iraqi women. Ala Talabani, a member of the Patriotic Union of Kurdistan (PUK) Party, for example, is a co-founder of WFFI, the Iraqi

Women's High Council and Iraqi Women's Network in 2004. Rand Rahim Francke, the Executive Director of the Iraq Foundation, moved on to co-found WFFI. Tanya Gilly, manager of the democracy program at the FFD is a founding member of WFFI and WAFDI. Zainab al Suaij, Safiya al Suhail, etc. are in more than three NGOs at the same time.

Projects in Iraq

U.S.-funded NGOs moved to work inside Iraq immediately after "mission accomplished." Most prominent have been WFFI, WAFDI, Iraq Foundation and AIC. Their funding came primarily from the U.S. State Department, U.S. Agency for International Development (U.S.AID), International Republican Institute (IRI), National Democratic Institute, (NDI- president Madeline Albright), and Independent Women's Forum (IWF). The budget allocated for women's NGOs has been several million U.S. dollars. The funds go mainly for organizing conferences, training selected women to be "leaders on democracy and women's rights."

An example of a conference was one attended by150 women in Iraq. "The Heartland of Iraq Women's Conference" on democracy and women's rights in Hilla, that was organized by WFFI in October 2003 with support from the FDD, the American Islamic Congress and the Iraq Foundation, and sponsored by U.S.AID's Office of Transition Initiatives and the Coalition Provisional Authority (CPA) in South-Central Iraq.[34]The conference chair was Ala Talabani who acted as a liaison between women's groups around the country, the CPA and the Iraqi Governing Council (IGC) which was perceived by a majority of Iraqis as the occupation authority and its puppet council. Zainab al-Suwaij, Safia al-Souhail and Rand Rahim Francke were the organizers. U.S.-Ambassador Paul Bremer delivered the closing remarks, and brought with him a taped address by Condoleezza Rice. The ending was described as "a momentous ending to four very intense days" during which "the participants meticulously read everything we gave them. We distributed the only democratic constitution we could find in Arabic, the Swiss constitution."[35]

The closing moment was described in emotional terms:

> The women stood up and clapped, tears streaming down their faces. We knew something very special, maybe even historical, had taken place, speakers and participants alike were transformed by the experience.[36]

WFFI described the conference as instrumental in orchestrating the cooperation between women, "positioned to take leadership roles in the new Iraq. In so doing, we went to the heart of the conflict between extremism and freedom, where it is taking place today: in the minds of the Iraqi people."[37]

FDD continues to support and finance WFFI, WAFDI and others, organizing their efforts when needed, in the service of U.S. policy.

> FDD arranged for Iraqi women to speak at the White House and to Members of Congress, organized letter-writing campaigns to Ambassador Bremer and the Iraqi Governing Council and built coalitions on behalf of Iraqi women that included liberal and conservative American women's groups.[38]

Here is an excerpt from one of their letters, dated 24 July 2003.

Dear President Bush:

> We are privileged that two of our representatives have the opportunity to meet with you once again, and convey our deepest gratitude for your leadership in launching Operation Iraqi Freedom and removing Saddam Hussein, a tyrant who endangered the whole world. The last time we had the honor of meeting with you at the White House on April 4th, you moved us with your heartfelt commitment to helping the Iraqi people build a new, democratic Iraq.
>
> The ongoing attacks against coalition soldiers remind us that the war to free Iraq is not over. Ba'athists and other anti-democratic forces in the region want to maintain Iraq in a state of chaos, and then use propaganda to turn Iraqis against the United States. They hope their attacks will pressure us to retreat. We must not allow that to happen: If our enemies succeed in Iraq, it will be a victory for tyrants and terrorists worldwide.

The letter goes on to denounce a woman member of the IGC, and a plead to censure the media:

> One critical issue is that the CPA continues to retain Ba'athists in positions of power…One of the members of the new Iraqi Governing Council, Aquila al-Hashemi said, "At the same time the CPA is not doing enough to counter anti-American propaganda. The coalition's spotty radio and TV broadcast service and local army newsletters are no match for the disinformation on the two television stations, four radio stations, and

dozens of newspapers that Iran operates in Iraq, the Saudi intelligence's radio service and major Gulf TV stations such as al-Jazeera and al-Arabiya—all of which purposely present the United States in a bad light."[39]

Alongside these efforts and during the U.S. election campaign WAFDI hoped "To be able to bring at least three more groups of women through November to visit the United States and take courses before election. These women are the best exposure to the American public to say thank you and to speak about what is really going on in Iraq."[40]

The U.S. Department of State awarded FDD a grant to run a comprehensive democracy training program for Iraqi women beginning in the fall 2004. Iraqi Women's Educational Institute (IWEI)in partnership with the AIC and the IWF also benefited. Paula Dobriansky, U.S. Undersecretary of State for Global Affairs, who announced the $10 million grant, said "we will give Iraqi women the tools. We will provide the information and experience they need to run for office, lobby for fair treatment in Iraq's emerging institutions."[41] The fact that the money will go mainly to organizations embedded with the U.S. Administration such as the Independent Women Forum (IWF) founded by Dick Cheney wife, Lynn Cheney, who has worked tirelessly over the years to oppose progress on women's issues in the United States, was not mentioned. Nor was it mentioned that Paula Dobriansky, who announced the grant, has also served on IWF board of advisers. Recipients of the grants also include the Bangalore-based Art of Living Foundation, a volunteer organization that promotes yoga and other breathing exercises to "eliminate stress, create a sense of belonging and restore human values"; and it has been running classes in Tikrit.[42]

These training conferences continue in tandem with the U.S.-designed "political process" in Iraq, i.e. the handing over of sovereignty, the elections, the drafting of a constitution, etc. In April 2005, IWEI hosted the "Iraqi Women leaders conference," where "150 pro-democracy Iraqi women leaders from every corner of Iraq to Jordan to participate in a historic five-day conference on the principles and practice of democracy and women's rights sponsored by the IWF and its partners in this endeavor, the AIC and FDD and funded by IRI and NDI (who are said to have received $80 million for the Iraqi elections) and IWF."[43] An Iraqi newspaper, *Al-Sabah*, said that the conference was being organized by the Iraqi Ministry for Women Affairs.

Other projects inside Iraq are bizarre. WAFDI implemented a multi-phase "love of Iraq essay" contest. The first phase took place during the 2003/2004 school year. They claimed that the prize of $100 per student per grade level was high for an average Iraqi family, but it was essential to attract the adults to help their children with this contest: "The love of the country will then be spread to the larger population much faster if it was approached through their children."[44]

Another WAFDI project was for Cultural Arts Paintings, designed to paint over all of Saddam's picture murals in Iraq with cultural and historical paintings. They claimed that "Will give the Iraqis a constant reminder of how wonderful, beautiful, and historical is the country they live in."[45]

A project with practical help to women in three locations in Baghdad and one in Nasiriyah was to provide women with sewing machines. The budget was exactly $700.[46] However, no matter how small the project is, the U.S.AID rules for NGOs had to be followed.[47] Therefore, the local project managers in Iraq who received the amount on 3 November 2004 collected the names and information on the families that are in need of financial support and hence needed sewing machines. To these families, they had to explain that "the project is organized by a women's organization called WFDI which is interested in improving the status of women in Iraq." [48]

A more public role for the women's NGOs has been in the political process, including more recently campaigning "to preserve women's rights in Iraq's new constitution." Representatives of two women's groups were in Washington, D.C. on 4 August to rally support for their cause. Zainab al-Suwaij, executive director of the AIC, and Basma Fakri, WAFDI, appeared at a "Newsmaker" event at the National Press Club. This time they came to represent other newly established Iraq-based organizations, the *More Than One Source* campaign and the Iraqi Women's Network (*Amal*), respectively. Leaders of the campaign in Iraq include Rend Rahim Francke, the former Iraqi representative to the U.S., and Safia al-Suhail, Iraq's ambassador to Egypt and known to American audiences for her appearance at the last State of the Union address, where she was personally welcomed by President Bush. The IWEI, a joint project of the AIC, the FDD, and the Independent IWF, supported the efforts by Iraqi women leaders in the Press Club event to establish equal rights for women in the new constitution.[49]

Reality of Iraqi Women

What about Iraqi women, their reality and aspirations? And how do they perceive the work of the colonial feminists in Iraq?

From the start, the U.S. Administration chose to characterize Iraqi women as silent, powerless victims in urgent need of social and political 'liberation' in a male-dominated society. This was borrowed from the image they created for Afghani women. The most striking example of this stereotyping comes from the CPA's representative, Joanne Dickow, who began working with Iraqi women in April 2003. Recalling the timid response she received in a meeting from Iraqi women, she stated: "There was this incredible sense by the Iraqi women of 'Oh my goodness, what do you mean we are going to get involved in politics?' And there was this sense of 'Oh, these are doctors, lawyers and engineers.'" Dickow explained that women had been largely excluded from the political process. "Getting them to understand that this was their time was probably the hardest job of all at the beginning," she opined.[50]

This image fits conveniently into the overall picture of the Iraqi people as passive victims who would "welcome the occupation of their country with flowers and sweets."[51] The reality is, of course, entirely different. Iraqi women have been actively involved in public life going as far back as the Ottoman Empire. This can be seen in Iraq's public schooling, in the media and in women's participation in political life. Women were involved in political activity, including combat, going back at least to the 1920 revolution against the British occupation. Feda'aha al Ezairjiya of Amara, the "poetess of the Twenties Revolution," joined the fighters to replace her brother who was killed in battle. Nazik al-Malaika (b. 1924), the most important poetess and critic in the Arab world, blended Iraqi nationalism and solidarity with Palestinian and Algerian struggles against occupation as well as broader struggles for freedom and social justice. Women were active in various political parties during the entire period, and, by 1952, there were 150 women political prisoners.[52] All of this reflected the same principle: fighting alongside men, women were also liberating themselves. This was proven in the aftermath of the 1958 revolution ending the British-imposed monarchy when, within two years, women's organizations achieved what over thirty years of British occupation failed to: legal equality.

These struggles and achievements, the result of slow organic processes, led UNICEF, to report in 1993:

Rarely do women in the Arab world enjoy as much power and support as they do in Iraq. The 1970 constitution affirmed the equality of all citizens before the law, and guaranteed equal opportunities without discrimination by sex. According to labor law number 71 enacted in 1987, men and women must receive equal pay for equal work. Women working in the government sector are entitled to a one-year maternity leave, receiving their full salary for the first six months and half salary for the next six months. A wife's income is recognized as independent from her husband's. She has the right to vote, hold office, acquire and dispose of agricultural land. In 1974, education was made free at all levels, and in 1979/ 80 it was made compulsory for girls and boys through the age of twelve. These legal bases provide a solid framework for the promotion of women and the enhancement of their role in society. They have had a direct bearing on women's education, health, labor and social welfare.[53]

Other developments were also reported by UNICEF in 1998: Women's industrial employment increased from thirteen percent in 1987 to twenty-one percent in 1993; in the same year, female employees constituted seventy-nine percent of the services sector, 43.9 percent of the professional and technical sectors and 12.7 percent of administrative and organizational posts.[54] Iraq also had one of the highest literacy rates in the Arab world, twenty-two universities, forty-five vocational colleges and approximately 14,000 schools. There were more professional women in positions of power than in almost any other Middle Eastern country.[55]

Despite all of this progress, the tragedy was, of course, that women were living under Saddam's oppressive regime. Members of the National Assembly were not elected but appointed. There was no legal protection for victims of crimes of the regime. It is true that women occupied high political positions, including twenty-seven out of 250 seats in the National Assembly, but they did nothing to protest the injustices inflicted on their sisters who opposed Saddam's regime. The same is now happening in "the new democratic Iraq."[56]

After "liberation," Bush had a vision for Iraq that trumpeted women's advancement as a centerpiece of his policy of 'democratization'. And, indeed, in the White House, Women for a Free Iraq recited what Bush desperately needed to hear, justifying the invasion of Iraq. Those women were rewarded generously in Allawi's CIA-backed government and the subsequently "elected" interim government. The U.S. political rewards to WFFI included three cabinet ministers, a deputy minister, Iraq's ambassador to Egypt, and Iraq's former representative to the United States.

The gap between those women members of the interim government and the majority of Iraqi women has widened daily. While cabinet ministers and the U.S.-UK embassies are cocooned inside the fortified Green Zone, Iraqis are denied the basic right of walking safely in their own streets. Iraqi women's daily lives are marked by this violent turmoil. Lack of security and a fear of kidnapping effectively prevent them from participating in public life. Occupation troops are immune from prosecution under Iraqi or international laws.

The killing of academics, journalists and scientists has not spared women. On 27 October 2004, Liqa Abdul Razaq, a newsreader at Al Sharqiya Television, was shot with her two-month old baby in the Aldoura district of Baghdad. Layla Al-Saad, Dean of Law at Mosul University, was slaughtered in her house. Maha Ibrahim, editor in chief of Baghdad TV, was killed on 3 July 2005. She was thought to be shot by U.S. military gunfire.[57] The Iraqi journalist Raeda Mohammed Wageh Wazzan of the regional public TV station Iraqiya was found dead on 25 February 2005, five days after she and her son were kidnapped by masked gunmen in the center of the northern city of Mosul. She was shot in the head.

As of this writing twenty-one journalists have been kidnapped in Iraq since the start of the war in March 2003.

It is important to emphasize that the reality of Iraqi women under occupation is that of all Iraqis, the reality of women as citizens. Gender issues are situated in an overall frame, whereby the family, health, education, and survival dominate every minute of the day.

Iraqi women are outraged to see their country's resources robbed while they live in slums, drink water mixed with sewage and have no say in the political process. They witness the looting of their country by Halliburton, Bechtel, mercenaries, contractors, and local subcontractors. According to a study conducted by Iraq's Health Ministry in cooperation with Norway's Institute for Applied International Studies and the UN Development Program, acute malnutrition has doubled among Iraqi children since 2003. This figure translates to roughly 400,000 Iraqi children suffering from 'wasting,' a condition characterized by chronic diarrhea and dangerous deficiencies of protein.[58] Unemployment at seventy percent is, of course, exacerbating poverty, prostitution, backstreet abortions and honor killing.

Ediba Nouman, a distinguished Iraqi academic who was dismissed by Saddam's regime in the Eighties, re-applied for her old job as a lecturer at Basra University. In order to start the process she was asked to provide a letter from al Hawze (scholarly Shia religious authority) to prove her affiliation with one of the sectarian parties controlling the IIG.

House raids and random arrest is a feature of the new Iraq. Women and children, though they might not be arrested themselves, are obvious victims of these. The raids seem to exhibit a general pattern which was summarized in a February 2004 report by the International Committee of the Red Cross, based on its own investigation of reported incidents:

> Arresting authorities entered houses usually after dark, breaking down doors, waking up residents roughly, yelling orders, forcing family members into one room under military guard while searching the rest of the house and further breaking doors, cabinets, and other property. They arrested suspects, tying their hands in the back with flexicuffs, hooding them, and taking them away. Sometimes they arrested all adult males in the house, including elderly, handicapped, or sick people. Treatment often included pushing people around, insulting, taking aim with rifles, punching and kicking, and striking with rifles. Individuals were often led away in whatever they happened to be wearing at the time of arrest sometimes pajamas or underwear....In many cases personal belongings were seized during the arrest with no receipt given.... In almost all incidents documented by the ICRC, arresting authorities provided no information about who they were, where their base was located, nor did they explain the cause of arrest. Similarly, they rarely informed the arrestee or his family where he was being taken or for how long, resulting in the de-facto disappearance of the arrestee for weeks or even months until contact was finally made.[59]

Since the nominal handover of sovereignty on 30 June 2004, Iraqis have witnessed an escalation of Israeli-style collective punishment of Iraqi cities. Civilian carnage, coupled with enormous damage to homes and infrastructure, has become a daily reality. Mass punishments have become the language of occupation. Twelve cities were attacked in 2004. Most devastated of all was Falluja. Camps around Falluja had been erected to receive displaced women and children. Men aged fifteen to twenty were not allowed to leave the city, so 150,000 waited in anguish for news of fathers, husbands and sons. The execution-style killing of the wounded Iraqi inside a Falluja mosque by a U.S. Marine, captured by NBC television, was one of many, according to an eyewitness interviewed by Al-Jazeera television at the time.

The plight of the people of Fallujah is not unique. In Tall Afar, a city of about 300,000 inhabitants in the north, U.S. troops cut off water for three days in September 2004 and blocked food supplies to 150,000 refugees. Then in Samarra, residents cowered in their homes as tanks and warplanes pounded the city. Bodies were strewn in the streets but could not be collected for fear of American snipers. Of the 130 Iraqis killed, most were civilians. Hospital access was denied to the injured. Tell Afar was besieged and its people were displaced again in September 2005.

The response of U.S.-Iraqi "feminist" women's organizations to the daily violations of human and women's rights in occupied Iraq has been highly selective. The suffering of their sisters in cities showered by U.S. jet fighters with napalm, phosphorus and cluster bombs, the destruction of archaeological sites, the daily killing of civilians by occupation forces, all of this is met with rhetoric about "training for democracy."

Iraqi Women and the National Liberation Movement

The architects of occupation claim that it is the Iraqis themselves who are beyond the reach of democracy. Hence the need identified by the occupation apologists for running the "training for democracy workshops for Iraqi women," so that in the future they may be involved in the peaceful democratic political process. But Iraqis including women are already practicing democracy albeit in a different frame than that designed by the colonial feminists. Over the last two years grass-root women's groups have organically grown within new movements or independently, unlike the colonial feminist NGOs. They have identified their own priorities and timing. They have joined protests, appeals, initiatives to set up a reasonable program for elections, the opening of human rights centers, lecturing at universities, even poetry writing. This torrent of activism is still being practiced by a broad variety of political parties, women's groups and individuals who oppose the foreign occupation. And they have been ignored. Newspapers were closed. Editors were arrested. Demonstrators were shot at, arrested, abused and tortured.

The Iraqi National Foundation Congress (INFC) , an anti-occupation umbrella of about twenty political, cross-sectarian religious associations, veteran political leaders, and civil society organizations, includes two women organizations, Iraqi Women's Resolve (Director Hana Ibrahim), and the Association of Iraqi Women (Director Dr. Maha Al-Hadithi). Individually women also participate in the Jurist Association and other unions affiliated with the INFC. The Popular Campaign to boycott Israeli and American goods is headed by Dr Haseeba Shia', a General Practitioner at the Sadr City hospital who is also a member of the INFC.

Summary

Colonial feminists were instrumental in lobbying for the invasion and occupation of Iraq. They are also a political card repeatedly used in imposing the time-table of the occupation. They apply U.S. policy by proxy, which has nothing to do the will of the Iraqi people.

George W. Bush has repeatedly utilized the colonial feminists when he needed justification for his policies or as a cover-up for his failures in Iraq. For his State of the Union address on 2 February 2005, Safia Taleb al-Suhail was invited. Guests are usually selected by the White House as living embodiments of crucial administration policies. To no one's surprise, Safia, who had recently voted in the Iraqi election, sat next to Laura Bush, and waved her index finger stained purple to the packed chamber of the House of Representatives below. Her appearance was staged to promote a president whose Iraq policy is increasingly unpopular at home. Bush spoke first of one of the objectives of the war: "Our men and women in uniform are fighting terrorists in Iraq, so we do not have to face them here at home." Then he praised by name Safia al-Suhail, a founding member of WFFI: "One of Iraq's leading democracy and human rights advocates .... She says of her country, 'We were occupied for thirty-five years by Saddam Hussein. That was the real occupation. Thank you to the American people who paid the cost, but most of all, to the soldiers.' And we are honored that she is with us tonight."[60]

Meanwhile an Iraqi poet and mother Nedhal Abbas writes:

Sura-Min-Ra'a
On Friday morning
In Sura-Min-Ra'a
A young man lays in pieces
Torn apart by sniper's fire
A woman
In Black A'baya
Passes by

Holding her toddler by the hand.
The child
Stares at the remains,
At a hand opened to the sky.
He reaches for a touch,
Wondering
Could it be his father's?[61]

Notes

1. Http://www.defenddemocracy.org/about_FDD/about_FDD_show.htm?doc_id=257042&attrib_id=7615.
2. Remarks to the National Foreign Policy Conference for Leaders of Nongovernmental Organization, Secretary of State Colin L. Powell, Washington, DC, 26 October 2001.
3. "Andrew Natsios, Speaking on the last day of Interaction's three-day Forum," 9 June 2003.
4. "Women and the Transition to Democracy: Iraq, Afghanistan, and Beyond," Paula J. Dobriansky, Under Secretary of State for Global Affairs, Remarks at the Heritage Foundation. Washington DC, 11 April 2003.
5. http://www.defenddemocracy.org/about_fdd/about_fdd.htm.
6. Ibid.
7. Http://www.defenddemocracy.org/about_FDD/about_FDD_show.htm?doc_id=257042&attrib_id=7615.
8. http://www.defenddemocracy.org/about_FDD/about_FDD_show.htm?doc_id=160895&attrib_id=7615.
9. http://www.defenddemocracy.org/about_FDD/about_FDD_show.htm?doc_id=257042&attrib_id=7615
10. "Human Rights and Women in Iraq: Voices of Iraqi Women," Paula J. Dobriansky, Under Secretary of State for Global Affairs;Foreign Press Center Briefing, Washington, DC 6 March 2003.
11. Ibid.
12. http://rightweb.irc-online.org/org/cli.php.
13. John B. Judis, "Minister Without Portfolio," *The American Prospect*, 1 January 2003 http://www.prospect.org/print/V14/5/judis-j.html.
14. http://www.acttogether.org/index.htm. AT statement reads: "We are a group of UK-based Iraqi and non-Iraqi women. We formed in 2000 to campaign against the economic sanctions on Iraq and, since late 2001, also campaigned against the U.S./U.S. invasion of Iraq. Now our focus is on the occupation and the support of independent grassroots women's initiatives in Iraq."
15. http://www.notinournames.org.uk/exiles/, 12 August 2002.

16. Ibid.
17. http://www.caabu.org/campaigns/arab-women-declaration.html
18. *The Guardian*, 26 September 2003.
19. www.oxfam.org.uk/iraqactnow.
20. http://www.caabu.org/campaigns/threat-of-war.html#campaigns, the World Alliance of Reformed Churches; War on Iraq is simply wrong
21. www.yachana.org/haw, More than 1,000 historians, members of the American Historical Association, called on 24January 2003 for a halt to the march towards war against Iraq, saying "We are deeply concerned about the needless destruction of human life, the undermining of constitutional government in the U.S., the egregious curtailment of civil liberties and human rights at home and abroad, and the obstruction of world peace for the indefinite future."
22. *The Guardian*, http://www.guardian.co.uk/Iraq/page/0,12438,793802,00.html.
23. Ibid.
24. Amid the casualties and chaos, there is a sudden appearance by Saddam, Suzanne Goldenberg, *The Guardian*, 5 April 2003.
25. See FDD success stories at http://www.defenddemocracy.org/about_ FDD/about_ FDD_show.htm?doc_id=257042&attrib_id=7615.
26. "Women and the Transition to Democracy: Iraq, Afghanistan, and Beyond," Paula J. Dobriansky, Under Secretary of State for Global Affairs, Remarks at the Heritage Foundation. Washington DC, 11 April 2003.
27. http://www.wafdi.org/background.
28. http://www.wafdi.org/objectives.
29. http://i.b5z.net/i/u/2003095/i/pdf/Falluja_attack.pdf.
30. http://www.georgiabizupdate.com/pdf/white-house-women-0408.pdf.
31. http://www.iraqfoundation.org/news/2003/knov/hilla.pdf.
32. http://www.untoldiraq.org/.
33. Ibid.
34. http://www.defenddemocracy.org/programs/programs_show.htm?doc_id=198780.
35. Ibid.
36. Ibid.
37. Ibid.
38. http://www.defenddemocracy.org/about_FDD/about_FDD_show.htm?doc_id=160895&attrib_id=7615.
39. See research topics at http://www.defenddemocracy.org.
40. See www.wafdi.org.
41. http://www.defenddemocracy.org/programs/programs_show.htm?doc_id=246637&attrib_id=10014.
42. "Foe of 'Radical Feminism' to Train Iraqi Women," Jim Lobe, IPS, 5 October 2004.

43. http://www.iwf.org/iraq/iraq_detail.asp?ArticleID=788.
44. http://www.wafdi.org/projects.
45. Ibid.
46. Ibid.
47. "We need to show the people of Iraq an improvement in their standard of living in the next year or two. And I have to have it clearly associated with the U.S. government, for diplomatic reasons which are, in my view, eminently defensible, ethically defensible, and good policy. So, proving results counts, but showing a connection between those results and U.S. policy counts as well." Remarks by Andrew Nastios, U.S.AID administrator at Interaction Forum, 21 May 2003.
48. http://www.wafdi.org/projects.
49. http://www.iwf.org/iraq/iraq_detail.asp?ArticleID=792.
50. See http://www.iraqcoalition.org/transcripts/20040426_women_net.html- 26/4/04.
51. Kanaan Makiya reassured President Bush during a meeting at the White House, *Al-Mutamer Weekly,* 24-30 January 2003, London.
52. Dr Souad Khayri, *Iraqi Women*, Stokholm, 1998.
53. UNICEF Report, "Iraq: Children and Women in Iraq, 1993."
54. Ibid.
55. UNICEF Report, "Situation Analysis of Children and Women in Iraq," 30 April 1998.
56. Haifa Zangana, "Quiet or I'll Call Democracy," *Guardian*, 22 December 2004.
57. See reporters sans frontiere http://www.rsf.org/article.php3?id_article=14353.
58. Karl Vick, "Children Pay Cost of Iraq's Chaos," *Washington Post Foreign Service*, 21 November 2004.
59. *On the Treatment by the Coalition Forces of Prisoners of War and Other Protected Persons by the Geneva Conventions in Iraq during Arrest, Internment and Interrogation* (Geneva: International Committee of the Red Cross, February 2004).
60. http://www.whitehouse.gov/news/releases/2005/02/20050202-11.html.
61. Translated by Haifa Zangana (Sura-Min-Ra'a : " A delight to the seer," the old name of the modern city of Samarra which (ءارماس) stands on the east bank of the Tigris, 125 Km north of Baghdad.

3

IRAQI HOSPITALS AILING UNDER OCCUPATION

ೞೲ

Dahr Jamail

I. Introduction

Although the Iraq Ministry of Health claims its independence and has received promises of over $1 billion in U.S. funding, hospitals in Iraq continue to face ongoing medicine, equipment, and staffing shortages under the U.S.-led occupation.

During the 1990s, medical supplies and equipment were constantly in short supply because of the sanctions against Iraq. And while war and occupation have brought promises of relief, hospitals have had little chance to recover and re-supply: the occupation, since its inception, has closely resembled a low-grade war, and the allocation of resources by occupation authorities has reflected this reality. Thus, throughout Baghdad there are ongoing shortages of medicine of even the most basic items such as analgesics, antibiotics, anaesthetics, and insulin. Surgical items are running out, as well as basic supplies like rubber gloves, gauze, and medical tape.

In April 2004, an International Committee for the Red Cross (ICRC) report stated that hospitals in Iraq were overwhelmed with new patients, short of medicine and supplies and lack both adequate electricity and water, with ongoing bloodshed stretching the hospitals' already meager resources to the limit.[1]

Ample testimony from medical practitioners in the interim in fact confirms this crisis. A general practitioner at the prosthetics workshop of Al-Kena Hospital in Baghdad, Dr. Thamiz Aziz Abul Rahman, said, "Eleven months ago we submitted an emergency order for prosthetic materials to the Ministry of Health, and still we have nothing." After a pause he added, "This is worse than even during the sanctions."[2]

Dr. Qasim al-Nuwesri, the chief manager at Chuwader General Hospital, one of two hospitals in the sprawling slum area of Sadr City, Baghdad, an area of nearly two million people, added that there, too, was a shortage of most supplies and, most critically, of ambulances. But for his hospital, the lack of potable water was the major problem.

"Of course we have typhoid, cholera, kidney stones…but we now even have the very rare Hepatitis Type-E…and it has become common in our area," said al-Nuwesri, while adding that they never faced these problems prior to the invasion of 2003.[3]

Chuwader hospital needs at least 2000 liters of water per day to function with basic sterilization practices. According to Dr. al-Nuwesri, they receive fifteen percent of this amount. "The rest of the water is contaminated and causing problems, as are the electricity cuts," added al-Nuwesri, "Without electricity our instruments in the operating room cannot work and we have no pumps to bring us water."[4]

In November, shortly after razing Nazzal Emergency Hospital to the ground,[5] U.S. forces entered Fallujah General Hospital, the city's only healthcare facility for trauma victims, detaining employees and patients alike.[6] According to medics on the scene, water and electricity were "cut off," ambulances confiscated, and surgeons, without exception, kept out of the besieged city.[7]

Many doctors in Iraq believe that, more widely, the lack of assistance, if not outright hostility by the U.S. military, coupled with the lack of rebuilding and reconstruction by foreign contractors has compounded the problems they are facing.

According to *Agence France-Presse*, the former ambassador to Iraq Paul Bremer admitted that the U.S. led coalition spending on the Iraqi Health system was inadequate. "It's not nearly enough to cover the needs in the healthcare field," said Bremer when referring to the amount of money the coalition was spending for the healthcare system in occupied Iraq.[8]

When asked if his hospital had received assistance from the U.S. military or reconstruction contractors, Dr. Sarmad Raheem, the administrator of chief doctors at Al-Kerkh Hospital in Baghdad said, "Never ever. Some soldiers came here five months ago and asked what we needed. We told them and they never brought us one single needle.... We heard that some people from the CPA came here, but they never did anything for us."[9]

At Fallujah General Hospital, Dr. Mohammed[10]said there has been virtually no assistance from foreign contractors, and of the U.S. military he commented, "They send only bombs, not medicine."[11]

International aid has been in short supply due primarily to the horrendous security situation in Iraq. After the UN headquarters was bombed in Baghdad in August 2003, killing twenty people, aid agencies and non-governmental organizations either reduced their staffing or pulled out entirely.

Dr. Amer Al Khuzaie, the Deputy Minister of Health of Iraq, blamed the medicine and equipment shortages on the U.S.-led Coalition's failure to provide funds requested by the Ministry of Health.[12]

"We have requested over $500 million for equipment and only have $300 million of this amount promised," he said, "Yet we still only have promises."[13]

According to *The New York Times*, "of the $18.4 billion Congress approved last fall, only about $600 million has actually been paid out. Billions more have been designated for giant projects still in the planning stage. Part of the blame rests with the Pentagon's planning failures and the occupation authority's reluctance to consult qualified Iraqis. Instead, the administration brought in American defense contractors who had little clue about what was most urgently needed or how to handle the unfamiliar and highly insecure climate."[14]

The World Health Organization (WHO) last year warned of a health emergency in Baghdad, as well as throughout Iraq if current conditions persist. But despite claims from the Ministry of Health of more drugs, better equipment, and generalized improvement, doctors on the ground still see "no such improvement."[15]

II. The Study

From April 2004 through January 2005, the author and his colleague surveyed thirteen hospitals in Iraq in order to research how the healthcare system was faring under the U.S.-led occupation. While the horrendous security situation in Iraq caused the researchers to confine the survey to hospitals primarily in Baghdad, hospitals west, north, and south of the capital are included in this report.

Hospitals surveyed:
Al-Karama Hospital, Sheikh Marouf, Baghdad
Falluja General Hospital
Saqlawiya Hospital
Amiriat Al-Fallujah Hospital
Balad General Hospital
Alexandria Hospital, Babylon Province (just south of Baghdad)
Al-Kena Hospital, Baghdad (Prosthetics/Rehabilitation)
Yarmouk Hospital, Baghdad
Baghdad Teaching Hospital (Baghdad Medical City)
Chuwader Hospital, Sadr City, Baghdad
Al-Noman Hospital, Al-Adhamiya, Baghdad
Al-Kerkh General Hospital, Baghdad
Arabic Children's Hospital, Baghdad

III. Summary of Findings

Early in 2004, prior to this report, Dr. Geert Van Moorter, a Belgian M.D., conducted a fact-finding mission to Iraq where he surveyed hospitals, clinics, and pharmacies. Van Moorter concluded: "Nowhere had any new medical material arrived since the end of the war. The medical material, already outdated, broken down or malfunctioning after twelve years of embargo, had further deteriorated over the past year."[16]

Findings in this report suggest that Dr. Van Moorter's statement remains true today, albeit with the continued deterioration of equipment, supplies, and staffing, further complicated by an astronomical increase in patients due to the violent nature of the occupation of Iraq.

This chapter documents the desperate supply shortages facing hospitals, the disastrous effect that the lack of basic services like water and electricity have on hospitals and the disruption of medical services at Iraqi hospitals by U.S. military forces.

This essay further provides an overview of the situation afflicting the hospitals in Iraq in order to highlight the desperate need for the promised "rehabilitation" of the medical system. Case studies highlight several of the findings and demonstrate that Iraqis need to reconstruct and rehabilitate the healthcare system. Reconstruction efforts by U.S. firms have patently failed, while Iraqi contractors are not allowed to do the work.

The current model in Iraq of a "free trade globalized system," limited in fact to American and a few other western contractors, has plainly not worked. Continuing to impose this flawed and failing system on Iraq will only worsen the current healthcare crisis.

Figure 1: Iraqi Hospital Occupancy Rates

Iraqi Hospital Occupancy Rates

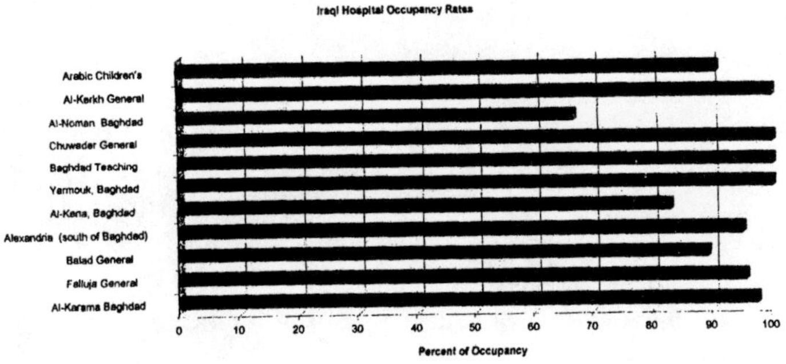

Compounding the problems due to a lack of equipment and medicine in Iraqi hospitals, occupancy rates at all but one of the hospitals surveyed was between 80-100% because of heavy fighting, car bombs, and an exceedingly high crime rate in occupied Iraq.[17]

IV. Case Studies

Highlighting some of the critical areas of need in the hospitals surveyed, the case studies focus on the following areas:

A. Shortage of Equipment and Medicine

In Baghdad, Al-Kena Hospital also serves as a prosthetics workshop and is the only facility in the entire country that provides rehabilitation services for persons with disabilities. It provides one example of how the U.S.-funded Ministry of Health is abjectly failing to provide Iraqi hospitals with equipment, medicine, and funding.

A General Practitioner at the prosthetics workshop, Dr. Thamiz Aziz Abul Rahman, said they even lacked the necessary machinery needed to make artificial prostheses. "We are using antiquated machinery from the 1970s which is missing parts," he said while pointing to broken machinery in the dusty workshop.[18] While holding a leg brace in need of repair, Dr. Rahman noted: "In addition to this, the lack of adequate funding means we are unable to treat more patients who need prostheses, as well as [having] a very long waiting list for people who need our care."[19]

Dr. Ahmed Kassen, a specialist in rheumatology at the hospital and supervisor of the workshop, said most of the materials used by the workshop for prostheses are imported from France and Germany. In a situation resembling that in other hospitals around the country today, Dr. Kassen added: "This takes time and we must await the shipments. They are also delayed by the security situation and delays at the Ministry of Health for approvals of these materials."[20]

The prosthetics workshop has only one wheelchair to transport patients in and out of the clinic, and there is not enough funding to hire wheelchair assistants or purchase more wheelchairs. Thus, simply to reach the clinic, patients must use friends or family members.

The clinic also received broken promises made by coalition authorities. After the invasion of Iraq, U.S. personnel from the Ministry of Health came to the workshop to find out what supplies were needed. Dr. Kassen said he provided both a catalogue and a computer disk of the materials the workshop needed but never heard from the officials again. "The Americans who came here didn't even know what a clinic like this was for," he exclaimed. "Of course we got no assistance."[21] Both he and Dr. Rahman said that the workshop had yet to receive any new materials from the Ministry of Health since the 2003 U.S.-led invasion of Iraq.

The workshop lacks even the most basic materials necessary for constructing prosthetics, such as leather, pins, metal bars and joints. Reliant upon the Ministry of Health for these supplies that are not forthcoming, hospital personnel are forced to obtain from the market what they can afford with their meager funds. "We don't have enough money, and barely enough of the most simple supplies we need to treat amputees," explained Dr. Rahman. "Of course we've had a dramatic increase in the number of amputees because of the invasion and now the occupation."[22] While helping a small boy with a new back brace to counter the effects of scoliosis, Dr. Kassen added: "We lack locking joints for prosthetics. Most of the time we are unable to serve smaller children and geriatrics. And if one component from the prosthetics is missing, we cannot help the people."[23]

Like nearly every hospital in Baghdad during the aftermath of the invasion, the hospital and workshop were looted heavily and have received neither funding nor supplies from the U.S.-funded Ministry of Health for compensation.

At the Arabic Children's Hospital which treats young cancer patients in Baghdad, Dr. Waad Edan Louis, the Chief Visiting Doctor, said that before the war most of the cancer cases came from the south, but now the doctor says there are numerous cases from Baghdad as well and this has caused a great strain on their supplies and staff.[24] While the extent of this increase in cancer rates is difficult to substantiate owing to inadequate disease surveillance or working cancer registries, this problem highlights the additional strain applied on the already struggling healthcare system overburdened by the costs of the invasion and military operations under the occupation.

Dr. Louis said the cancer rate jumped dramatically in the late 1990s, and his hospital alone is treating four new cases each week.

While the Pentagon admits to using over 300 tons of Depleted Uranium (DU) munitions on Iraq in the 1991 Gulf War, the actual figure is closer to 800 tons. Thus far in the current war there have been 200 tons of DU used in Baghdad alone, according to Al-Jazeera.[25]

As far as availability of medical supplies, Dr. Louis said there are always shortages, and what they need varies from week to week. At present they are lacking IV sets for blood transfusions and cannulas. Patients are compensating for this by purchasing their own supplies that they bring with them to the hospital.[26]

Dr. Louis stated that these deficiencies are due to a lack of money from the U.S. that supplies the Ministry of Health with its funding.[27]

Dr. Namin Rashid, the Chief Resident Doctor at Yarmouk Hospital, echoed this opinion when he stated that the only medical help his hospital had received lately had been a load of medical supplies from Grand Ayatollah Ali Al-Sistani.

He complained that the Ministry of Health consistently does not give them enough supplies, and his hospital currently only had one hundred sets of IVs and blood transfusion equipment. He added: "We are getting less medical supplies now than we were during the sanctions!"[28]

He said his hospital is receiving only one half as much supplies as it was prior to the invasion. This is also compounded by the fact that Iraqi companies have yet to be identified or allowed to participate in supplying equipment and medicine to the hospitals.

A doctor at the Al-Karama hospital speaking on condition of anonymity also said: "Things for us here now are worse than they were during the sanctions. We have certain items that we have shortages of—kidney transplant supplies, immuno-suppressive drugs, anti-rejection drugs, gauze, IV supplies and antibiotics."[29]

He said that they have received no funding from the U.S. reconstruction funds, and that most of the minimal funding they are receiving has come from NGOs.[30]

A doctor at Al-Kerkh Hospital said that the hospital is lacking IV supplies and blood transfusion fluids. Most operating tables there were broken. Also speaking on condition of anonymity due to fear of U.S. military reprisals, a second doctor working as an administrator doctor there reported, "the hospital is currently in a very bad situation. Before the invasion we had a much better supply situation, eighty percent better than now."[31]

B. U.S. Military Interfering With Medical Care

Another common impediment affecting Iraqi hospitals under occupation is interference by the U.S. military. While this intrusion has most often taken the form of soldiers entering hospitals to interrogate or detain alleged resistance fighters, perhaps the most glaring example of the U.S. military impeding medical care of Iraqis occurred in Fallujah during the heavy fighting of April 2004.

Doctors from Fallujah General Hospital, as well as others who worked in clinics throughout the city during the U.S. siege of Fallujah, reported that U.S. Marines obstructed their services and that U.S. snipers intentionally targeted their clinics and ambulances.

The Marines have said they didn't close the hospital, but essentially they did," said Dr. Abdulla, an orthopedic surgeon at the General Hospital who spoke on condition of using a different name. "They closed the bridge which connects us to the city [and] closed our road . . . the area in front of our hospital was full of their soldiers and vehicles.

Figure 2: Availability of Critical Necessities at Iraqi Hospitals

Hospital	X-Ray	Ventilator	Ambulances
Al-Karama Baghdad	Have .... 6 Working.......... 2 Total Needed.....6	Have .... 10 Working........ ....4 Total Needed 10	Have .... 4 Working.......... 2 Total Needed 5
Fallujah General	Have .... 5 Working.......... 2 Total Needed 7	Have .... 8 Working........ ....3 Total Needed 8	Have .... 5 Working.......... 2 Total Needed 6
Balad General	Have .... 3 Working.......... 1 Total Needed 4	Have .... 5 Working................2 Total Needed 5	Have .... 3 Working...........1 Total Needed 3
Alexandria (south of Baghdad)	Have .... .3 Working...........1 Total Needed 3	Have .... 3 Working................1 Total Needed 3	Have .... 4 Working.......... 1 Total Needed 4
Al-Kena, Baghdad	Have .... 2 Working.......... 1 Total Needed ... 4	Have .... 4 Working................ 2 Total Needed 4	Have .... 2 Working............ 1 Total Needed.....3
Yarmouk, Baghdad	Have .... 4 Working.......... 3 Total Needed. ...5	Have .... 28 Working................ 16 Total Needed.............28	Have .... 6 Working...........4 Total Needed.....6
Baghdad Teaching	Have .... 7 Working.......... 4 Total Needed ... 4	Have .... 20 Working............ ...20 Total Needed............0	Have .... 4 Working......... .4 Total Needed 6
Chuwader General	Have .... 13 Working......... 6 Total Needed ... 13	Have ....14 Working................ 7 Total Needed 12	Have .... 5 Working........... 3 Total Needed.. ..10
Al-Noman Baghdad	Have .... 2 Working.......... 1 Total Needed 3	Have .... 5 Working................ 3 Total Needed 6	Have .... 2 Working...........1 Total Needed 3
Al-Kerkh General	Have .... 6 Working...........5 Total Needed..... 5	Have .... 9 Working....... ....3 Total Needed.. 9	Have ....5 Working.......... 2 Total Needed......5
Arabic Children's	Have .... 3 Working......... 1 Total Needed 5	Have .... 6 Working................ 3 Total Needed 8	Have .... 3 Working.......... 3 Total Needed. 0

Virtually all of the areas have critical needs, i.e., an area with an unsustainable level of operation. Yarmouk and Baghdad Teaching, Ambulances, have a difficult level of operation that needs immediate attention, and Baghdad Teaching, Ventilator, and Arabic Children's, Ambulances, are areas in which the hospitals are operating sufficiently and do not need assistance.[1]

---

[1] Saqlawiya and Amiriat Al-Fallujah Hospitals were not used in this graph as time constraints at each hospital prevented collection of this data.

He added that this prevented countless patients who desperately needed medical care from receiving medical care. "Who knows how many of them died that we could have saved," said Dr. Abdulla. He also blamed the military for shooting at civilian ambulances, as well as shooting near the clinic at which he worked. "Some days we couldn't leave, or even go near the door because of the snipers," he said. "They were shooting at the front door of the clinic."[33]

Dr. Abdulla also said that U.S. snipers shot and killed one of the ambulance drivers of the clinic where he worked during the fighting.

Dr. Ahmed, who also asked that only his first name be used because he feared U.S. military reprisals, said: "The Americans shot out the lights in the front of our hospital. They prevented doctors from reaching the emergency unit at the hospital, and we quickly began to run out of supplies and much needed medications."[34] He also stated that several times Marines kept the physicians in the residence building, thereby intentionally prohibiting them from entering the hospital to treat patients.

"All the time they came in, searched rooms, and wandered around," said Dr. Ahmed, while explaining how U.S. troops often entered the hospital in order to search for resistance fighters. Both he and Dr. Abdulla said the U.S. troops never permitted the delivery of necessary medicine or supplies to assist the hospital when they carried out their incursions. Describing a situation that has occurred in other hospitals, he added: "Most of our patients left the hospital because they were afraid."

Dr. Abdulla said that one of their ambulance drivers was shot and killed by U.S. snipers while he was attempting to collect the wounded near another clinic inside the city.

> The major problem we found were the American snipers," said Dr. Rashid who worked at another clinic in the Jumaria Quarter of Fallujah. "We saw them on top of the buildings near the mayor's office.[35]

Dr. Rashid told of another incident in which a U.S. sniper shot an ambulance driver in the leg. The ambulance driver survived, but a man who came to his rescue was shot by a U.S. sniper and died on the operating table after Dr. Rashid and others had worked to save him. "He was a volunteer working on the ambulance to help collect the wounded," Dr. Rashid said.[36]

During a visit to the hospital in May, two ambulances in the parking lot sat with bullet holes in their windshields, while others had bullet holes in their back doors and sides.

"I remember once we sent an ambulance to evacuate a family that was bombed by an aircraft," said Dr. Abdulla while continuing to speak about the U.S. snipers. "The ambulance was sniped—one of the family died, and three were injured by the firing."[37]

Neither Dr. Abdulla nor Dr. Rashid said they knew of any medical aid being provided to their hospital or clinics by the U.S. military.

Targeting ambulances and impeding operations of medical facilities in Fallujah directly violates the Fourth Geneva Convention, which strictly forbids attacks on emergency vehicles and the obstruction of medical operations during wartime.[38] Chuwader General Hospital in Sadr City has reported similar illegalities, as have other hospitals throughout Baghdad.

Dr. Abdul Ali, the ex-Chief Surgeon at Al-Noman Hospital, admits that U.S. soldiers have come to the hospital asking for information about resistance fighters. To this he said: "My policy is not to give my patients to the Americans. I deny information for the sake of the patient."[39]

During an interview in April, he admitted this intrusion occurred fairly regularly and interfered with patients receiving medical treatment. He noted: "Ten days ago this happened—this occurred after people began to come in from Fallujah, even though most of them were children, women and elderly."[40]

A doctor at Al-Kerkh Hospital, speaking on condition of anonymity, shared a similar experience of the problem that appears to be rampant throughout much of the country: "We hear of Americans removing wounded Iraqis from hospitals. They are always coming here and asking us if we have injured fighters."[41] The November 2004 U.S.-led siege of Fallujah posed similar difficulties for the operation of health care services in that city.

Burhan Fasa'a, a cameraman with the Lebanese Broadcasting Corporation (LBC), witnessed the first eight days of the fighting. "I entered Fallujah near the Julan Quarter, which is near the General Hospital," he said during an interview in Baghdad. "There were American snipers on top of the hospital," who, he testified, "were shooting everyone in sight."[42] The Iraqi Red Crescent would have to wait a full week before being permitted to dispatch three ambulances into the city.[43]

Similar testimony emerged from hospitals in other cities during the same period. In Amiriyat al-Fallujah, for instance, a city some ten kilometers east of Fallujah, the main hospital was raided twice by U.S. soldiers and members of the Iraqi National Guard, doctors say. "The first time was 29 November at 5:40 a.m., and the second time was the following day," said a doctor at the hospital who did not want to give his real name for fear of U.S. reprisals. "They were yelling loudly at everyone, both doctors and patients alike," the young doctor said. "They divided into groups and were all over the hospital. They broke the gates outside, they broke the doors of the garage, and they raided our supply room where our food and supplies are. They broke all the interior doors of the hospital, as well as every exterior door." He was then interrogated about resistance fighters, he said. "The Americans threatened to do here what they did in Fallujah if I didn't cooperate with them," he added.[44]

A second doctor, speaking on condition of anonymity, said that all of the doors of the clinics inside the same hospital were kicked in. All of the doctors, along with the security guard were handcuffed and interrogated for several hours, he said. The two doctors pointed to an ambulance with a shattered back window. "When the Americans raided our hospital again last Tuesday at 7 pm, they smashed one of our ambulances," the first doctor said. His colleague pointed to other bullet-riddled ambulances, saying: "The Americans have snipers all along the road between here and Fallujah. They are shooting our ambulances if they try to go to Fallujah."[45]

In nearby Saqlawiyah, Dr Abdulla Aziz reported that occupation forces had blocked any medical supplies from entering or leaving the city. "They won't let any of our ambulances go to help Fallujah," he said. "We are out of supplies and they won't let anyone bring us more."[46]

"We were tied up and beaten despite being unarmed and having only our medical instruments," Asma Khamis al-Muhannadi, a doctor who was present during the U.S. and Iraqi National Guard raid on Fallujah General Hospital told reporters later. She said troops dragged patients from their beds and pushed them against the wall. "I was with a woman in labor, the umbilical cord had not yet been cut," she said. "At that time, a U.S. soldier shouted at one of the (Iraqi) national guards to arrest me and tie my hands while I was helping the mother to deliver."[47]

Clearly, the U.S. Federal Government needs to launch a broad inquiry into these matters so that those responsible for these acts are brought to justice and Iraqi medical personnel are free to perform their jobs.

C. Lack of Water and Electricity Affecting Medical Care

Dr. Qasim al-Nuwesri, the head manager of Chuwader Hospital, was quick to point out the struggles his hospital is facing under the occupation. "We are short of every medicine," he said while telling that the extent of these shortages rarely occurred before the invasion. "It is forbidden, but sometimes we have to reuse IVs, even the needles. We have no choice."[48]

His hospital treats an average of 3000 patients each day. Dr. Nuwesri said that one major issue that compounds all of their other problems is the lack of clean water. "Of course we have typhoid, cholera, kidney stones...but we now even have the very rare Hepatitis Type-E (HEV)... and it has become common in our area."[49]

HEV, transmitted via the fecal-oral route, is also primarily associated with ingestion of feces-contaminated drinking water. While it has a low fatality rate in the general population, fetal loss among pregnant women infected with the disease is common, along with casualty rates between fifteen and twenty-five percent among pregnant women as well. There have also been reports of perinatal transmission. Obviously, the best prevention from being infected with HEV is to avoid contaminated water. But in a place like Sadr City, a sprawling slum area of Baghdad with over two million residents, this is impossible for most of the residents.

Dr. Qasim al-Nuwesri said that one German non-governmental organization was bringing in water trucks, but the hospital still only had fifteen percent of the necessary clean water supply to operate hygienically.

In a room upstairs in the hospital with seven younger doctors, one of their top concerns was also the water. "The most important thing is no clean water," said Dr. Amer Ali, while the other six doctors in the room nodded in agreement. The twenty-five-year old resident doctor continued: "This problem is affecting us so much."[50]

Dr. Ali also described more of the horrendous conditions the hospital has faced under the occupation. These conditions include the ongoing power, water, medicine and equipment shortages. The other doctors nodded in agreement. "I think the cause of these worse conditions is the Americans," he said firmly.[51]

Highlighting the difficulties medical personnel faced because of electrical shortages, Ahlan Bari, the Manager of Nurses at Yarmouk Teaching Hospital in Baghdad told of a horrendous incident.

"We had a power outage while someone was undergoing surgery in the operating room," she said in her office, "And [he] died on the table because we had no power for our instruments."[52] While the hospital has generators, at times the generators do not perform correctly because the hospital lacks parts or runs out of fuel due to ongoing fuel shortages.

Most of the hospitals surveyed did not have fully functioning backup generators and lacked either funds or parts to have them repaired.

V. Corruption and Crime

Corruption and crime existed under the regime of the former ruler Saddam Hussein, but both are much more rampant under the U.S.-led occupation. One of the glaring instances of corruption is evident in the lack of proper allocation of U.S. funds within the Ministry of Health.

The Deputy Minister of Health, Dr. Amer Al Khuzaie, said the Ministry of Health was allocated $1 billion of the $18.6 billion the U.S. set aside for rebuilding Iraq. During an interview in his office in June 2004 he clearly stated that Bechtel, via U.S.AID, had the contracts for distributing the subcontracts and money for rebuilding/rehabilitating the hospitals.

When asked why he felt the work of rebuilding/rehabilitating the hospitals and medical infrastructure was not being done, Dr. Khuzaie replied: "Usually they use the excuse of the security situation in Iraq. But then why don't they allow Iraqi companies to do the work?"[53]

Dr. Khuzaie said frankly, "Surely every country passes their money through their contractors," when referring to what he felt was the root of the problem that the hospitals are facing under the occupation. "We could do the work and use Iraqi subcontractors," he continued. "The problem is that they [U.S.AID/Bechtel] want their own companies to do it."

According to the Deputy Minister, the Ministry of Health was supposed to have received $300 million of the $1 billion of U.S. funds allocated for the medical infrastructure, but still had not received any money.

While Dr. Khuzaie stated that the rampant looting of hospitals and warehouses following the invasion has aggravated the shortages of equipment and medicine, the main reason for the shortfalls has been that the former Coalition Provisional Authority (CPA) was slow to issue "Letters of Credit" for the Ministry of Health. "Letters of Credit are simply how we ask them for the money we need to operate," said Dr. Khuzaie, "and the CPA consistently holds these up for two months for us and this hurts us very much."

"The U.S. has opened the door to share the contracts with its companies and this made the delay for us," said the Deputy Minister while leaning forward to make his point. "This is what caused the delay in opening our Letters of Credit and this contributed to the drug shortages. This delay with the Letters of Credit happens every time we make a request. We have requested over $500 million for equipment, and only have $300 million of the Letters of Credit, but none of the money yet. We only have promises."[54]

Dr. Khuzaie's comments highlight the imperative need for U.S. funds to be released to the Ministry of Health so that the necessary medicine and equipment can be purchased and distributed to hospitals throughout Iraq. Along with releasing the funds, proper monitoring and oversight of their dispersion is necessary as well.

Iraqi drug companies are another source of corruption. According to the Deputy Minister, the lack of oversight, since the infrastructure in his country was shattered and the former regime overthrown, has led to this corruption. "Kymadia is the Iraqi company [that] used to supply the drugs," added Dr. Khuzaie. "They still do, but due to no infrastructure and lack of oversight, the company has become completely corrupted."[55]

Dr. Sarmed, a medical doctor who specializes in ophthalmology, voiced a similar concern. "There is no government office to complain to when the pharmacies are overcharging us or patients because we have no infrastructure," he said in his Baghdad home.[56] Dr. Sarmed pointed out that the black market for medicine was common before the invasion because doctors only made three dollars per month and some doctors illegally sold medications to augment their incomes; however the situation is worse now.

"Medicines used to be limited because of the sanctions, but now the drugs are pouring in from everywhere; thus [they] are unregulated and not certified," said Dr. Sarmed. He then added that another problem is that the distribution of narcotics is out of control and is thus being abused.[57]

Wa'al Jubouri, a student of Pharmacology at Baghdad University who is currently interning at a pharmacy, also felt that corruption is a greater problem now than prior to the invasion. "Each pharmacy now is like a black market," he said of his experience working in a pharmacy. "They can sell drugs for a very high price because there is no regulation like before."[58] Mr. Jubouri added that the medicine Iraq is receiving from other countries is usually outdated and unregulated material, further complicating the medicine shortage.

Another problem consistently plaguing the struggling healthcare system in occupied Iraq is that important and vital drugs are oftentimes available on the black market, but not in the hospitals. Dr. Sa'alm Shadid, a resident doctor in Baghdad, believes that the black market is a very big problem. "We don't get the drugs we need now, whereas even during the sanctions we were able to get them," he said. "So people smuggle them in and make more on the black market for them."[59]

The fact that drug companies have been forced to by-pass normal sales methods in order to make up for funds lost during the rampant looting which followed the fall of Baghdad also exemplifies how the lack of infrastructure in Iraq after the U.S.-led invasion has led to corruption that affects medical services.

Dr. Thadeb al Sawah is the assistant manger of Samarah Drug Industries. He is also the head of Inspections and Quality Control at the factory of Samarah Drug Industries. Dr. Sawah said: "After the invasion, my company owed the Ministry of Health 1.5 million Iraqi dinar and had to begin selling our drugs to the pharmacies to make up our money to pay the Ministry of Health… We sold them medicines we knew were on the Ministry's list of needs at slightly higher prices. Consequently, the pharmacies could sell these medicines in turn to the Ministry of Health."[60]

Practices such as these have further aggravated the lack of funds of the struggling Ministry of Health and have contributed to shortages of medicine for both hospitals and patients.

Criminal activity in occupied Iraq has further deteriorated the healthcare system. Organized crime is running in Baghdad, resulting in the kidnapping of doctors and severe staffing shortages at some of the hospitals. "The prominent docs are being warned and told to leave by organized crime," said Dr. Sa'alm Shadid in Baghdad. "It is very unsettled here for us. People want to leave mostly because of the security situation."[61]

Dr. Shadid explained that since doctors are now paid more than before the invasion, they have become higher profile targets for organized crime gangs who kidnap them for large ransom sums. In addition, street criminals have been targeting doctors' homes as well. "Kidnapping for money is happening often with doctors because we don't have bodyguards," added Dr. Sarmed while further explaining the problem.[62]

Dr. Sarmed cited several instances of the kidnapping of doctors: a famous neurosurgeon was kidnapped, humiliated and beaten before a ransom of $30,000 was paid; a famous ophthalmologist was released when a ransom of $70,000 was paid; the son of a famous surgeon was released for $30,000 and many, many others. "The most famous one is Dr. M. al-

Rawi, ex-president of Baghdad University and ex-dean of my medical college," added Dr. Sarmed. "Right after the war he was shot in the head in his private clinic."

All of the doctors interviewed about this topic believe that the horrible security situation under the occupation permits organized crime gangs in Baghdad to kidnap and rob doctors at will.

There is no indication that conditions have improved in the time since these interviews were conducted. According to the Iraqi Ministry of Health, such violence against doctors is increasing.[63] A recent study of corruption in the healthcare sector found that "bribery, nepotism and theft are rife, with the problem so serious that the health of patients is suffering."[64] Kareem al-Ubaidy, a senior official at the Medical City Hospital in Baghdad, said that corruption had left the medical sector in a worse state than it was under the previous regime.

VI. Brain Drain

Iraqi hospitals are also attempting to cope with brain drain—an event that commonly occurs during wars where trained and talented personnel emigrate to other nations because of the troubled situation in which they are living.

Doctors and medical students in Iraq today agree that this is occurring at an alarming rate, again with kidnapping being a large part of the impetus. "Security is causing so many doctors to leave, as are the kidnappings," said Dr. Wijdi Jalal, the executive manager of Baghdad Teaching Hospital.[65] Dr. Sarmed, an ophthalmologist working in the capital city, agreed. "The brain drain here is very bad," he said. "Regular doctors still don't make enough money to leave Iraq, so they don't. But the more senior doctors are leaving because they can afford to."[66]

Doctor Sarmed also claimed that the situation is so desperate that medical universities in Iraq have ceased providing their graduating doctors with certificates in order to force them to remain in Iraq to practice medicine.

Even though the pay for doctors in Iraq is now far superior to what it was prior to the U.S.-led invasion, morale has dropped because Iraqi doctors remain acutely aware of the fact that they are still paid very little compared to doctors practicing in other countries. "We all know that we don't make much money compared to if we were practicing in a western country," said Dr. Sarmed. "Everything is worse now for doctors in Iraq than during the sanctions, except the pay."[67]

Dr. Sarmed is paid $161 per month from the Ministry of Health. His colleagues with higher training are paid up to $313 per month, but are still not satisfied with this amount. Why? Because, according to Dr. Sarmed, they are paid the same amount as other government workers with far less education. Yet, they have much greater responsibilities and face many more difficult working conditions. Furthermore, compared to doctors in developed countries, Iraqi doctors are only earning a fraction of that income.

He said that while he was optimistic after the invasion, because he believed he would be allowed to travel and earn degrees abroad, he was suffering from poor morale since none of his aspirations has occurred. In addition, religious sects and political parties have begun struggling for control of the hospitals in Baghdad. This means Sunni are excluding Shia members, and Dawa Party members are discriminating against other political parties, and so on.

Wa'al Jubouri, a pharmacology student at Baghdad University said; "Everyone is asking himself if he'll go or stay. But we just live day by day. We all want to get out because the situation is so bad."[68]

VII. Reconstruction Contract Work in Limbo

But the present crisis in Iraqi healthcare is dwarfed, perhaps, by the new Iraqi government's promise of free enterprise to reconstruct healthcare services.

Let us briefly consider some preconditions of this promise.

Antonia Juhasz recounts that prior even to the war in Iraq, U.S.AID requested proposals to bid on contracts to select firms. "Excluded from the secret bidding process, were, among others: Iraqis, humanitarian organizations, the United Nations and any non-U.S. businesses or organizations."[69] Billions of dollars in U.S. and Iraqi public funds have already been doled out in such "expedited" reconstruction contracts, with billions more on the way. From the outset, "free enterprise" in Iraq, then, was anything but free.

Such contracting, as well as subsequent changes in ownership, was facilitated by transformations in existing Iraqi law. (The transformation of an occupied country's laws violates the Hague regulations of 1907, the

1949 Geneva conventions—both ratified by the United States—and the
U.S. Army's Law of Land Warfare.) These transformations were largely
made possible by the executive orders of Presidential Envoy to Iraq and
Administrator of the Coalition Provisional Authority, L. Paul Bremer.
Juhasz describes the impact of the executive orders on public services as
fundamental and far-reaching. Order #39, for example, "allows for the
following: (1) privatization of Iraq's 200 state-owned enterprises; (2) one
hundred percent foreign ownership of Iraqi businesses; (3) "national
treatment" of foreign firms; (4) unrestricted, tax-free remittance of all
profits and other funds; and (5) forty-year ownership licenses. Thus, it
allows the U.S. corporations operating in Iraq to own every business, do all
of the work, and send all of their money home. Nothing needs to be
reinvested locally to service the Iraqi economy, no Iraqi need be hired, no
public services need be guaranteed, and workers' rights can easily be
ignored. And corporations can take out their investments at any time."[70]
Little surprise, perhaps, that in such a context U.S. corporations are
essentially unaccountable for their actions. "Order number seventeen grants
foreign contractors, including private security firms, full immunity from
Iraq's laws. Even if they do injure a third party by killing someone or
causing environmental damage such as dumping toxic chemicals or
poisoning drinking water, the injured third party can not turn to the Iraqi
legal system, rather, the charges must be brought to U.S. courts under U.S.
laws."[71] As David Fidler suggests, such ordinances are reminiscent of a
system of political, economic, and legal thinking that created and maintained the colonial order of the late nineteenth and early twentieth
centuries.[72] In the colonies, as one contemporary account put it, the idea
was

> To exempt foreigners from the civil and criminal jurisdiction of the local
> magistrates and tribunals, and make them subject only to the laws and
> authorities of their own country, thus creating a kind of extra-territoriality
> for all citizens of the contracting States resident in or visiting any part of
> the East where the treaties obtained.[73]

Little surprise, then, that despite the ample reconstruction contracted
by the U.S. Agency for International Development, the Iraqi healthcare
system remains dysfunctional. Bechtel Corporation was hired to deliver a
comprehensive analysis of all damage following the U.S. invasion and to
identify priority reconstruction projects, including those in the healthcare

sector. Bechtel completed minor repair work in about fifty primary healthcare centers around the country and handed the rest over to U.S.AID.

On 30 April 2003, U.S.AID awarded Boston-based Abt Associates a contract worth up to $43.8 million[74] to "ensure the rapid normalization of health services in Iraq while strengthening the overall health system in the country."[75] According to the Center for Public Integrity, Abt Associates had earlier agreed to pay the U.S. government $1.9 million as part of a settlement in October 1999 after being "accused of billing several federal agencies prematurely during a 10-year period starting in 1988."[76]

A full year and a half later, reconstruction of Iraqi medical facilities can at best be called superficial. As Baghdad Medical City began to look nice in its new coat of paint, Dr. Hammad Hussein, ophthalmology resident at the center noted: "I have not seen anything which indicates any rebuilding aside from our new pink and blue colors here where our building and the escape ladders were painted." He said that "what this largest medical complex in Iraq lacks is medicines. I'll prescribe medication and the pharmacy simply does not have it to give to the patient." The hospital is "short of wheelchairs, half the lifts are broken, and the family members of patients are being forced to work as nurses because of shortage of medical personnel," he added.[77]

That very day, the Yarmouk hospital in Baghdad was given new desks and chairs. The new desk delivered to Dr Aisha Abdulla sits in the corridor outside her office. "They should build a lift so patients who can't walk can be taken to surgery, and instead we have these new desks," she said. "How can I take a new desk when there are patients dying because we don't have medicine for them?"[78]

The latest reports are not hopeful. "The cost of maintaining the gardens of Medical City was 68 million dollars, the cost of painting the building was 150 million dollars and the cost of repairs was 18 million dollars, but when you enter the hospital you don't feel any changes from the time of Saddam's regime. On the contrary, it's getting worse. There's theft and embezzlement."[79] As a consequence, according to pharmacist Muhamad Abbas at the Adnan Khairulal Surgical Hospital, "We can only give patients half the drugs that have been allocated to them because we don't have enough," and "we don't even have some varieties of drugs, such as insulin and certain antibiotics." Amir Batrus, who led the inquiry, found a more generalized restriction of basic services.[80]

VIII. Conclusions

This report takes as its central subject Iraqi healthcare as reflected by the condition of Iraqi hospitals. Such an approach necessarily excludes considerations that, however unrelated to hospitals, are fundamentally related to healthcare. Such exclusions from our thinking about healthcare reflect prior exclusions of persons from comprehensive medical care. Their mention here, however passing, is hoped to broaden avenues whereby medical care for all Iraqis can be envisioned and, without further delay, delivered.

One such exclusion is that of a civilian population, having already been subject to attack and displacement, from basic medical services. Interviews conducted in the aftermath of the November siege of Fallujah indicate a comprehensive denial of such services to the refugees who emerged from the rubble. "The Ministry of Health instructed us not to provide aid for Fallujans," said Dr. Aisha Mohammed from Baghdad.[81] "But then they have not done anything to help them during the siege, and very little at the refugee camps in Baghdad." Dr. Mohammed reported that she and several doctors from her hospital had struggled to get supplies from the Ministry of Health to refugees stranded in camps around Baghdad. "Only when we fought them did they allow us to have some supplies. What they eventually let us have after we demanded it, is still not nearly enough for all of the camps. We are in a crisis." Shehab Ahmed Jassim of the Iraqi Ministry of Health admitted that "in the camps now there are severe problems of diarrhea, colds, flu and lack of electricity and clean water."[82] Abel Hamid Salim, spokesman for the Iraqi Red Crescent (IRC) in Baghdad, reported that "while the MOH (ministry of health) gave their approval to transport aid to the refugees of Fallujah, they had provided the IRC no support of materials."[83]

There is increasing evidence that such shortages are especially pronounced in detention facilities. A recent report from the Abu Ghraib Field Hospital, for instance, describes the situation accordingly.

At times the hospital lacked basic supplies, according to members of the clinical staff, and at times it maintained a surgical service without surgeons. Sometimes the hospital ran out of chest tubes, intravenous fluids or medicines. Medical staff members improvised, taking tubes from patients when they died and reusing them, without sterilization.

Physician's assistants and general practitioners amputated limbs, a dentist did heart surgery, and Dr. Auch begged and bartered with other medical units for drugs and intravenous fluids. When they ran out of blood sugar test strips for Abu Ghraib's many diabetics, according to a medic assigned to the unit, they gave insulin by guessing the dose and watching for bad reactions.[84]

The same report cites the underlying basis for the now famous photographs of Dr. David Auch's response to an episode of psychosis at the prison. Without straitjackets and psychiatrists who could prescribe medication, Dr. Auch prescribed a leash to restrain the patient, recounting, "My concern was whatever it took to keep him from getting hurt."

The account resembles those emerging from detention pens at Guantanamo Bay, where former prisoners describe medical treatment as contingent on their "cooperation,"[85] and when offered, as often little more than "prescribing Prozac across the board."[86] Individual Iraqis, such as Sadiq Zoman, have undergone similar treatment. Fifty-five year old Zoman, detained in a home raid by U.S. soldiers that produced no weapons, was taken to a police office in Kirkuk, the Kirkuk Airport Detention Center, the Tikrit Airport Detention Center and then the 28th Combat Support Hospital, where he was treated by Dr. Michael Hodges. Dr. Hodges' medical report listed the primary diagnoses of Zoman's condition as hypoxic brain injury (brain damage caused by lack of oxygen) "with persistent vegetative state," myocardial infarction (heart attack), and heat stroke. The same medical report did not mention the bruises, lash marks, head injury, or burn marks found on Zoman's body upon his arrival at Tikrit hospital days later.

Such evidence that doctors, nurses, and medics have been complicit in torture and other illegal procedures in post-Saddam Iraq is already ample. As Dr. Robert Lifton writes,

We know that medical personnel have failed to report to higher authorities wounds that were clearly caused by torture and that they have neglected to take steps to interrupt this torture. In addition, they have turned over prisoners' medical records to interrogators who could use them to exploit the prisoners' weaknesses or vulnerabilities.[87]

Far more common, of course, than the direct administration of torture by medical authorities is the role that medical treatment has played in rehabilitating those subject to torture (often followed by further detention) while doing nothing to report and thereby abate its cause. Dr. Lifton writes that

> Even without directly participating in the abuse, doctors may have become socialized to an environment of torture and by virtue of their medical authority helped sustain it. In studying various forms of medical abuse, I have found that the participation of doctors can confer an aura of legitimacy and can even create an illusion of therapy and healing.[88]

By failing to report on the root of the physical and psychological trauma caused by torture—this root being the torture itself—medical authorities, by mitigating its excesses (providing temporary respite, tending to mere symptoms, suggesting alternative interrogation techniques, whatever the particular case may require) and thereby conferring legitimacy upon the military-clinical institutions that they serve—effectively facilitate the torture that they treat. As billions of dollars are deployed to create Iraqi security forces and hundreds of millions more for the reconstruction and modernization of detention facilities,[89] there seems little to indicate that Iraqi sovereignty over the police-state that is emerging represents a meaningful improvement for the healthcare of Iraqis. The exclusions from comprehensive health care here touched on suggest that medical facilities in Iraq serve as petty functionaries of this police-state. I write with regret that the contents of this report appear to do little more than confirm this reality.

Where does this leave us? "Security" has made several appearances throughout this report; it has been the basis for a primary complaint leveled by medical providers against occupation authorities—that of the latter's failure to create safe, secure conditions in which to work. But in the presiding language of occupation authorities—language that in fact prefigured such complaints in the form of a promise—"security" means home raids, capable weaponry, and state of the art detention facilities, which is to say security for property above persons. Although life would seem a necessary prerequisite to liberty, and the pursuit of happiness, today in Iraq there is, at best, security for expropriated property. In this light, then, the following conclusions represent only a return to old principles.

> This report supports the conclusion of many observers that the war and occupation—and sanctions prior to that—are primarily to blame for the

appalling state of healthcare in Iraq today. Up to 1990, Iraq had one of the best healthcare systems in the Middle East. This was the result of a deep commitment by the Iraqi health professionals to serve their patients well; a long-term, quality-oriented planning by successive Iraqi governments since the 1930s; and well-functioning and disciplined—albeit sometimes heavy-handed—government structures.

Currently an autonomous government is claimed in Iraq, although both its legitimacy and its autonomy are highly questionable. It can easily be argued, based on international law, that the existence of this government doesn't change the U.S.'s status as an occupying power. In any case, the U.S. was the occupying power in Iraq for the period covered by this report. As such, the U.S. was responsible for conforming with all international law, especially humanitarian law and human rights law, regarding the situation of healthcare in Iraq.

The Fourth Geneva Convention contains specific provisions pertaining to the delivery of healthcare services:

Article 55: To the fullest extent of the means available to it the Occupying Power has the duty of ensuring the food and medical supplies of the population; it should, in particular, bring in the necessary foodstuffs, medical stores and other articles if the resources of the occupied territory are inadequate. (...)

Article 56: To the fullest extent of the means available to it, the Occupying Power has the duty of ensuring and maintaining, with the cooperation of national and local authorities, the medical and hospital establishments and services, public health and hygiene in the occupied territory, with particular reference to the adoption and application of the prophylactic and preventive measures necessary to combat the spread of contagious diseases and epidemics. Medical personnel of all categories shall be allowed to carry out their duties. (...)

This report clearly illustrates the abject failure of the U.S. to carry out even minimal humanitarian duties as the occupying power. More importantly, it paints a picture of a healthcare system that has deteriorated since the start of the war, and of a failure to fundamentally reverse this decline. From a public health point of view, an end to occupation, with a scheduled withdrawal of all foreign troops, appears to be a major requirement.

In the meantime, actions must be undertaken that would constitute small but important steps in securing a more functional healthcare system for the Iraqi people. Thus, this report concludes with the following calls to action:

1. The fact that the U.S. government has released so little of the one billion dollars in reconstruction funds allegedly allocated to the Ministry of Health should be subject to an immediate congressional investigation to scrutinize the U.S. government's expenditures and actions, as well as the expenditures and actions of western companies that have been awarded contracts in Iraq regarding the healthcare system. Investigators should be given the power to impose or seek punitive measures for contract violations and over-expenditures and to provide oversight, regulation and accountability of the work of these companies in regard to their individual contracts.

2. This abuse of resources and widespread corruption seems a natural consequence of the lack of oversight of multinational corporations, owing perhaps primarily to their immunity under Iraqi law as established by Executive Order #17. An institutional regime consisting of international oversight, which would include a legitimate body of experts on essential services and representatives of the country's medical society, should be created and put to work immediately.

3. An independent investigation should be launched to probe the actions of the U.S. military regarding its alleged interference with Iraqi healthcare personnel and facilities, specifically with regard to the city of Fallujah. This investigation should include a more general appraisal of U.S. military actions that have interfered with efforts to provide both healthcare and emergency services to a population under occupation. The investigation should also examine the issue of accountability to clearly identify who is accountable for this state of affairs. In order to facilitate independent inquiries into these and other human rights issues, the post of UN Human Rights Rapporteur, vacant since 2003, should be filled immediately.

4. Every Iraqi who has suffered the loss of a loved one, injury or property damage as a result of the invasion and ensuing occupation should immediately be compensated in full by western standards, not the

$2500 payout the U.S. military has set as the standard fee for a dead Iraqi.

Contributors

I would like to acknowledge the following people for their invaluable contributions to this report. Without their assistance, this report would not have been possible:

Abu Talat (Interpreter-Iraq)
Dr. Bert De Belder (Coordinator of Medical Aid for the Third World)
Dirk Adriaensens (coordinator, SOS Iraq)
Professor Jean Bricmont (scientist, specialist in theoretical physics, U.C. Louvain-La-Neuve)
Emad Ahmed Khammas (Former co-director of Occupation Watch-Iraq)
Abdul Ilah Al-Bayaty (Writer-Iraq/France)
Dr. Imad Khadduri (Nuclear scientist-Iraq/Canada)
Hans von Sponeck (Former UN Assistant Secretary General & United Nations Humanitarian Coordinator for Iraq-Germany)
Karen Parker (Attorney-U.S.A)
Amy Bartholomew (Law professor-Canada)
Dr. Geert Van Moorter (Medical Aid for the Third World)
(as well as the other members of the Brussels Tribunal Executive and Advisory Committee).

X. Sections of Geneva Conventions I, III and IV of 1949[90] Relevant to Health Rights and Health Care

Geneva Convention I
(Protection for sick and wounded combatants on land)[91]

Article 7: Wounded and sick, as well as members of the medical personnel and chaplains, may in no circumstances renounce in part or in entirety the rights secured to them by the present Convention...[92]

Article 12: [Combatants] who are sick and wounded...shall be treated humanely and cared for by the Party to the conflict in whose power they may be without any adverse distinction founded on sex, race, nationality, religion, political opinions, or any similar criteria. Any attempts on their lives, or violence to their persons, shall be strictly prohibited; in particular, they shall not be murdered or exterminated, subjected to torture or to biological experiments; they shall not be willfully left without medical assistance and care, nor shall conditions exposing them to contagion or infection be created.

Only urgent medical reasons will authorize priority in the order of treatment to be administered.

Article 15: At all times, and particularly after an engagement, Parties to the conflict shall, without delay, take all possible measures to search for and to collect the wounded and sick, to protect them against pillage and ill-treatment, to ensure their adequate care, and to search for the dead and prevent their being despoiled.

Article 16: Parties to the conflict shall record as soon as possible, in respect of each wounded, sick or dead person of the adverse Party falling into their hands, any particulars which may assist in his identification.

Article 19: Fixed establishments and mobile medical units of the Medical Service may in no circumstances be attacked.

Article 24: Medical personnel exclusively engaged in the search for, or the collection, transport or treatment of the wounded or sick, or in the prevention of disease, staff exclusively engaged in the administration of medical units and establishments, as well as chaplains attached to the armed forces, shall be respected and protected in all circumstances.

Article 33: The material of mobile medical units...shall be reserved for the care of wounded and sick.

The material and stores defined in the present Article shall not be intentionally destroyed.

Geneva Convention III
(Protection for prisoners of war)

Article 13: Prisoners of war must at all times be humanely treated. Any unlawful act or omission by the Detaining Power causing death or seriously endangering the health of a prisoner in its custody is prohibited, and will be regarded as a serious breach of the present Convention.

Likewise, prisoners of war must at all times be protected, particularly against acts of violence or intimidation and against insults and public curiosity.

Article 30: Prisoners of war suffering from serious disease, or whose condition requires special treatment, a surgical operation or hospital care, must be admitted to any military or civilian medical unit where treatment can be given ... The cost of treatment... shall be borne by the Detaining Power.

Geneva Convention IV
(Protection of the civilian populations)

Article 18: Civilian hospitals organized to care to the wounded and sick, infirm and maternity cases, may in no circumstances be the object of attack, but shall at all times be respected and protected by the Parties to the conflict.

Article 20: Persons regularly and solely engaged in the operation and administration of civilian hospitals, including the personnel engaged in the search for, removal and transportation of and caring for the wounded and sick civilians, the infirm and maternity cases, shall be respected and protected.

Article 21: Convoys of vehicles or hospital trains on land conveying wounded and sick civilians, the infirm and maternity cases, shall be respected and protected in the same manner as the hospitals for in Article 18.

Article 23: Each High Contracting Party shall allow for the free passage of all consignments of medical and hospital stores...intended only for civilians of another High Contracting Party, even if the latter is its adversary. It shall likewise permit the free passage of all consignments of essential foodstuffs, clothing and tonics intended for children under fifteen, expectant mothers and maternity cases.

Article 55: To the fullest extent of the means available to it, the Occupying Power has the duty of ensuring food and medical supplies of the population; it should, in particular, bring in the necessary foodstuffs, medical stores and other articles if the resources of the occupied territories are inadequate.

Article 56: To the fullest extent of the means available to it, the Occupying Power has the duty of ensuring and maintaining, with the cooperation of national and local authorities, the medical and hospital establishments and services, public health and hygiene in the occupied territory, with particular reference to the adoption and application of the prophylactic and preventive measures necessary to combat the spread of contagious diseases and epidemics. Medical personnel of all categories shall be allowed to carry out their duties.

In adopting measures of health and hygiene and in their implementation, the Occupying Power shall take into consideration the moral and ethical susceptibilities of the population of the occupied territory.

Article 147:[93] Grave breaches shall be those involving any of the following acts, if committed against persons or property protected in the present Convention: willful killing, torture or inhumane treatment, including biological experiments, willfully causing great suffering or serious injury to body or health, unlawful deportation or transfer or unlawful confinement of a protected person...taking of hostages and extensive destruction and appropriation of property, not justified by military necessity and carried out unlawfully and wantonly.

Notes

1. Naomi Koppel, "Red Cross Says Iraq Hospitals Overwhelmed," Associated Press, 9 April 2004.
2. Dahr Jamail, interview with Dr. Thamiz Aziz Abul Rahman at Al Kena Hospital, 28 April 2004.
3. Dahr Jamail, interview with Dr. Qasim al-Nuwesri at Chuwader General Hospital, 14 June 2004.

4. Ibid.
5. BBC News, "U.S. strikes raze Fallujah hospital," 6 November 2004.
6. Richard A. Oppel Jr., New York Times, "Early Target of Offensive Is a Hospital," 8 November 2004.
7. Fares Dulaimi, Agence France-Presse, "Doctors, Medical Supplies Scarce in Fallujah as Major Assault Begins," 8 November 2004.
8. Bremer Admits Coalition Spending on Iraq Health Grossly Inadequate," Agence France Press, 15 February 2004.
9. Dahr Jamail, interview with Dr. Sarmad Raheem at Al-Kerkh Hospital, 19 June 2004.
10. This doctor also asked that only his first name be used, due to his fear of military reprisals.
11. Dahr Jamail, interview with Dr. Mohammed at Fallujah General Hospital, 10 May 2004.
12. Dahr Jamail, interview with Dr. Amer Al Khuzaie at Ministry of Health, 24 June 2004.
13. Ibid.
14. "The Iraq Reconstruction Fiasco," *The New York Times*, 9 August 2004.
15. Matthew Price, "Hospitals Endure Iraqi Paralysis," BBC News, 17 March 2005.
16. Dr. Greet Van Moorter, M.D., "One year after the fall of Baghdad: how healthy is Iraq?," *Medical Aid for the Third World*, 28 April 2004
17. Saqlawiya and Amiriat Al-Fallujah Hospitals were not used in this graph as time constraints at each hospital prevented collection of this data.
18. Dahr Jamail, interview of Dr. Thamiz Aziz Abul Rahman at Al-Kena Hospital, 28 April 2004.
19. Ibid.
20. Dahr Jamail, interview of Dr. Ahmed Kassen at Al-Kena Hospital, 28 April 2004.
21. Dahr Jamail, interview of Dr. Ahmed Kassen at Al-Kena Hospital, 28 April 2004.
22. Dahr Jamail, interview of Dr. Thamiz Aziz Abul Rahman at Al-Kena Hospital, 28 April 2004.
23. Dahr Jamail, interview of Dr. Ahmed Kassen at Al-Kena Hospital, 28 April 2004.
24. Abu Talat, interview of Dr. Waad Edan Louis at Arabic Children's Hospital, 24 July 2004.
25. Lawrence Smallman, "Iraq's real WMD Crime," Al-Jazeera, 30 October 2003.
26. Abu Talat, interview of Dr. Waad Edan Louis at Arabic Children's Hospital, 24 July 2004.
27. Ibid.

28. Dahr Jamail, interview of Dr. Namin Rashid at Yarmouk Hospital, 8 April 2004.
29. Dahr Jamail, interview of a doctor who asked to remain nameless at Al-Karama Hospital, 8 April 2004.
30. Ibid.
31. Dahr Jamail, interview of doctor who asked to remain nameless at Al-Kerkh Hospital, 8 April 2004.
32. Dahr Jamail, interview of "Dr. Abdulla" at Fallujah General Hospital, 10 May 12004.
33. Ibid.
34. Dahr Jamail, interview of "Dr. Ahmed" who asked to use this false name to protect his identity at Fallujah General Hospital, 10 May 2004.
35. Dahr Jamail interview of "Dr. Rashid" who asked to use this false name to protect his identity at Fallujah General Hospital, 10 May 2004.
36. Ibid.
37. Dahr Jamail, interview of Dr. Abdulla at Fallujah General Hospital, 10 May 2004.
38. Martin Zwanenburg, "Existentialism in Iraq: Security Council Resolution 1483 and the law of occupation," *International Review of the Red Cross*, Number 856, p. 750.
39. Dahr Jamail, interview of Dr. Abdul Ali at Al-Noman Hospital, 22 April 2004.
40. Ibid.
41. Dahr Jamail, interview of doctor who asked to remain anonymous at Al-Kerkh Hospital, 8 April 2004.
42. Dahr Jamail, interview of Burhan Fasa'a, Baghdad, 4 December 2004.
43. Dahr Jamail, *The Ester Republic*, "An Eyewitness Account of Fallujah," 16 December 2004.
44. Dahr Jamail, interview of Amiriyat al-Fallujah doctor who asked to remain anonymous, Baghdad, 13 December 2004.
45. Dahr Jamail, interview of a second Amiriyat al-Fallujah doctor who asked to remain anonymous, Baghdad, 13 December 2004.
46. Dahr Jamail, Inter Press Service, "U.S. Military Obstructing Medical Care," 13 December 2004.
47. Dahr Jamail, interview of Dr. al-Muhannadi, Baghdad, 13 December 2004.
48. Dahr Jamail, interview of Dr. Qasim al-Nuwesri at Chuwader Hospital, 14 June 2004.
49. Ibid.
50. Dahr Jamail, interview with Dr. Amer Ali at Chuwader Hospital, 14 June 2004.
51. Ibid.

52. Dahr Jamail, interview with Ahlan Bari at Yarmouk Teaching Hospital, 8 April 2004.
53. Dahr Jamail, interview with Dr. Amer Al Khuzaie at Ministry of Health, 24 June 2004.
54. Dahr Jamail, interview with Dr. Amer Al Khuzaie at Ministry of Health, 24 June 2004.
55. Ibid.
56. Dahr Jamail, interview with Dr. Sarmed at his home in Baghdad, 26 June 2004. Dr. Sarmed spoke on condition of using a pseudonym.
57. Ibid.
58. Dahr Jamail, interview with Wa'al Jubouri at his home in Baghdad, 26 June 2004. Mr. Jubouri spoke on condition of using a pseudonym.
59. Dahr Jamail, interview with Dr. Sa'alm Shadid at his home in Baghdad, June 26, 2004. Dr. Shadid spoke on condition of using a pseudonym.
60. Abu Talat, interview with Dr. Thadeb al Sawah in his office in Samarra, 26 July 2004.
61. Dahr Jamail, interview with Dr. Omar Sa'ad at his home in Baghdad, 26 June 2004.
62. Dahr Jamail, interview with Dr. Sarmed at his home in Baghdad, 26 June 2004.
63. Institute for War and Peace Reporting (IWPR), *Iraqi Press Monitor*, No. 227, "Attacks on Iraqi Doctors Rising," 25 April 2005.
64. Yaseen al-Rubai, *Iraqi Crisis Report* (ICR) No. 119, "Health Service Mired in Corruption,"1 April 2005.
65. Dahr Jamail, interview with Dr. Wijdi Jalal at Baghdad Teaching Hospital, 12 June 2004.
66. Dahr Jamail, interview with Dr. Sarmed at his home in Baghdad, 26 June 2004.
67. Ibid.
68. Dahr Jamail, interview with Wa'al Jubouri at his home in Baghdad, 26 June 2004.
69. Antonia Juhasz, *Left Turn Magazine*, "The Corporate Invasion of Iraq," August/September 2003.
70. Antonia Juhasz, Foreign Policy in Focus, "The Hand-Over That Wasn't: How the Occupation of Iraq Continues" July 2004.
71. Ibid.
72. David Fidler, "A Kinder, Gentler System of Capitulations?" *Texas International Law Journal*, Summer 2000.
73. Sir Sherston Baker, *Halleck's International Law*, 3rd edition, 1893, pages 387-88.
74. U.S. AID, *Fact Sheet*, 1 May 2003.
75. Abt Press Release, 30 April 2003.

76. André Verlöy, Windfalls of War, Center for Public Integrity.
77. Dahr Jamail, interview of Dr. Hammad Hussein, Baghdad, 7 December 2004.
78. Dahr Jamail, interview of Dr. Aisha Abdulla, Baghdad, 7 December 2004.
79. Yaseen al-Rubai, *Iraqi Crisis Report* (ICR) No. 119, "Health Service Mired in Corruption," 1 April 2005.
80. Ibid.
81. Dahr Jamail, interview of Dr. Aisha Mohammed, Baghdad, 30 November 2004.
82. Dahr Jamail, interview of Shehab Ahmed Jassim, Baghdad, 30 November 2004.
83. Dahr Jamail, interview of Abel Hamid Salim, Baghdad, 30 November 2004.
84. M. Gregg Bloche and Jonathan H. Marks, "Triage at Abu Ghraib," *The New York Times*, 5 February 2005.
85. Shafiq Rasul, Asif Iqbal and Rhuhel Ahmed, "Composite statement: Detention in Afghanistan and Guantanamo Bay," 23 July 2004, 299.
86. Ibid., 274. Also see 151.
87. Dr. Robert Jay Lifton, "Doctors and Torture," *New England Journal of Medicine*, Volume 351:415-416, July 2004.
88. Ibid.
89. Tens of millions were recently reallocated from penal to detention facilities; see U.S. Department of State, Section 2207 Report to Congress on the use of Iraq Relief and Reconstruction Funds, Appendix 1, p. 19, 5 April 2005. Such reallocations would seem to serve the interest of interrogations and confinement less hampered by legal considerations.
90. Geneva Convention II addresses wounded, sick and shipwrecked naval personnel, and does not apply to the conflict in Iraq. The United States has not ratified the two Protocols Additional, adopted in 1977. However, some of their provisions are viewed as binding customary international law and should be consulted in the context of health rights and health care.
91. The whole of Convention I addresses the medical rights of sick and wounded combatants. This selection is only meant to provide the framework articles.
92. The rule of non-renunciation of rights is found in all four Conventions, and applies to the particular persons addressed in each. As the language is essentially identical it will not be set out under the other Conventions.
93. There is a grave breach (war crimes) article in each Geneva Convention. In Convention I it is Article 50; in Convention III it is Article 130; in Convention IV it is Article 147. While nearly identical, each specifically addresses the "protected" persons or property, so we have set out Article 147 of Convention IV as the most relevant here.

4

RECONSTRUCTING CIVIL SOCIETY AND CITIZENSHIP IN IRAQ

෨෨

Jacqueline S. Ismael

Civil Society
Theoretical Conceptions

T he notion of "civil society" is Western in origin. It came into existence as a way of conceptualizing the rapidly shifting dynamics of
the interlinkages between atomized individuals and the state in societies
that were experiencing rapid changes in industrialization, urbanization and
bureaucratization. Tocqueville pointed at civil "intermediate associations"
as prerequisites to democratization, while Hegel viewed it as a manifestation of the bourgeoisie's attempt to organize and harmonize conflicting
interests within its body. In addition, the American Founding Fathers
identified plurality of interests as one of the main foundational concepts of
the new American Republic.[1] All definitions of "civil society" oscillate
around the notion of the very important "patty in the hamburger"—the link
between the state and its citizenry. Operating independently from the state,
yet obeying the laws of the land, civil society organizations articulate the
diversity of interests that cannot be included willy-nilly in free and fair

elections alone. While a reductionist definition of democracy does not go beyond free and fair elections,[2] no healthy democracy has empirically existed without some kind of independent civil society.

As a working definition, we will think of the civil society concept as the sphere of activity outside the political-legal authority of the state where citizens band together in free association to promote and pursue non-profit objectives.[3] In other words, civil society denotes the sphere of autonomous social action. Antonio Gramsci conceptualized civil society in terms of the superstructure, which justifies the socio-economic formation of bourgeois capitalism. According to Gramsci, civil society functions as an obstacle to state encroachment on personal autonomy as well as an ideological carrier that serves to legitimize the state. Thus, the hegemony of liberal democracy as an organizing ideology does not rely on the state's coercive apparatus alone—instead, it is legitimated by academia, intellectuals and countless civil society organizations which act within the liberal democratic order often questioning its outcomes but never questioning its right to decision-making. In Gramsci, civil society becomes the nexus of the ideological struggle. Whichever ideology wins over civil society will win over the state.

Civil Society Traditions in the Middle East

Western skepticism on the notion of civil society in Islamic polities is connected to Weber's verdict that the norms of Arab culture were fundamentally nonconducive to the flourishing of a plurality of voluntary associations. But, his analysis was grounded in the Mameluk period alone, and his generalizations on Islamic civilization were invalid. Civil society flourished in the Abbasid period (723 A.D.-945 A.D.) when urban activity reached its zenith. Islamic law successfully protected associational formations and societies that developed and sustained business and industrial activities. The Abbasid house successfully encouraged industry and trade by establishing protocol houses, markets and banking institutions, thus stimulating industry and trade. This gave rise to a plurality of interests that had to be protected and articulated through civil society organizations.[4] The practices and ethical conventions of each society found para-judicial legitimation and were invoked in case of legal conflicts. These organizations often provided a basis for political action. For example, when the Buwayids in 976 imposed taxes on cotton and silk textiles, affected societies rose in active protest until the tax was repealed.

State regulatory activity of professional and economic undertakings was minimal because of the independent religious stratum that was the source of law-making and legitimation. The state engaged in assessing a nominal tax regime on local industry and trade and protected businesses from foreign impingement. Ibn Khaldun's dictum "The state is the greatest commercial market" epitomized the support of the state for free enterprise.

The Buwayid and Seljuk invasions in the tenth and eleventh centuries proved to be detrimental to the Abbasid socio-economic heritage. Both regimes were based on military hereditary rule and were inimical to industry and trade. Instead, land control akin to the hereditary feudal system provided the main pillar of economic life. Finally, the transformation of the stratum of religious legal jurists into the state administration brought an end to judicial independence. The resulting religious vacuum was filled by Sufi orders that emphasized self-salvation through rejection of worldly pleasures and prosperity. This was the period which was analyzed by Weber.

In Islam, both the state and civil society delineate their boundaries and forge their relationships by relying on independent law. The primary principles of law exist *a priori* and transcend the interests of state and civil society. As an analogy, this is not very different from the interpretive tradition that exercised an absolute monopoly on the Anglo-Saxon legal tradition up to the nineteenth century. Lost to the conceptualizations of post-modernism to which it is inimical, the interpretive tradition held that the principles of law already existed. Law was to be discovered and not to be made. God, human nature and the basic principles of life in society were unchangeable. The issue was how they applied to particular questions that came in front of judicial authorities.

The Mongol invasions delivered the *coup de grace* to Muslim civil society. Neither the Ottoman Empire, where social prestige was to be attained in the civil service and the army, nor Western economic domination which centered on the development of export crops and the infrastructure necessary for economic exploitation, proved conducive to the growth of an autonomous civil society.

Civil Society in Contemporary Arab History

Independence found Arab societies living in polities created by the West for its own, mainly short-term, goals with a socio-economic heritage that was not conducive to economic development and civil society organization. These imposed polities were not designed, institutionally and even in terms of physical boundaries, to be responsive to the needs of the societies encompassed by them. The Arab elites in power were quasi-Europeanized individuals drawn from either military cliques or tribal elites empowered by Britain to ensure the safety of her vast oil concessions. The post-independence era witnessed the increasingly erratic functioning of rather unnatural polities where the elites were in constant need of reinforcing their grip on power through mass-propaganda, grandiose development projects and the neutralization of potentially autonomous social formations—civil society.

The detrimental effects of the Arab authoritarian state, a heritage of Western imperialism, on Arab societies are too well-documented to warrant extensive attention here. However, in recent years this state has been on the retreat and, following the dictum "nature abhors a vacuum," civil society has slowly surged forward to fill the gap. By 1995, 70,000 civil society organizations existed—20,000 of them in Egypt.[5] Women and human rights organizations were the first to emerge, may with the aid of foreign funding. With the withdrawal of state support for social programs under the impact of the IMF's structural adjustment agenda, faith based civil society organizations grew rapidly throughout the Muslim world to fill the vacuum left by the state's withdrawal of social welfare programs and services.

Democracy, the Arab State and Civil Society

In recent years, the democratization of the Arab world has become a hot political topic outside the exclusive concern of political scientists and Arab opinion-makers alone. In the West, the debate has taken a racist overtone where a whole society is often assumed to be incapable of self-rule. There are two main camps—the first claims that there is no reason to think that the Arabs cannot democratize and American occupation would help move things along,[6] and the other brings forth cultural reasons to underline the incapacity of the Arabs to create a functioning, tolerably efficient, democratic society.[7] A systematic critique of these views need not be carried out here. They suffer from imperialist assumptions and, what Edward Said called "orientalism." Even worse, the arguments used by both sides ignore notions that political science has discovered long ago. This paper will argue that the question of democratization cannot be analyzed without taking into account the state as the arbiter of the rules governing a political order and citizenship as the link between the democratic order and the arbiter. The formulation and implementation of a well-defined and predictably enforced notion of citizenship by the state is a necessary precondition for the transition to and consolidation of a democratic system of governance.

When considering the possibilities of democratization in the Arab world, and Iraq in particular, we must deal with the notions of citizenship and the state. As Przeworski has pointed out, "modern citizenship entails a bundle of predictable and enforceable rights and obligations for every member of the political community."[8] Historically, in certain nineteenth century European countries, membership in the political community has been defined in terms of property and/or income. That is to say that citizenship was restricted by clear prerequisites that were enforced in a universal and predictable manner. Democracy as a political system existed through the exercise of rights and obligations by these members of the political community—the citizens. The advent of universal suffrage extended citizenship to all individuals of a certain age. The boundary between citizens and non-citizens was pushed outwards in favour of reducing the exclusiveness of the political community.

Democracy and citizenship co-exist. One cannot conceptualize the former without the latter or vice versa. This becomes apparent when considering the very meaning of "democracy" as an organizing ideology of the political system. One of the foremost scholars on democracy and democratization, Juan Linz, has stated that a system can be regarded as democratic "when it allows the free formulation of political preferences, through the use of basic freedoms of association, information, and communication, for the purpose of free competition between leaders to validate at regular intervals by nonviolent means their claim to rule,... without excluding any effective political office from that competition or prohibiting any members of the political community from expressing their preference."[9] Leaving aside the procedural elements of the definition, Linz's definition points out that civil and political liberties are to be enjoyed by members of the democratic community in order for democracy to function. The exact range of civil and political liberties to be legislated and protected by the system of authority is encompassed within the notion of citizenship. Hence, theoretically as well as empirically, democracy cannot occur without some well-defined notion of citizenship—the bundle of predictable and enforceable rights and obligations for every member of the political community. Citizenship can be exercised only when the system is guided by universal criteria, when the rule of law is effectively enforced, when the power centers are willing and able to protect rights, and when individuals enjoy some social and economic prerequisites.[10]

All of the requirements of citizenship fall within the domain of the state. The state is the unit, which constructs and enforces the universal criteria of citizenship, protects the rights entailed within that concept, and ensures the stability necessary for the pursuit of interests in the economic, social and political spheres. Since the Treaty of Westphalia which brought about the existence of the nation-state system, and especially during the twentieth century when that system was globalized, the sphere of political activity independent of the boundaries and rules of engagement set out by the state became almost impossible. Certainly, the exercise of citizenship occurs within the web of state-regulated human relations. Therefore, it is imperative that, in the words of Theda Skocpol, "we bring the state back in"[11] when we consider democratization and citizenship in the Middle East.

In his famous definition, Max Weber conceptualized the state as "a human community that claims the monopoly of the legitimate use of physical force within a given territory."[12] While the concept monopoly of the use of force' from this oft-repeated definition is widely recognized, the other key concept, "legitimacy," is rather less so. Legitimacy can be objective or subjective. Objectively, legitimacy would mean a systematic "title to rule" based on well defined political processes.[13] Objective legitimacy may be conceptualized as legitimacy *a priori*. When it is lacking, the state's existence may be questioned irrespective of the benevolence of its rulers. The rulers simply lack the "title to rule" because of the way in which the state was conceived and its institutions were built. On the other hand, subjectively, a political unit is regarded as legitimate to "the degree to which it is generally accepted by its citizens."[14] In this case, the state as an abstract unit may have legitimacy but the behaviour of the ruling elites since the state's conception has been such that they have personalized the state. When the ruling elites lose legitimacy, the state loses legitimacy as well. When the state lacks subjective legitimacy, it usually lacks the institutions to challenge the ruling elites within the realm of normal politics and thus, the overthrow of the elites brings about the destruction of the state. In its subjective sense, the degree of legitimacy is highly fluid and the struggle to maintain an acceptable "balance of legitimacy" must be on-going.

The very fluidity of the concept leaves open the possibility that a state may not continually enjoy legitimacy. In this paper, the state that satisfies Weber's definition will be called a *civil state*. The civil state enjoys a monopoly on the use of force as well as the authority to legitimately exercise its power. On the other hand, the state that has a monopoly on the use of force but not the authority to legitimately exercise that power,[15] will be called the *uncivil state*. It is our contention that the modern Arab state is an uncivil state. It only enjoys a monopoly on the use of force without the legitimacy to exercise that power. Because the Arab state system was designed by Western powers and imposed on Arab societies, Arab states have never enjoyed objective legitimacy. Furthermore, because the Arab ruling elites have failed to govern according to domestic expectations, they have personalized the state and weakened its institutions. Arab states lack subjective legitimacy. The modern Arab state can coerce but it cannot persuade.[16] In this sense, the exercise of citizenship is by definition impossible. The individuals living under the shadow of the *uncivil state* are subjects and not citizens. Finally, without citizenship, democracy is realistically unattainable. The uncivil state is an obstacle to democratization and cannot be a fair referee of the democratic process. Hence, we conclude that the arguments used in favour of the democratization of the existing political system in the Arab world do not hold.

The superimposition of the modern state on the local population by Western powers, and their sponsorship of these states thereafter, is the inherent reason for the inevitability of the emergence of uncivil states in the region. Thus, the Arab states failed *a priori*. The local political elites were empowered by the colonial powers with symbols of state sovereignty rather than by institutionalized political processes.[17] In their efforts to maintain power, these elites had to rely on coercion internally and dependence on external power for regime stability. This dependence on coercion and external powers for the very existence of the post-colonial Arab state, reflects its failure to take root in the region's political culture.

Moreover, economic development since the genesis of the modern Arab state has relied on Western economic aid and trade. This has undermined regionally-oriented and non-market oriented economic constituencies.

Socially, modern education has crowded out traditional patterns of socialization, marginalizing the cultural foundations of economics and politics, which has brought about a fragmentation between popular culture and political realities.

The impact of these structural dynamics on Arab political development has produced an antagonistic relationship between Arab politics (the process of interest articulation and aggregation) and the political culture of Arab society (the process of value determination and articulation). Because the contemporary Arab state system is essentially culturally alien to Arab society, Arab political actors have sought cultural legitimacy by appealing to Arab history, religion, customs and tradition to buttress their authority. However, because the state has proved to be incapable of formulating and incorporating a viable notion of citizenship, Arab elite discourse has remained outside popular political culture. Increasingly uncertain of its hold on power, the Arab state has relied on coercion and control of the modern instruments of cultural articulation, cutting off avenues for the expression of popular political culture. As a result, the development of popular political culture has become distorted, confined to traditional religious channels and modes of articulation. Consequently, by the 1980s, Islamic revivalism had a partial-monopoly on the anti-elite, populist discourse in the Arab world.

By its nature, the *uncivil state* cannot tolerate independent activity because of the threat that it potentially poses to the state's very existence. In terms of power, the uncivil state may be strong. But, in terms of legitimacy, it lacks genuine political resilience. The sense of insecurity that follows, induces the state to incorporate autonomous civil society into its apparatus—as indeed happened in almost all Arab states where they were either directly absorbed by the state (Nasserite Egypt and Ba'athist Iraq), co-opted by the state (oil rich Gulf sheikhdoms) or banned outright (Palestine under Israeli occupation, Syria under Hafez al-Assad). While the recent withdrawal of the state from the public sphere under pressure from the IMF and World Bank has allowed for some Western-oriented civil society organizations to exist, the Middle East is structurally very far from creating a robust, culturally relevant civil society in the economic, cultural, social and religious spheres. That is because the modern Arab state remains uncivil. As long as this state system continues to exist, political instability and very low levels of institutionalization will continue. Only a governing structure that takes into account Arab culture, history and traditions can conceivably have the legitimacy to arbitrate harmonious development in the Arab world.

The Concept of "Citizenship" in Islamic Scholarship

In 1951, when Egypt was still under indirect British control, Khaled M. Khaled, an Egyptian intellectual, raised the slogan "We are citizens not subjects" from his analysis of the Middle Eastern culture and human nature. He argued that human nature has a number of drivers that configure its actions, which if institutionalized would create equality, democracy, and a harmonious society. He described these drivers as the emotions of anger, repulsion, civic pride, possession, compassion and the propensity for freedom.[18] He argued cogently from history that freedom of expression is equivalent to the institutionalized anger, which preserves society from the destabilizing effects of suppressed anger. When human feeling of repugnance has the legitimate means of discharge, it culminates in the institution of free opposition and the release of human will for positive change. Compassion is the basis of solidarity and the spring of *esprit de corp*, which requires the institutionalized freedom of thought and conscience in an atmosphere of free reasoning because human rationality forms the basis of selfless community bonds, and dispels fear. Civic pride derives from the genuine political freedom, which encompasses the freedom to run for office, free voting and other mechanisms of democracy. The human propensity for freedom is enshrined in the freedom of choice that both Islamic religion and culture propound. The tool of change in the author's analysis is the social formations of society because it is their destiny that is at stake under any regime of dictatorship. His prescription is one of open socio-political space where the plurality and the freedom of the social forces could bring about the representative state.[19] He does not hesitate to aver that there is no cost high enough for the struggle to attain a *free* democratic society.

From a historical perspective, Khaled's concepts are not new in the Islamic world. Islamic chronicles have denoted the co-operative and harmonious society that Islam stands for as *Al-Mugtam'a al-Ahli*. In the process of creating the Caliphate, urban Muslims ordered their social and economic formations according to an Islamic set of laws, whose makers, until 945 A. D. enjoyed relative autonomy from the Caliphate. Furthermore,

Islamic lawmakers were independent of the executive government because the profundity and strenuousness of the pre-requisites for attaining the status of law-making were such that public recognition and deference granted them immunity from coercive attempts from the executive to co-opt them.

These practices did not exist in a vacuum. Theoretically, they were firmly bound to the Qu'ran. There are two relevant verses in the Qur'an, which lay the political foundation for the polity: chapter three verse 159, and chapter forty-two verse thirty-eight. Variations of the Arabic root *shawar* are used. This root means group deliberation to extract the most successful course of action. Such definition necessarily pre-supposes the existence of a plurality of different opinions, otherwise group deliberation becomes meaningless. Chapter three, verse 159 is a Qur'anic injunction to the Prophet in his capacity as a leader (which excludes his function as a medium of revelation and its explicator) of the Muslim community to deliberate the mundane issues, including the political with the *people* in order to decide what course of action to pursue; the *people*, not the leader are the basis of action. Hence political sovereignty lies with the *people*. The mode for manifesting the sovereignty is left to vary with *time* and place. Chapter forty-two, the Qur'anic verse thirty-eight characterizes the Muslim community as one of a plurality of opinions, where no group is allowed position of hegemony or ideological monopoly. Indeed, the procedures for appointing the head of the Muslim community are not laid out explicitly in the Qur'an. The political underpinning in the Qur'an, however, generalizes the primacy of the people in deciding issues of the mundane.

The organization of socio-economic life from the Ummayyads until the beginning of the decline of the Abassid dynasty in 945 A.D. shows the practical application of these concepts. Urban society, particularly during the apex of the Abassid rule, organized itself on the religious norm of the *Umma,* and within the boundary of Islamic law. *Umma* is an abstract concept denoting a community of human groupings that exist in a location. The unity of the members of the community is premised on the commonality of the creation, which implies the equality and brotherhood of all believers. The Muslim *Umma* has never historically consisted solely of Muslims. It included from its very inception, during the life of the Prophet Muhammad, Jews and Christians, which made the *Umma* a quasi-federal structure. The Islamic term that refers to them is *dhimmi,* which etymologically emphasizes a moral commitment to the Jews and Christians. It is as such a moral commitment, notwithstanding events of deviations from the

Islamic teachings, which permitted these groups their courts and laws, customs and cults, manners and language. It further entitled them to the same rights of Muslims in the spheres of education, work, public service and social welfare.[20] Because the ontological foundation of the Islamic law is the protection of life, freedom of conscience, property, family, reason and health, it was congruent to the emergence of an urban bourgeoisie that engaged in associational formations that developed and sustained business and industrial activity during the apex of Islamic civilization.[21] It is not the concern of this paper to classify and enumerate the various bourgeois economic activities of the urban Muslim society of that time to prove the existence of *al-Mugtama' al-Ahli*.[22] Such details are available in both primary and secondary sources.[23] What is important is the existence of intersecting vertical structures of similar economic occupations and interests organized in a hierarchy of voluntary associations. The heterogeneity of the vertical structures at intersectional points did not cause disharmony or lasting conflict of interests because such associations internalized the concept of the brotherhood of the *Umma* and most of them were tied to Sufi orders in various ways, which enabled *al-Mugtama' al-Ahli* to act as a coherent unifying bond that mediate their interests into the state when needed. Further, because of sharing the same worldview of the *Umma* and articulating the same cultural discourse, *al-Mugtama' al-Ahli* assumed educational and social responsibilities towards its members and society at large. It was through the system of private endowments that learning became accessible to those who aspired to it and it was the social responsibility of the head of the association to care for the private lives of the members of the association. The state was excluded from the socio-economic activity of *al-Mugtama' al-Ahli* to such an extent that product pricing was beyond state control, and left to market mechanisms.[24]

However, the foreign invasions that followed the demise of the Abassids as well as intra-Muslim infighting led to the closure of the Gate of Ijtihad, and resulted in the increasing ossification of Islamic culture as Ijtihad had functioned as the dynamic link between jurisprudence and society. The widening gap between an Islamic culture and an ever-changing reality led to increasingly reactionary cultural resistance to the increasing foreign interference. For example, the Ottoman Sultan, Sulayman the Magnificent, issued an edict to the effect that no woman was permitted to be seen in public, even when veiled unless she was "old." Disobedience would result in physical punishment and humiliating parade in the city.[25][vii] The debased status of women was an Ottoman nomadic norm, which also introduced and enforced the veil when early Muslim women engaged in learning and teaching and in market activities.

Iraq: Case Study

The above concepts of the populist potentialities of Islamic theory as well as the reality of a political system dominated by the *uncivil* state are all true of Iraq. An analysis of the recent history of Iraq, from the British occupation to dictatorship and, now to the American occupation, reveals the damage that has been done not only to human rights, but to civil society as well. Yet, the theoretical and historical notions of citizenship, *Ijtihad*, and *al-Mugtama' al -Ahli* expose the myth that civil society and citizenship are western constructions and require western patrimony.

On the eve of British occupation in 1917, the territory of present day Iraq consisted of 3 independently administrated provinces under the Ottoman Empire: Mosul, Baghdad and Basra. Because the Ottoman Empire espoused the Sunni school of religious thought, and Muslims perceived in it a moral symbol of Muslim unity, the Sunnis at the head of the administration have been historically dominant though the lower administrative ranks in touch with the daily discharge of the affairs of the state were left to local officials in each province. The Ottoman State did not constitute an integral component of power dynamics in Iraq. Rather, Iraq was localized, provincialized and mediated through notables, figures accorded high social status, tribal chiefs and heads of clans.

Congruent with provincialism was the social structure, which derived from segmented and agrarian communities. The communities were held together by overlapping bonds: tribal norms, blood relationships, ethnic or religious identities. There were also within the city whole amalgams of internal migrants that dwelt in one place, which was assigned the name of the origin of the migrant amalgam, as in the cases of the Tekritti and Ukyddat zones.[26] Britain merged the three provinces into the new state of Iraq under its colonial administration.

Direct British rule, the presence of the British military, the British failure to honor their promise to end the occupation and the exorbitant taxes that were at a much higher scale then than those of the Ottomans[27] provided the catalyst that precipitated the Revolt of 1920 and cost the British Exchequer up to 56 million Pounds.[28] It should be remembered that it was Winston Churchill, then the British Secretary of State for War, who introduced the military tactics of blanket bombing of villages as the original "shock and awe" doctrine, which eight decades later the U.S. military continued. In ordering the gassing of Iraqi civilians, Churchill said, "I do not understand the squeamishness about the use of gas. I am strongly in favor of using poison gas against uncivilized tribes."[29] Whole villages were bombed and gassed. Men, women and children fleeing from gassed villages in panic were mercilessly machine-gunned by low-flying British planes. The Royal Air Force routinely bombed and used poison gas against the Kurd, Sunni and Shi'ite tribes without discrimination.[30]

Britain was the architect of the modern Iraqi state. The British prototype for the Iraqi state was further developed and invigorated by the unexpected abundance of petro-dollars and the pervasiveness of the security apparatus throughout the era of the Ba'ath regime, (1968-2003.) The British contrived a parliamentary regime, in which the king was Faisal, a descendant from the Prophetic line, with the state structure comprising local power groups that represented the notables, the social elite, merchants and land owners, and the Iraqi officers in the Ottoman army who had allied with the British during the First World War and joined the rebellion against the Ottoman empire. The local power groups were integrated into the modern bureaucratic machine of the state imposed by the British, and the elected parliament was designed constitutionally to place minimal constraint on the pro-British Iraqi monarchy.

After about three decades the British design of the modern Iraqi state had unwittingly generated a volatile new stratum that hailed from the urban middle class and made up the military of the armed forces. They led the 1958 military coup and put an end to the royal regime. The process that gave birth to this new stratum was the spread of education and state suppression of organized opposition. The tone of the discourse of the new middle class was not religious, but one that emphasized nationalism, Arabism and revolution. This was characteristic of the pattern of Middle Eastern politics in the mid 20th century. While the rhetoric of the new military rulers paid lip service to the idea of the will of the people, they did not constitute the institutions that would operationalize these slogans, and suppressed civil society development, in effect forcing it underground and politicizing it. Clandestine political groups became dependent on external funding, opening them to the influence of foreign intrigues. Catalyzed by Cold War rivalry, the absence of democratic institutions intensified the element of violence as an instrument in civic culture. The process of centralization of the dictatorship and the economy, abetted by Cold War rivalries, intensified under Saddam.[31]

By the time Saddam occupied the presidency in 1979, the Ba'ath had already established the foundations for a totalitarian regime. According to a report from the U.S. Institute for Peace, the combination of totalitarianism and traditional social formations resulted in an entire social layer united by blood, as well as economic and financial ties that engulfed society. What gave the totalitarian Ba'ath state its pervasive and oppressive power was not the fact that it was the largest employer by virtue of ownership of the public sector. It was rather the fact that the state was the producer and the owner of the oil sector, which after the phenomenal price increase in 1974, the state became independent of the production capacity of the Iraqi society (the primary, secondary and tertiary sectors combined) and hence unaccountable to it. All other socio-economic formations and political agents diminished in power vis-à-vis the owner \ producer status of the Iraqi state that monopolized petro-dollar wealth. Oil revenue helped create the political economy of patron-client relations where personal relationships and crony capitalism were the driving forces. This distorted state-society relations by reshaping the business class in the image of the ruling clan-class.[32] The emerging self-image of an all powerful state that was the employer of, and unaccountable to its society was brought to a head under Saddam who catapulted Iraq into disaster with his projection of this image into global politics—first with the Iraq-Iran war and then with the invasion of Kuwait.

Following Saddam Hussein's assumption of the presidency in 1979, the regime's human rights abuse intensified with the introduction of ethno-cultural cleansing. With the initiation of the Iraq-Iran war in 1980, an ethnic cleansing campaign was initiated against Iraqis of real or hypothetical Iranian descent, with the forced expulsion of over 300,000 Iraqi Shi'ites. An ethnic cleansing campaign of genocide against the Kurds of northern Iraq was initiated in the 1980s in the infamous Anfal Campaign in which 4,000 Kurdish villages were destroyed and tens of thousands of Kurds disappeared.[33]

Thus, under Saddam Hussein's regime, the Iraqi state had in effect been centralized to the point of its complete personification in the ruler, Iraqi society totally absorbed into the state apparatus, and the Iraqi economy absorbed in the state's rentier economy. In this context, civil society—the dynamic component of public life in Iraq from classical to modern times—had ceased to function in the public sector. In fact, there was no more public sector. It had been colonized by the state, and through a complex web of secret service agencies, the state was increasingly encroaching on the private sector. Iraqis were subjects not citizens, and consumer culture had replaced civic culture in community life. The UN Security Council sanctions imposed on Iraq from 1990 to 2003 essentially wiped out consumer culture by impoverishing the society. While the Saddam regime effectively maneuvered to survive the dilapidating impact, the Iraqi middle class and the poor shouldered the brunt of the burden.

The public image of Iraq portrayed through the UN and the world media was of a society in collapse. According to a report from Associated Press on 8 February 1998, the long years of destitution resulted in widespread depression and paranoia, the spread of prostitution, and the rise of crime. The collapse of the rentier economy and consumer culture constructed under the Baath regime was well monitored by the international community. After the 1991war Iraq's GDP fell by nearly two-thirds owing primarily to an 85 percent reduction in oil production and the destruction of the both the industrial and service sectors of the economy.[34] "Per capita income fell from $2,279 U.S. dollars in 1984 to $627 in 1991 and...less than $700 by 1998. Other sources estimate a decrease in per capita GDP to be as low as $450 [U.S.] dollars in 1995."[35] The 1999-2000 Report of UNDP Iraq Country Office summarised the situation in Iraq on the cusp of the new millennium:

> Iraq's economy has been in crisis since the imposition of economic sanctions in 1990. Despite the Oil-for-Food program, the country continued its decline into poverty, particularly in the south. Food supplies continue to be inadequate in the centre and south of the country; the prevalence of general malnutrition in the centre and south has hardly changed. Although the rates have stabilised, this happened at "an unacceptably high level." In the area of child and maternal health, in August 1999, UNICEF and the Government of Iraq released the results of the first survey on child mortality in Iraq since 1991. The survey showed that under-five child mortality had more than doubled from 56 deaths per 1000 live births in 1984 to 131 deaths in the period 1994-1999. At least 50% of the labour force is unemployed or underemployed; a shortage of basic goods, compounded by a drought, has resulted in high prices and an estimated inflation rate of 135% and 120% in 1999 and 2000 respectively...Most of the country's civil infrastructure remains in serious disrepair. GDP per capita dropped to an estimated U.S. $715 [from U.S. $3508 before the Gulf War], which is a figure comparable with such countries as Madagascar and Rwanda.[36]

The Anglo-American invasion of Iraq in March 2003 occurred in this context. Iraqis, already occupied by the Saddam regime and impoverished by sanctions, may well have hoped for liberation (as the invading forces touted) but instead found themselves under foreign occupation, and with nothing to lose. They had already endured the ruthless brutality of the Saddam regime for thirty-five years and the callous brutality of sanctions for thirteen years. Rather than invading a society in disarray, what the occupying forces found was a population with nothing to lose and well organized in underground civil society formations—that is, associations driven from the public sector under the Saddam regime and entrenched in the private sector under sanctions as a buffer against the regime and sanctions in the struggle of everyday life. The loose social groupings formed in mosques, neighbourhoods, clans, and tribes had served as the seedbed for dynamically interlinked and overlapping networks of solidarity, mutual aid and exchange in the struggle to sustain daily life under conditions of economic collapse and political oppression. Their resistance to the U.S. enterprise in Iraq (discussed in detail in other chapters) and its effort to reconstruct citizenship and civil society on an American model has demonstrated a dynamic capacity and resilience unexpected by the occupying power.

The nature of the underground civil society can be gleaned from an examination of the Iraqi Federation of Workers' Trade Unions (IFTU). Since the initial development of the oil industry in Iraq and up until the establishment of Saddam Hussein's government in 1979, the union movement in Iraq was a relatively important factor in Iraqi civil infrastructure. The Iraqi General Federation of Trade Unions (GFTU) boasted of a membership of 275,000 workers in 1959 and enjoyed a relatively substantial level of autonomy.[37] That same year, the May Day demonstrations were attended by an estimated 500,000 people.[38] However, upon the Ba'ath coup of 1963, and more dramatically Saddam's ascension to power in 1979, the Ba'ath government managed to effectively seize control of the GFTU by arresting many of its leaders and appointing loyal Ba'athists, and later Saddamists, to its ranks, thus transforming the organization primarily into a tool for the state's repressive measures and espionage. Union headquarters were transformed into interrogation centres and, according to Abdullah Muhsin of the Iraqi Federation of Workers' Trade Unions, the very term "trade union" had come to be "associated with oppression for many Iraqis."[39] As a result of this repression, an alternative, underground trade federation, the Workers Democratic Trade Union Movement (WDTUM) was formed in 1980 by a number of passionate trade unionists, along with a number of intellectuals, liberals, communists and other social justice activists.[40] Although the WDTUM was involved in at least one strike, involving over 4000 tobacco workers in Iraqi Kurdistan, it seems that the organization operated primarily as political vehicle to collect and disseminate information about the abuses emerging from the Saddam regime to unions and social justice movements outside of Iraq.[41] Repression of the union movement was further intensified with the passage of a new Labour Code on 11 March 1987, which not only abolished the eight-hour day altogether, but also stipulated that all public service workers were to be considered state employees and no longer able to join or form trade unions.[42]

However, with the fall of the Saddam regime in 2003, the WDTUM resurfaced and organized a public meeting on 16 May in which it announced the formation of the IFTU, which now represents twelve independent union organizations, including the Oil and Gas Union, the Railway Union, the Transport and Communication Union, The Mechanics, Printing and Metal union, the Textile and Leather Products Union and the Agriculture and Food Staff Workers' Union.[43] Within just over a year, the IFTU has managed to lay the groundwork for the emergence of a relatively strong labour movement in post-Saddam Iraq, despite a number of significant handicaps and obstacles, not the least of which is the occupation and the critical lack of human security. According to Muhsin,

> We have organised strikes, marches and [are] entering into negotiation[s] with both public and private enterprises in defence of workers rights to [achieve] just wages and better working conditions. And we are campaigning for a labour code that adheres to the ILO conventions.
>
> In Baghdad, the Mechanic, Printing and Metal Union organized industrial action in a bicycle factory near Baghdad. The president of the union committee, Najim Al Daham, called for a 24-hour strike and won pay increases from 17,000 to 60,000 Iraqi Dinars. The IFTU was able to bring solidarity delegations from seven Baghdad work places representing several unions, to demonstrate outside the main gate of the bicycle factory in support of the strikers' demands.[44]

Additionally, the Electricity and Energy Workers' Union in Basra elected the first woman trade union leader in Iraq's history on 13 May 2004: Hashimia Muhsin Hussein, who is a fervent advocate for women's and workers' rights.[45]

However, despite the significant progress of the IFTU, there have been a number of major impediments to its progress in developing a vibrant labour sector of Iraq's civil society. The most obvious has been the security situation, which has raged out of control and seems to be steadily deteriorating, but another major factor has been the occupation itself. Not only did the Coalition Provisional Authority and its Governing Council (and now the Interim Government) fail to repeal the brutally anti-union Labour Law of 1987, but American forces were even utilized to close down the Baghdad office of the IFTU-affiliated Transport and Communication Workers' Union on 6 December 2003, arresting 8 of the union's leaders.[46] The offices were only reopened after union members and its supporters marched to the office premises on 1 July 2004 and took direct action to re-open it.[47] The difficulties experienced by the IFTU are reiterated by numerous other non-governmental organizations (NGOs) throughout Iraq, which, according to Ray Salvatore Jennings of the Daily Star, is resulting in a tendency for civil society organizations to form most predominantly along insular, often tribal, business, religious or familial lines.[48]

The IFTU leadership has outlined three major goals that they feel the organization must work on in order to be able to develop a strong labour movement, which include the establishment of a new Labour Code that is worker friendly, the achievement of affiliation with international labour federations, and the overseeing of not just the end of the occupation, but also the establishment of "a sovereign and democratic Iraq."[49] This is in sharp contrast to the vision of the occupying power. To sap the strength of the indigenous civil society emergent in the early months of the occupation, the U.S. unleashed an army of American funded NGOs in Iraq as missionaries of the American model to flood the illusory public space of occupation with American images of democratic society, to co-opt socially concerned Iraqis with funding for social projects, and to create the illusion of freedom for the American public. For example, in 2004 the American press reported

> Iraqis have registered 965 local civic organizations, including human rights, democracy promotion, humanitarian and women's empowerment groups, with the Coalition Provisional Authority (CPA) in Baghdad. For every registered group there are many more organizations that are not registered. Unfortunately, only 35 registered groups are prepared to implement a long-term agenda of activities. The Kurdish north is an

exception because 10 years of development under semi-autonomy led to a more robust and sophisticated civic infrastructure.[50]

Conclusion

The drafting of Iraq's proposed constitution[51] provides a focus for bringing this discussion to summation. As both citizenship and civil society are bound to the state, the constitution sets the formal-legal framework for their reconstruction. Their nature is embedded in the principles enshrined with the constitution, in effect legitimating some reconstruction options, and perhaps more significantly in terms of the barriers to reconciliation being laid, delegitimating others. The constitution has gone through three drafts by the Constitutional Assembly. Under the tutelage of the U.S., the document has been honed to legitimate the ideological principles of neoliberalism and delegitimate the basic cultural principles of social justice common across the spectrum of Iraq's political forces, principles of government that even those most willing to cooperate with the United States, members of the constitutional Assembly, could not disdain without arm-twisting.

Notes

1.   *The Federalist Papers* http://www.law.ou.edu/hist/federalist/
2.   Samuel Huntington, *The Third Wave: Democratization in the Late Twentieth Century*, (Norman: University of Oklahoma Press, 1991), 7.
3.   Tareq Y. Ismael and Jacqueline S. Ismael, *Civil Society and the Oppressive State in the Arab World*, 2.
4.   Corporations alone were organized according to their character into partnerships and limited partnerships (*shaman*); limited liability (*al-mufawadha*); shareholders (*al-wujuh*); marketing companies (*al-rakkadh*); and monopoly (*al-khazan*).
5.   Augustus R. Norton (ed.), *Civil Society in the Middle East,* Vol. 1, (New York: E. J. Brill, 1995), 9.
6.   For the evolution of this view within influential U.S. foreign policy circles, see for example, Spencer Ackerman, "The Radical," *New Republic*, 12/1/2003, Vol. 229 Issue 22/23: 17-24.
7.   Of these advocates, Bernard Lewis is perhaps the best known. For a good example of this perspective see Bernard Lewis, *Islam and the West* (New York: Oxford University Press, 1993)

8. Adam Przeworski et. al., *Sustainable Democracy*, (Cambridge: Cambridge University Press, 1995), 34.
9. Juan J. Linz, *Totalitarian and Authoritarian Regimes*, 182-83.
10. Przeworski, 34. The requirement of "social and economic prerequisites" as part of the notion of citizenship is as old as Aristotle: "neither life itself nor the good life is possible without a certain minimum standard of wealth." See, Aristotle, *The Politics*, trans. by T. A. Sinclair, (Suffolk: Penguin Books, 1978), 31. See p. 38 on the connection between a minimum standard of wealth and citizenship.
11. Evans, Rueschemeyer and Skocpol, 1985 in Joel S. Migdal, "Studying the State," in Mark Irving Lichbach and Alan S. Zuckerman, *Comparative Politics: Rationality, Culture, and Structure*, (Cambridge: Cambridge University Press, 1997), 215.
12. Max Weber, *From Max Weber: Essays in Sociology*, (New York: Oxford University Press, 1946).
13. Seymour Martin Lipset, "The Social Requisites of Democracy Revisited," *American Sociological Review,* Vol. 59, No. 1: 1-22.
14. Seymour Martin Lipset, *Political Man: The Social Bases of Politics*, expanded ed., (Johns Hopkins University Press, 1981), 22.
15. Partially thanks to the international system that recognizes states and states alone, some states have neither legitimacy nor a monopoly on the use of force. They can be called states only insofar as they are recognized as such by the international community but they certainly are not Weberian states.
16. There is no room for too literal a reading of this thesis. Obviously, legitimacy and the degree of *uncivility* varies from state to state in the Arab world. The history and the culture of the Arabs display too much intravariation for us to equate all Arab states. Instead, this is but a conceptual exercise. For more on interstate variation of oppression, see Tareq Y. Ismael and Jacqueline S. Ismael, *Civil Society and the Oppressive State in the Arab World.*
17. For more on the negative effects of low institutionalization of decision-making on the civility of the state, see, Guillermo O'Donnell, "Delegative Democracy?" *East-South Systems Transformation*, University of Chicago, Working Paper No. 21.
18. Khaled M. Khaled, *Muwatonoun la Ra'yya*, (Citizens not Subjects), Dar al-Kitab al-Arabi, Beirut, 7ᵗʰ edition 1974, 64-102.
19. Ibid., 105-171.
20. Hasan Hanafi, "Alternative Conceptions of Civil Society: A reflective Islamic approach," in *Islamic Political Ethics*, Sohail H. Hashmi, Ed. Princeton University, 2002, PP. 58-63
21. Ellis Goldberg, "Khatima Nadhariyya wa Tarikhiyya:Al-Mujtama' al-Madani," in *al-Dimuqratiyya fi al-Sharq al-Awast*, Ahmad Abdulla, Ed. Cairo, Markaz al-Gil, 1995; P. 384

22. For more details on these activities, see Hassan Ibrahim Hassan, *Islam:A religious, political, social and economic study*, Baghdad, the Times Printing and Publishing, 1967, PP. 462-465

23. Examples of primary sources are Taqi al-Din al-Maqrizi, "Al-Khetat" and "Ighathat al-Umma bikashf al-Ghumma" and Abu al-Hasan al-Masoudi, "Morouj al-Dhahab" and "Al-Tanbih wa al-Ishraf." Good secondary sources are Hussien Mu'nis, *Alam al-Islam*, Dar al-Ma'rif, Egypt, 1973; and Abdel Aziz al-Dury, *Muqadima fi al-Tarikh al-Iqtesadi al-Arabi*, Al-Tali'a, Beirut, 1967.

24. Hussien Mu'nis, *Alam al-Islam*, Dar al-Ma'rif, Egypt, 1973; PP. 229-248

25. Ibid., 36.

26. Faleh A. Jabar, *Al-Dawla, al-Mugtam'a al-Madani wa al-Tahawul al-Demokrati fi al-Iraq*, Markaz Ibn Khaldoun li al-dirasat al-Inma'iyya, Cairo, Egypt, 1995; PP. 52-53

27. Henry C K Liu, "Geopolitics in Iraq an old game," *Asia Times*, 18 August 2004 in http://www.atimes.com/atimes/Middle_East/FH18Ak02.html

28. Ibid. Faleh A. Jabar, P. 194

29. Ibid. Henry C. K. Liu

30. Ibid.

31. Ibid. Faleh A. Jabar, PP. 54-59

32. Faleh A. Jabar, May 2004, U.S. Institute for Peace in http://www.usip.org/fellows/reports/ 2004/0415_jabar.html

33. Tareq Y. Ismael and Jacqueline S. Ismael, *The Iraqi Predicament: People in the Quagmire in Power Politics*, (London: Pluto Press, 2003)

34. United Nations. "Report of the second panel established pursuant to the note by the president of the Security Council of 30 January 1999 (S/1999/100), concerning the current humanitarian situation in Iraq" 30 March 1999. *http://www.un.org/Depts/oip/panelrep.html*; as quoted in Tareq Y. Ismael and Jacqueline S. Ismael, Op. cit. p. 131

35. Ibid.

36. United Nations Development Program (UNDP). "1999-2000 Report" *Iraq Country Office. http://www.iq.undp.org*

37. Abdullah Muhsin, ," Iraqi Federation of Workers' Trade Unions (IFTU): Outline History and Future Tasks," (25 August 2004) http://www. iraqitradeunions.org/archives/000072.html

38. Ibid.

39. Ibid.

40. Ibid.

41. Ibid.

42. "Iraqi Federation of Workers' Trade Unions (IFTU): A Short History of Trade Unionism in the Iraqi Oil Industry" (24 August 2004) http://www.iraqitradeunions.org/archives/000071.html

43. Abdullah Muhsin, Op. cit.
44. Ibid.
45. "First Woman Elected to Lead Iraqi Trade Union" Iraqi Federation of Workers' Trade Unions (23 August 2004) http://www.iraqitradeunions.org/archives/000070.html
46. "IFTU-Transport & Communication Workers' Union Takes Direct Action to Re-Open its National Office" Iraqi Federation of Workers' Trade Unions (4 August 2004) http://www.iraqitradeunions.org/archives/000062.html
47. Ibid.
48. Ray Salvatore Jennings, "A new Iraqi civic culture is emerging" *The Daily Star* (26 May 2004), http://www.dailystar.com.lb/article.asp?edition_id=10&categ_id=5&article_id=4351
49. Abdullah Muhsin, Op. cit.
50. Ray Salvatore Jennings, Op. cit.
51. Table 1: Constitutional Revisions

Area	1990 Constitution	June 30, 2005 Draft	July 20, 2005 Draft	August 25, 2005 Final Draft
General principles	Article 12: "The State assumes the responsibility for planning, directing, and steering the national economy for the purpose of (a) establishing the socialist system on scientific and revolutionary foundations (b) realizing Arab economic unity"	Article 5: 1) "Social justice is the basis of building the society..." Article 18: 1) "The basis of the economy is social justice. It is composed of cooperating between public and private activity. Its goal is economic growth in accordance with a decreed plan and the realization of prosperity for citizens..." 2) "The state shall bear the responsibil-	No similar provisions.	No similar provision.

Area	1990 Constitution	June 30, 2005 Draft	July 20, 2005 Draft	August 25, 2005 Final Draft
		ity for growth, developing production and services, building a solid infrastructure for the economy of the country, and providing services."		
Ownership of Iraq's resources	Article 13: "Natural resources and the basic means of production are owned by the People. They are directly invested by the Central Authority in the Iraqi Republic, according to exigencies of the general planning of the national economy."	Article 17: "All natural resources and the [resulting] revenues are owned by the people. The state shall preserve and invest them well."	No similar provision.	Article 109: Oil and gas is the property of all the Iraqi people in all the regions and provinces."
Foreigners' right to own Iraqi assets	Article 18: "Immobile ownership is prohibited for non-Iraqi, except otherwise mentioned by law."	Article 8: "Iraqis have the complete and unconditional right of ownership in all areas of Iraq without limitation."	Article 10: "The Iraqi citizen has a complete and unconditional right to ownership in all parts of Iraq without limitation.	Article 23: "An Iraqi has the right to ownership anywhere in Iraq and no one else has the right to own real estate except what is exempted by law."
Right to work	Article 32: 1) Work is a right which is	Article 12: 1) Work is a right for every	No similar provisions.	Article 22: 1) Work is a right for

Area	1990 Constitution	June 30, 2005 Draft	July 20, 2005 Draft	August 25, 2005 Final Draft

	ensured to be available for every able citizen.
	    "The state undertakes to improve the conditions of work, and raise the standard of living, experience, and culture for all working citizens."
		citizen and duty for him. The state and the governments of the regions shall strive to provide work opportunities for every able-bodied citizen.
		    2) The state is responsible to support the provision of work opportunities for all qualified and pay monthly salaries for all unemployed for any reason until opportunities are provided in the case of disability, handicap, or illness until the malady ceases.
				all Iraqis in a way that guarantees them a good life.
				    2) The law regulates the relation between employees and employers on an economic basis, while keeping in consideration rules of social justice.

Private property	Article 16:
	    "Ownership is a social function, to be exercised within the objectives of the Society and the plans of the State, according to stipulations of the Society."
		No similar provision.	Article 10:
			    "Private ownership is protected. Nobody may be prevented from using his property except within the boundaries of law."
				Article 23:
				    "Private property is protected and the owner has the right to use it, exploit it, and benefit from it within the boundaries of the law."

Taxes	No similar provision.	Article 17: "The basis for taxes and public expenditures is social justice."	No similar provision	No similar provision.

Area	1990 Constitution	June 30, 2005 Draft	July 20, 2005 Draft	August 25, 2005 Final Draft
Education	Article 27: "The State undertakes the struggle against illiteracy and guarantees the right of education, free of charge, in its primary, secondary, and university stages for all citizens."	Article 6: "The state and regional governments shall combat illiteracy and provide their citizens with the right of free education at the various stages."	Article 25: "Iraqi citizens have the right to enjoy security, education in all its stages, health care, and social insurance. The Iraqi state...shall ensure these rights within the limits of their resources, taking into consideration that the state shall strive to provide prosperity and employment opportunities for all members of the Iraqi people."	Article 24: 1) "Free education is a right for all Iraqis in all its stages" 4) Private and national education is guaranteed and regulated by law.
Health	Article 33: "The state assumes the responsibility to safeguard the public health by continually expanding free medical services, in protection, treatment, and medicine, within the scope of cities and rural areas."	Article 7: "Iraqi citizens have the right to enjoy security and free health care. The Iraqi federal government and regional governments must provide it and expand the fields of prevention, treatment, and medication by the construction of various hospitals and	Article 25: "Iraqi citizens have the right to enjoy security, education in all its stages, health care, and social insurance. The Iraqi state...shall ensure these rights within the limits of their resources, taking into consider-	Article 31: 1) "Every Iraqi has the right to health service, and the state is in charge of public health and guarantees the means of protection and treatment by building different kinds of hospitals and health institutions." 2) Indi-

Area	1990 Constitution	June 30, 2005 Draft	July 20, 2005 Draft	August 25, 2005 Final Draft
		health institutions."	ation that the state shall strive to provide prosperity and employment opportunities for all members of the Iraqi people."	viduals and associations have the right to build hospitals, dispensaries, or private clinics under the supervision of the state."
Agriculture	No similar provision.	Article 17: "The state shall take the necessary measures to realize the exploitation of land suitable for agriculture, stop desertification, and work to raise the level of the peasant and help farmers and their land ownership in accordance with law."	No similar provision.	No similar provision.
Terrorism	No similar provision.	No similar provision.	No similar provision.	Article 8: "The state will be committing to fighting terrorism in all its forms and will work to prevent its territory from being a base or corridor or an arena for its activities."
Free trade	No similar provision.	No similar provision.	No similar provision.	Article 24: "The

Area	1990 Constitution	June 30, 2005 Draft	July 20, 2005 Draft	August 25, 2005 Final Draft
				state shall guarantee the freedom of movement for workers, goods, and Iraqi capital between the regions and the provinces."
Economic reforms	No similar provision.	No similar provision.	No similar provision.	Article 25: "The state shall guarantee the reforming of the Iraqi economy according to modern economic bases, in a way that ensures complete investment of its resources, diversifying its sources and encouraging and developing the private sector."
Investments	No similar provision.	No similar provision.	No similar provision.	Article 26: "The country shall guarantee the encouragement of investments in the different sectors."
Oil	No similar provision.	No similar provision.	No similar provision.	Article 110: "The federal govern-

Area	1990 Constitution	June 30, 2005 Draft	July 20, 2005 Draft	August 25, 2005 Final Draft
				ment and the governments of the producing regions and provinces together will draw up the necessary strategic policies to develop oil and gas wealth to bring the greatest benefit for the Iraqi people, relying on the most modern techniques of market principles and encouraging investment."

5

NATION BUILDING OR CULTURE WAR?
America's Credentials as an Honest Broker in the Middle East

ഇ‍ൂ‍ൽ

Fuad Shaban

For over fifty years, the United States of America has been deeply involved in the affairs of the Middle East, especially in the Arab-Israeli conflict, but the pressures of domestic politics have prevented any chance of an even-handed American stand in resolving the conflict. To begin with, the financial-industrial-military complex has exercised a powerful influence on America's policy in the Middle East. Moreover, political and religious lobby organizations have made it very improbable for the United States to be objective in its dealing with the Arab-Israeli conflict.

A close examination of the election platforms of both political parties during the past fifty years will reveal a pattern of competition between the two parties as well as individual politicians to show their pro-Israeli stands. Since presidential and congressional elections in the States are held every four years, and given the fact that even the most modest move towards peace in the Middle East takes years to accomplish, it is politically unlikely for America to have and sustain any objective policy in the Middle East.

But there is an additional factor which makes it virtually impossible for the United States to be an honest broker in the Arab-Israeli conflict; this is the rise to power of an administration which publicly describes itself as a right-wing religious administration. The situation has been further aggravated by acts of terrorism committed by self-described Islamic fringe groups, thus strengthening the hands of advocates of a brutal Israeli-style military "containment policy" in the Middle East.

This chapter will present an analysis of these factors and will show why they make it impossible for the United States to play the role of an honest broker in bringing about a peaceful settlement in the Middle East.

By September 2001, according to Bob Woodward and other analysts, the political administration of the U.S. had decided that this time America would not resort to limited strikes or half-way measures. That would seem to be mere punitive action against only the band of terrorists who planned the attacks on the World Trade Center and the Pentagon. There was a period of eerie expectation throughout the world of what the U.S. would do next. Most people knew that there would be some action, perhaps swift and decisive. And the look on President Bush's face when the news was whispered to him twice as he spoke to school children in Florida was pained but determined. We heard later that the reaction which built up during the next few days was that "this is it"; this is all-out war, a total war that would pit the U.S.—and, of course, the Free World—against the "evil doers." Translated later, the "evil doers" became "those who are not with us." There is no need to remind ourselves of the numerous expressions used to explain what that meant in concrete terms. For, if you are not with us, you are against us; you are an enemy of the free civilized world. You are also evil, which puts you squarely in the army of the Devil. Early on, President Bush said the U.S. would do "whatever it takes" to hunt down and bring to justice all those who were responsible for the 11 September 2001 attacks. And the Deputy Secretary of Defense, Paul Wolfowitz stated in the *New York Times* (14 September 2001) that the all-out war would not simply be "a matter of capturing people and holding them accountable, but removing the sanctuaries, removing the support systems, ending states who sponsor terrorism" As for those states that chose not to join the campaign, the consequence of their choice would be dire indeed. An editorial in the *Washington Post* (13 September 2001) clarified what the Bush Administration had in mind: "Cooperation in the war effort must be an absolute requirement for friendly relations with the United States. A rejection of that cooperation, or support for the terrorists, should define an adversary of this

country and bring about serious political, economic or military consequences."

Later on, in fact about four months later, the *Washington Post* (7
January 2001) reported that immediately after the attack President Bush
told his war cabinet that 11 September was in fact "a great opportunity." So
the tragic event was a "great opportunity" to be seized for the United States
to wage an all-out war against the "evil ones." referred to on another
occasion as "the Axis of Evil." And although this term, as well as the
"crusade" announced by the President, was described later as rhetorical
rather than historical, the "opportunity" presented itself for a remaking of
the world and reshaping of cultures. "Ending states" became the unspoken
but official policy of the United States.

After invading Afghanistan and ousting the Taliban and Al-Qaida, the
Bush administration declared that the war on terror was going to be a long
war which aimed at eliminating the tens of thousands of terrorists alleged
to be stationed all over the world. The American psyche after the September attack became obsessed with the terror threat that may originate
anywhere in the world. No one specific source of terror was named, giving
the Bush administration a reason to launch an attack at will against any
perceived enemy of the Free World. By keeping the field wide open, the
administration would pick targets that suited its purposes at any given time.
The goal was to rid the world of evil; and evil was to be found everywhere.
Ergo, the world was the battle ground.

With my interest in literature and cultural studies, I cannot pretend to
fully recognize the implications of this kind of thinking from the perspective of the political scientist. What concerns me most is the global cultural
ramifications of this attitude, especially when one considers that this was
going to be an all-out war—i.e. a global war on terror and evil—to be
waged by an administration whose members either believe in the apocalyptic view of the world or are allied to believers in this ideology.

This may seem irrelevant to the world of *real politique*. Yet let us
consider the background and the backdrop of these crucial, and I think,
fateful times.

The President of the U.S., besides being a seasoned politician, is, in his
own words, a devout born-again Christian. He has repeatedly declared that
God is present in his life as He should be in the life of the nation. In his
thinking, there is a plan in God's mind for him and for the nation. When he
was Governor of Texas, he was reported to have told his friends that God
wanted him to run for the presidency because there was a mission in God's

mind for him to fulfill.[1] As part of his political-religious upbringing, Bush, we are told, when he was forty, prayed with the Rev. Billy Graham for a whole weekend, after which he believed that he found Christ and was born again.

More importantly, and more realistically, "although Bush was taught by Billy Graham how to live in expectation of the Second Coming, the person who shaped his ideology," according to Michael Ortiz Hill, was his close friend Dr. Tony Evans. The overlapping of political principles and end-times expectations is at the core of Evans' teachings and of the goals of his "Promise Keepers" organization. Hill said that "Evans taught Bush how to look at the world from the vantage point of the Lord, and that the only way to 'save the world' is to return it to the control of the 'people of God'." So, when following the 11 September terrorist attacks on America, the President and his lieutenants repeatedly spoke of "ridding the world of evil," they were actually crossing the line between the current political situation of defending America and the larger divine plan of saving the world. In fact, as Hill suggested, by going against the opinion of millions across the world, including some of his military and political advisors, Bush was "literally and determinedly drawn, consciously and unconsciously, toward the enactment of such a scenario, as he believes, for God's sake. Indeed, the stark relentlessness of his policy in the Middle East suggests as much."[2]

It is this combination of Judeo-Christian beliefs and the ideology of Islamic extremists that may become a volatile recipe for a global disaster. "Islamic" extremists, out of despair over the injustices committed by Western powers against the Muslim world and the encroachment of an alien Western culture in their midst, claim that they are fighting a holy war. The Christian Right, especially the Christian Zionist brand, that lives in expectation of the Second Coming, also think that they are privy to God's mind and are working to fulfill His plan.

Unfortunately, the Christian Zionist perception of God's plan and its ultimate fulfillment are conditioned on the destruction of the third most sacred Islamic mosque, Al-Aqsa in Jerusalem.

The perception of "God's Plan" is not new in American beliefs. A telling example of this belief is the quote by Vice President Cheney in his speech at the Republican Convention on 1 September 2004, from the historian Bernard De Vote that "when America was born, the stars must have danced in the sky." Cheney and Bush are the descendents of people who held on to this belief in America's special place in God's Plan. The best modern example of this belief is the late President Reagan whose son Ron announced during the 2004 election campaign that his father "believed that God had a plan for his life, for everyone's life, and for the life of the nation." ("CNBC," show hosted by Pat Buchanan and Ronny Reagan during the 2004 Republican National Convention). Reagan himself, on one of many occasions, told Barbara Walters ("20/20," December, 1981) that "when God put this continent here He had a plan that it would be peopled by people who uprooted themselves from the comfort of their homes to found the most wonderful nation called America." There was a plan in the mind of God for him also.

This is the cultural context of statements by President Bush and his administration about the "call of history" and America's destined role to rid the world of evil.

This bi-polar, good-vs.-evil concept of the world is evident in many statements Bush has made since 2001. One of his earliest comments on the duty of America in the present crisis was that "history calls on us to rid the world of evil," and indeed, as Woodward reported, Bush told him: "our responsibility to history is already clear: to answer these attacks and rid the world of evil."[3] The number of times the President mentioned the call of history and the war against evil and evil doers is an indication of the direction of his thinking. As recently as September 2003, Bush went before the United Nations General Assembly to proclaim to the whole world that "events during the past two years have set before us the clearest divides between those who seek order and those who spread chaos." It is the religious equivalent of the political Armageddon foreseen by those who predicted that the terrorists could unleash acts that would lead to global chaos. The call of history, according to the President, has come to the right nation.

The apocalyptic undercurrent of this language of "order" and "chaos" and the "call of history" to "rid the world of evil" is precisely what the Fundamentalist literal interpreters of the sacred texts like to hear. President Bush, according to Woodward, "was casting his mission and that of the country in the grand vision of God's master plan."[4]

But this modern trend of thought had started before September 2001, in fact, on the day of the President's inauguration. On 5 March 2000, the day after the public swearing-in ceremony, a service was held on the occasion at the Washington National Cathedral. The Convocation was given by the Rev. Franklin Graham. Now the name, Franklin Graham, should conjure images of bi-polar good- vs.-evil concepts, besides the anti-Islamic statements that he has been notorious for.

The sermon itself, however, is a curious religious exercise of lecturing Bush on how to govern the country. The restless soul of America, Graham told Bush, can be treated only through igniting it with the Old Testament example of David, the King of Israel. For, "God worked in a mighty way through the life of King David, the greatest king of Israel, most likely all of human history." Most of the sermon was devoted to presenting a case for David as a model for a God-fearing "chosen community." One paragraph is worth quoting in full as an illustration of Graham's mix of politics and religion in the lesson he gave the new President:

> God said that David was a man after His own heart. Throughout David's life, from the time he was a small boy tending his father's flocks, he inquired of the Lord what he should do, regardless of whether the decision was great or small. David did not test the political winds of the day to see which direction he should go. David's only concern was to find the will of God for his life and then to do it. God blessed him and God blessed the nation of Israel because of David. Today I believe that God will bless our President and Vice President and our nation if we will humble ourselves before the Almighty and seek his will and then do it.

The cultural stage was set for the present administration in the President's religious education and in the company he keeps. It is not necessary to dwell at length on the religious convictions of members of the administration. Most of them make no secret of the importance of prayer in their lives and of the guidance they seek from God in times of crisis. Attorney General John Ashcroft's statement that "there is only one King in this country, and that is King Jesus Christ"[5] is representative of the religious orientation of the administration and of the conservative ideologues who stand behind it. Condoleezza Rice has said on many occasions that she is a religious person and that her religious convictions play a vital role in her life.

The larger picture of the U.S. political-religious stage is crowded with the motifs of the good-vs.-evil theme. In the 8 October 2004 Presidential Campaign Debate, both Bush and Kerry emphasized that religion plays an important role in their lives. Bush, in particular, stated in no uncertain terms that freedom is God's gift to every man and woman in this world, and that these beliefs play a role in his foreign policy. These statements are to be combined with his numerous claims that the "evil doers" in this world hated the United States because they hated freedom. The logical conclusion is that 'they' work against God's will. Thus, America, and the Free World, are the natural allies of God and are doing God's work, while the "enemy" is doing Satan's work. The cultural divide between "us" and "them" is clearly drawn in the circles of the neo-conservatives and the religious right, both of whom are openly allied to the present administration. Some public statements made by persons of diverse backgrounds will illustrate the point: Writing in the *Washington Post* on 12 September 2001, George Will set the tone of the looming battle between "us" (Americans) and "them" (the evil ones). He said: "Americans are slow to anger but mighty when angry, and their anger should not be alloyed with pride. They are targets because of their virtues—Principally democracy, and loyalty to those nations which, like Israel, are embattled salients of our virtues in a still-dangerous world." Clearly, Will's seemingly casual mention of Israel among "those nations" is another example of the need to martial the Judeo-Christian factor to this battle with evil. It is indeed in line with Graham's emphasis on King David and Israel as the model of a virtuous God-fearing society, presented in the general term of "our virtues."

Retired General Charles G. Boyd wrote also in the *Washington Post* (12 September 2001) that "this nation represents freedom, strength, tolerance and democratic principles dedicated to both liberty and peace. To the tyrants, the despots, the closed societies, there are no alterations to the policies, no gestures we can make, no words we can say that will convince those determined to continue their hate." Another representative of this trend of thought wrote on 13 September, asking "Are Americans afraid to face the reality that there is a significant portion of this world's population that hates America, hates what freedom represents, hates the fact that we fight for freedom worldwide, hates our prosperity, hates our way of life?" (*Washington Post*, 13 September 2001)

"They," meaning the terrorists, or anyone who does not agree with America, are natural haters, people who are instinctively inclined to spread chaos, while America's political and religious role in this world of evil and chaos is to spread freedom and democracy, besides—in fact in order to—bring about the fulfillment of biblical prophecies.

Then there is the highly decorated General William Boykin who occupies the important position of Deputy Assistant Secretary of Defense in charge of the war on terror—who, donning his military uniform and medals, gave sermons in churches, and asked his audiences: "And we ask ourselves this question, "Why do they hate us? Why do they hate us so much?" He does not wait for an answer. "Ladies and gentlemen," the General announces, "the answer to that is because we're a Christian nation, because our foundation and roots are Judeo-Christian. Did I say Judeo-Christian? Yes, Judeo-Christian." The general then launches a diatribe against "Allah" who is a "false cruel god" totally different from "Our God" (www.msnbc.com/news/ 980841.asp).

And the Attorney General also had his say on the difference between the two religions. Ashcroft was reported to have stated that whereas "our God" sent his Son to die for us, the god of Muhammad orders his followers to die for him (as quoted in an interview with Cal Thomas, radio commentator, 9 November 2001).

And between the generals and the Attorney General there is a chorus of voices that have been constantly singing the same tune. The result is that the American public perception of "those who hate us" becomes blurred and includes a wide variety of images from Bin Laden to Saddam to Muhammad, and to all Muslims in many cases. The statement by the respected journalist Dan Rather represents what I think is a conscious effort to keep the concept blurred. Rather stated authoritatively that "they see themselves as the world's losers and it drives them batty. There's no rationality to it. These are crazy people, they are haters." (*Washington Post*, 12 September 2001)

A few years ago, the former Secretary of State, Madeline Albright, described Saddam Hussein as a "congenital liar." It appears now that there is a species of humans who are "congenital haters."

The ambivalent terms, "they" and "them" become synonyms for the enemy, and therefore for Muslims, especially in the minds of the millions who attend the churches of the Religious Right and who listen to the words of wisdom coming from leaders like Pat Robertson, Jerry Falwell, Franklin Graham, Jack Graham, Jerry Vines, Benny Hinn and scores of others who joined the chorus of vilification of Islam and Muslims. Politicians like Peter King, Congressman from New York, and Cass Ballenger, Congressman from North Carolina, had their say about the subject. King accused eighty-five percent of the mosques in the U.S. of being breeding grounds for terrorists. "The vast majority of Muslim community leaders are enemies living amongst us."[6] Ballinger accused the Muslim community which had a mosque near his house of being the cause of his marriage breakup. "They" bugged the hell out of his wife.[7]

The picture of the difference between "us" and "they" takes shape, and it allows for the launching of a global war in which anything goes. For, according to Phillip Steel, "when all is said and done, most men, and especially men from non-Western cultures and less developed areas, are capable of taking pleasure in great evil."[8] And the point is made clearer to the minds of those who doubted the generalizations by right-wing journalists like Barbara Amiel who recently commented on the Madrid bombing by claiming that "they [again unspecified] inhabit a different moral universe from us... They partake of the satanic nature of the terrorist culture." She admonished those who are satisfied to stay home and pray: "Let us pray by all means, and then pass the ammunition."[9]

It is very crucial to demonize the enemy and to draw as vague a public image of them as possible in order to mobilize everyone in this global war. And here begins the story of the reconstruction of the world; to build nations and to change the world. A total war, a war of destruction, was needed because only by totally destroying the enemy can America reconstruct them in her own image. The concept of total war was ingenuously described by Michael Ledeen as a war of "creative destruction." "The purpose of total war," Ledeen said, "is to permanently force your will onto another group of people. Limited war pits combatants against combatants, while total war pits nation against nation, and even culture against culture." Writing in the *National Review Online* (7 December 2003), Ledeen drew out the rules of this "creative destruction" strategy:

> By total war, I mean the kind of warfare that not only destroys the enemy's military forces, but also brings the enemy society to an extremely personal point of decision, so that they are willing to accept a reversal of the cultural trends that spawned the war in the first place... We should have no misgivings about our ability to destroy tyrannies. It is what we do best. It comes naturally to us, for we are the only truly revolutionary country in the world. Creative destruction is our middle name... A total war strategy does not have to include the intentional targeting of civilians, but the sparing of civilian lives cannot be its first priority.

Crazy as this may sound, consider statements like General Schwarscof's "that Americans were not in the Iraqi body-count business," another general's boast that "we can bomb Baghdad back to the dark ages" and Secretary of State Albright's statement that the death of half a million Iraqi children was "worth it" ("acceptable" on other occasions) as a price for the success of the embargo (Leslie Stahl, *60 Minutes*, 12 May 1996).

Ledeen's total war between cultures is only an echo of the trend that has been promoting a clash of cultures between the Muslim East and the Christian West.

Some months ago, the American Defense Secretary, Ronald Rumsfeld, announced that the U.S. is engaged in a "war of ideas," and that the enemies in this war are the "*medrassa*" and the "clerics." Now, it is often difficult for me to understand fully all the oblique statements and gestures that the Secretary makes, but I think here he was speaking of this total cultural war in which the enemy will not lose the military battle only but will be brought to Ledeen's "desperate state of mind that he would experience a reversal of cultural trends," and, perhaps, join the community of the civilized.

Examples from recent history show the practical application of Ledeen's theory by successive U. S. administrations: The use of "agent orange" and the murdering of civilians in Viet Nam; the flattening of villages and towns in Somalia and Afghanistan; the killing of over 100,000 civilians in Iraq since the beginning of the invasion. These are but a few cases where brutal force is used to effect a "reversal of cultural trends." Sometimes, this policy seems to work, if only by intimidation. When critical statements of the oil-producing Arab states mounted in the Pentagon and other American official and public forums, suddenly we saw television cameras focusing on young princes and sheikhs on official occasions dressed in suits and ties, most probably Ive Saint Laurant or a similar brand. And following a lecture given at an Arab Gulf think-tank-like center by the French journalist Terry Maisson who treated with suspicion the 11 September attacks, an order was promptly issued closing that center. Similarly, foreign students were banned from studying Islamic subjects in some Arab countries, and Imams were ordered to avoid political subjects in their sermons.

I remember also seeing on television a Western reporter talking to a young Arab somewhere in the Arabian Peninsula showing off his gold watch, his American car, his expensive cigarette lighter, while telling someone on his cell phone: "I will be spending my Christmas in New York." I also remember the young man in an Arab city walking into the mosque to perform the Friday prayer, wearing a T-shirt which had "I love Michael Jackson" inscribed on it. (I am rather relieved that this happened before his sister's "wardrobe malfunction." Her picture on the young man's shirt would really indicate a "reversal in cultural trends." So, you see, Western efforts to reconstruct the enemy seem to be working.

But this is not something new. During the second half of the nineteenth century, missionaries were hard at work to save souls and regain the Arab world to Christ. The results were rather encouraging, at least to some persistent souls. One such person was David Porter, the American Counsel in Istanbul, who reported back home that the Sultan was now wearing western shoes about his palace, and that dancing parties—balls, he called them—were held in the city without the interference of the authorities or the Mullas. Beirut was reported by missionaries to be a beacon of Western culture and civilized behavior.

If there is one thing in common among all of these appearances of "modernization" in the Arab East, it is that the Sultan's Western shoes, the balls in Istanbul, the "I love Michael Jackson" shirt, and the suits and ties of the young princes, all, in and of themselves, mean nothing, except as indications of the naivety—dare I say "stupidity"—of those who consider them signs of victory over "the inferior culture." For, whatever they may mean to the Western observer, these manifestations hide a deep resentment that is only strengthened by them.

The resentment can only increase when members of the "inferior" culture hear American statesmen claim that they are doing God's work, and that "God is on their side." At a time when one is too helpless to argue against this claim, one could only use Abraham Lincoln's reply: "Are they on God's side?"

Notes

1. Paul Harris, "Bush Says God Chose Him to Lead His Nation," *The Observer* (2 November 2003).
2. Michael Ortiz Hill, "Mine Eyes Have Seen the Glory: Bush's Armageddon Obsession, Revisited," www.gatheringin.com.
3. Bob Woodward, *Bush at War* (New York, Simon & Schuster, 2003), p. 67.
4. *Ibid.*
5. Commencement Address at Bob Jones University, 1999, reported in *Newsweek* (11 January 2001), p. 15.
6. Representative Peter King (R-NY), on Sean Hannity's nationally-syndicated radio program, 9 February 2004.

7.   Representative Cass Ballenger (R-NC), an interview with the Charlotte Observer newspaper (4 October 2003), www.charlotte.com/mid/charlotte/news/politics/6929935.htm.

8.   Phillip Steele, *Terrorism: Past and Present* (New York, Prentice Hall, 1992), p. 27.

9.   Barbara Amiel, "Let Us Pray By All Means, and Then Pass the Ammunition," *The Daily Telegraph*, 15 March 2004.

6

IRAQ, THE U.S. AND
INTERNATIONAL LAW
Beyond the Sanctions

ഇരുൻ

Richard Falk

W hat accounts for the obsessiveness of American policy toward Iraq over the course of more than a decade? Is it another Vietnam in the sense that the U.S. Government cannot bring itself to acknowledge the failure of its approach to regime change in Baghdad since the end of the Gulf War, Saddam Hussein having withstood comprehensive sanctions, a variety of covert assaults, and repeated American harassment from the air without flinching? Is it pique at the White House and Pentagon associated with the electoral removal from the scene of Bush, Sr. contrasting with the persistence of Saddam Hussein, posing a filial challenge to Bush, Jr.? Is it some sort of Freudian response by the younger Bush in retaliation for Saddam Hussein's alleged plot to assassinate his father? Is it the long deferred payback to Israel for staying on the sidelines during the Gulf War, despite the Scud missiles being fired from Iraq? Is it a matter of securing U.S. control of the oil reserves being linked to periodic displays of regional dominance, especially through the denial of weaponry of mass destruction to those states in the Middle East that might seek at some point to deter or challenge the U.S. in some future crisis? Or is it part of the American empire-building strategy that views Iraq as both an obstacle, but also as an opportunity to demonstrate the extent of military dominance possessed by the U.S. and its political will to deal harshly with states that stand in its way? Or is it the new cover story, frequently repeated by Bush and senior political aides, that the Baghdad regime has become more dangerous since 11 September because it may enable al-Qaida to obtain weapons of mass destruction that would then be used against American targets?

Undoubtedly there is no single correct answer because different members of the Bush inner circle are drawn to various combinations of these lines of analysis and advocacy, and they seem mutually reinforcing in any event. But what is beyond doubt is that American policy toward Iraq since the ceasefire in 1991 that ended the Gulf War has violated the most basic precepts of international law, including the UN Charter, and the fundamental economic and social rights of the Iraqi people.[1] To the extent that the UN Security Council has endorsed American policy, it has weakened respect for the UN around the world. In 1991 Iraq was defeated in a war, accepted humiliating conditions for a ceasefire, which effectively encroached upon the basic sovereign rights of Iraq as a state. In the ensuing period, Iraq was not offered any kind of protection by the international community even in the face of an armed attack by the United States.

This chapter discusses the changing context of U.S. policy toward Iraq, followed by a consideration under international law of sanctions and war threats, concluding with a criticism of the approach taken by the United States and by the United Nations over this period of more than a decade. In sum, for more than a decade, the international community, as shaped by the United States, imposed an extremely punitive peace on Iraq, abruptly forgetting the lessons supposedly learned as a consequence of the disastrous effects of the punitive peace imposed by the victorious powers on Germany after World War I. In contrast, these lessons were self-consciously and successfully applied to Germany and Japan to promote the recovery of these defeated countries in the aftermath of World War II. In retrospect, it seems reasonable to wonder whether these "lessons of Versailles" were only meant for those countries associated with the North in some integral way. The South, subordinate in any event, has remained fertile ground for indefinite punishment of a political actor that challenged the established geopolitical order. Iraq, formerly a strategic junior partner in the maintenance of such an order, especially during its long war with the Islamic Republic of Iran during the 1980s, became the arch enemy of this post-Cold War American design for the region. Iraq for a decade after the first Iraq war faced dire threats of invasion and attack that were openly discussed by American political leaders, with alternative plans for the military operation openly debated in mainstream media.[2] The debate focused on means, their supposed effectiveness and their anticipated costs and risks, and treated the acceptability of the ends as taken for granted or irrelevant, although in stark violation of the most basic rules of the UN Charter prohibiting recourse to non-defensive force in the setting of an unresolved international dispute. To look sympathetically at the plight of Iraq as a beleaguered state should not be confused with an endorsement of the former Baghdad regime, or its brutal and bloody past behavior, both with respect to neighbors and its own internal minorities. In this regard, there is little doubt that Saddam Hussein is indictable for crimes against humanity and crimes against the peace. But the criminality of a head of state or of official policies pursued does not impair the sovereignty of that state, nor does it provide grounds for suspending the application of international law. The reclassification of Iraq as "enemy" and "rogue state" in the 1990s was purely a consequence of altered geopolitical priorities as the worst excesses of the Iraqi government were committed years prior to its attack on Kuwait, and provoked no change of strategic relationship.

The Changing Context

From every perspective except that of geopolitics, American policy toward Iraq since the end of the first Gulf War has been a disaster. The imposition and retention of comprehensive sanctions for more than a decade after the devastation of the Gulf War resulted in hundreds of thousands of civilian casualties, more than a million according to some estimates.[3] This assessment has been abundantly documented by reliable international sources, and affecting most acutely the very young and the poorest sectors of the Iraqi population.[4] Although regrettably formally backed by the United Nations through a strained interpretation of Security Council Resolution 687, with some modifications, the cruel impact of sanctions so appalled the most senior international civil servants of the UN entrusted with administering programs of oil-for-food programs as to prompt that rarest of bureaucratic impulses, successive resignations by the lead administrators on principle![5] The political objective of this highly punitive diplomacy was justified as a way to destabilize and contain the repressive regime of Saddam Hussein, but the evidence clearly indicated that as the years passed, the government in Baghdad gathered political strength while the internal and external opposition among Iraqis seemed ever more inconsequential. It was ordinary Iraqi people who paid the main price for the encounter between Saddam Hussein and the United States Government.

Throughout this period, as well, American and British planes continued to patrol extensive no-fly zones that had been established in the north and south of Iraq, initially justified by the U.S. Government as indirectly authorized by Security Council Resolution 688 as a way to protect endangered minorities, but later maintained as a way to challenge Baghdad militarily on a daily basis, exhibiting its helplessness as a sovereign state. Unlike sanctions, these military incursions lacked clear Security Council authorization, were quite unconnected with their original protective function benefiting the Kurds in northern Iraq and the Shi'ia minority in southern Iraq during the immediate aftermath of the Gulf War during which period Baghdad was seeking revenge against those elements in the Iraqi population that had sided with the American-led military campaign.

At issue all along was the UN mechanism, the United Nations Special Commission (UNSCOM), that was imposed on Iraq after the 1991 ceasefire in the form of an inspection mechanism that claimed extensive rights to oversee the destruction of existing Iraqi stockpiles of weapons of mass destruction and ensure that no activities were continuing secretly to acquire such weaponry in the future.[6] There was much controversy surrounding UNSCOM activities, associated with alleged Iraqi evasions and denials of access, but also counter-charges by Iraq contending that the inspection procedure was being used for espionage purposes and to harass and humiliate the Iraqi government. Finally, Iraq refused to grant further access to UNSCOM, creating a pretext for the current war, as well as debates about whether such inspections, however extensive, could ever provide confidence about Iraqi compliance with the conditions of disarmament imposed by UN Security Resolution 687. In the early years of the Bush II presidency there were assertions that without inspection a pre-emptive war was needed to ensure that Iraq did not pose a threat to the United States, but also assertions from Washington that inspections would never provide sufficient confidence to overcome the justification for a military attack designed to impose a regime change. Complicating the picture further, the UN, with strong backing from Secretary General Kofi Annan, had been seeking to negotiate a renewal of an inspection arrangement positing an UNSCOM arrangement as an alternative to war, and coupled with some indication that sanctions could be ended if the new scheme worked successfully. It became clear that Washington rejected such an approach, and viewed the inspection issue as a diversion and distraction from its goal of regime change. But the U.S. played a double game: If Iraq resisted inspection, it would validate the need for intervention, but if it assented, then the unreliability of inspection would validate the need for intervention, a deadly Catch-22!

In the meantime during the latter half of the 1990s, a cruel stalemate arising from the imposition of sanctions and intrusive U.S. claims persisted. It had long been apparent to objective observers that these undertakings were not succeeding, but policymakers in Washington lacked the political courage to acknowledge, even indirectly, that their approach had failed to dislodge Saddam Hussein and was doing great damage to the people of Iraq, as well as to the humanitarian reputation and political autonomy of the United Nations. The Clinton Administration had so committed itself to the support of sanctions, as well as the continuation of periodic bombings within the no-fly zones, that it seemed completely unable and unwilling to re-evaluate the policy in light of the harm being done to Iraqi civilian society. Such a reluctance was consistent with the overall approach in the Clinton years to exhibit "toughness" in foreign policy, especially in the Middle East, so as to minimize criticism from the hard right that made little secret of its push all along for a renewal of outright war against Iraq with the goal of coercing a regime change in Baghdad.[7] Reminiscent of Vietnam, leaders in Washington could not bring themselves to admit that their policy was a dreadful failure, and so it went on and on, with no end in sight. During his presidential campaign and upon arrival in Washington, George W. Bush announced that sanctions against Iraq would be continued, and intensified, although the undisclosed intention was to move from sanction to the more proactive option of intervention and war.

From the perspectives of international law and morality these policies directed at Iraq were of a highly dubious character, yet their continuation despite widespread criticism from most governments in the region and the world, revealed the extent of American influence within the United Nations specifically, and international politics generally. The whole experience was a demonstration of the primacy of geopolitics at the expense of basic standards of law and morality. Despite the pragmatic and humanitarian misgivings of many governments, there was little disposition to challenge openly the American position.

And then came the 11 September attacks on the World Trade Center and the Pentagon, which inflicted heavy symbolic and substantive damage on the United States, and produced a claim to use force in self-defense. Despite some criticisms directed at the way the claim was formulated and applied to Afghanistan, it did represent a reasonable effort to retaliate against the main locus of al-Qaida operations and to diminish the prospect of future attacks.[8] In the face of these attacks, President Bush in his 20 September 2001 address to a Joint Session of Congress, outlined the resolve of the U.S. Government to wage an overall war against "every terrorist group of global reach."[9] Iraq was mentioned by name in the speech only to make the point that the character of the war being launched was different than the Gulf War: "This war will not be like the war against Iraq a decade ago, with a decisive liberation of territory and a swift conclusion." True, a generalized warning declared that "...from this day forward, any nation that continues to harbor or support terrorism will be regarded by the United States as a hostile regime."

But the hawks in Washington smelled Iraqi blood from the moment of the al-Qaida attacks. There were early statements by right wing think tank analysts urging the extension of the military response to Iraq. Leading members of Congress sent a bipartisan letter to the President, coordinated by Senators Joseph Lieberman and John McCain, insisting that the war on terrorism could not succeed unless the threat posed by Saddam Hussein was confronted by military force. Israel, as well, made little secret of its wish to extend the battlefields of Afghanistan to Iraq (and Iran). Various efforts were made to encourage war against Iraq by trying to show (on the basis of slim and unconvincing evidence) that there were links between Baghdad and al-Qaida agents prior to 11September, or to imply that Iraq was the source of the anthrax distributed via the U.S. Postal Service. Throughout this period there were inconsistent and inconclusive comments deriving from top members of the Bush security team. The Secretary of State, Colin Powell, was seen soon after 11 September as still reluctant to endorse such a belligerent stance, realizing that it would interfere with his diplomatic priority, which involved building up a global coalition against the al-Qaida network and finding some way to dissipate anti-Americanism arising from the unresolved fate of the Palestinians. Such caution seems to have disappeared in the wake of the successful campaign by American military forces to turn the tide of battle within Afghanistan so quickly and decisively in favor of the Northern Alliance, producing the collapse of the Taliban regime, the destruction of the Afghan nerve center of al-Qaida and the dispersal of its leadership. This American victory was achieved with almost no American casualties sustained during the air campaign. At first, it seemed far more dangerous to be a journalist covering the U.S. war in Afghanistan than to be a soldier on the American side. Later on, this state of affairs changed somewhat, as American forces were used on the ground to deal with enclaves of Taliban and al-Qaida resistance and some deadly fire-fights occurred. A new wave of American triumphalism emerged, being painted in vivid colors of geopolitical achievement in the course of President Bush's State of the Union Address on 29 January 2002.[10] This occasion was seized to expand the scope of the war against global terror by extending its goals to include a series of countries, Iraq, Iran, and North Korea, which were provocatively labeled "the axis of evil". Ever since that speech, the assumption permeated media treatments and public attitudes that a U.S. decision to wage war against Iraq had been made by the White House, and the only uncertainty that remained was related to the adoption of specific war plans, the extent, timing, and nature of the attack, the degree of dependence on a ground attack, and the availability and relevance of Iraqi opposition forces both inside and outside of the country.

This further turning of the screw by the U.S. Government moved the sanctions debate into the background, shifting world attention to the avoidance of war. The UN was still pursuing a course that would suggest that a reliance on the inspections mechanism authorized by UNSC Res 1441 could avert a second Gulf War. Despite this sidelining of sanctions, it remains important even today to consider the sanctions regime, which continued to impose hardships on the civilian population of Iraq, from the perspective of international law and morality. The sanctions regime, though now ended, stands before our political understanding of liberty as a severe descent by the organized international community into criminality, subjecting it to serious analysis as to whether the wrongdoing and harm amount cumulatively to genocide or not.[11]

The Sanctions Regime

It seems helpful to separate the former sanctions regime into five distinct phases, each of which poses the question of legality and morality in a different way:

1. Pre-war reliance on sanctions in the months after the Iraqi invasion of Kuwait in August 1990;
2. Immediate post-war reliance on sanctions to achieve compliance with Security Council Res. 687;

3. Persisting reliance on sanctions during the UNSCOM period in the face of growing evidence of civilian suffering;

4. Shift to "smart sanctions" to deflect criticism of early sanctions regime, and to sustain UN consensus for their imposition;

5. Maintenance of sanctions as a secondary policy, with increasingly blatant "war talk" as the primary policy, threatening a military attack unless a satisfactory regime change in Baghdad occurs.

Pre-War Sanctions

It is of great importance to distinguish sharply between the imposition of comprehensive sanctions by virtue of UNSC Resolution 661 prior to the initiation of the Gulf War on 15 January 1991. In the months following Iraq's conquest and annexation of Kuwait in August 1990, the approach advocated publicly by the United States, and adopted by the United Nations Security Council, was to endorse Kuwait's right of self-defense and to seek a resolution of the conflict by a combination of diplomacy and sanctions. The limited goals of this policy were to restore fully the sovereign rights of Kuwait, and to impose on Iraq the costs of the harm inflicted. The issue of Iraqi actual and potential possession of weaponry of mass destruction was not part of the UN engagement in this phase. Such a response to the Iraqi invasion was widely and genuinely supported, including by the members of the Security Council with the sole exception of Yemen's abstention. Reliance on sanctions, even if imposing hardships on Iraq's population, were seen as a reasonable and appropriate approach to constructive diplomatic efforts to obtain Iraqi withdrawal, and the best way to fulfill the Charter goals of protecting states that have been victims of international aggression while doing everything possible to avoid recourse to war. In this fundamental sense, sanctions prior to the Gulf War were fully consistent with international law and morality, and enjoyed the virtually unanimous backing of the membership of the United Nations, including most of the countries of the Middle East.

Indeed, to the extent criticism was made, it moved in the direction of advocating a greater reliance on the mix of sanctions and diplomacy, especially providing more time to generate effective pressure on Baghdad. A related criticism was that the United States did not genuinely seek a diplomatic resolution of the dispute, and put forward the demand for withdrawal in such unconditional and rigid terms as to ensure that the Iraqi government would respond negatively, thereby building the U.S. case for war. The UN Secretary General at the time, Javier Perez de Cueller, supported the view in his memoirs that a somewhat more flexible approach might well have achieved the stated UN goals without war.[12] But even then, for undisclosed reasons, Washington preferred a military solution that would eliminate Iraq as a regional power, as a threat to the Gulf oil reserves, and to Israel. Part of this preference was the possibility of connecting the aggression against Kuwait with the quite separate concerns arising from Iraq's efforts to acquire weapons of mass destruction, including biological, chemical, and nuclear weaponry. Only with war, and an imposed ceasefire, could this wider security concern be addressed, as was done in Resolution 687 establishing the mandate for destruction and inspection of such capabilities.

Post-War Realities

In contrast, the perpetuation of sanctions by way of UNSC Resolution 678, in the period after the ceasefire and Iraqi withdrawal from Kuwait, was justified initially as leverage needed to ensure compliance with Iraq's various obligations to make various amends for the harm inflicted, as well as to satisfy the most serious disarmament demands imposed on a sovereign state since the end of the two world wars. It is to be noted that after World War II, in contrast to the punitive reparations burdens put on Germany after World War I, the defeated countries were not subject to economic sanctions. On the contrary, despite the terrible harm inflicted, these countries were given help with economic reconstruction, and soon achieved positive economic growth.

The devastation wrought by the first Iraq war was extensive, including the civilian infrastructure. The former president of Finland, Martti Ahtisaari, presented a report to the UN on the basis of a fact-finding mission shortly after the military campaign ended, that indicated the destruction of Iraq's entire industrial and modern sectors, suggesting that it had literally been bombed back to a pre-industrial reality.[13] Declassified documents from the U.S. Defense Intelligence Agency (DIA) confirm early complaints that the United States deliberately targeted the civilian infrastructure of Iraq, especially the water treatment system, with the acknowledged purpose of disrupting civilian life throughout the country.[14] Under these circumstances, the imposition of comprehensive sanctions was legally and morally dubious from the outset. It was perfectly obvious that the war had left Iraq in a situation of great vulnerability to a health crisis of a major magnitude, and that increasing pressures by sanctions would exact a heavy toll on the civilian society.[15] To go ahead with comprehensive sanctions under these circumstances would seem certainly to have the foreseeable effect of imposing massive indiscriminate death and illness on the civilian population, with the ironic effect of exempting the military and political leadership of Iraq from harm, and as such would engage the moral, and possibly, the legal responsibility at some level of those countries that supported post-war sanctions. Such an approach to implementing the agreed ceasefire also eroded the legitimacy and moral standing of the United Nations, first, for agreeing to sanctions given its knowledge of their probable effects, and then, extending the ceasefire to cover aspects of coercive disarmament and inspection that were not closely connected with the claim of collective security that was properly put forward as a proper justification for the war.

Sustaining the Sanctions

As the months and years went by evidence accumulated to confirm what should have been anticipated: the sanctions were exacting an enormous toll among the civilian population, and were doing virtually nothing to hamper the activities and life style of the Iraqi elite. The U.S. Government favored the maintenance of a tough sanctions regime even in the face of the well-documented reports detailing the suffering of the Iraqi people, contending in the notorious words of Madeline Albright in 1996, while serving as U.S. ambassador at the UN, not long before becoming Secretary of State, when confronted by statistics as to the loss of life among Iraqi women and children, "...we think the price is worth it."[16]

The humanitarian considerations were only part of the discontent experienced by governments when periodically asked to extend the sanctions under UN auspices. Similar hostility was expressed in various ways by public opinion outside of the United States. Another part of the growing anti-sanctions movement within the UN had to do with the degree to which the United States was seen as throwing its weight around in the UN and elsewhere, without finding a path that could lead to a quick resolution. Closely related here was the European concern that lost business opportunities in the Middle East, especially in the field of energy development, were being sacrificed for no plausible reason.

Maintaining sanctions under these conditions certainly seemed to run counter to international humanitarian law, as well as to the more general just war doctrine in its application to sanctions. The most basic conception embedded in the law of war at the close of the 19th century, in the Hague Convention, was the idea of agreements by governments that force could be legally used in warfare only if directed against military targets and the related broad injunction against the "unlimited" use of force against an enemy state. Admittedly, there are conceptual and interpretative issues present. International law is directed at states, not at international organizations such as the UN, the imposition of sanctions in this comprehensive form was initially authorized and periodically reaffirmed by the Security Council. Is the Security Council bound by the restraints of international humanitarian law? There are no clear answers given by existing international law to such questions. By analogy and by moral reasoning, it would seem that the UN as political actor should not be freed from rules of behavior seeking to protect civilians from the ravages and excesses of warfare, but can such an analogy be legally relied upon in the absence of its acceptance by the UN Security Council? Cautiously, then, it could be concluded that the maintenance of sanctions, given the evidence of their effects, is both immoral and in violation of the just war doctrine, involving three separate aspects: sanctions as applied seem indiscriminate, disproportionate, and have little prospect of achieving the ends being pursued.[17]

The Move to Smart Sanctions

In response to the rising tide of anti-sanctions sentiment, especially in Europe, the United States took a series of backward strides from its preferred unyielding position so as to prevent the international consensus from falling apart. It had earlier agreed to an oil-for-food program that allowed Iraq to sell its oil on the world market, importing civilian goods, with the use of the revenues by Iraq scrutinized by the UN Office of the Iraq Program (OIP) in such a cumbersome and restrictive way as to compromise the humanitarian rational.[18] In May 2001 after elaborate diplomatic negotiations in which the United States did its best to maximize sanctions while retaining support of the Security Council, a much heralded move to "smart sanctions" was finally approved by the UN.[19] Then in November 2001, with the adoption of UNSC Resolution 1382, the sanctions regime somewhat modified this focus, banning all traded goods that had military or dual use applications. Any Iraq overseas contract was subject to scrutiny, and rejection by UN administrative action. Any member of the Security Council could delay a contract almost indefinitely by seeking review if any of the challenged items appeared on the extensive Goods Review List. The OIP turned any questionable contract with Iraq over to the United Nations Monitoring, Verification and Inspection Commission (UNMOVIC) and the International Atomic Energy Agency (IAEA) to determine whether the trade goods were related to Iraqi military applications. The so-called 661 Committee of the Security Council had the last word on whether a contract survived this review process.

In fact, Iraq appears to have circumvented many of the constraints associated with the early years of sanctions via internal adaptation and regional smuggling arrangements designed to sell oil outside the sanctions regime, especially with Syria. Iraq and the UN played a cat-and-mouse game related to the renewal of inspection, which at times was made to be a bargaining move, exchanging access by inspectors for a gradual lifting of sanctions. Also, the smuggled goods tended to reflect state priorities relating to security and regime stability, and did not emphasize the alleviation of the humanitarian tragedy. While the U.S. at times seemingly endorsed this approach, it maintained a degree of ambiguity by stressing the inability to have confidence that inspection would be able to determine whether Iraq was upholding its obligation to refrain from the production, development, and possession of weaponry of mass destruction.

What became clear long before 11 September is that to the extent that sanctions were seeking political results beyond a punitive effect, their impact was negligible although maintained for more than a decade in the face of strong objective evidence that massive loss of civilian life was being caused on a monthly basis over the course of many years. Consequently, it can be concluded that the indiscriminate civilian harm caused was not "collateral," especially after the initial period when it might have been reasonable to suppose that over time the sanctions would erode internal support for Saddam Hussein's leadership, possibly stimulating internal and external Iraqi forces to achieve a regime change. Without the intervening reality of 11 September, despite this assessment, and by making adjustments of the sort involved in the adoption and administration of smart or selective sanctions, American-led policy toward Iraq would in all likelihood have maintained its futile course indefinitely, squeezing the people of Iraq without any realistic hope of achieving political objectives. Of course, some supporters of the U.S. approach argued that sanctions did succeed to the extent of keeping Saddam Hussein pinned down, "within his box" to use Beltway jargon.[20] Further, without sanctions, Iraq would have acquired a formidable arsenal of weaponry of mass destruction. Even if this latter conjecture is accurate, there is no reason to doubt, particularly in light of the Gulf War and U.S./Israeli regional security policy, that containment and deterrence would be relied upon, with every prospect of success, to minimize the risk of Iraqi expansionism. A careful examination of Iraqi behavior under Saddam Hussein discloses an ambitious approach to the use of power in regional settings, but also a rational approach to gains and losses, and a willingness to back down rather than to engage in self-destructive warfare. In effect, then, sanctions after 1991 were essentially punitive, and although supported by the UN, seemed to violate the most fundamental values embodied in international humanitarian law, and arguably raise plausible allegations of genocide. Some have argued that although atrocities did occur, the sanctions do not qualify as genocide because there was no showing of specific intent.[21]

From Sanctions to War

There is no doubt that 11 September created an opportunity for those seeking regime change in Iraq to acknowledge tacitly the failure of the sanctions approach, yet escalate their demands with respect to Iraq. Recourse to war against al-Qaida gave the Bush Administration a wide berth in foreign policy. There were attempts in the immediate aftermath of the September attacks to intimate that there were Iraqi connections with al-Qaida, a supposed meeting in Prague between an Iraqi intelligence official and Mohammed Atta, the claim that Iraq was behind the anthrax dispersal, and other more generalized allegations of the connections between Iraq as a rogue state and the new threats posed by mega-terrorism.

But the decisive move was made in the 2002 State of the Union address when Iraq headed the list of "axis of evil" states, and a doctrine of pre-emption was set forth by President Bush. Drawing on public anxieties about mega-terrorism, Bush declared that "axis of evil" countries with the will and capability to produce weaponry of mass destruction posed severe threats, not by the likelihood that such weapons would be directly used, but rather by the prospect that the weaponry would be transferred to al-Qaida and possibly other terrorists groups with global agendas. Without explicitly indicating that an attack upon Iraq was forthcoming, the clear implication of what Bush and others in Washington were saying was that it would do what was necessary to supersede the Saddam Hussein regime thus achieving regime change comparable to that which took place in Afghanistan.

It is important to underscore the degree to which such war talk was at odds with the most fundamental rules and principles of international law, as well as being incompatible with the just war tradition that continues to be influential in religious and ethicist circles. Throughout the 20th century, there were major efforts to outlaw non-defensive wars, the core undertaking of the UN Charter designed to fulfill the pledge of the Preamble "to save succeeding generations from the scourge of war." The Nuremberg/Tokyo prosecutions of German and Japanese leaders after World War II proceeded on the premise that aggressive war was a crime against the peace, and that, as such, was the most serious form of international criminality. The Charter was drafted to minimize the role of subjective factors, self-serving explanations by governments as to why war was justifiable. The Nicaragua decision of the World Court in 1986 upheld this Charter approach as also contained in general international law applicable under all circumstances of conflict. It is arguable that the 11 September attacks by al-Qaida cannot be addressed within this template of modern international law as the threat and capability cannot be territorialized, and the idea of defensive force needs to be extended to enable a threatened state to protect its people and uphold its security.[22] Such reasoning does not apply in the setting of the axis of evil states as deterrence offers an adequate way to reconcile containment with the avoidance of war, the security policy used by both sides in the Cold War for over 40 years. In this regard, the war talk directed at Iraq was a direct challenge to the overall framework of modern international law with respect to war/peace issues. When war was unleashed against Iraq a second time, it established a dangerous and unacceptable precedent validating recourse to international force in a wide range of circumstances. First of all, anticipatory defense and preventive war were used as a rationale. Secondly, recourse to war was undertaken by the United States without a UN mandate, and without even the collective procedures invoked to justify recourse to war in 1999 in relation to Kosovo.

Conclusion

The Iraq experience with sanctions needs to be understood by reference to the five distinct temporal intervals discussed above. No blanket generalizations can be applied to the sanctions regime as a whole. The imposition and maintenance of sanctions after the Gulf War needs to be condemned as a deliberate and indiscriminate policy designed to inflict harm on the civilian population of Iraq. The UN discredited itself by endorsing sanctions, although efforts were made to mitigate the humanitarian catastrophe being caused by initiatives of the Secretary General and others, and the UN generally is no stronger and more accountable under international law than it is leading members permit. In this regard, the United States and the United Kingdom, the most ardent proponents of sanctions and the enforcers of the no-fly zones, bear a particularly heavy political, legal, and moral responsibility for the harm inflicted on the people of Iraq during the 1990s.

The debate about sanctions was superseded as of the end of the Afghanistan War by the debate about recourse to an American-led war against Iraq. President George W. Bush claimed that such a war was necessary as part of the anti-terrorist campaign that represented the American response to September 11. Most of the world disagreed, despite the general recognition that Saddam Hussein was an oppressive ruler who had committed numerous Crimes Against Humanity during his period as head of state. In an attempt by the Bush administration to build greater international support for the war, the United States agreed to work through the UN in September 2002 so as to give Iraq one last chance to avoid war. The Security Council was persuaded to establish a very intrusive mechanism of unconditional inspection that Iraq accepted, presumably seeking to avert the threatened American attack. This inspection process was tasked with the job of ensuring the complete "disarmament" of Iraqi weapons of mass destruction, with Iraq facing the prospect of "serious consequences" if it foiled the inspectors or was found to be in "material breach" of the operative Security Council resolution, 1441. As the process went forward it was evident that there was a widening gap between the American-led war party and the French-led inspection party.

Despite this overshadowing of sanctions by the clouds of war, it is important to assess the sanctions imposed on Iraq that set the stage for the initiation of an aggressive war. What we should learn from this reliance on sanctions first to induce Iraq to withdraw from Kuwait, and then for more than ten years as a punitive peace in the aftermath of the Gulf War, is that such a policy can be extremely devastating with respect to the civilian population. This is especially true when the sanctions are imposed on a country whose centralized water purification system has been destroyed. Indeed, in such a setting sanctions are both more indiscriminate than war itself and more life-threatening as the experience of Iraq since 1991 demonstrates. In such circumstances, sanctions amount to the continuation of war, without even the loose constraints of international humanitarian law. For the United Nations to have formally endorsed such a sanctions policy when these realities were widely reported, and essentially uncontested, is a severe blight upon its own mission to prevent war and to raise the moral standards of the world politics, especially with regard to the protection of vulnerable peoples confronting a humanitarian disaster. Though the second Iraq war has added immeasurably to the suffering of the Iraqi people, Let us hope that the dismal lessons of the Iraq sanctions will not be forgotten, and the suffering caused to the people of Iraq not repeated elsewhere in the future.

Notes

1. For an excellent overview that covers these issues see Roger Normand & Christoph Wilcke, "Human Rights, Sanctions, and Terrorist Threats: The United Nations Sanctions Against Iraq," *Transnational Law & Contemporary Problems* Vol. 11, No. 2:(Fall 2001), pp. 299-343.
2. See Eric Schmitt, "U.S. Plan for Iraq is Said to Include Attack on 3 Sides," *New York Times*, 5 July 2002; see also: editorial, "Battle Plans for Iraq," *New York Times*, 6 July 2002, p. A26.
3. A valuable overview has been provided by Sarah Graham-Brown (1999) *Sanctioning Saddam: the politics of intervention in Iraq*. New York: I.B. Tauris.
4. See the early and respected assessment of the civilian impact of the sanctions imposed after the Gulf War by the Harvard Study Team that visited Iraq several times during 1991. Albert Acherio and others, "Effect of the Gulf War on Infant and Child Mortality in Iraq," *New England Journal of Medicine* Vol. 327 p. 931; see also "Unsanctioned Suffering: A Human Rights Assessment of United Nations Sanctions on Iraq," Center for Economic and Social Rights, May 1996.
5. These two civil servants have become prominent civil society campaigners against sanctions in the years following their resignation. See Denis Halliday & Hans von Sponeck, "The Hostage Nation: Former UN Relief Chiefs Hans von Sponeck and Denis Halliday Speak Out Against an Attack on Iraq," *The Guardian*, 29 November 2001.
6. For accounts of this controversial inspection process under UN auspices see Richard Butler. (2000) *The Greatest Threat: Iraq, Weapons of Mass Destruction and the Growing Crisis in Global Security*. New York: Public Affairs; Scott Ritter and others (1999) *ENDGAME: Solving the Iraq Problem:*

Once and For All. New York: Simon & Schuster; Tim Trevan. (1999) *Saddam's Secrets: The Hunt for Iraq's Hidden Weapons.* London, UK: HarperCollins.

7. As is consistently the case when liberal militarism seeks to appease the hard right, the criticisms of Clinton's foreign policy that have surfaced since 11 September have emphasized its reluctance to use force sufficiently to intimidate Islamic extremism. Bernard Lewis and Fouad Ajami have been particularly influential in mounting such lines of criticism, partly to support moves toward waging war against Iraq, and partly to give assent to the approach taken in the Afghanistan War.

8. For an argument along these lines see Richard Falk. (2003) *The Great Terror War.* Northhampton, MA: Interlink.

9. For text see White House website <www.whitehouse.gov>.

10. For text see White House website <www.whitehouse.gov>.

11. Compare George E. Bisharat. (2001). "Sanctions as Genocide," *Transnational Law & Contemporary Problems.* Vol. 11, No. 2, pp. 379-425 with Joy Gordon. (2002) "When Intent Makes All the Difference in the World: Economic Sanctions on Iraq and the Accusation of Genocide," *Yale Human Rights & Development Law Journal.* Vol. 5 pp. 1-27. Gordon argues against the inference of genocide by stressing the degree to which specific intent is an essential element of the crime, and not present in relation to the sanctions policy.

12. See Javier Perez de Cueller. (1997) *Pilgrim for Peace: a secretary general's memoir.* New York, NY: St. Martin's Press.

13. Ahtisaari, a respected international figure, revealing the conditions prevailing in Iraq when comprehensive sanctions were re-imposed, wrote in the report: "The recent conflict has wrought near-apocalyptic results upon the economic infrastructure of what had been, until January 1991, a rather highly urbanized and mechanised society. Now, most means of modern life support have been destroyed or rendered tenuous. Iraq has, for some time to come, been relegated to a pre-industrial age, but with all the disabilities of post-industrial dependency on an intensive use of energy and technology." (1991) "Report to the Secretary-General on Humanitarian Needs in Kuwait and Iraq in the Immediate Post-Crisis Environment by a Mission Led by Mr. Martti Ahtisaari, Under-Secretary-General for Administration and Management, 10-17 March 1991," UN SCOR, Annex, UN Doc. S/22366.

14. See the devastating account based on these declassified documents by Thomas J Nagy, "The Secret Behind the Sanctions: How the U.S. Intentionally Destroyed Iraq's Water Supply," *The Progressive*, August 2001; also Felicity Arbuthnot. "Allies Deliberately Poisoned Iraq's Public Water Supply in Gulf War," *Sunday Herald.* (Scotland), 17 September 2001.

15. As Bisharat observes, note 11, fn 4, p. 381; beyond other considerations, Iraq's particular vulnerability to sanctions "was increased by its relative geographical isolation, its reliance on oil pipelines, and its limited shipping access, which made an embargo simple to enforce," citing Graham-Hughes, note 3, p. 73 as source.

16. This statement was made in the course of the following exchange on Sixty Minutes: "We have heard that a half million children have died," said 60 Minutes reporter Lesley Stahl, speaking of U.S. sanctions against Iraq. "I mean, that's more children than died in Hiroshima. And ... and you know, is the price worth it?" To which Ambassador Albright replied, "I think this is a very hard choice, but the price ... we think the price is worth it." Michael Schwartz, "U.S. Takes Selfish Stance in Relations Throughout the World," U-Wire, 14 February 2001, available at <http://www.uwire.com/content/topops 021401001. htm>.

17. The just war criteria are well expressed in the context of Iraq in an article primarily concerned with the prospect of war against Iraq, but is applicable to the sanctions discussion as well. See: George Hunsinger. (2003) "Iraq: Stop the War," in Robert McAfee Brown in Memoriam. See also, Drew Christiansen & Gerard F. Powers. (1995) "Economic Sanctions and the Just-War Doctrine," in *Economic Sanctions: Panacea or Peacebuilding in a Post-Cold War World* (Boulder, CO: Westview Press), pp. 97-117.

18. See Richard Garfield. (2001) "Health and Well-Being in Iraq: Sanctions and the Impact of the Oil-for-Food Program," *Transnational Law & Contemporary Problems* Vol. 11, No. 2, pp. 277-298.

19. See helpful summary assessments by Sarah Graham-Brown. "Sanctions Renewed on Iraq," MERIP Information Note 96, 14 May 2002. See also: George A. Lopez. (2001) "Toward Smart Sanctions on Iraq," Policy Brief, No. 5, April; Marc Lynch. "Smart Sanctions: Rebuilding Consensus or Maintaining Conflict?" MERIP, 28 June 2001.

20. Even *The Nation* in an editorial endorsed an approach to Iraq that rests on renewed inspection and selective sanctions, partly as an alternative to war, partly as a containment plus strategy of meeting what it acknowledges to be an Iraqi threat. "War on Iraq is Wrong," *The Nation*. 19 June 2002, pp. 3-4.

21. See Bisharat and Joy articles referred to in Note 11 for serious scholarly explorations of the relevance of genocide to the sanctions regime.

22. This position is fully developed in Falk (2003) *The Great Terror War*, Chapters 2 and 3.

PART II

Palestine and Israel

7

THE ISRAELI ALLIANCE
WITH CHRISTIAN ZIONISTS

℘ℭ℞

Norton Mezvinsky

In the spring of 2003, I traveled to Waco, Texas to deliver a lecture on Christian Zionism at Baylor University, the premier Baptist University in the United States. When leaving the Waco airport to drive to the campus in the car of one of my academic hosts, I saw a huge billboard on the side of the road near the entrance to the airport. The billboard message was: "and the Lord said to Jacob…unto they offspring will I give this land." *Genesis* 35:11-12. Pray that president Bush honors God's covenant with Israel. Call the White House with this message 202-456-111." The message was signed "The Religious Roundtable," which is a Christian Zionist grouping. Baylor University and Waco are in a major evangelical, Christian Zionist location; the George W. Bush ranch and the White House retreat are also in that same vicinity. I began my lecture at Baylor last spring by citing this hometown billboard as being indicative of major sentiment in the area in which I was then lecturing.

During a political visit to the United States in late November and early December 2003. Binyamin Elon, an Orthodox Rabbi who lives in the West Bank, is Israel's Minister of Tourism, an Israeli cabinet member and the head of the political party Moledet reported that he saw a large, identical billboard in downtown Memphis. Roberta Combs, president of the Christian Coalition; Ed McArteer, one of the founders of the Christian Right Moral Majority; Mike Evans, founder of the Jerusalem Prayer teams; Gary Bauer, the head of American Values, a conservative, Christian grouping; Pat Robertson, the founder of the Christian Broadcasting Network and a host of other Christian Zionist leaders have cited this same billboard message. Yechiel Eckstein, an Orthodox Rabbi, who has fostered and deepened Christian Zionists and Israeli governmental links and because of this was named by *The Forward*, a major American Jewish weekly publication, as one of the three most important Jews in the United States, has cited this and similar messages. Tom De Lay, a leading conservative Republican member of Congress from Texas, who is an avowed evangelical Christian Zionist, cited this billboard message when addressing the Israeli Knesset a few months ago as a preface to his statement: "I stand before you today in solidarity as an Israeli of the heart who believes biblically that the struggle in the Middle East is between Israel's godly good and Arab-evil." Understandably, numerous Israeli and other politicians and commentators have opined that evangelical Christian Zionists are more important allies for Israel then are American Jews.

Jerry Falwell claims that as a Christian Zionist leader he speaks for one hundred million Americans. That is probably an exaggeration, but he may well be speaking for forty to fifty million Americans who are evangelical Christian Zionists. In addition other tens of millions of Americans are part of a more liberal, sometimes termed "main-line," Christian Zionist contingent.

The first point I am making, therefore, is that when I write about Christian Zionism, which I shall soon define in more depth, I am writing about something adhered to by a great number of citizens of the United States. Many of these Americans actively support the government of the state of Israel and its Arab-Israeli conflict policies. Christian Zionists exist in numerous other countries as well. There can be no reasonable doubt, based upon an abundance of empirical evidence, that Christian Zionism and Christian Zionists have significantly and increasingly affected the Arab-Israeli conflict especially since the 1980s, that this influence in the United States—both in regard to public opinion and the government—is currently more of a force than ever before.

As already indicated, I shall in this chapter focus primarily upon evangelical Christian Zionism. Before going further in that regard, however, I need to provide some additional context and background by defining Zionism per se.

Zionism is one, not the only, theory of Jewish nationalism. As such it postulates a definition—or at least a partial definition—of the Jewish people. From the late nineteenth century, three distinct and in many ways contrasting versions of Zionism appeared; two were secularist, and one was religious in orientation. One of the secular strains, which I term humanistic Zionism, originated by the great Jewish thinker and writer, Ahad Ha'am, and developed further by Martin Buber and Judah Magnes, was overwhelmed by the other secular version, political Zionism. Until the Holocaust occurred, the third version, religious Zionism, was advocated by a relatively small number of Orthodox Rabbis. Although keeping their own identity and continuing their separate advocacies, political and religious Zionism joined together after the Holocaust. It was nevertheless political Zionism that became and has remained the essence of this Jewish nationalism. The state of Israel came into existence in 1948 as a political Zionist state and has remained such to date. Political Zionism has been legislated into the character of the Jewish state.

Theodore Herzl, a Viennese journalist and writer in the late nineteenth century, was the father of political Zionism. A few other individuals had earlier suggested some of what became political Zionism, but Herzl creatively added substance and put it together in a coherent, rational way. Herzl's advocacy is based upon the following absolute theory of anti-Semitism: Jews at some point in time in all nation-states wherein they are in a minority will be persecuted by non-Jews. Jews therefore need a state of their own wherein they constitute the majority of the citizenry. As a secularist, Herzl did not at first specify historic Palestine as the locale for the Jewish Zionist state. He accepted the designation of Palestine only because the majority of the Jews in his Zionist movement at that time were Orthodox religious Jews who threatened to leave the movement if Palestine; the land they believed God had promised to the Jews was not so designated.

The religious Jews in Herzl's Zionist movement wanted a Jewish, theocratic state. They were the early advocates of the religious strain of Zionism. They constituted only a tiny minority of the worldwide community of Orthodox Jews in the late nineteenth and early twentieth centuries. The great majority of Orthodox Jews until World War Two and the Holocaust opposed Zionism. They based their opposition primarily upon the pronouncement by the great Jewish sage, Rabbi Akiva, following the

Bar-Kochba revolt against the Romans in 135-136 C.E. Rabbi Akiva stated that God would restore the Jewish State again only when the Messiah came and that it would be a sin for Jews to attempt to establish this state prior to the Messiah's coming. Rabbi Akiva's pronouncement resulted in three Talmudic oaths to which religious Jews swore. (Most reform Jews for differing reasons also opposed Zionism as well as all forms of Jewish Nationalism until the late 1930s.)

The relatively few Orthodox Jews who were religious Zionists in the period from the 1890s until the 1940s did not directly disagree with Rabbi Akiva's pronouncement. Rather, they argued that the messianic age had begun and that therefore a theocratic Jewish state, based upon the Halacha (Jewish religious law), should be established. This has to date remained the platform of religious Zionism.

After the Holocaust and World War Two most Orthodox Jews converted to religious Zionism. A significant minority of Orthodox Jews and their rabbis has nevertheless consistently remained anti-Zionist and are to this day still virulent critics of both Zionism and numerous Israeli state policies and actions, especially those that are oppressive to Palestinians.

Zionism became most significant when the state of Israel came into existence in 1948. Israel is a Zionist state; in its public policy, i.e. laws, it grants rights and privileges to Jews not granted to non-Jews. Israel is a demographic Jewish state. The Zionist objective is to keep it as such.

Having briefly defined and sketched an outline of the development of Zionism per se I now return to my discussion of Christian Zionism: It is a well-known fact that the state of Israel has enjoyed and continues to enjoy Christian support in the western world, especially in the United States. This support—religious, economic and political—has been broadly based, coming from liberal and conservative Protestant churches, church associations, church leaders, theologians and lay people. To a lesser degree support has come from Roman Catholicism. A good deal of support has been largely uncritical and sometimes unconditional, deriving mainly from the Holocaust and the resultant guilt felt by Christians that they and their spiritual, religious brethren contributed—at least indirectly—to the killing of the six million Jews by not criticizing and by not attempting to combat the onslaught. This feeling or attitude has to date often overridden serious appraisals and criticisms of how the Jewish state was created and how it has behaved. Zionism, the philosophy of Jewish nationalism legislated into the character of the Jewish state, has been glorified. The literature for all of this is voluminous and contains advocacies by a number of distinguished and significant Christian theologians, e.g. Reinhold Niebuhr, and commentators, e.g. Franklin Littell, Paul Van Buren, Alice and Roy Eckardt, Robert Mcafee Brown, John Paulikowski and others. Jewish—Christian dialogue for the past half-century has been dominated by Holocaust concern.

It nevertheless is also a fact that numerous liberal and conservative, including some fundamentalist and evangelical, Christian churches, church associations, church leaders, theologians and lay people have expressed concerns for and have supported the cause of the Palestinians. They have been—and to a great extent have remained—critical in varying degrees of certain aspects of Zionism, and most particularly some specific Israeli state policies and actions.

As already stated, my major focus will be fundamentalist, evangelical Christian Zionism. The term evangelical refers to the pietistic strands of Christianity, which stress a literal interpretation of scripture as a framework for the "born again" conversion experience. The Christian Zionists, to whom I shall refer, are certainly evangelicals, but all evangelicals are not Christian Zionists. Much of the Southern Baptist Convention and the charismatic Pentecostal and independent churches support and advocate Christian Zionism as do the evangelical wings of main-line Protestant churches (Presbyterian, United Methodist and Lutheran). The reach of Christian Zionism extends through Christian television, radio and publishing. The National Religious Broadcasting Organization, for example, which controls ninety percent of religious radio and television in the United States, is dominated by Christian Zionists.

Christian Zionism is a central plank of what is often referred to as the Christian Right. The Christian Right includes a growing number of churches, organizations, fellowship groupings and individuals; it is particularly influential in the United States. While allowing for variations in location and among groups, characteristically Christian Zionism takes its cue from a particular reading of certain passages of the Bible, including specific theological interpretation of the state of Israel. It is largely insensitive to the human rights of Palestinians, demonizes Islam, and assists in the immigration of Jews to Israel. It supports Israeli governments indiscriminately, as a step in the direction of the coming millennium, while too often having little respect for Judaism as such. Since 1980 Israeli prime ministers in particular, have exploited those specific fundamentalist, evangelical individuals and groupings that argue specifically and in some depth that the ingathering of the Jewish people and the rebirth of the nation of Israel are in fulfillment of the Biblical prophecies. Since God gave the land to the Jewish people as an everlasting possession, it is further alleged, Jews have absolute rights over all of it, including the occupied West Bank (Judea and Samaria), Gaza and the Golan Heights. God will bless or curse nations in accordance with their treatment of the Jewish People. In evangelical Christian theology there is a strong emphasis on a certain literalist fulfillment of biblical prophecy, on eschatology and, in some circles, on millenarianism, that brand of eschatology which affirms that the Second coming of Christ will be followed by a thousand year reign of blessedness. With regard to the state of Israel, there are two major strands: fulfillment of biblical prophecy and the association of the state with a theology of end-time. Some scholars, e.g. Regina Sharif in her book, *Non-Jewish Zionism*, argue that the basis for such an association can be traced back to religious changes that accompanied the Protestant reformation in Europe.

John Nelson Darby (1800-82), perhaps more than anyone else, laid the foundations for the development of fundamentalist evangelical Christian Zionism. A minister of the Church of Ireland, Darby renounced the visible Church and organized a group of "Brethren," whose distinctive theology was devised for the final days of history. While the division of history into a number of periods (dispensations) antedated his theological speculations, Darby divided it into seven epochs, beginning with creation, and ending with the millennial Kingdom of Jesus, following the battle of Armageddon, views he claims to have derived from his exegesis of Scripture and from personal proddings of the Holy Spirit.

Rather then subscribing to the view that the Church replaced Israel, Darby claimed that Israel would replace the Church, which was a mere parenthesis to God's continuing covenantal relationship with Israel. Those portions of biblical prophecy and apocalyptic that had not been fulfilled already would be completed in the future. He invoked apocalyptic language to postulate a two-stage Second Coming of Christ. The first "invisible appearing" would involve the rapture of the saints: the faithful remnant of the Church. This remnant especially his own followers, would return to earth with him after seven years. The seven-year long rapture in the air would be marked on earth by the "great tribulation" of natural disasters, wars and civil unrest. After the rapture, the faithful Jewish remnant would observe Law, and rule on earth for a millennium.

B.W. Newton, Darby's chief assistant in Plymouth, proposed a variant: the Jews would be restored only after the return of Christ, who would bring them to the faith in the Messiah, making them into a kingdom of priests and a holy nation. With his authority waning in Britain, Darby concentrated on North America, where he influenced such evangelical leaders as Dwight L. Moody, William E. Blackstone, and C.I. Schofield with his emerging Bible and Prophecy Conference movement that set the tone for the evangelical and fundamentalist movements in North America between 1875 and 1920. Typically, dispensationalists predict that that the present age is a penultimate one: biblical prophecy finds its fulfillment in the birth of the state of Israel, and soon Christ will come in glory to bring matters to a cataclysmic triumph over the forces of evil at Armageddon.

There has been strong support for the establishment of a Jewish commonwealth among American evangelicals for well over a century, due in no small measure to Darby and those whom he influenced. For William E. Blackstone Zionism was the fulfillment of prophecy. He visited Palestine in 1889 and was impressed by the agricultural settlements in the first Aliya (movement of Jews to Palestine); these settlements were all "signs of the time," indicating that the end-time would come very soon. Zionist leaders passed over Blackstone's real hopes for the Jews and his disparagement of the Jewish law as an agent of salvation. Zionist leaders sought as the price Blackstone's support for the Zionist venture regardless of the qualifications he suggested.

The evangelical constituency was critical of the British policy after 1920 that sought to limit the number of Jewish immigrants; this constituency was disdainful of Arab opposition for which, these evangelicals claimed, Arabs would pay dearly for their rebellion against God. A coalition between Christian evangelicals and secular Jewish Zionists had enough advantage for each party to co-operate on the one issue of the establishment of a Jewish state. Their example has been followed by all Israeli prime ministers since Menachem Begin in 1977. Up to the 1970s, the evangelicals did not have significant influence over American policy, but they have since exerted considerable influence. When it came to power in 1977, the Likud Party in Israel began to use religious language to advance its revisionist Zionist agenda, which was popular with some branches of American Christianity; efforts were made to forge bonds between evangelical Christians and pro-Israel lobbies. The evangelical Christian constituency was a major factor in the election of Jimmy Carter to the Presidency in 1976 and of Ronald Reagan in 1980. In 1980 more then eighty percent of the Christian Right supported the candidacy of Reagan. The stage was set for promoting an alliance between the conversionist goals of evangelical Christianity and the political aspiration of Zionism. The establishment of the state of Israel is an important element in such a worldview. The Jews have allegedly returned to their ancient homeland and will themselves be ruled by a Jewish imposter of the Messiah. But the return of Jesus, the true Messiah, will end the anti-Christ's rule and establish the millennial kingdom. Those Jews who survive will welcome Jesus as their savior. During the 1,000 year reign, Jesus would establish his capital in Jerusalem, the center of the world government, and the Jewish people, now living within the boundaries of the ancient kingdom of David, would assist him in his administration. Most of the evangelical world viewed the birth of Israel as the first clear sign of the fulfillment of biblical prophecy and the final countdown to Armageddon. Israel's amazing victory over Arab armies in June 1967 confirmed the prophetic scenario. Immediately after the war L. Nelson Bell, editor of the mouthpiece of conservative evangelicalism, wrote, "That for the fist time in more than 2,000 years Jerusalem is now completely in the hands of the Jews gives the student of the Bible a thrill and a renewed faith in the accuracy and validity of the Bible."

Hal Lindsey's book, *The Late Great Planet Earth* (1970), of which well over twenty-seven million copies have been sold, reflects a typical evangelical mixture of biblical literalism and political analysis with biblical prediction fulfilled almost to the letter. In Lindsay's interpretation of the fig tree the most important sign for Matthew was to be the restoration of the Jews to the land in the rebirth of Israel: When the Jewish People, after nearly 2,000 years of exile became a nation again on 14 May 1948, the fig tree, according to Lindsay, put forth its first leaves. But the restoration was only a stage in Lindsay's eschatology. Under attack from godless communism and militant Islam the state of Israel would fight an apocalyptic battle at the mount of Megiddo, in which Jesus Christ would come to the rescue, be proclaimed King of the Jews and rule over the nations form the rebuilt temple in Jerusalem. At this point, "Jerusalem will be spiritual center of the entire world… All people of the earth will come annually to worship Jesus who will rule there."

From the early 1990s until 2003 the *New York Times* best-selling *Left Behind Series*, co-authored by Tim LeHaye and Jerry B. Jenkins, a 12 book sequence of novels about the end-time has sold sixty-two million copies. The series emphasizes all of Christian Zionist belief in the second coming of Jesus Christ and in the necessity for a Jewish state in historic Palestine and beyond prior to the second coming. In the *Left Behind Series,* Israel is the only nation God favors.

The October War of 1973 gave further fuel to Armageddon theology. President Carter shocked the fundamentalists with his concern for human rights, and used the words, "Palestinian homeland" in a speech in March 1977. Full-page newspaper advertisements then appeared throughout the country, proclaiming, "The time has come for evangelicals to affirm their belief in biblical prophecy and Israel's divine right to the Holy Land." Reflecting its concern that Carter's advocacy of Palestinian rights might conflict with their evangelical interests, the text went on, "We affirm as evangelicals our belief in the promised land to the Jewish people. ... We view with belief in the Promised Land to the Jewish people. ... We would view with grave concern any effort to carve out of the Jewish homeland another nation or political entity." The swing of the evangelical Christian Right from Carter to Reagan in the 1980 election was a major factor in the former's defeat.

Jerry Falwell's "friendship tour to Israel" in 1983 included meetings with top Israeli government and military officials, a tour of Israeli battlefields and inspections of defense installations. Falwell's tour and trips to Jerusalem supposedly heralded the immigration of Jews into Israel as the sign of the imminent second coming of Jesus Christ. Jews would rapture true Christians into the air, while the rest of humankind would be slaughtered below. Then 144,000 Jews (some dispensationalists say a few more) would bow down before Jesus and be saved, but the remainder would perish in the mother of all holocausts, Armageddon. This could happen even while the evangelical pilgrims were in Jerusalem, thus giving them a ringside seat at the Battle of Armageddon. (A few Christian Zionists recently changed their position and amended this prophecy of destructions of all but 144,000 Jews. In agreement with some other Christians they now maintain that God in a separate covenant put Jews in a special category, by which they, or at least most of them, would avert destruction.)

The views summarized here are at the core of the normal creed of evangelicals. Of some influence in this creed was the carefully orchestrated and heavily financed campaign, coordinated by Jerry Strober, a former American Jewish Committee employee, who recognized the value of the evangelicals to the Israelis. As the American Jewish Committee's national inter religious affairs director, moreover, Rabbi Marc Tannenbaum attested later that the pro-Israeli lobby felt abandoned by the mainstream Protestant Churches and National Council of Churches, both of which were sympathetic to Third World countries and supported the Palestinians. The Israeli lobby then targeted the evangelicals, who, as already mentioned, number as many as fifty-to-sixty million Americans. Prime Minister Begin presented Jerry Falwell with the Jabotinsky Award from the Government of Israel in appreciation of his support. Pat Robertson charted the Israeli invasion of Lebanon in 1982 with daily reports on CBN, interpreting the events according to the end-time fulfillment of biblical prophecy. Israeli's attack was for Robertson a modern Joshua event. Robertson urged American viewers to phone President Reagan immediately, offering encouragement to Israel in its war against the Palestinians.

Together with the power of the Israeli lobby, the influence of the North American evangelical right wing has been and remains a major factor preventing the United States from exercising even-handedness in the Middle East. On 27 January 1992, for example, a full-page advertisement in the *Washington Times* claimed: "Seventy Million Christians Urge President Bush to Approve Loan Guarantees for Israel." That same day, Hal Lindsay became a consultant on Middle East affairs to both the Pentagon and the Israeli government. The evangelical Right was responsible for the pro-Israel advertisement in the *New York Times* on 10 April 1997, titled "Christians Call for a United Jerusalem," supporting the uncompromising Likud Party position on Jewish sovereignty over the entire city. Some evangelical bodies, moreover, have compensated in recent years for the fall-off of some American Reform and Conservative Jewish support of the Jewish National Fund by providing substantial financial donations.

In Jerusalem the leader of the International Christian Embassy has continued to insist that Israel be faithful to its role within God's cosmic plans. He has consistently maintained that Israel should listen to God rather than to the United Sates Secretary of State and should not give up territory. In his apocalyptic reading of human history, Islam is satanic, and the mosques on the Temple Mount must be destroyed in order to prepare of the coming of the Lord and the rebuilding of the temple. Indeed, no event in everyday Israeli political life is above the possibility of being interpreted as a fulfillment of a biblical prophecy. In the United States Pastor John Hagee from San Antonio established himself as not just a prophetic voice on the end-time but a "prophet for our generation." According to Hagee, whose books have each sold well over 500,000 copies, even the assassination of Prime Minister Rabin was in fulfillment of biblical prophecies, auguring the imminent arrival of Armageddon and the end of days. The peace process, Hagee and others have maintained, will result in the most devastating war Israel has ever known, after which the Messiah will come.

For their part, successive Israeli governments have entered into a marriage of convenience with the International Christian Embassy, happy to use this as a means of gaining support for Israel from some groups of Christians, while ignoring its eschatological expatiations. Prime Minister Netanyahu addressed its annual conference at the Jewish Feast of Tabernacles again in 1998. Ehud Olmert, the Mayor of Jerusalem, assured the gathering, "I'm going to tell the Prime Minister, The Defense Minister, the Chief of Staff you are part of our army, of our power, of our defense." The audience contained representatives of Christian Friends of Israeli Communities, an organization that matches churches in the United States with Israeli settlements.

In 1996 the Proclamation of the Third International Christian Zionist Congress clearly and simply outlined the position of many fundamentalist, evangelical Christian Zionists. This proclamation, which has often been reiterated since, stated: 1) God judges all people on how well they treat Jews. 2) Islam comprises an anti- Jewish and anti-Christian distortion of the true faith of Abraham. 3) Jews have the absolute right to possess and dwell in the Golan Heights and all of what are now the occupied territories as an everlasting possession by an eternal covenant with God. 4) Islamic claims to Jerusalem derive not from the Quran or early Islamic traditions but from later, more secular origins. 5) Jerusalem must remain undivided under Israeli sovereignty and the capital of Israel alone.

In the late 1990s, as previously noted, donations to Israel and the Jewish National Fund declined because of the tensions between Orthodox Jews in Israel and the Reform and Conservative Jews in the United States. The loss of funding caused the Likud Party to turn to Christian Zionists for assistance, an appeal that met with quick response. Additional support came from campaigns led by the International Fellowship of Christians and Jews and headed by a former Anti-Defamation League employee, Rabbi Yechiel Eckstein. In 1997 this campaign claimed that it had raised over five million dollars from fundamentalist Christians. John Hagee's Cornerstone Church in San Antonio, Texas, presented Eckstein with more than one million dollars for resettling Jews from the former Soviet Union in the West Bank and Jerusalem. Again, these American Christian Zionists send millions of dollars each year to the Israeli government. The conservative estimate is that these people have sent at least seventy-five million dollars just to settle Jewish immigrants in the West Bank and to support the settlers. The Reverend James Hutchens, president of the Christians for Israel/United States, claims that his organization alone had by 1999 financed that immigration of 65,000 Jews to Israel. These Christians have for years urged the United States Congress to increase its aid to Israel. The Reverend John Hagee, among others, is especially keen about all of this, because he believes that God will greatly expand the boundaries of the state of Israel. As Hagee wrote in book, *Beginning of the End* (1996):

> Given these boundaries found in Holy Scripture, we discover that Israel will have far more land when the Messiah comes than she presently does. Israel's boundaries established time and time again in the Old Testament, will include all of present-day Israel, all of Lebanon, half of Syria, two-thirds of Jordan, all of Iraq and the northern portion of Saudi Arabia... God told Abraham that the land would belong to his offspring forever (Hagee, *Beginning of the End*, p.23-4, 30).

American Christian Zionists have for a number of years said that they are a more important source of support of Israel than are American Jews and the Israeli lobby. Jerry Falwell in 2002 stated publicly: "It is my belief that the Bible belt in America is Israel's only safety belt right now."

In December 2000, Israeli Prime Minister Ariel Sharon told a group of 1500 Christian Zionist pilgrims who were in Jerusalem: "We regard you as our best friend in the world."

In a 15 November 2001 article in the *Jerusalem Post*, titled "U.S. Christians Care More than U.S. Jews," Jonathon Rosenblum observed that many of Israel's staunchest supporters in Congress have been influenced more by Christian Zionists than by Jews. Rosenblum noted, as many others have pointed out, that significantly intertwined relationships exist between American Christian Zionist and Israeli political leaders. After being elected prime minister in the late 1990s, Binyamin Natanyahu, for instance, established an Israeli Christian Advocacy Council and flew seventeen prominent Christian Zionist supporters to Israel. Included in the seventeen were the president of the National Association of Evangelicals and the president of the National Religious Broadcasters, whose oversight includes almost ninety percent of all Christian Radio and television broadcasting in North America.

Christian Zionist influence in the current Bush administration, as covered in greater detail in Haddad's chapter, reflects the political reality of almost three decades. In 1987 polls indicated that twenty-six percent of the total membership of the Republican Party adhered to the positions, including Christian Zionism, of the Christian right. By 1999 the percentage had risen to the thirty-three and has since continued to rise. The influence of pro-Israel groups and Christian Zionists in such vital swing states as Texas and all-important Florida may have been the deciding factor for George W. Bush in the 2000 election. Bush is certainly aware that he owes a political dept to this voting bloc. George W. Bush, who became a born again Christian when he was thirty-nine years old, is clearly a sympathetic follower of evangelical Christian Zionism. His personal minister, Franklin Graham—the son of Billy Graham—is an outspoken Christian Zionist advocate, who in writing and speaking had called Islam evil and Israel God's nation. President Bush has often had Franklin Graham lead prayer meetings at the White House and at the Pentagon.

After 11 September 2001, the pro-Israeli lobby and Christian Zionists began to close ranks, fearing that George W. Bush's support for Israel was beginning to waver. At the April 2002 Washington Rally for Israel, for example, an impressive group of politicians were joined by leading voices from Israel and the American Jewish community to address the audience of well over 1,000,000 people on the Washington Mall. The list included former Israeli Prime Minister Binyamin Netanyahu, Deputy Secretary of Defense Paul Wolfowitz, New York Governor George Pataki and others. The loudest cheers of the rally, however, were reserved for Janet Parshall, who hosts her own nationally syndicated radio program, *Janet Parshall's America*, and serves as a spokesperson for the Family Religious Council. Parshall drew an immediate ovation when she said: "...we represent millions of Christian broadcasters in this country. We stand with you now and forever." She went on to loud applause and sustained cheers: "I am here to tell you today [that] we Christians and Jews together will not labor any less in our support for Israel. We will never limp, we will never wimp, and we will never vacillate in our support of Israel." At this rally Gary Bauer, the president of American Values, told the crowd: "Whoever sits in Washington and suggests to the people of Israel that they have to give up more land in exchange for peace [is uttering] an obscenity."

In April 2002 Jerry Falwell reacted to President Bush's call for Israel to withdraw its troops from Palestinian towns in the West Bank by sending a letter of protest to the White house. More than 100,000 emails from self-identified Christian Zionists followed Falwell's letter. President Bush did not again ask Israel to withdraw. In October 2002 Falwell commented during a sixty-minute television program interview:

We can now count on President Bush to do the right thing every time…
There's nothing that would bring the wrath of the Christian public in this
country down on the government like abandoning or opposing Israel in a
critical matter… I really believe that, when the chips are down, Ariel
Sharon can trust George Bush to do the right thing every time. The Bible
is Israel's safety net in the U.S..

Falwell speaks for a large number of Christian Zionists in the United
States. To reiterate, these Christians believe that the modern state of Israel
is the fulfillment of biblical prophecy and thus deserves unconditional
political, financial and religious support. Christian Zionists work closely,
as they have for many years, with religious and secular Jewish Zionist
organizations and the Israeli government. A recent Religious News Service
report noted: "The Israeli Embassy has begun monthly strategy discussions
with evangelicals about increasing Israeli tourism, sponsoring pro-Israeli
events on United States campuses and doing more political lobbying in
Washington." On 15 February 2004, Israeli Tourist Minister Binyamin
Elon, as previously noted, honored Pat Robertson of CBN at the National
Association of Broadcasters Convention in Charlotte. Elon said that
Robertson's leadership saved Israeli tourism from bankruptcy by promoting
pilgrimages to the Holy Land despite the United States Government's travel
warnings. After 11 September and an increase in hostilities between Israel
and the Palestinians, the pilgrimages continued. Elon estimated that over
400,000 evangelicals traveled to Israel in 2003 and contributed millions of
dollars to the Israeli economy. Elon reiterated what Prime Minister Ariel
Sharon said in Jerusalem in the fall of 2003 when he addressed three
thousand Christian Zionist evangelicals who had come from the United
States, Europe and South Africa: "Coming here, I heard many people say,
'We love you, we love Israel.' I tell you now: we love YOU. We love all
of you." Sharon continued: "You did not come here as normal tourists, you
came because your souls and hearts brought you here. And when you come
here you don't need a 'guide book.' You have the guide book, you have the
Bible in your hands." Many of the Christian Zionists called out to support
Sharon in "finishing the job" and encouraged him to "annihilate" Yassir
Arafat.

The Israeli Embassy in Washington has recently begun to expand its
work with evangelical Christian Zionists in sponsoring pro-Israeli events
on United States campuses and doing political lobbying work in Washing-

ton. This work was largely initiated in the 1990s during the Clinton administrations.

At first glance it might appear that Christian Zionists and Israeli Jews are strange bedfellows. After all, Christian Zionist theology—or at least most of it—portends doom for the great majority of Jews when the end-time arrives. According to most Christian Zionists only 144,000 Jews will accept and follow Jesus and thus be saved. When in Israel in the summer of 2003, I asked officials of and other individuals close to the Sharon government about all of this, I received a standardized answer. These Israeli Jews considered the Christian Zionist theology "nonsense," but, of course, they accepted with great thanks the aid and support given by Christian Zionists. The Christian Zionists, with whom I spoke in Israel, said they knew that Israeli Jews viewed their theology as nonsense, but they nevertheless were not dismayed. They merely told me that they were neither receiving direction nor taking orders from Israeli Jews but rather from above. And when they said this, they looked up towards heaven. Be that as it may, Christian Zionists are playing a significant role in the Arab-Israeli conflict. This will likely continue for at least the foreseeable future.

8

ON THE TRAIL OF THE
PALESTINE STATE

ഇൗരു

John Strawson

There is much talk of the creation of the Palestinian state. The Israeli disengagement from Gaza might be a step towards one. The issue has been in the air for some time. Since 2002 the United Nations Security Council has called for one,[1] the roadmap for peace provides its creation[2] and even Ariel Sharon's first disengagement plan refers to it.[3] Indeed in his first press conference after re-election President George W Bush re-affirmed U.S. policy as the creation of a "Palestinian state living alongside Israel."[4] In this chapter I will argue that the widespread use of the term masks fundamental differences as to what a Palestinian State might be. The argument here will be based on the indeterminate character of international law and the very specific character of the Palestinian-Israeli conflict as revealed through the discourse of the Oslo peace process, the roadmap for peace and the Israeli disengagement plan. The dissonance over the questions of whether there should be a Palestinian state and what it might be has haunted the past decade of Palestinian-Israeli relations. In the flurry of international activity following the Gaza disengagement it might be cautionary to identify the contours of this issue.[5]

International Law

A state has a juridical character which is determined by international law. However, international law, as Marrti Koskenniemi has argued, combines utopian rhetoric about justice with a rather more mundane service of legitimating power.[6] This combination, what he calls utopia and apology, takes place at the same moment. This approach will be used suggestively here. International legal terms such as state, sovereignty and self-determination have developed a specialized meaning that is somewhat different to the way in which we might understand them in the context of politics or international relations. As a legal concept the state is endowed with sovereignty and based on a people with a recognized right to self-determination. Sovereignty once assumed that there was exclusive jurisdiction over the over the territory and people of the state. However, this exclusivity is modified by current developments in international law including the provisions of United Nations Charter and international treaties such as those on genocide, torture and human rights. However, it still remains the case that whatever the potential role for international institutions other states do not have jurisdiction over another and generally must abide by the obligation of "non-interference."

In the dominant liberal theory of international law states are equal one with each other. This notion of equity is, however, unrelated to power and refers to the idea that the state has legal personality simply meaning that it can appear before international courts and tribunals, sign treaties and apply to be a member of the United Nations. The legal definition of a state which has come to be widely accepted involves four criteria: defined borders, a settled population, an effective government, and capacity to enter into international relations.[7] The latter subjective test is perhaps the most important indicating that a state is an entity that the international community agrees to accord legal personality to. The other elements have been modified by international practice as illustrated in the recognition of the State of Israel despite its undefined borders and unsettled population (note the Law of Return which offers instant citizenship to any Jew).[8] Many states continue to act in the international community despite lacking an effective government, for example Lebanon during its seventeen-year civil war or the Democratic Republic of Congo today. This general legal indeterminacy also extends to the notion of states being sovereign. The United Nations Security Council for example has passed a series of resolutions on Iraq 2003-2004, affirming its sovereignty while recognizing the American led occupation (see for example resolution 1483 (2003)). The doctrine of sovereignty is made all the more problematic with the U.S. proposal for "regime change" based on the assumption that some states should be characterized as "failed states" or "rogue states." This principle has now been incorporated albeit more elegantly in the United Nations reform plan which proposes a new peace-building commission to aid in the administration of failed states.[9]

There is also a specialist use of the term "self-determination," which legal doctrine attaches to "a people," although fails to define the concept of people. The Palestinians, however, have been explicitly recognized as such a people by the United Nations in many resolutions since 1969.[10] However, even this clarification carries with it the seeds of problematic application as the Palestinian people live in four main jurisdictional situations: in the West Bank and Gaza, in Jerusalem, in Israel and as refugees in many countries. This necessarily raises critical questions of legal representation and what exercising the right of self-determination would mean for all four categories.

Reading legal texts and applying legal doctrine thus requires great effort to encompass many differences of interpretation and requires great sensitivity to the many silences that are encountered.[11] The texts of the Palestinian-Israeli conflict whether found in United Nations resolutions, the Oslo agreements, the roadmap and instruments which, are said to implement them, contain many such silences. With the issue of the Palestinian state we shall see that first there is silence and then gradually the term emerges. Both stages contain many perplexities.

The Oslo Agreements

It is against the background of this legal discourse that the Oslo agreements were negotiated between Israel and the Palestine Liberation Organization between 1992 and 1993.[12] The negotiations produced the Declaration of Principles that was signed with such fanfare on the White House lawn in September 1993.[13] The negotiations had concentrated on providing a solution to the status of the territory Israel occupied in the 1967 war and to address at least one consequence of the creation of the State of Israel in 1948, the Palestinian refugees. .The Oslo process is contained in a series of documents, the principal ones being: the 1993 Declaration of Principles, the 1994 Cairo Agreement[14] and the 1995 Interim Agreement.[15] The first set out the objectives, the framework for the negotiations and the time frame of completing the negotiations within five years of the first Israeli withdrawal. The second affected the Israeli withdrawal from most of Gaza and the Jericho area and created the Palestinian Authority. The third provided for further Israeli deployments from the occupied territories and provided for the emergence of state-like institutions for the Palestinian Authority including elections for the President and for the Palestine Legislative Council.[16] For the first time since 1948 Palestinian institutions and leadership were based on Palestinian soil.

The implementation of the Cairo Agreement saw the return of the PLO leadership in the summer of 1994. The leadership was accompanied by several thousand officials and personnel including from the Palestine National Liberation Army, the latter forming the backbone of the "strong police force" referred to in the agreements. The return of Arafat to Palestine was seen as highly symbolic both in Israel and Occupied Territories. For the Israelis it broke a long running taboo on seeing Arafat as anything other than a terrorist. For the Palestinians of the Occupied Territories it marked a qualitatively new relationship between them and previously exiled leadership. As the Palestinian Authority established a measure of normal political life resumed as nationalist, secular and religious based political groupings were now able to operate relatively freely.

The Cairo Agreement and the Interim Agreement provided for Israeli withdrawal and redeployments from the occupied territories. The initial withdrawal was from 68% of Gaza and a tiny area around the city of Jericho—about one percent of the West Bank. The Cairo agreement's maps were careful to ensure that all Israeli settlements and military installations were left under Israeli control. In the Interim Agreement the West Bank was divided into three designations: area A under the exclusive control of the Palestinians, area B under the civil administration of the Palestinians but with security in the hands of Israel and area C under full Israeli control. Again great pains were made in the accompanying maps to ensure that Israeli settlements and military installations were kept under Israeli control. When at the end of December Israeli forces were withdrawn from area A comprised about three percent of the West Bank. By 1999 Israel still controlled fifty-nine percent of the West Bank under area C while the Palestinians were running all civilian affairs in areas A (twenty-two percent) and B (nineteen percent), while possessing exclusive powers over the former. These territories were discontinuous and thus divided by Israeli controlled areas including settlements. The road system linking them was regulated through a series of checkpoints which began to be a permanent feature of Palestinian life. Six years after signing the Oslo agreements the Palestinians had only achieved some form of control over about ten percent of what had been British Mandate territory.

The Palestinian Authority, under the agreements was only able to exercise powers over issues of internal self-government. Even here the Authority had powers somewhat less than local government in many countries as it had to rely on finance not from raising taxes but from Israel handing the receipts from VAT to the Palestinian treasury. The rest of the money came from donors. These limited powers were further diminished by the checkpoints, and the system travel permission passes which frustrated the ability of even officials to move freely.

Despite some suspicions, the Oslo agreements did produce a degree of optimism in the occupied territories that life could change for the better. Some important advances did take place. The emergence of Palestinian institutions and, in particular the holding of possibly the freest and fairest election in the Arab world in 1996, was significant. This institutional progress was not matched by any serious evidence of "land for peace" as the deal was often colloquially described. Despite the impression at the time of the signing of the Declaration of Principles there was no freezing of Israeli settlement activity. In fact settlement activity increased dramatically and since 1993 the number of new settlers on the West Bank more than doubled.[17] The influx of the new population meant increasing land appropriations. This was exacerbated as new road system linking the settlements to each other and to Israel resulted in yet more land seizures. At the end of the Oslo process while the Palestinian institutions came to be seen as more state-like the land on which they stood was less like a conventional state and recalled the Bantustans of apartheid South Africa. While the map of the West Bank looked eerily similar to the Bantustans, the experience of the Palestinians negotiating checkpoints, carrying identity cards and requesting passes for travel increasingly resembled life under apartheid. The territorial arrangements were also highly problematic for economic life. The Palestinian economy declined, unemployment increased and the standard of living of the average Palestinian fell. With rates of unemployment in Gaza at upwards of sixty percent in 1999 it was not surprising that life expectancy fell to two years less than before the agreements.[18]

The founding text, the Declaration of Principles, of what came to be called the peace process was accompanied by letters from each the first time formally recognizing each others existence. The recognition, although mutual in the sense that this was reciprocal, was not between equal parties. The PLO recognized a state while Israel recognized a national liberation organization. Although the latter had observer status at the United Nations it was decidedly not equal to a state. This legal imbalance reinforced the political differences between the parties. The objectives of the Declaration were to achieve the "mutual legitimate rights" of the two peoples although these rights were left undefined. The text created a framework for negotiations between the two parties which would provide for "interim self-rule" for the Palestinians and then conduct negotiations of what were called "permanent status" issues. A time frame was established which gave the parties five years to complete the agreement. According to the terms of the agreement Israel would withdraw from the Gaza Strip and the Jericho opening the way for a Palestinian administration in those areas. There would then be second phase which would see the election of a Palestinian Council to represent all the Palestinians of the West Bank, Gaza and East Jerusalem. Once the Council was installed the permanent status talks would commence.

The permanent status issues were five: Israeli settlements, Jerusalem, refugees, borders and relations with neighbors. The text does not mention the creation of a state nor does it refer to the Palestinian right to self-determination. This was not unintentional or the lack of skilled drafting but the deliberate formulation of a Labor-led Israeli government which at the time, actively opposed the creation of a Palestinian state. Thus the parties began with no agreed destination for the process. Nor did they start form the same legal or political assumptions. Whereas the Palestinians regarded the West Bank, East Jerusalem and Gaza as occupied territory the Israelis referred to areas as "disputed" territories. The legal gulf between the parties was therefore very wide indeed. The Palestinians began with the assumption that their legal rights had been established and that the purpose of the process was to recognize them. The Israelis saw the agreement to negotiate as evidence that the Palestinians were prepared to consider all possibilities for a settlement. Palestinian rights in short had become negotiable by virtue of Oslo.

This uncertainty can be exemplified by a consideration of the first three issues for these permanent status talks; settlements, Jerusalem and refugees. For the Palestinian side it would be argued that each had settled legal status governed by various international treaties, customary law and in particular by United Nations General Assembly and Security Council resolutions. The

Israelis would argue that such sources of law were either inappropriate to open to different interpretations.

As far as the Israeli settlements were concerned the Palestinians regarded this as a breach of the Geneva Convention IV 1949. The Geneva Convention is concerned with civilians during war and includes their rights during an occupation. Article 49, provides that the "Occupying Power shall not deport or transfer parts of its own civilian population into the territories it occupies." The settler population is thus reasonably interpreted to be the transfer that the Convention prohibits. Internationally this interpretation has widespread support. The United Nations Security Council has regularly upheld the position that the settlements have "no legal validity" and have called on Israel to "rescind" its policies and "not to transfer its own civilian population into the occupied Arab territories," (UN Security Council resolution 446, 22 March 1979). However, successive Israeli governments have argued that while they accept the spirit of the Convention it does not apply to the situation as they reject the notion that the territory is occupied referring instead to it as "disputed land." This designation stems for an analysis of the status of East Jerusalem and the West Bank at the time of the 1967 war. The Israeli case is that there was no legitimate sovereignty over the territories at that time. This was due to the questionable character of Jordanian possession. Jordan occupied the areas in the 1948 war ands formally annexed it to the Hashemite Kingdom in 1950. However, the annexation was not internationally recognized—not even by the Arab League—and so was a doubtful legality. This leads the Israelis to argue that as there was no settled sovereign in 1967, it would be impossible to become an occupier as such.[19] Further arguments are then advanced about Israel's historic claims dating back over 3,000 years to areas the known as Judea and Samaria. These arguments are then used to justify the building of Israeli settlements on the grounds that there is a genuine dispute as to whose land it is.

As has been said the Israeli approach to this question does not receive much support among international lawyers. However, it is important to note that the Israelis attempt to frame the building of settlements within an alternative legal framework rather than merely rejecting the idea of law at all.[20] The difficulties that this position encounters nevertheless are serious. The status of the territory of the West Bank was subject to judicial review by the International Court of Justice in the advisory opinion on the Israeli wall in the West Bank as recently as July 2004.[21] The Court certainly rejected the Israeli position and found the wall to be illegal and confirmed that the territory on which it was being built was occupied in the terms of the Geneva Convention. This strengthens an already wide international consensus on the issue. However, it is important to take into account different legal arguments in order to understand the starting points of the parties. For the Palestinians the settlements were illegal and therefore either had to be evacuated. For the Israelis it was a matter of faith that the most of the settlements would remain while those that they gave up would be a major concession.

The status of Jerusalem is regarded as yet to be determined as a result of the United Nations General Assembly partition resolution (UNGA resolution. 181 (1947).[22] Under this resolution Jerusalem was to be a separate territory[23] and not to be included in either the Arab or Jewish state that the resolution proposed. The city would have an international status and would be administered under United Nations auspices for ten years at which time the citizens could chose by a referendum which state Jerusalem would join. As a result all of Jerusalem has been regarded as outside Israeli jurisdiction. This position has received the status of international customary law as virtually no state with diplomatic relations with Israel maintains an Embassy in Jerusalem—preferring Tel Aviv. The Israeli unilateral annexation of East Jerusalem—together with additional districts from the West Bank—has been declared illegal by Security Council. Resolution 478 (20 August 1980) declared that the Israeli annexation law was "null and void." For the Palestinians therefore Jerusalem's special status remained and like the West Bank constituted part of the occupied territories that the Israelis were not entitled to govern. In East Jerusalem vast Israeli settlements have been built with a population that now exceeds 170,000. At the same time Palestinians living in Jerusalem are regularly denied planning permission by the municipal authority to extend existing property or to build new ones. Both the settlements and these restrictions appear contrary to the Geneva Convention which in addition to banning the transfer of civilians also prohibits an occupying from changing the existing civil law. This is the case with the planning restrictions and with the new municipal powers extending over all of East Jerusalem. The Israelis do not regard any part of Jerusalem as disputed but claim it as the "united and eternal capital of Israel and the Jewish people." A frequent Israeli argument here is that General Assembly resolution 181 does not apply as the Palestinian side rejected it at the time, and that the city has long historic links to the Jewish people.[24]

The status of Palestinian refugees is covered by a different legal regime that the one created by the United Nations Convention on Refugees 1951.[25] This has been created through United Nations General Assembly resolution 194 (1948) and the resolutions creating the United Nations Works and Relief Agency. These instruments do recognize the "right to return."[26] The issue of the refuges is a fundamental issue for the Palestinians as the PLO was created in exile and was for much of its existence the voice as much as for the Palestinian in exile as it was for those in Palestine. According to United Nations statistic some 3,700,000 Palestinians are refugees and thus constitute a major segment of the nation. As their rights are enshrined in international legal instruments there are some who would argue that those rights are not collective but individual and no other entity has the capacity to renounce them on their behalf. Israel sees the issue as entirely collective, believing that a symbolic return to Israel of a few thousand under family reunification schemes would suffice while the remainder should be financially compensated or possibly (accounts differ) have the right to return to the West Bank and Gaza. Israel explicitly rejects any right to return to Israel on the basis that millions of Palestinian would undermine the Jewish character of the Israeli state—and thus right of the Jewish people to self-determination. This, the Palestinians regard as inconsistent with the Israeli acceptance of the United Nations partition resolution which provided for the creation of a Jewish State in Palestine but did not provide for any movement of population.[27]

It is increasingly clear that the Palestinians began the negotiations on the assumption that the permanent status matters were already clarified and that the issue for the negotiators was to establish the modalities for their implementation. For the Israelis the opposite interpretation was the case as they saw Palestinian agreement to the Declaration of Principles as a signal of their willingness to negotiate on fundamental legal rights. The disagreement on the status of East Jerusalem and the West Bank is of course of critical for the discussion of borders. For the Israelis their starting assumption is that all of Jerusalem belongs under its sovereignty and that potentially all and most likely, some, of the "disputed" West Bank could also fall under it. Thus any agreement that cedes any part of the West Bank to the Palestinians is seen as a compromise on Israel's part. This becomes even more significant in the case of agreeing to any kind of Palestinian presence in Jerusalem. The Palestinians, however, assumed that as international law is on their side they were entitled to all the territory that Israel occupied in 1967. As Raja Shehadeh has stressed the divergent Palestinian and Israeli legal narratives made very urgent the need for what he calls a "sovereign legal consciousness."[28] As events unfolded it is clear that Shehadeh's advice went unheeded.

Code for a State

Eugene Cotran makes a case that probably had wide support among Palestinians lawyers at the time that the inclusion in Oslo of negotiations about borders logically meant the permanent status talks would include the creation of Palestinian state on the basis that only states have borders.[29] This implicit code for a state seems plausible. However, it must also be said that all that has been agreed is to discuss the implied state not to its creation. For most of the years of Oslo the Israeli negotiating team represented governments that did oppose the creation of a Palestinian state. The Labor party only changed its position in 1996 when it dropped its opposition to a state, although it did not embrace the idea of one. In reality it must have been clear to both Rabin and Peres that a state would result. However, they seemed to think that not stating this publicly would give them an additional leverage in the talks so that the state could be presented to the Palestinians as a major Israeli concession—and in exchange for which the Palestinians would concede on other issues such as Jerusalem and the size and character of the state.

Labor's policy change was never tested at the time as the party lost the 1996 election to Benjamin Netanyahu and the Likud party. Netanyahu and Likud opposed the creation of a Palestinian state but did not reject the Oslo Agreements. Indeed their acceptance of them, however grudging, was made possible because of the ambiguity on this point. Indeed Netanyahu himself made this point when he talked about "lowering Palestinian expectations." Netanyahu did carry out negotiations with the Palestinians and did redeploy Israeli forces from parts of the West Bank—more than under the previous Labor government. However, his option for the Palestinians had been outlined in his book, *A Place Amongst the Nations*[30], where he argued in favor of Palestinian self-management within Israel on about 40% of the West Bank and in most of the Gaza strip. As he put it

There is no reason why every lonely cluster of Arab houses should need to claim autonomy over an entire mountain on which it is perched. This *autonomy is primarily applicable to urban centres* in which the Arab population can make decisions about its daily life.[31] [emphasis in the original]

In his long term view he thought that if the Palestinians behaved well during the self-management period which would last for twenty years, they might then be offered Israeli citizenship as a reward. The book assumes large scale Jewish immigration to Israel and no right of return for Palestinian refugees.

However, Netanyahu's rival for the Likud leadership and eventual Prime Minister, Ariel Sharon had a much subtler approach to the question. Sharon as with other members of the Likud had campaigned against the Oslo agreements and had been opposed to ceding any land to the Palestinians. Nevertheless he did see the advantage that the amount of land in Palestinian hands was small—at the time Likud came to power in the summer of 1996 only three percent of the West Bank and about two-thirds of Gaza. Sharon wrote an interesting opinion piece in the *Jerusalem Post* in December 1995 saying that in fact a Palestinian state already existed which was very bad, but what was good was how small and weak it was.[32] This began the political reorientation of Sharon from outright opponent of Palestinian statehood to a supporter of what I will term as the weak state solution.

However, at the time Netanyahu who occupied the office of Prime Minister resisted the formal endorsement of a state although increasingly talked in terms that implied one was a possible option. In a speech during a tour of the United States after a year in office he outlined his view of final settlement in the following terms:

I have not drawn any precise maps to define what I have in mind for an agreement with the Palestinians. But I do know that I represent a very broad national consensus when I declare that the Jordan Valley must be Israel's strategic border, that Israel must not give up control of airspace, and water resources, that it must keep strategic zones that it considers vital; that it will not allow a Palestinian army equipped with heavy or non-conventional arms to form West of the Jordan, and above all that Jerusalem will stay the undivided capital of Israel for ever.[33]

It appears that Netanyahu was also moving to the weak state solution. The language carefully avoids referring to the legal status of Palestine but by talking about borders and restrictions on an armed force there does emerge a sub-text that the projected entity could be some sort of state, providing it was on Israeli terms. In the Likud administration it appears that the key leaders could envisage such a state, small in territory and weak in power. There are examples of states coming into existence with conditions attached. The re-emergence of Austria in 1955, for example, under the Austrian State Treaty committed the country to permanent neutrality. Other states have had their independence "guaranteed" by others such as the three power agreement over Cyprus in 1960 and the now well-known 1903 Guantanamo Bay Treaty by which the United States pledged to ensure Cuban sovereignty. These examples indicate that a precedent exists for imposing external limitation on the exercise of state sovereignty. However, the detailed restrictions on a possible Palestinian state that Netanyahu outlined appears to exceed their scope. In any event the Netanyahu government never got to stage of seriously negotiating even on this proposal as it dragged the talks on implementing the interim agreement for so long. This delay meant that the date by which the Oslo process should have been completed 4 May 1999 passed as Netanyahu prepared for new elections.

As the date approached, however, there was much speculation as to whether the Palestinian leadership would unilaterally declare a state. At the time the Palestinians Authority had about twenty percent of the West Bank under its exclusive control. This together with the Gaza strip could form the territorial basis for a state. At first it appeared that the Palestinian held a strong card in that they could use a unilateral declaration to seek recognition form other states and thus put pressure on the Israelis. However, there were also many disadvantages to the plan. Internationally the Clinton Administration opposed it. In Israel the Labor party opposed it and as it had a strong possibility of winning—which it did—the up-coming elections it could offer a more amenable partner in concluding Oslo. These factors were undoubtedly were significant, however, there was one other major consideration which was a realization in some Palestinian quarters than the Likud government—and perhaps other Israeli forces cool on Oslo, such as Labor leader Ehud Barak—might welcome such a declaration of statehood. Far from putting pressure on Israel on to conclude the agreement it could relieve then of their obligations. The entity created on scattered parts of the West Bank and Gaza could be passed off as the Palestinian state with no necessity for further negotiations. In any event the Palestinian leadership let the deadline pass and hoped that a Labor government would revive realistic negotiations.

Barak and the "Generous Offer"

The June 1999 elections saw a crushing defeat for Netanyahu and the triumph for Ehud Barak who won the election for Prime Minister by a margin of ten percent. Barak formed a broad coalition government that included the religious party Shas and the left-wing secular Meretz along with Labor. Barak, however was not an enthusiastic supporter of Oslo and had in fact abstained in the cabinet on the vote on the 1995 Interim Agreement. Perhaps reflecting this background Barak did not turn to implementing the full terms of the interim agreement that Netanyahu had failed to do. In particular this would have meant completing the third redeployment of troops form the West Bank and engaging in serious negotiations on a final settlement. Instead Barak turned his attention to new negations with Syria, and only when these failed did he belatedly turn his attention to the Palestinians.[34] By the time that he did he wanted one final conference that would address all unresolved issues of the interim agreement and the permanent status at once. This became the Camp David talks of July 2000 hosted by President Bill Clinton that brought together Israeli and Palestinian delegations lead by Barak and Arafat. It was these talks that led to the much-publicized "generous offer" that Barak allegedly made and Arafat rejected. Before looking at the terms of this "offer" it is important to place these talks within their political context.

All three leaders arrived at the talks with ebbing political capital. Clinton was in the last six months of his presidency, Barak's coalition had collapsed and was facing elections in six months and Arafat led a people increasingly frustrated by the apparent lack of any progress. While the Palestinian Authority increasingly took on the trappings of a state as the Basic Law providing for the creation of a cabinet,[35] including a Minister of Foreign Affairs, something that the Interim Agreement excluded, the lives of Palestinians in the West Bank and Gaza were lived increasingly under Israeli regulation. While the institutions looked more state-like they were unable to protect the lives of the citizens. Although the redeployments from the West Bank gave the appearance of the transfer of land and powers to the Palestinians a simultaneous process of the expansion of Israeli settlements and the road system connecting them saw a consolidation of Israel's presence in the West Bank. The vast growth in the population of the settlements which doubled between 1992 and 2000 also saw a more aggressive use of the system of checkpoints designed to the protect them. After the signing of the Interim Agreements checkpoints increasingly began to dominate the lives of Palestinian and after the outbreak of the second intifada in September 2000 movement became extremely difficult. This had drastic effects on the economy and the living standards declined as unemployment rose. However, perhaps it was the daily humiliation of Palestinians that became their worse feature, as they stood in line waiting to have papers checked by Israeli soldiers as they attempted to go to school, work, hospital or visit relatives. The entire apparatus of the checkpoint turned Palestinian towns and cities in area "A" into large prisons. The ability to leave area "A" became dependent on having the correct pass. Arafat thus far from representing a people who were running their own affairs, was in fact negotiating against the background of seething discontent borne of increasingly oppressive policies and a worsening economic outlook.

Barak and the Israeli team did not just have the handicap of weakened government but were constrained by an Israeli law that required a referendum must be held before any final agreement could go ahead. This meant that the negotiators knew that they would have to be able to persuade the Israeli public to agree to any final settlement. The law of course is highly problematic in an international context as it appeared to give a veto to one people over another's right to self determination. However, for the Israelis it provided an additional pressure on the Palestinians as it created a central position for Israeli concerns in the talks.

In the Israeli narrative it was at the Camp David talks in July 2000 and the subsequent discussion that the Palestinian leadership rejected an "Israeli generous offer" that would have seen a Palestinian state on some ninety to ninety-five percent of the West Bank and almost all of Gaza. This "offer" was rejected and the Palestinian leadership turned to violence instead. Accounts of the Camp David talks differ but the testimony of Robert Malley, a special assistant to President Clinton for Arab-Israeli affairs and Ehud Barak, then Israeli Prime Minister who were both at the talks do challenge this version of events. Malley was the first participant to suggest that there was no offer from the Israelis in the sense of a written version and that in fact no real face to face negotiations on the "offer" between Barak and Arafat.[36] What appears to have happened is that President Clinton and Ehud Barak discussed a negotiating position and then Clinton put the formula verbally to Arafat. Dennis Ross, who was the chief American negotiator and Yossi Beilin one of the key Israelis at the talks confirm this version. It was President Clinton, working closely with Ross who drafted "parameters" for a settlement based on his assessment of what the parties might agree to. This is the origin of the "generous offer" story. While Clinton's proposals have now been published[37] there is some disagreement amongst the participants of the details of their implementation. It also has to be born in mind that the Camp David talks themselves ended without agreement although the talks continued until January and even after the end of Clinton's time in office. Much of what had been referred to as the Camp David deal in fact emerged during these later discussions.

The basic terms of this deal begin with the allocation of territory. Here Clinton articulates the position that "the solution will need to provide for sovereignty over somewhere between 90 and 100 percent of West Bank territory."[38] The principle that is being established here is that Israeli is to keep the main settlement blocks although "there will need to be swaps and other territorial arrangements" to compensate the Palestinians.[39] This is further defined as meaning that Israel will annex between four and six percent of the West Bank while the Palestinians would receive an equivalent of between one and three percent in compensation. Clinton also suggests that land could be leased—that is by Israel. In Beilin's account it appears that that the deal on land meant Israel annexing six percent of the West Bank and leasing a further two percent with the Palestinians gaining an equivalent of one percent. It is these figures that gave rise to the idea that the Palestinians were offered ninety-five percent of what they wanted. On Jerusalem the Palestinian areas would have become Palestinian and Israeli ones Israeli with a complex arrangement for Haram al Sharif/Temple Mount. Again the principle is established that Israeli settlements will remain. This also means that the Israelis are in fact annexing much more of the occupied territories than six percent as the extended boundaries of East Jerusalem have been excluded from the West Bank. Overall the territorial deal would mean that Israel would acquire permanent position of about ten percent of the occupied territories in exchange for swap of about a tenth of that from Israel to the Palestinians. It would also appear from Barak's later comments that there would have been a small Israeli corridor running from Jerusalem to the Jordan Valley dividing the West Bank—and this area seems not have been included in the calculations.[40]

However, there is more to a state than merely territory and as the Clinton proposal make clear Palestine would be "non-militarized." This we are told would mean that there would be a "strong Palestinian security force," and that its borders would be protected by an "international force." Israel, however would maintain three early warning military bases on the

West Bank. In addition there would also be provision for Israel to deploy armed forces in the West Bank—along agreed routes—providing that Israel declared "a state of national emergency." While Palestine would have sovereignty over its airspace the two sides should "work out special arrangements for Israeli training and operational needs." It appears that the physical control over the territory would be somewhat tenuous and subject to the dictates of Israeli security requirements. The international borders of the state would not be its own hands. In the first three years Israeli would be in control and after that the task would be handed to a permanent international force. These are certainly special arrangements that few states would probably accept. It is particularly difficult to imagine that Israel would accede to them.[41]

On the question of the Palestinian refugees and the "right to return" Clinton proposes one of two formulas, either "both sides recognize the right of Palestinian refuges to return to historic Palestine," or "Both sides recognize the right of Palestinian refugees to a homeland." Clinton assumes that either of these positions would mean concretely that there would be "five possible homes"

1. The state of Palestine
2. Areas in Israel being transferred to Palestine in the land swap
3. Rehabilitation in a host country
4. Resettlement in a third country
5. Admission to Israel.[42]

On the latter the text adds that would have to be "consistent with Israel's sovereign decision." Essentially the Palestinian refugees are being offered the actual right to live in the new state as a collective right and all individual claims to property and land inside Israel would be forfeited.

The overall shape of the deal is described by Clinton at the conclusion of the text thus;

> It gives the Palestinian people the ability to determine their future on their own land, a sovereign and viable state recognized by the international community, al Quds as its capital, sovereignty over the Haram, and new lives for the refugees.

> It gives the people of Israel a genuine end to the conflict, real security, the preservation of sacred religious ties, the incorporation

of 80% of the settlers into Israel, and the biggest Jerusalem in history, recognized as your capital.[43]

The idea of the "generous offer" is based of course on the assumption that the party making it has it to give. All the negotiations appear to have been conducted on the basis that Israel would keep the settlements despite their rejection as illegal by the United Nations, that the refuges would be dealt with collectively over the heads of the individuals concerned and that Israel's security needs would take precedence over Palestinian sovereignty and territorial integrity. The Palestinian starting point that the occupation of all the territory was illegal and that any negotiations should ensure the withdrawal of Israel, together with its settlers and the creation a normal sovereign state on that territory was clearly off the agenda. The Israeli ability to create a framework based in the main on its legal narrative is impressive. This was assisted by the role of the United States whose negotiating stance, which as Dennis Ross admits, was heavily tilted in Israel's favor.[44] So pervasive was this pro-Israeli outlook that Arafat was portrayed as irrationally rejecting a reasonable offer. In fact there was no rejection as such and the Labor government and the Palestinians continued to negotiate at Taba even after Clinton left office. It was the Israeli election of Ariel Sharon in January 2001 that brought that process to an end. For Sharon and for those who voted for him this deal went too far.

Ehud Barak's attitude towards the talks and his view of Yasser Arafat are also revealing. In his interview with Benny Morris in June 2002 Barak claims that the Palestinians "want a state in all of Palestine."[45] Although he argued that in the short term this would be difficult to achieve because "Israel is too strong...their game plan is to establish a Palestinian state while leaving an opening for further 'legitimate' demands down the road."

They will exploit the tolerance and democracy of Israel first to turn it into "a state for all its citizens," as demanded by the extreme nationalist wing of the Israel's Arabs and extremist left-wing Jewish Israelis. Then they will push for a binational state and then demography and attrition will lead to a state with a Muslim majority and a Jewish minority. This would not necessarily mean kicking out all the Jews. But it would mean the destruction of Israel as a Jewish state. This I believe is their vision.[46]

Barak thus sees ulterior motives on the part of Palestinian negotiators. However it is more than that, Palestinians come from a culture which is characterized by lying;

> They are products of a culture in which to tell a lie…creates no dissonance. They don't suffer from the problem of telling lies that exists in Judeo-Christian culture. Truth is seen as an irrelevant category. There is only that which serves your purpose and that which doesn't. They see themselves as emissaries of a national movement for whom everything is permissible. There is no such thing as "truth."[47]

These statements are striking in their rather crude Orientalist language. For Barak the Palestinians are not negotiating in good faith. They have a secret plan and in any event they will systematically lie due to their culture. It might be asked why he is bothering to discuss with Palestinians at all given his determinist and frankly racist views. Barak suggests that perhaps Arafat "would rise to the occasion." Hussein Agha and Robert Malley see this as Barak setting a test for Arafat.[48] One might add that given his attitudes it is a test that he knows will be failed. Indeed the more considers Barak's analysis of the failure of Camp David the stranger it appears that he wanted to engage in any negotiations at all as he would have known that failure would be inevitable. The point of it seems to be that the Camp David process was aimed at unmasking Arafat and show the world that no solution would be possible.[49] Indeed according to him the *intifada* that was sparked by Ariel Sharon's visit to Al Aqsa (or Temple Mount) in September 2000 was "preplanned, pre-prepared. I don't mean that Arafat knew that on a certain day in September," it would begin "but it was definitely on the level of planning, of a grand plan."[50] This Barak says was known as a result of "hard intelligence." What is interesting is not so much the evaluation of factual issues as the way in which the Barak narrates the Camp David experience so that Arafat is portrayed as devious, untruthful and with a hidden terrorist plan. He is the typical Orientalist Other. The campaign to ensure that the world understood who was responsible for the failure of the talks and how that was linked to the second *intifada*—the plan all along—was fairly effective. Although as the vigorous debate in the *New York Review of Books* shows there was some serious resistance to this view—and from some important U.S. sources. The final break-down of the process was confirmed as the Taba talks collapsed and President Clinton left the White House in January 2001. Within a month Ehud Barak had been replaced by Ariel Sharon as Israeli Prime Minister. While Sharon was opposed to Barak's "generous offer" and indeed the entire Oslo accords, he was none the less to stick to his predecessor's account of Arafat's failings. Sharon turned almost immediately to complete the process of sidelining Arafat. This process was given a new international context with 11 September 2001. At once "Islamic terrorism" became the main enemy of the United States and the Sharon government seized the opportunity to link Palestinian violence and Arafat's alleged leadership of it, to the war against terrorism.[51]

The Bush and Sharon Plan for the Palestinian State

As in the Gulf war 1991 so in the Iraq war 2003, the United States promised in return for support for the "coalition of the willing," there would be a major engagement with the Palestinian-Israeli conflict once Saddam Hussein's government was removed. In 1991 the promise had been vague but did lead to the Madrid peace conference the fall of that year which created the atmosphere for the Oslo agreement. However a decade later the situation was somewhat different. The ten years of the Oslo had transformed the situation on the ground. The residue of a failed peace process added the dashed hopes of resolving the conflict to the complexities of a new initiative. Suicide bomb attacks against Israeli civilians and other violent actions by some Palestinian groups saw an increasing death toll on either side, as Israel opted for the military solution. Israel's robust response to the new *intifada* saw the re-conquest of the West Bank including area "A" which no longer enjoyed exclusive Palestinian governance.

Against this dire situation, the United States had participated in initiating a new policy that supported the creation of a Palestinian state and with the United Nations, the European Union and Russia known as the quartet. The roadmap aimed at creating a Palestinian state by 2005 through three phases. First violence should end, Palestinian life should return to normality and Palestinian institutions would be built. Second a Palestinian state with provisional borders would be created. In the last phase all the negations would be completed and the conflict would end. The main theme of the performance-related plan was that the Palestinians would have to reform their institutions, including security services and cleanse their leadership from the "taint of terror." The first two phases were meant to be completed by the end of 2003.

In the immediate aftermath of the Iraq war 2003 the roadmap dropped down the agenda. However, it proved a useful foil in an elaborately choreographed dance between Washington and Tel Aviv. On 14 April 2004 an exchange of letters and statements between President George W. Bush and Ariel Sharon marked a new stage in the Palestinian-Israeli conflict.[52] The Gaza disengagement plan had international origins. The basic idea that Israel would withdraw from the Gaza Strip including from its military installations and settlements as well from some (tiny) parts of the West Bank was introduced to the international public through the publication of these letters. While this policy will be unilateral and there will be no negotiations with the Palestinians, in his letter to President Bush, Ariel Sharon claims that these steps are entirely within the framework of the Roadmap for Peace, described as

> The first time a practical and just formula was presented for the achieve-ment of peace and, opening a genuine window of opportunity for progress toward a settlement between Israel and the Palestinians, involving two states living side-by-side in peace and security.[53]

However, Sharon carefully conditioned the acceptance of the road map in the previous sentence when as he put it "Israel has accepted the road map, as adopted by our government." The latter phrase indicating the Sharon government never whole heartedly accepted the entire road map in particular the obligations that imposed on Israel to halt settlement construction. The question at stake therefore is what prospect does the Sharon-Bush plan hold for the creation of Palestinian State, the goal of the road map?

The Sharon letter makes clear the Israeli government's interpretation of the road map's obligations as they affect the Palestinians.

> A Palestinian state will never be created by terror, and the Palestinians must engage in a sustained fight against the terrorists and dismantle their infrastructure. Moreover there must be serious efforts to institute true reform and real democracy and liberty, including new leaders not compromised by terror.[54]

For Sharon this has not occurred and he concludes, "we are committed to this formula as the only avenue through which an agreement can be reached. We believe that this formula is the only viable one."[55] Thus Sharon constructs not only an interpretation of the road map's obligations but also transforms them into central and imperative ones. There is no alternative.

The next stage of his argument is that the Palestinian Authority has failed to honor the "only viable" formula.

> The Palestinian Authority under its current leadership has taken no action to meet its responsibilities under the Roadmap. Terror has not ceased, reform of the Palestinian security services has not been undertaken, and real institutional reforms have not taken place.[56]

Thus Sharon's view of the roadmap becomes universalized as he also now adds to his interpretation an assessment of how the Palestinians have discharged their responsibilities. The Palestinians have simply failed in their undertakings. The implication is that this is an irrational response to Israel's compliance. In this discourse Israel it is assumed has acted with due diligence in implementing all its obligations. Israel has been the main victim on the Palestinian non-compliance.

> The State of Israel continues to pay the heavy cost of constant terror. Israeli must preserve its capacity to protect itself and to deter its enemies, and thus we retain our right to defend ourselves against terrorism and to take actions against terrorist organizations.[57]

In this way the Sharon letter makes it clear that the Oslo process is quite dead and indeed that that meaningful negotiations only began with the publication of the roadmap—and in particular United States' sponsoring of it. The Oslo framework was never seen by Sharon as favorable enough to the Israelis, despite its elliptical formulations which were to Israel's advantage. Now the language of the letter has the purpose to de-legitimize Oslo entirely. The acceptance of the roadmap is conditioned by the Israeli cabinet's reservations, however even this is insufficient as "there exists no Palestinian partner with whom to advance peacefully toward a settlement."[58] Israel is portrayed as the wronged party. The roadmap's obligation's on Israel to cease settlement activity is ignored. The Sharon government's use of military provocations, regular raids, re-occupations at will, targeted assassinations (e.g. Sheikh Yassin Abd-al Azziz Rantisi) which have been used to frustrate cease-fires and negotiations are simply ignored. The Palestinians alone are at fault.

Sharon is quite honest about the purpose of the disengagement plan which is "designed to improve security for Israel and stabilize our political and economic situation." This plan is not part of the roadmap and although it is claimed not to be inconsistent with it although it represents an "independent Israeli plan." The main planks of the plan are then outlined. There are, that:

> Israel intends to relocate military installations and all Israeli villages and towns in the Gaza Strip, as well as other military installations and a small number of villages form Samaria [the Northern part of the West Bank]. In this context, we also plan to accelerate construction of the Security Fence, whose completion is essential in order to secure the security of the citizens of Israel.[59]

The plan now becomes clear, disengagement from Gaza is accompanied by the building of the wall. It is interesting to note how settlements in Gaza and the West Bank are re-named "Israeli towns and villages." The withdrawal from Gaza is linked to the building of the wall in the West Bank. Sharon protests that the wall is "a security rather than political barrier, temporary rather than permanent and therefore will not prejudice the outcome of any final status issues including final borders."[60] The route of the wall will "take account consistent with security needs, its impact on the Palestinians not engaged in terrorism."[61] The plan is thus entirely dictated from the viewpoint of Israel. The reason for the withdrawal from Gaza is explained in terms of improving Israel's security, its political and economic situation and the extension of the plan to the West Bank has the same purpose. Palestinians remain secondary to Israeli interests. The wall dividing Palestinians from each other, from their land and indeed its threatening physical presence are all to be balanced against Israel's security needs. This issue is returned to when Sharon refers to Israeli obligations under the roadmap. These are described as, "limitations on the growth of settlements; removal of unauthorized outposts and steps to increase the freedom of movement of Palestinians not engaged in terrorism."[62] Again, these obligations are subject to being "permitted by security needs."

The interests of the Palestinians are referred to but in the context of a people who are not yet ready to assume their responsibilities. This attitude has been common in many colonial situations where Imperial powers deem the colonized not yet to be able to act for themselves due to lack of education, level of civilization, or administrative abilities.[63] In Sharon's language "terrorism" is used in the same way civilization once was in the past. The military and security activities of Israel, as with the European imperial powers, are portrayed as the use of rational force by a legitimate state against an unruly occupied people. Their very rebellion against colonial rule is seen as evidence of their lack of readiness to rule themselves. In the case of the Palestinians the refusal to accept the Israeli occupation is enough even to question their right to self-determination. As Sharon says of his current plan it has "the inherent potential to improve the lot of the Palestinian Authority, providing that it demonstrates the wisdom to take advantage of this opportunity."[64] The Palestinians are able to benefit from the plan providing they act "wisely" which must be a thinly veiled code for acting in ways approved by Israel. At the end of his letter Sharon spells out what this might mean.

> The government of Israel supports the United States efforts to reform the Palestinian security services to meet their roadmap obligations to fight terror. Israel also supports the American efforts, working with the international community, to promote the reform process, build institutions and improve the economy of the Palestinian Authority and to enhance the welfare of the people, in the hope that the Palestinian leadership will prove able to fulfill its obligations under the roadmap.[65]

Again the "welfare" of the Palestinians is subject to the way in which the Palestinians behave. They have no rights as an independent political or legal community. What is also significant about this passage is the way in which the Israeli government invokes the "authority" of the United States. Israel is merely serving the interests of "American efforts, working with the international community." Despite the plan being described as an "independent Israeli" one it now appears that its legitimacy actually stems from the approval of the United States. Indeed this is precisely why Ariel Sharon is symbolically announcing it in Washington and not in Tel Aviv. Far from being independent the initiative is dependent on the United States' active support. Sharon made this position clear when reflecting on the plan a year later in an interview he gave to the *Jerusalem Post*. It is put to him that the disengagement plan had not been negotiated with the Palestinians but with the Americans. He replies "I agree. I made an agreement with the Americans. And as much as I desire good relations with the Arabs and to make progress in that regard, I place more faith in an agreement with the Americans than in an agreement with the Palestinians."[66] The protected character of Israeli nationalism is very much on display here. Despite the rhetoric of Israeli security needs Sharon needs to appeal to the U.S. as the representative of universal power in order to legitimate the plan.

The United States is a willing participant in the process as the letter in reply from President George W. Bush makes clear. Bush says that he remains committed "to my 24 June 2002 vision of two states living side by side."[67] We should note the use of "my" before vision, as this formula is repeated later and implies a particular version of what the characteristics of the two states might be. He welcomes the plan and thinks that it would "mark real progress to realizing my June 24, 2002 vision." Bush then continues to flesh out what U.S. acceptance of the Sharon proposals mean. He assures Sharon that the roadmap is the only process available. Then he makes three specific commitments. First he summarizes Palestinian obligations:

> Palestinians must undertake an immediate cessation of armed activity and all acts of violence against Israelis anywhere, and all official Palestinian institutions must end incitement against Israel. The Palestinian leadership must act decisively against terror, including sustained targeted and effective operations to stop terrorism and to dismantle terrorist capabilities and infrastructure. Palestinians must undertake a comprehensive and fundamental political reform that includes a strong Parliamentary democracy and an empowered Prime Minister.[68]

Bush conveniently repeats the Israeli formulations on fighting terrorism and just makes concrete what reform means for the Palestinians. It is clear that the evaluation of whether a "strong Parliamentary democracy" or an "empowered Prime Minister" have emerged will rest with the United States, no doubt ably assisted by the Israelis. The use of the term "empowered Prime Minister" we must assume to be meant to eclipse the key powers of the late President Arafat. This is perhaps regime change by another name.

Bush's second proposition is that both Israelis and Palestinians must "join together in the fight against terrorism." However, this apparently equal obligation is conditioned by a commitment to Israel's security which is expressed as support for "secure, defensible borders, and to preserve Israel's capability to deter and defend itself, by itself, against any threats or possible combination of threats."[69] It is notable that the United States has extended to Israel the right of preemption that was so central in the United States National Security Strategy 2002.[70]

The third point is the most far-reaching and contains three discrete aspects. First he recognizes the right of Israel to maintain the occupation in parts of the West Bank it does not withdraw from, "existing arrangements regarding the control of airspace, territorial waters and land passages of the West Bank and Gaza will continue."[71] Second he recognizes Israel as a Jewish state and that the Palestinian refugees must be settled in an eventual Palestinian state, "rather than Israel." And finally he returns to the key issues of borders. While paying lip service to the two key United Nations Security Council resolutions 242 (1967) and 338 (1973) he announces for the first time United States public support for the creation of Israeli settlements on occupied Palestinian territories. Writing in the vein of former Israeli Prime Minister Yitzhak Shamir he says,

> In the light of new realities on the ground, including already existing major Israeli population centers, it is unrealistic to expect that the outcome of the final status negotiations will be a full return to the armistice lines of 1949…It is realistic to expect that any final status agreement will only be achieved on the basis of mutually agreed changes that reflect these realities.[72]

As Bush concludes his letter he returns to theme of his vision. Now the parameters of this have become quite clear. "As you know the United States supports the establishment of a Palestinian state that is viable, contiguous, sovereign, and independent, so that the Palestinian people can build their own future in accordance with my vision." The right of self-determination of the Palestinian people is thus brought within the discourse of the United States. It appears from what has gone before that the Palestinian state must have a governmental structure in accordance with the wishes of the United States. It must have a reformed security service that must join with the United States in the "war on terror." The borders of the state will be determined by the needs of Israel to have secure, defensible ones and by the scope of the "already existing major Israeli population centers." Self-determination in this account means living within a territorial unit defined by Israel's colonial conquest and with a government that fully accepts the right of conquest including the permanent exile of the Palestinian refugees from the homes that they fled in 1948. This is the end result of the roadmap. In the meantime it is also clear that there is no Palestinian leadership to deal with, as it appears unless a Palestinian leadership emerges which signs up to this "vision" there is no one responsible enough to negotiate with.

The status of these arrangements is in itself interesting. While the letters do not make a treaty, their exchange does seem to be more than political rhetoric. The subsequent letter from Ariel Sharon's bureau chief, Dov Weisglass to the United States National Security Adviser Condoleezza Rice take the agreement to a formal level and appear to give rise to mutual obligations. The letter says that its purpose is to "reconfirm the following understanding, which has been reached between us."[73]

Conclusion

The plan that Bush and Sharon plan launched in April 2004 has some echo's of early Zionist views on the creation of a Jewish state in the Middle East advanced by Vladimir Jabotinsky in the 1920s and 1930s. At the time very much the outsider Jabotinsky headed the revisionist wing of Zionism which advanced the policy a Jewish state could only be created by force of arms against the Arab population. Once established it would have to remain by force until the Arab population just got used to its immovability—this might take two or three generations. His politics rejected any idea of any negotiations with Arabs but projected the building of an iron wall to protect the state.[74] Sharon as the political heir of Jabotinksy is adapting this approach to current realities some fifty-seven years after the creation of the State of Israel and some thirty-eight years after it occupied the West Bank and Gaza. While Sharon might have hoped that the occupation could be made permanent in its entirety—the greater Israel project—he has lowered the scale of conquest. This would mean a larger state of Israel possibly extending over about eighty-five percent of British Mandate Palestine leaving the rest for a Palestinian state. This tiny state would in George Bush's vision not only be the territory where the Palestinians "can build their own future" but also be the home for the Palestinian refugees.

Ariel Sharon used the high level of U.S. involvement in the disengagement plan to launch it in Israel. It proved unpopular with many in his Likud party and a majority of its members rejected it in a vote shortly after.

Nonetheless, Sharon persisted and the Knesset finally adopted the policy in the fall of 2004. This revised plan interestingly removed the explicit reference to a Palestinian state using a more elliptical formation, the "State of Israel is committed to the peace process and aspires to reach an agreed resolution of the conflict based upon the vision of President George Bush."[75] It adds that Israel has "come to the conclusion that there is currently no reliable Palestinian partner with which it can make process in a two sided process."[76] The tenor of the text and the political discourse that accompanied it appeared to clear the way for an Israeli unilaterally imposed process in which Israel would withdraw from Gaza and some parts of the West Bank while integrating as many of the settlements into Israel.[77] The death of Yasir Arafat, however, undermined such calculations and a change of tone has been noticeable in Israeli government pronouncements, indicating that negotiations might be possible.[78] However, the package remains very much the same.

In the period since Oslo it has become evident that the Palestinian right to self-determination has become literally subject to negotiation. Since the Beilin-Abu Mazen understandings in 1995[79] it appears that there has been an assumption that the main Israeli settlements will be allocated to Israel, despite the international consensus that they are illegal. Although George Bush was the first U.S. President to publicly state that they were "major Israeli population centers" he was following an already well trodden path and stood very much in the position of Bill Clinton. The borders of a Palestinian state are thus dictated by the results of Israeli conquest. If its territory is subject to Israel's needs, so apparently will be its powers as it will be a non-militarized state unable even to police its own borders. It is extraordinary the extent to which a gulf has opened between the apparent legal rights of Palestine and the Palestinians and political expediency. The settlements have to be accepted, the refugees are not to return and Israel's security is to be paramount. This seems to be the formula for a Palestinian state. As the wall continues to be built it appears that a form of caged self-determination is to be offered to the Palestinians. As the Israeli academic, Benny Morris put it in graphic terms, "something like a cage has to be built for them. I know that sounds terrible. It is really cruel. But there is no choice. There is a wild animal there that has to be locked up."[80] The current danger is that the international community will be asked to agree to such an arrangement and to praise the Israelis for being bold and courageous. Colonialism has perhaps reached its limits in Palestine and Israeli leaders may be forced to leave more of the occupied territories than they want. For the Palestinians far from being offered ninety-five percent of what they want they are likely to be offered about fifteen percent of historical Palestinian territory to found their state. As Edward Said, wrote, the "roadmap ...is not about a plan for peace as a plan for pacification, it is about putting an end to the Palestinian problem."[81]

The disengagement from Gaza however opens a new historical window in the Palestinian-Israel conflict. For the first time Israel has dismantled—and forcibly removed—settlements in Palestinian occupied territory. Gaza is without a direct occupying power for almost the first time in history. The Israeli right's national project is in disarray. Unlike at the time of the Oslo Agreements the international community now favors the creation of a Palestinian state and has the machinery through the Quartet and its envoy James Wolfensohn to pursue it. The United States has General William Ward on the ground arguing against the Israelis over the need to arm and equip the Palestinian security forces. The Palestinians have created state-like institutions and the Islamists of Hamas now contemplate the possibility of dealing with Israel. Ariel Sharon's plan for a small weak Palestinian state without Jerusalem may yet be undermined by the political dynamic that he has unleashed.

Notes

1. United Nations Security Council resolution 1397 (12 March 2002), affirms "a vision of a region where two states, Israel and Palestine, live side by side within secure and recognized borders."
2. See: "A Performance-Based Roadmap to a Permanent Two State Solution to the Israeli-Palestinian Conflict" at: http://www.un.org/News/dh/mideast/roadmap122002.pdf (last visited 6 December 2004).
3. See: Israeli Prime Minister's office, "The Disengagement Plan—General Outline," 24 April 2004 at: http://www.mfa.gov.il (last visited 7 October 2004).
4. Richard W. Stevenson, "Confident Bush Outlines Ambitious Plan for Second Term," *New York Times*, 5 November 2004.
5. For the way Gaza took place generally see: http://electronicintifada.net/bytopic/379.shtml (Last visited 18 August 2005.)
6. See generally; Marrti Koskenniemi, *From Utopia to Apology: The Structure of international legal Argument* (Helsinki: Finish Lawyers Publishing Company, 1989).

7. This is based on the definition of state contained in the Montevideo Convention on the Rights and Duties of States 1933, see: *Rosalyn Higgins, Problems and Process: International Law and How We Use It* (Oxford: Clarendon Press, 1994), 39-46.

8. Israel is not alone, however, as many states have long running border disputes and special rules on citizenship. For example, the United Kingdom's borders with the Republic of Ireland only became clear after the Good Friday Agreement in 1998.

9. See: United Nations Report of the Secretary-General's High-Level Panel on Threats, Challenges and Change, "A More Secure World, Our Shared Responsibilities," at http://www.un.org/secureworld/ (last visited 7 December 2004). It can be argued that the United Nations itself is founded on the idea of regime change as it began as a military alliance (founded 1 January 1942) with the purpose of removing the criminal regimes of the Axis powers.

10. See: United Nations General Assembly Resolution 2535 (XXIV), 10 December 1969.

11. See: Jacques Derrida, Force of Law: The "Mystical Foundation of Authority," In Drucilla Cornell, Michel Rosenfeld, David Gray Carlson (eds.) *Deconstruction and the Possibility of Justice* (New York and London: Routledge, 1992), 3-67.

12. See: Geoffrey R. Watson, *The Oslo Accords: International Law and the Israeli-Palestinian Agreements* (Oxford and New York: Oxford University Press, 2000)

13. See: "Israel-Palestine Liberation Organization Declaration of Principles on Interim Self-Government Arrangements," 13 September 1993 *International Legal Materials*, Vol. 32 (1993), 1525.

14. See: "Israel-Palestine Liberation Organization Agreement on the Gaza Strip and the Jericho Area," May 4, 1994, *International Legal Materials*, Vol. 33 (1994), 622.

15. See: "Israeli-Palestinian Interim Agreement on the West Bank and the Gaza Strip," 28 September 1995, *International Legal Materials* Vol. 34 (1995), 650. There are many others such as the Hebron Agreement and the Note for the Record, 1997, and Wye Plantation Agreement 1998.

16. See: As'ad Ghanem, *The Palestinian Regime: A "Partial democracy."* (Brighton, Portland: Sussex Academic Press, 2001), 51-86; Nathan J Brown, *Palestinian Politics after the Oslo Accords: Resuming Arab Palestine* (Berkeley, Los Angeles, London: University of California Press, 2003), 59-93; and Ghassan Al-Khatib (ed.) *The Palestinian Council* (Jerusalem: Jerusalem Media and Communications Centre, 1996)

17. Yossi Beilin writes "in the six years between 1994 and 2000, the Jewish population in the territories increased by as much as it had during the twenty-six years between the Six-Day War and Oslo," see: Yossi Beilin, *The Road*

to Geneva: The Quest for a Permanent Agreement, 1996-2004 (New York: RDV Books, 2004), 278.

18. *Ibid.*, 281.
19. On this position see: Allan Gerson, *Israel, the West Bank and International Law* (London John Cass, 1978) and Julius Stone, *Israel and Palestine: Assault on the Law of Nations* (Baltimore: John Hopkins University Press, 1981).
20. Indeed Israeli governments have gone to great lengths to argue that land acquired for settlements accords with the Ottoman and British Mandate law.
21. "Legal Consequences of the Construction of a Wall in Occupied Palestinian Territory, Advisory Opinion of the International Court of Justice," 9 July 2004, for the text see: http://www.icj-cij.org (last visited 7 December 2004).
22. This was certainly the accepted legal position for the period under discussion (1992-2004). However, it might be argued that the opinion of the International Court of Justice in the Wall case might have now altered the situation as the court treated the West Bank and East Jerusalem in the same territorial category. The implication of this Opinion may be that the Green Line, demarcated in 1949 has acquired something of the status of an international boundary which would result in West Jerusalem being in Israel and East Jerusalem in Palestine. In paragraph sixty-seven of the opinion the Court refers to land west of the Green line as "the territory of Israel itself."
23. The actual area for the *corpus separatum* included not only Jerusalem but also Bethlehem, Abu Dis, Ein Karim and Shu'fat.
24. The argument about whether the UN partition resolution does, or does not have legal force is in fact argued by both sides at different times. In 1947 the Palestinians and the Arab world regarded the resolution as "null and void." Israeli governments which for most of the time since 1948 refused to recognize the rights of the Palestinians to a state took a similar position. However, when political negotiations began in the early 1990s attitudes on both sides began to change. The ICJ in the Wall Advisory Opinion certainly found that it had relevance.
25. See: Siraj Sait, "International Refugee Law: Excluding the Palestinians," in John Strawson (ed.) *Law after Ground Zero* (London, Sydney, Portland: GlassHouse Press, 2004), 90-107.
26. For thorough presentation of the legal status of Palestinian refugees see: Guy Goodwin-Gill and Susan M Akran, "Forward to Amicus Brief on the Status of the Palestinian Refugees under Palestinian Refugee Law," *Palestine Yearbook of International Law*, Vol. XI (2000/2001), 185-260.
27. There are major differences as to the relevant populations assigned to each state. The total population of Palestine was about 1.9 million in 1946 of which 608,000 were Jews. The Arab State would have had a population of about 800,000 (of whom 10,000 were Jews), Jerusalem's population would

have been 205,000 (100,000 Jews) and the Jewish State's 900,000 population would have included at least 400,000 Arab Palestinians. While the minorities could opt to vote for the legislature of their choice, the two states and Jerusalem were to be part of an economic union and all land and property would have been retained by their existing owners. See: Paul J.I. M. de Waart, *Dynamics of Self-Determination in Palestine: Protection of Peoples as a Human Right* (Leiden, New York, Koln: E.J. Brill, 1994), 126-143.

28. Raja Shehedeh, "The Weight of Legal History: Constraints and Hopes in the Search for a Dovereign Legal Language," in Eugene Cotran and Chibli Mallat, *The Arab-Israeli Accords: Legal Perspectives* (London, the Hague, Boston: Kluwer Law International, 1996), 3-20.

29. Eugene Cotran, "Some Legal Aspects of the Declaration of Principles: A Palestinian View" in Cotran and Mallat (eds.), *The Arab-Israeli Accords*, 67-77.

30. Benjamin Netnayahu, *A Place Among the Nations: Israel and the World* (London, New York: Bantham Press, 1993)

31. Ibid., 352.

32. See: John Strawson, "Netanyahu's Oslo: Peace in the Slow Lane," *Soundings* Vol. 8 (1998), 49-60. Sharon was not alone in thinking that a Palestinian state already existed, see: John Whitbeck, "The Palestinian State Exists," *Palestine-Israel Journal*, Vol. III, no 2 (Spring 1996).

33. Address by Prime Minister Benjamin Netanyahu to the Council of Jewish Federations General Assembly in Indianapolis, *Prime Ministers Reports*, Vol. I, No 11, 17 November 1997 (Prime Minister's Office, Israel.)

34. See: Denis Ross, *The Missing Peace*, 549-590.

35. See: Nathan J Brown, *Palestinian Politics after the Oslo Accords*, 18-58 and 94-137.

36. See: Hussein Agha and Robert Malley, "Camp David: The Tragedy of Errors," *New York Review of Books*, Vol. 48, No. 13 (9 August 2001)

37. See Denis Ross, *The Missing Peace* (2004), 801-805 and Yossi Beilin, *The Path to Geneva* (2004), 321-235. Both contain the text that was issued on 23 December 2000. There are some slight differences between the texts, however. the overall shape of the proposals is similar on each permanent status issue is the same.

38. Dennis Ross, *Missing Peace*, 801.

39. Ibid.

40. See: Benny Morris, "Camp David and After: An Exchange" (An Interview with Ehud Barak), *New York Review of Books*, Vol. 49, No. 10 (13 June 2002). In the interview Morris writes, "Barak says that the Palestinians were promised a continuous piece of sovereignty territory except for a razor thin Israeli wedge running from Jerusalem through Maale Adumin to the Jordan River." This is a highly significant remark as Dennis Ross produces his own

map of what the "offer" was without the "wedge" that Barak refers to, see: Dennis Ross, *The Missing Peace: Inside the Story of the Fight for Middle East Peace* (New York: Farrar, Straus and Giroux, 2004), xix. This certainly indicates the lack of any actual maps presented at the talks has allowed each participant to remember events differently.

41. Denis Ross, *The Missing Peace*, 802.
42. Ibid., 804-805.
43. Ibid., 805.
44. Ibid., 765.
45. He is referring to all of British Mandate Palestine, including Israel.
46. Dennis Ross, *The Missing Peace, 765.*
47. *Ibid.*
48. See: Hussein Agha and Robert Malley, "Camp David: An Exchange" (A Reply to Ehud Barak), *New York Review of Books*, Vol. 49, No. 10 (13 June 2002).
49. Dennis Ross seems to have the same approach, see: Dennis Ross, *The Missing Peace*, 767-769
50. See: Benny Morris, "Camp David and After" (An interview with Ehud Barak).
51. See: Rafiq Latta, "Palestine/Israel: conflict at the crossroads," in John Strawson (ed.) *Law after Ground Zero*, 170-186.
52. All letters and statements referred to derive from the web-site of the Israeli Ministry of Foreign Affairs http://www.mfa.gov.il last visited 15 April 2004.
53. See ibid: Exchange of Letters between PM Sharon and President Bush, 14 April 2004.
54. Ibid.
55. Ibid.
56. Ibid.
57. Ibid.
58. Ibid.
59. Ibid
60. Ibid.
61. Ibid.
62. Ibid.
63. Although these excuses have been deemed as inconsistent with the doctrine of self-determination since 1960, see: UN General Assembly resolution 1514 (1960).
64. Exchange of Letters between PM Sharon and President Bush, 14 April 2004.
65. Ibid.
66. David Horovitz and Herb Kienon, "Prime Minister Speaks to 'The Post'," *The Jerusalem Post*, 22 April 2005.
67. Ibid.

68. Ibid.
69. Ibid.
70. See: National Security Strategy of the United States of America, September 2002 at: http://www.whitehouse.gov/nsc/nss.html (last visited 7 December 2004).
71. Exchange of Letters between PM Sharon and President Bush, 14 April 2004
72. Ibid.
73. Letter from Dov Weisglass to Condoleezza Rice, *Haaretz*, 19 April 2004.
74. See: Avi Shalayim, *The Iron Wall; Israel and Arab World* (London: Penguin Books, 2000), for a discussion of the impact on this outlook on the Oslo peace process see: David Thompson, "Climbing the Iron Wall: Palestine and Self-Determination," *Griffith Law Review*, Vol. 12. No. 2 (2003), 288-310.
75. "The Government Resolution Regarding the Disengagement Plan," published by the Prime Minster's office, 6 June 2004, see in particular "Addendum A—Revised Disengagement Plan, Main Principles" at http://www/mfa.gov.il (last visited 7 December 2004).
76. Ibid.
77. It is significant that Ariel Sharon's bureau chief did reveal that that the purpose of the plan was to freeze the idea of a Palestinian state at all, see: Ari Shavit, "The Big Freeze," *Haaretz*, 8 October 2004, English Edition.
78. See Herb Keinon, "'Disengagement' Out, 'Leaving Gaza' In," *Jerusalem Post*, 10 December 2004.
79. See: Yossi Beilin, *The Path to Geneva*, 299-312.
80. *Haaretz*, 16 January 2004, English Edition.
81. Edward W. Said, *From Oslo to Iraq and the Roadmap* (London: Bloomsbury, 2004), 282.

9

GREATER ISRAEL AS AN
UNDEMOCRATIC STATE

℘CⳢ

Glenn E. Perry

The essence of the Palestinian cause always has been a struggle against violations of democratic principles if not one for democracy per se. The whole idea of creating a Jewish national home in a country in which the Jews were only a small minority and still less than a third of the population when the Zionist movement in 1942 officially declared its goal of making the country a Jewish Commonwealth—as well as when the majority population underwent ethnic cleansing in1948 in order to allow the smaller colonial settler community to create a state in seventy-eight percent of the territory—collided head on with all principles of democracy.

The focus long has been on seeking independence for the West Bank and Gaza, twenty-two percent of the Palestinians' homeland. But now increasing numbers of Palestinians, Israelis, and others are coming to see the issue as one of rights for the disenfranchised in their whole homeland. After all, the state of Israel that the Zionists established in most of Palestine over half a century ago and that only eighteen years later took control of the rest of the country to become Greater Israel constitutes a democracy for Jews. Representing a type of political system that is variously known as a *Herrenvolk* democracy[1] (i.e., one in which a *Herrenvolk* or "master race" runs its affairs democratically but rules undemocratically over others), "ethnocracy"[2] or "half a democracy,"[3] citizenship and the suffrage in Israel exist for the Jewish population (notably, without regard to whether they reside in the territories acquired in 1948-1949 or in 1967) but not to the indigenous population of the more recently incorporated territories (or people in those territories or outside who are refugees from the previously acquired seventy-eight percent of the country). Citizenship and the right to vote are extended to the remnant of the indigenous Christian and Muslim Palestinians left within the territory the state gained control of by 1949, although they have not acquired full democratic rights.

Whatever the extent of democratic rights practiced by the Jewish population within their own community, it is the denial of such to the others that concerns us here. In this regard, both Greater Israel and the former South Africa parallel the situation in ancient Athens and the nineteenth-century United States (and, to a lesser extent in the latter case, until the implementation of civil rights legislation of the 1960s). Robert A. Dahl[4] describes each of these as "a competitive system that was inclusive with respect to one part of the population but hegemonic with respect to another." The application of what Dahl says about the former situation in the United States—then with the help of much "resignation and hopeless-ness on the part of the subordinated people"—to Greater Israel is compel-ling:

> To enforce a long-standing condition of extreme deprivation upon the black people of the South, southern whites (like the free Athenians) had to develop two political systems, one superimposed on the other: a more or less competitive polyarchy in which most whites were included and a hegemonic system to which Negroes were subject and to which southern whites were overwhelmingly allegiant.[5]

While Dahl suggests that the effective right to vote in freely contested elections makes it unlikely that any large group will be subjected to severe repression, he incisively argues that democracies can not be expected to behave better than non-democracies toward those who are excluded from citizenship.[6] Thus the problem for places such as Jenin and Rafah is that they are incorporated into the territory of Greater Israel without obtaining the kind of political rights that would protect them from repression.

Occupation or Absorption

The extension of Israeli rule to the West Bank (including East Jerusalem) and the Gaza Strip since 1967 is ordinarily seen as a case of occupying foreign territory. And that paradigm indeed is useful to an extent for understanding the situation. The international community sees these areas as Israeli-occupied territories rather than as parts of an enlarged Israel. And there is admittedly a danger that any challenge to this will play into Israeli hands.

Israeli Deputy Prime Minister Ehud Olmert complained that Palestinians are beginning to shift their views of the conflict "from an Algerian paradigm to a South African one."[7] If so, this represents a return to the objective nature of the conflict with Zionism. The West Bank and Gaza are not a country that is being occupied by another country, as in the case of Algeria under French rule. The French settlers in Algeria were from places such as Paris and Marseilles. The Algerians were not from those places and had no claim to them. But the Palestinians are not just from Nablus and Gaza. They also are from Nazareth and from Haifa and Jaffa and nearly four hundred other former cities, towns, and villages within the Green Line. Even with such uprooting of the Palestinians in 1948, they make up nearly twenty percent of the population within the Green Line today. The whole region between the Mediterranean and the Jordan River is ruled today by an alien settler community (the existence of a few indigenous Jews notwithstanding), much like South Africa in the past (where indeed the white presence began in the 1600s). For the Israelis to withdraw from the West Bank and Gaza would be like the white South Africans withdrawing from "the Bantu homelands," not like the French rulers of Algeria returning to France. The conflict in Palestine/Israel, in the words of Meron Benvenisti, is "Between a society of immigrants and a society of natives... the story of natives who feel that people who came from across the sea ...dispossessed them."[8]

The democratic one-state solution to the Palestine question is nothing new. This was the position of cultural Zionists such as Martin Buber and Judah Magnes before 1948. Even mainline Zionists such as David Ben Gurion once articulated it (if only because this was the only morally defensible position), although revelations about plans for "transfer," and the way such "transfer" or ethnic cleansing actually took place in 1948 demonstrate their lack of sincerity in this matter. Furthermore, the Palestinian resistance movement's original call for a "secular democratic state" was eventually abandoned only because the defeat of Israel proved impossible, while the goal of achieving independence in twenty-two percent of their homeland seemed attainable. It is ironic that the idea of a unified democratic Palestine/Israel now has emerged as the more realistic alternative, although this results not from Israel being defeated but as part of the ultimate blowback of its victory. In the words of Daniel Gavron, who blames the settlers in the West Bank for the demise of the separate Jewish state, "unfortunately, given the choice between sovereignty and land, we chose land. We have manifestly preferred settlement in the whole Land of Israel to a state of Israel in part of the land." He tells the settlers: "Okay, you've won, let's have one state. But don't tell me we're not going to be democratic."[9] Ehud Barak has warned his fellow Jews that the failure to establish a separate Palestinian state will play into the hands of the Palestinians, for "a single state will have to be in the spirit of the twenty-first century: democratic, secular, one-man, one-vote. One man, one vote? Remind you of something? Yes. South Africa. And that's no accident. It's precisely their intention."[10]

And indeed it is this specter of democratization that made Ariel Sharon see the need to withdraw from some densely populated areas and perhaps ultimately to allow the creation of a truncated Palestinian state. But the kind of state Sharon foresees would be so small and its "sovereignty" so fraudulent that this could not ward off demands for a democratic solution as in South Africa. Writing about Sharon's plan to disengage from the Gaza Strip, Akiva Eldar pointed to the remarkable parallel between this and future enclaves in the West Bank on the one hand to the "homelands" for Blacks in South Africa that represented "one of the last inventions of the white minority...to perpetuate its rule over the black majority" but eventually "became part of united South Africa."[11] Professor Ali Jerbawi has proposed that the Palestinian Authority threaten to disband itself as a way of bringing this threat of democracy home to the Israelis.[12] Former Prime Minister Ahmad Qureia once announced that if Israel goes ahead with plans to absorb much of the West Bank, the Palestinians would adopt the one-state approach.[13]

The "occupation" paradigm is misleading in two senses. In the first place, it does not fit the historical facts. The whole area between the Mediterranean and the Jordan River is one entity, with the State of Israel the successor to the Palestine Mandate. No legal partition ever occurred. The plan—itself of dubious legality—proposed by the United Nations General Assembly in 1947 was never implemented. Thus when the Jewish ethnocracy invaded the West Bank and Gaza in 1967, it was reunifying Palestine but imposing its ethnocratic political system on the whole entity. The appropriate solution was to enfranchise those to whom its rule now extended.

In the second place, the description of the Israeli presence in the West Bank and Gaza as a mere occupation does not fit the post-1967 reality. Aside from East Jerusalem, there has been no formal annexation, but the Israeli settlers are not treated as living outside Israel. According to B'Tselem, the Israeli Information Center for Human Rights in the Occupied Territories, settlers controlled 41.9 percent of the land in the West Bank by 2002.[14] Children born to the settlers have been defined as native-born Israelis, not as people born in a foreign country under temporary military occupation. Jews in the new settlements do not have to go inside the Green Line to vote or to cast absentee ballots as they would if they were outside the country. The allegation that "Israel is the only country in the world where government ministers and parliament members [and 'seven percent of the citizenry'] live permanently outside its borders"[15] overlooks the fundamental reality that the territories conquered in 1967 have been incorporated into the state's borders. Furthermore, while hiding the fact of de facto incorporation without enfranchising the local population behind the transparent veil of an absence of formal annexation, the Israelis and their supporters often have rejected the term "occupied." Prime Minister Menachem Begin used to say that there was no need for annexation, as the West Bank and Gaza were already part of Israel. While admitting the ultimate need for "some sort of entity" in the West Bank and Gaza Strip, U.S. Secretary of Defense Donald H. Rumsfeld dismissed references to "the so-called occupied territories."[16] As Tony Judt put the matter, it is too late to think of partition, for "There are too many settlements, too many Jewish settlers, and too many Palestinians," thus dooming a two-state solution and leaving only two alternatives: "an ethnically cleansed Greater Israel and a single, integrated, bi-national state."[17] For Meron Benvenisti, "Israel and the Palestinians are sinking together into the mud of the 'one state.' The question is no longer whether it will be bi-national, but which model to choose."[18] Having during the early 1980s already decided that the presence of 20,000 Israeli settlers in the West Bank "had created an irreversible situation," he points to their increase to 230,000 today (not including those in Jerusalem) that makes for "a bi-national reality"[19]—though not a democratic one.

The Starting Point for A Democratization Movement

Only someone out of touch with reality might imagine that Greater Israel would consider democratizing now. What I am suggesting is that the Israeli policy of absorbing the areas conquered in 1967 has made way for future demands for democratization. Pointing out that the construction of settlements in the West Bank has made the preservation of the Jewish state unviable in the long run, Daniel Gavron maintains that the future of the Israeli Jews requires that they act now "to abdicate Jewish sovereignty and move quickly, while the balance of power still tilts in their favor, to a multiethnic democracy."[20] This would obviate a long struggle by the Palestinians for justice and at the same time provide guarantees for the Jews, but his suggestion is purely utopian. It is a non-starter for the vast majority of Jewish Israelis.[21] Far more realistic is the alternative that Gavron warns against, one in which "the one-state reality will ultimately be imposed on them—in a slow but savage process."

What I am suggesting is that we will eventually reach the point that the Israeli territorial aggrandizement will leave democratization as the only alternative to continuing the state's *Herrenvolk* character. That will be the time for a movement, made up of both Palestinians and moderate Jews, to demand the democratization of the state. When Palestinians and a few Israelis committed to democracy fully realize that the solution to their problem is not partition but an end to the *Herrenvolk* nature of the state they live in, they will have created a long dark tunnel filled with many obstacles blocking it that they likely will not be able to pass through quickly but through which they can see a ray of light at the other end.[22]

Already, many who are committed to the idea of a Jewish state see the trap that this aggrandizement unwittingly has set for their ethnocratic regime. Thomas L. Friedman has repeatedly warned of this threat. Thus in projecting a Palestinian majority in Palestine by 2010, after "the de facto or de jure Israeli annexation of the West Bank, Gaza and East Jerusalem," he grimly predicts that the only options for Israel will be continuing "apartheid" or expulsion,

> ...or they will grant Palestinians the right to vote and it no longer will be a Jewish state. Whichever way it goes, it will mean the end of a Jewish democracy. [23]

He warns of the difficulty awaiting Israel's defenders on American college campuses when the issue comes to be seen in terms of majority rule versus apartheid.[24]

A realization of the demographic danger to the idea of an exclusively Jewish state is propelling Israelis to accept the need to avoid absorbing all the territory they gained control of in 1967. Former Knesset Speaker Avraham Burg warned in 2003 that if Israelis want democracy, they must "abandon the greater land of Israel...or give full citizenship and voting rights to everyone, including Arabs."[25] Indeed, Likud leaders recently have been talking about the need to create a Palestinian state (though they have in mind one that is gerrymandered to allow for the retention of maximum territory with a minimum number of Palestinians) as a way of saving Israel as a Jewish state, and Dan Meridor—warning that "The problem now is not that we lose. The problem is that we might win"—has spoken of his fear that Palestinian leaders soon will be rejecting a separate state and calling instead for annexation.[26] In 2003, Israeli Vice Prime Minister Ehud Olmert, in calling for unilateral withdrawal from areas densely populated by Palestinians to allow a Palestinian state to be formed, expressed the fear that Palestinians would drop the idea of a two-state solution in light of "the emerging majority of Arabs in Greater Israel."[27] He admitted "shudder[ing] to think that liberal Jewish organizations that shouldered the burden of the struggle against apartheid in South Africa will lead the struggle against us."[28] A *New York Times* editorial[29] soon after this warned that if the two-state solution were bypassed, "Two options will remain: an apartheid state run by a heavily armed Jewish minority, or a new political entity without a Jewish identity," i.e., a democratized Greater Israel. Similarly, Henry Siegman recently warned that it may not be long until the only alternatives will be South African-style apartheid or even the completion of the 1948-style ethnic cleansing on the one hand or else the emergence of a Greater Israel in which "the emerging majority of Arabs...will reshape the country's national identity," which he considers "a tragedy of historic proportions for the Zionist enterprise."[30]

But truncating the West Bank in a way that is designed to enable Israel to retain maximum territory and minimal numbers of Palestinians may not suffice to ward off the dangers of democratization. Repeating almost verbatim his scenario of the problem pro-Israel students will have on American college campuses, Friedman warned again a year later that Sharon's wall will prove to "be the mother of all unintended consequences by destroying Palestinian hopes for a two-state solution and resulting in demands—"very problematic for Israel"—for one state in which the Palestinians will have a majority. Friedman warns in particular that many of those Palestinians that the wall leaves "isolated in pockets next to Jewish settlers—who have the rule of law, the right to vote, welfare, jobs, etc. ... will throw in the towel and ask for the right to vote in Israel" and cites a poll by Khalil Shikaki showing that twenty-five to thirty percent of the Palestinians already have come around to that way of thinking.[31] Thus while most Palestinians would acquiesce in forfeiting their rights in the seventy-eight percent of their homeland that the Israelis controlled during 1948-1967, any insistence on keeping much of the area they gained control over in 1967 will undermine this goal. "Sharon's monstrous wall," Avi Shlaim thus warns, "is not a prelude to a viable two-state solution."[32] While the ideal starting point for democratization would be formal annexation by Israel of all the already-incorporated areas, the more likely prospect is partial annexation—what Jeff Halper describes as Sharon's "vision of a Palestinian state [as] a truncated Bantustan with no control of its borders, no freedom of movement, no economic viability, no access to its water resources, no meaningful presence in Jerusalem and no genuine sovereignty, one that leaves Israel with 90% of the country."[33] This would make the ten percent left to the Native Palestinians hardly more than a reservation of disenfranchised subalterns still under Israeli rule if technically outside its borders ("pathetic Palestinian Bantustans," as Robert D. Kaplan predicts, "that are kept quiescent by the police-state tactics of a Jibril Rajoub"[34]) and might only delay the demand for a democratic one-state solution.

Some Israelis are worrying about the future difficulty of maintaining a Jewish state in the face of the Palestinian minority within the Green Line even if this actually became an international border. Binyamin Netanyahu has warned that, "when their [the Palestinian citizens of Israel] numbers reach thirty-five to forty percent of the Israeli population, the Jewish state will, at that point, cease to exist."[35] He even opined that the democratic and Jewish fabric of the country would be damaged if the Arab population remained at the twenty percent level[36] Benvenisti predicts that in ten years the Palestinians will constitute twenty-five percent of the population within the Green Line, making it impossible for Israel to remain a Jewish state.[37] If Israel wound up with only a small proportion of the West Bank Palestinians within its ultimate boundaries, the problem for it would be exacerbated, resulting in some suggestions—e.g., by Ephraim Sneh, A.B. Yehoshua, and Amos Oz—that a future Palestinian state should get some

Palestinian-inhabited areas within the Green Line in exchange for uninhabited territories in the West Bank.[38] Further ethnic cleansing might arguably create new possibilities for maintaining a Jewish Greater Israel. This may occur to some degree as people find alternatives to living under the harsh conditions imposed on them. But it is difficult to foresee a situation in which relatively thoroughgoing ethnic cleansing on the model of 1948 could be implemented. If such did occur, it likely would create severe divisions in Jewish Israeli society and have unintended demographic consequences that to some degree would undo the advantages of ethnic cleansing by inducing disillusioned liberals to leave the country. Another unintended consequence of partial ethnic cleansing likely would be to make the Israeli leadership more daring about absorbing a maximum amount of territory, but while the demographic danger to the Zionist project would be slowed down, it still would exist, making the idea of a Jewish state still incompatible with democracy in the fairly short term. Thus the Israelis' greed to keep as much of Palestine as possible may lead them into the trap of keeping more Palestinians than ultimately will prove compatible with maintaining their state as a "Jewish" one.

Could a Democratic Greater Israel Work?

One must consider the inevitable argument that an essential prerequisite of democracy is missing in the case of Palestine/Israel. Robert A. Dahl,[39] points out that "the greater the conflict between a government and its opponents, the more costly it is for each to tolerate each other." Some would argue that in an extreme case of conflict and of costly suppression the only solution would be partition or ethnic cleansing or some combination of the two.

Dahl develops his argument in relationship to subcultures and cleavage patterns. Referring to John Stuart Mill's assertion that only a state whose boundaries correspond to a nationality (i.e., a common identity), he points out that in some cases, conflict precludes democracy. Thus

Any dispute in which a large section of the population ... feels that its way of life or its highest values are severely menaced by another segment of the population creates a crisis in a competitive system.[40]

He concludes that a particularly unsuitable situation for democracy is where one subculture has a majority, that is, where the country either is divided into two or more groups and with one comprising a majority. In such a situation, the majority group may hope to dominate without exercising restraint and is able to exclude other groups from the government.[41] In a classic article on democratization, Dankwart A. Rustow treated as an essential background condition of democracy the lack of doubt on the part of "the vast majority of the citizens" regarding what "political community they belong to" and quotes Ivor Jennings's statement that "the people cannot decide until somebody decides who are the people."[42] Indeed, the problem for democracy in the face of rival national identities within the same state is obvious, and one should not underestimate the century of intense conflict between two peoples in Palestine/Greater Israel as an obstacle. But in fact there are few states in which nationhood coincides with the state's population, and yet many of them practice democracy. Some aspects of Greater Israel would provide assets for future democratization.

Polarization?

Several factors could prevent the sort of polarization that Dahl refers to in which each side faces the intolerable specter of the other winning an electoral majority. There is no prospect of a settlement in which, as happened in South Africa, the one-person-one-vote principle emerges immediately. The Jews at first would remain dominant, with the Palestinians focused on democratization rather than being distracted by calls for partition. When democratization eventually is achieved, the Palestinians likely will form at most only a small majority, making the transition fundamentally easier than in the South African case.

A Palestinian majority would not be monolithic. The Palestinians within the Green Line constitute an integral part of the Palestinian people, but their experience for over half a century has been different from those in the West Bank and Gaza Strip. Note how the patronage of Zionist parties has drawn support from many of them. Some of the Palestinians in the territories whose annexation will formally be proclaimed will, as experience shows, be drawn into the patronage of Jewish parties or otherwise will collaborate, demonstrating a pattern that some elements of long-subjected population are prone to engage in. Whatever moral judgment we assign to such collaboration, it will help the ethnocracy avoid the kind of sudden authentic democratization that most Jews would not be able to contemplate and prepare them gradually for the ultimate reality. Also, as long as a disproportionate percentage of the Palestinians are too young to vote, that would reduce their electoral capability for a while. Even with a considerable Palestinian majority a large degree of Jewish predominance in elections likely would continue. This would be particularly true if democracy were diluted at first by electoral devices—gerrymandering, educational requirements, and the like—designed to reduce the Palestinian vote, something that would be fundamentally unacceptable in principle and would emerge as the object of demands for change.

A Favorable Path to Polyarchy

Dahl's comparative analysis of "the paths to polyarchy"[43] points to one reality that helps explain the transition to democracy in South Africa and could be even more decisive in the case of Greater Israel/Palestine. Showing that polyarchy has two dimensions—contestation (or liberalization) and inclusiveness (moving toward something like universal adult suffrage)—Dahl concludes that an attempt to jump from a purely autocratic system (a "closed hegemony"), that is, a regime previously lacking either of the two dimensions, at one time is unlikely to be successful, making it conducive to the ultimate goal of democratization to develop one of the two dimensions before moving on to the next one. And it matters which dimension one starts with. The "path to polyarchy" that moves first from "closed hegemony" to a "competitive oligarchy" (i.e., contestation within a narrow group) before moving on to greater inclusiveness stands a much better chance of making polyarchy work than does one that proceeds in the opposite manner. In the more favorable path, new groups admitted into the increasingly inclusive contestation process can be "more easily socialized into the norms and practices of competitive politics" that already have emerged.[44]

Samuel P. Huntington suggests that this was mainly applicable when the previous exclusion was "based on economic, not racial grounds." He argues that "communal systems ... have been highly resistant to peaceful change" and that the South African exception resulted from "competition within the oligarchy."[45] In fact, one could expect the same kind of "conflict within the oligarchy" to occur in Greater Israel, perhaps to a larger extent than in South Africa. Some Jewish support for a democratic single state has already emerged, as is obvious from various people quoted above.[46] But the

Palestinian leadership has, in effect, been demanding a Bantustan, and so it is understandable that peace-oriented Israelis have supported that idea, just as might have been the case with liberal whites in South Africa if their government—hypothetically—had been rejecting calls by blacks for sham independence for tribal statelets. When finally partition ceases to be the issue, many Israelis who have favored a two-state solution can be expected to join with Palestinians in calling for the democratization of Greater Israel/Palestine.

A Strong State

Joel Migdal gives Israel as an example of a "strong state."[47] The Israeli state is strong in that power in it is institutionalized rather than representing a web of kinship and other personalistic relationships. This distinguishes it from the situation in most Third World countries in which the state, however authoritarian, is entangled in webs of social forces (clans, sects, etc.) that leave it largely impotent.

I am suggesting that this is the sort of state that would be able to incorporate a large population into its participatory structure. With Israel having ruled the West Bank and Gaza since 1967, the only change called for is that the rights of citizenship be extended to their populations. A weak state likely would not be able to do so.

Proportional Representation and the Multiparty System

The Israeli system of proportional representation could facilitate the extension of inclusiveness to the population of the West Bank and Gaza. Single-member districts in which the candidate with a plurality in each wins tend to produce exaggerated majorities in parliaments, thus putting the losing side in a deeply divided society in peril. Israel's list system, by contrast, produces a legislative chamber that reflects the divisions in the electorate more accurately. Considering that even in a society such as Greater Israel neither of the two main ethnic groups is monolithic but divided along lines of ideology (e.g., secularists versus both Islamists and Orthodox Jewish parties) and along lines of extremism versus moderation, the present multiplicity of political parties undoubtedly would be perpetuated—and presumably intensified—in a future democratized Greater

Israel. With no one party holding a majority of seats and with no majority coalition that would not be in danger breaking up in the face of extreme proposals, neither Jews nor Arabs in Greater Israel would be likely to exercise majority tyranny. This would constitute a much more favorable situation for democracy than the one in South Africa, in which the overwhelming majorities won by the African National Congress may result in its becoming dangerously entrenched in power.[48] As Arend Lijphart has argued, the existence of "segmental parties" is favorable to "consociational democracy" in such deeply divided countries (that is, a system in which elites representing each group collaborate with one another and avoid imposing majority control), [49] as "They can act as the political representatives of their segments, and they provide a good method of selecting the segmental leaders who will participate in grand coalitions."[50] In a democratized Greater Israel, perhaps more than in the present ethnocracy, the number of parties likely would be greater than the four or five that have been considered optimal, but Lijphart also suggests that in societies in which there are "either only two or more than five or six significant segments," a two-party system or more than the usual maximum number may better facilitate the clear representation of each segment.[51]

Consociational Features?

It is too early to propose the sort of mutual guarantees that will assure each of the country's two peoples that it will not face the tyranny of majority rule. These will emerge only as the demand for Palestinian enfranchisement gains momentum and as what by then may be a Jewish minority in Greater Israel begins to offer such only in return for limits on majority rule. Lijphart identifies four such techniques of consociational democracy: (1)grand coalitions, (2)mutual vetoes, (3)proportionality, and (4)segmental autonomy and federalism.[52] As for the grand coalition concept (one in which all major parties participate in each government, unlike in the majoritarian system in which there is a division into a government and an opposition), its gradual emergence on an informal basis provides the most likely scenario, with future governments of a democratized Greater Israel including various moderate parties—i.e., those committed to the bi-national approach—representing the two ethnic groups. The difficulty of working with extreme parties on each side likely would require the inclusion of moderates from both ethnic groups in order to have a governing majority. A full-fledged grand coalition on the Swiss model that includes all the major parties might seem less realistic, particularly at first, in light of the deep division between Jews and Palestinians. But as Lijphart tells us, "the prospect of participating in the government is a powerful stimulus to moderation and compromise,"[53] thus making a complete grand coalition at some stage a more likely possibility.

Some sort of mutual veto over decisions objectionable to either of the two main communities will seem reasonable. This might be based on an informal understanding rather than on legally binding constitutional provisions. Considering that neither Jews nor Palestinians likely will form an overwhelming majority, the usual objection to the veto, namely that it constitutes a form of minority rule, would not be compelling, although the danger of *immobilisme* would be present. But such an arrangement will not be realistic until democratization has proceeded so far that the Jewish population demands it as a condition for further inclusiveness.

Similarly, the principle of proportionality in the civil service and economic benefits might develop only in the long run as Palestinians gradually call for more equal representation and as some sort of affirmative action eventually emerges. Continued Jewish domination of the civil service—and notably the military—for a considerable period, though objectionable to the disadvantaged group, might help to make the transition to democracy more gradual and thus more acceptable to the present ethnocracy, while the realistic prospect of eventually changing this (the light at the end of the long tunnel) might give the presently excluded group some grounds for patience.

As for federalism,[54] those who make proposals today for guarantees such as a division into cantons along federal lines, demonstrate utopianism.[55] Gavron makes an excellent point in suggesting a structure in which there would be maximum autonomy for a variety of groups, including "the Muslim Arabs and the secular Jews" and also such "communities...as the ultra-Orthodox Jews" and "the various Christian communities...and the large community of foreign workers."[56] But this will come only after Jews and Palestinians stop talking about partition—notably, when the Jews see that some sort of federalism will provide an important kind of autonomy for them as well as the Palestinians as a way of sheltering each from total control by a countrywide majority representing the other. Aside from a kind of personal (non-territorial) federalism similar to that provided to different religious communities in both the Islamic world and Israel but on a basis of complete equality, it would be desirable to avoid the sort of federalism that would leave the country divided into two territorial ethnic entities, for the one-state solution presumably would allow for the continuation and perhaps proliferation of the Jewish presence in "Judea and Samaria" (but with the privileged status of the settlers curtailed as democratization proceeded) while Palestinian communities such as Nazareth would of course remain, along with new ones eventually established, perhaps on the ruins of villages destroyed in 1948. More desirable would be a high level of autonomy for local communities—some of which would be purely Palestinian or Jewish (or based on another principle of exclusivity) at least for the immediate future as a concession to the reality of segmental differences but with the option of mixed communities as well. Like other aspects of consociationalism, this hopefully could eventually be phased out as the plural society ceased to need such crutches.[57]

The first step in the process I am proposing is simply for it to become obvious that partition is no longer a viable solution. If the Israelis could be induced to formally declare that the whole West Bank and Gaza are annexed or even if the Palestinians find themselves relegated to only a small part of these territories (as seems increasingly likely in 2006), that stage would be imminent. The symbolic importance of the name of the state notwithstanding, the change to something that is not ethnically exclusive can be deferred to the future, as most Jews inevitably will resist ideas such as changing the name from "Israel" to Jerusalem[58] (or, as Mu'ammar al-Qadhdhafi has proposed, to "Isratine") even long after the country clearly is on the road to being a bi-national democracy. Perhaps this will mean formal annexation without citizenship and suffrage rights at the outset for the Palestinians of the West Bank and Gaza. Or perhaps there will be citizenship for only a few, with the rest relegated to walled-in enclaves that are not annexed but will be clearly recognizable as ghettos under continuing Israeli domination and unsuitable for separate statehood even if a fictional sovereignty is recognized. That is when I see the acceleration of the movement among Palestinians and some liberal Jews for democratization. The consociational elements—deviations from simple majority rule that arguably represent deviations from full democracy—will emerge then as ways of sweetening democratization for the group that now will be losing sole control of the country. Only in the long run can one hope that the division between the two main ethnic groups will be ameliorated to the extent that these features can be dropped. Although not all the conditions that Lijphart identifies[59] as favorable to the success of consociationalism present themselves in this case, the situation would be far from hopeless.

We already have dealt with the favorable conditions presented by the Israeli electoral and party systems.

Lijphart also points to the advantage of having a multiplicity of segments rather than a dual balance (i.e., a multipolar rather than a bipolar division). While the division in this case into Jews and Palestinians might seem to represent an excessive degree of bipolarity, careful consideration justifies greater optimism, as several kinds of division within each community could make for a multipolar balance. For example, the division between Orthodox and secular Jews might actually overshadow the overall Jewish hostility to the Arabs in the future, thus contributing to the development of a multipolar situation.

Lijphart's suggestion that a small country has an advantage would not necessarily apply to this case. He considers smallness to be an asset for two internal and two external reasons. One internal reason is that "elites are more likely to know each other personally and to meet often" and thus "not regard politics as a zero-sum game."[60] The indirect internal reason for smallness being conducive to consociationalism is that small countries are less complex and therefore more governable. Lijphart's external factor include the fact that small countries are more likely to feel threatened, thus providing an incentive to internal solidarity. But he cautions that this is true only if all sides feel equally threatened by a common danger, a condition that cannot be assumed in the case under consideration. He also points to small states' "tendency to abstain from an active foreign policy" and consequently to avoid "difficult choices in this realm."[68] While such a scenario might smack of naiveté, the path toward reconciliation based on justice, particularly with international guarantees, could have a powerful impact.

Other factors identified by Lijphart offer less promise. The extent to which cleavages in Greater Israel are crosscutting is low. Aside from the decreasing percentage of Arab Palestinian Christians, the ethnic division follows the same lines as religious identity (though not of practicing religion). The impoverishment of the bulk of Palestinians makes for relatively little crosscutting of the ethnic/religious division and that of socioeconomic class (but more than in the case of South Africa). As for "overarching loyalties," there is little ground for optimism, although a love for the same country, particularly once the democratic system begins to function, might turn into this eventually. An existing tradition of elite accommodation is perhaps the factor mentioned by Lijphart that clearly is almost completely absent in the case of Greater Israel. But his suggestion that the encapsulation or "segmental isolation" of the segments into separate communities—contrary to his emphasis on crosscutting cleavages, as he recognizes—is conducive to consociationalism in that it helps to limit antagonism and also is favorable to creating territorial federalism seems to offer promise, although one hopes that the kind of apartheid he is pointing to could eventually make way for an integrated society.

Conclusions and Further Thoughts

The two-state approach to the Palestine question, which once appeared to be a realistic twenty-two-percent-of-the-loaf solution for the country's indigenous population, has proved itself unattainable in fact. Without saying so formally (and, as in the case of "the Emperor's New Clothes," few noticing that the now-enlarged state did not qualify as a "democracy"), Israel effectively annexed the West Bank and the Gaza Strip after 1967, as shown by the establishment of Jewish settlements and acquisition of land. While the Palestinian Resistance Movement's original goal of defeating Israel and establishing a "secular democratic Palestine" stood no chance of success, the Israelis themselves ironically have created a situation in which it will increasingly be obvious that this is a state in which a *Herrenvolk* now sitting astride the pre-1967 frontier rules Palestinian *Untermenschen*, making this a question of democratizing Greater Israel rather than of freeing territories from foreign occupation. And in fact as a few liberal Israelis are beginning to call for transmuting Israel into a bi-national democracy, those who give priority to the maintenance of a Jewish state now resort to the goal of a separate Palestinian state—but only one so truncated that it cannot avoid being recognized as a sham—in order to get themselves off the hook of calls for democratization.

It is clear that democratization will be difficult. Even to propose any attempt to get this accepted now would be useless. What I am suggesting is that we may reach the point soon where the demand of the Palestinians becomes democratization rather than partition of Greater Israel/Palestine and where they are joined by liberal Jews and others—as in the parallel case of South Africa under apartheid—in an extended campaign that may take decades fully to succeed.

Democracy in Greater Israel will face some harsh conditions, as it would in any country that is so deeply divided into two long-mutually-hostile peoples. But the experience of other countries, as distilled in the writings of scholars in the field of democratization, offers some important bases for optimism. As Dahl has shown and as the recent South African transition has confirmed, countries that have established contestation within a limited group stand a better chance of succeeding when they add inclusiveness to the mix than do those who start with inclusiveness and then try contestation. Furthermore, the state in Israel is strong in relationship to its society, making it able to withstand such a traumatic development as incorporating the Palestinians of these territories into its electorate. The institutions of the Israeli state, notably the system of proportional representation that avoids the kind of exaggerated majorities expected when the plurality principle is applied to single-member districts, could provide a fortuitous starting point, while the multiparty pattern will allow each political tendency to be adequately represented in the parliament. A slow move toward such full inclusiveness might suffice to keep Palestinians on the track of peaceful democratization while allowing the members of the present ethnocracy to test the waters gradually. As the process unfolds, various consociational devices such as grand coalitions and federalism could be offered to those who would fear unimpaired majority rule, at least for a while, although not all the conditions favorable to such practices are present.

In this alternative to partition, neither the Jews nor the Palestinians would alienate themselves from any part of Palestine. It would be a win-win situation for both sides. It would not leave the Palestinians of Nazareth and Nablus divided by the Green Line, as do two-state proposals. While full equality for the Palestinians would not emerge suddenly, this would open up the prospect of such. By contrast, a separate Palestinian state that Israel would agree to could not be democratic, for its regime would have to act as Israel's "enforcer" against its own people, who could never accept this as anything more than an unjust arrangement that only their weakness forced them to accept.

A word about the Palestinian refugees' right of return is in order. The democratic bi-national solution could be expected eventually to result in a partial realization of this, at least in the case of those living within Greater Israel, for as they gained citizenship in the state they presumably would obtain freedom to move to the other side of the Green Line and to acquire the sites of some of their forebears' homes. And as democratization gained more and more reality, the political influence of the Palestinians in Greater Israel could be expected to work in favor of recognizing a broader right of return. As the bitterness of the conflict subsided, fewer Jewish Israelis would object to immigration from surrounding areas, whether or not the newcomers were descendants of those uprooted in 1948. At the least, this would not involve signing away any meaningful right of return, a sine qua non of any two-state solution. In short, the route to a democratized single state promises to be more conducive to this basic right of the Palestinians than does any other foreseeable option.

The positive effects of a truly democratized Greater Israel would be difficult to overestimate. This could constitute a basis for peace in the whole region. And by making it no longer necessary for Israel and its superpower backer to have authoritarian regimes such as those in Cairo, Amman, and Riyadh as enforcers to keep the population of the Arab world in line, democratization would have a much greater chance in those countries too. This is not the place to make gushy predictions, and I have tried to keep within the bounds of realism. Admittedly, a bi-national Palestine/Greater Israel would not remove Israel as a major geographical obstacle to Arab unity. But who can say that a secular Greater Israel/Palestine identity could not emerge as part of a larger pan-Semitic nationalism?

Notes

1. Meron Benvenisti, "The Second Republic," *Jerusalem Post*, international ed., 11 January 1987, pp. 8-9.
2. See Oren Yiftachel, "Ethnocracy: The Politics of Judaizing Israel/Palestine," *Constellations* 6 (September 1999), pp. 364-391. Also, by the same author: "The Shrinking Space of Citizenship: Ethnocratic Politics in Israel," *Middle East Report*, no 223, Summer 2002 (http://www.merip.org/mer223_yiftachel. html).
3. Overlooking the original undemocratic character of a state made Jewish by ethnic cleansing in 1948 (but pointing to the inequality imposed on even those 1.3 million Palestinians within the Green Line), Gideon Levy bluntly asserts that "Once Israel became an occupying state, it ceased to be a democracy." He calculates that democratic rights are extended to only 5.3 million of its 10.6 million inhabitants that include not only Palestinians but also "300,000 to 400,000 foreign workers." "Half a Democracy," *Haaretz*, 26 January 2002.
4. Robert A. Dahl, *Polyarchy: Participation and Opposition* (New Haven, Conn. and London: Yale University Press, 1971), p. 93.
5. Dahl, pp. 93-94.
6. Dahl, p. 29.
7. "Is the Two-state Solution in Danger?" *Haaretz*, 22 January 2004.

8. See Ari Shavit, "Cry the Beloved Two-State Solution," part 2, *Haaretz*, 6 August 2003.

9. Quoted in Peter Hirschberg, "One-State Awakening," *Haaretz*, 16 December 2003.

10. Quoted in Ahmad Samih Khalidi, "A One-State Solution," *Haaretz*, 29 September 2003.

11. Akiva Eldar, "Analysis/Creating a Bantustaan in Gaza," *Haaretz*, 16 April 2004.

12. Danny Rubinstein, "Back to the Future in the PA," *Haaretz*, 13 January 2004.

13. "Qureia: Israel's Unilateral Moves Are Pushing Us Toward a One-State Solution" (Reuters), *Haaretz*, 9 January 2004.

14. Nadav Shragai, "B'Tselem Report: Settlers Control 41.9% of West Bank," *Haaretz*, 13 May 2002.

15. Neve Gordon, "Most Israelis Don't Believe It (or Support It): The Only Democracy in the Middle East?" *CounterPunch*, 3 February 2004 (http://www.counterpunch.org/gordon02032004.html).

16. Todd S. Purdum, "Palestinians, Meeting Powell, Urge Pullout," *New York Times*, 9 August 2002, p. 6.

17. Tony Judt, "Israel: The Alternative," *The New York Review of Books*, 23 October 2003.

18. "Which Kind of Binational State," *Haaretz*, 20 November 2004.

19. Avi Shavit, "Cry, the Beloved Two-State Solution," part 2.

20. Peter Hirschberg, "One State Awakening," *Haaretz*, 16 December 2003.

21. A poll conducted by the Peace Index Project in 2003 showed that 6 percent of Israeli Jews supported the binational solution and that seventy-eight percent prefer a two-state solution. Considering that the binational alternative only recently has come to be discussed, this might be interpreted as a promising beginning. However, only 11 percent believe that the two peoples could live together on a basis of equality. Ephraim Yaar and Tamar Hermann, "The Peace Index/Israeli Jews Fret Over Possibility of a Binational State," *Haaretz*, 5 November 2003. Even the longtime dove, Uri Avnery rejects the idea as dangerously utopian. Uri Avnery, "The Bi-National State: The Wolf Shall dwell with the Lamb," *CounterPunch*, 15 July 2003 (http://www.counterpunch.org/).

22. Michael Tarazi's statement welcoming a step-up in Israeli settlement activity as leading to a situation in which the world will impose democracy on it within ten to twenty years and to a Palestinian counterpart of Mandela taking the helm (see Akiva Eldar, "Peace Can't Be Bought on the Layaway Plan," *Haaretz*, 6 September 2003) may overestimate the speed with which the transformation from apartheid can be expected to occur.

23. Thomas L. Friedman, "The New Math," *New York Times*, 15 January 2003, p. A23.

24. Thomas L. Friedman, "Campus Hypocrisy," *New York Tiimes,* 16 October 2002, p. A27.
25. Avraham Burg, "The End of Zionism," *The Guardian,* 15 September 2003. Also see Alex Brummer, "Why Greater Israel Vision Has Perished," *The Observer,* 11 January 2004; Yehiam Prior, "Israel Can Still Be Saved," *Haaretz,* 15 August 2003. Asserting the immediate need for Israel to define itself "according to the demographic border," Prior declares that not much time is left for Israel to remain "a democratic Jewish state."
26. James Bennet, "Likud Debates a Palestinian State to Save Israel," *New York Times,* 13 December 2003, pp. Al, A8.
27. Henry Siegman, "Israel: The Threat from Within," *The New York Review of Books* 51, no. 3, 26 February 2004 (wysiwyg:////http:www.nybooks.com/articles/16916) .
28. James Bennet, "An Ally of Sharon Foresees a Palestinian State," *New York Times,* 6 December 2003, p. A6.
29. "Middle East Math," *New York Times,* 12 September 2003, p. A26.
30. Siegman, "Israel: The Threat from Within."
31. Friedman, 14 September 2003, p. E11. Also see his "The Wailing Wall?" 9/17/03, p. A13, "The End of Something," 30 June 2002, p. A15, and "Breaking and Entering," *New York Times,* 11 December 2003 and Friedman, "One Wall, One Man, One Vote," 14 September 2003, p. 11.
32. Avi Shlaim, "Two Peoples and a Single Land," *The Observer,* 18 January 2004.
33. Jeff Halper, "End of the Road Map: Preparing for the Struggle Against Apartheid," *CounterPunch,* 19 September 2003 (http://www.counterpunch.org/halper)9192003.html).
34. Robert D. Kaplan, "Israel Now," *Atlantic,* January 2000, p. 77.
35. Avirama Golan, "Enough of This Demographic Panic," *Haaretz,* 17 February 2004.
36. Yaair Ettinger, "Herzliya Conference Sees Verbal Attacks on Israeli Arabs," *Haaretz,* 18 December 2003 and Aluf Benn, "MKs Slam Netanyahu's Remarks about Israeli Arabs," *Haaretz,* 18 December 2003.
37. Ari Shavit, "Cry, the Beloved Two-State Solution," *Haaretz,* 8 October 2003.
38. Oren Yiftachel, "The Shrinking Space."
39. Dahl, pp. 15-16.
40. Dahl, p. 105.
41. Dahl, pp. 115-116.
42. Dankwart A. Rustow, "Transitions to Democracy: Toward a Dynamic Model," *Comparative Politics* 2 (no. 3), pp. 350-351.
43. Dahl, pp. 34ff.
44. Dahl, p. 36.

45. Samuel P. Huntington, *The Third Wave: Democratization in the Late Twentieth Century*. (Norman and London: University of Oklahoma Press, 1991), p. 112.
46. See, for example, Ari Shavit, "Cry, the Beloved Two-State Solution," *Haaretz,* two parts, 6 and 8 August 2003 for statements by Haim Hanegi and Meron Benevisti.
47. Joel S. Migdal, *Strong Society and Weak States: State-Society Relations and State Capabilities in the Third World* (Princeton, N.J.: Princeton University Press, 1998), p. xiv. For a fuller analysis of the phenomenon in relationship to Israel, see pp. 142-143.
48. See Martin Woollacott, "The Greatest Threat to the ANC Is Its Own Dominance," *The Guardian*, 16 April 2004.
49. Arend Lijphart, *Democracy in Plural Societies: A Comparative Exploration* (New Haven and London: Yale University Press, 1971), p.1 and *passim*.
50. Lijphart, pp. 62-63.
51. Lijphart, p. 64.
52. See Lijphart, pp. 25ff.
53. Lijphart, p. 31.
54. On the relationship of federalism to consociationalism, see Lijphart, 41-44, 87-99.
55. For example, those of Benvenisti in Shavit. "Cry, the Beloved Two-State Solution" (part 2).
56. Peter Hirschberg, "One-State Awakening," *Haaretz*, 16 December 2003.
57. Lijphart (p. 228) notes that "an extended period of consociational government...may also create sufficient mutual trust ... to render itself superfluous."
58. Gavron, in Hirschberg, "One-State Awakening."
59. Lijphart, pp. 53ff.
60. Lijphart, p. 65.
61. Lijphart, p. 69.

10

LOCATING SOVEREIGNTY IN INTERNATIONAL LAW
Reflections on the Construction of a Wall in Palestine

ഇരു

Barry Collins

Every legal decision involves an exploration of the relation between law and politics. However, the Advisory Opinion issued by the International Court of Justice (ICJ) on the *Legal Consequences of the Construction of a Wall in Occupied Palestinian Territory* of 9 July 2004[1] is notable for its explicit examination of this terrain. This Advisory Opinion delivered a powerful indictment of current Israeli policy in the West Bank into the field of international law. While not a "binding" judgment of the ICJ, the Advisory Opinion confirmed the illegality of the construction of the Israeli wall in international law by a majority of fourteen votes to one. It further declared that Israel was under an obligation to cease construction of the wall, to dismantle those parts of the wall already constructed, to make reparation for all damage caused by its construction and (by a majority of thirteen votes to two) advised that states should not recognize the "illegal situation" resulting from the wall's construction.

This chapter will not focus on the legality or political consequences of the construction of the wall itself, nor will it seek to assess the issues of international humanitarian law or self determination discussed in the Advisory Opinion. Instead, the intention here is to explore how the relationship between the legal and the political became central to the case. In particular, this chapter will examine how much of the "international community" (notably most Western states), while expressing opposition to the construction of the wall, also opposed the intervention of the ICJ in such a "political" matter. In their written submissions to the ICJ, many states argued that the "political" nature of the question before the ICJ meant either that the Court could not or should not issue an Advisory Opinion. In doing so, these written submissions insisted on a rigid distinction between law and politics that is at odds both with the experience of international law and with the settled jurisprudence of the Court. This chapter will explore some of the theoretical assumptions that underlie such claims, and ask: What can such an insistence on the distinctness of international law from the field of politics tell us about notions of sovereignty in an international legal order?

The Request for an Advisory Opinion

Israel's decision to construct a wall to isolate Palestinian population centers continues to have disastrous humanitarian consequences for the people of the West Bank. The wall cuts deeply into territories on the Palestinian side of the Green Line, effectively enclosing many of the Israeli settlement blocs into a contiguous whole with pre-1967 Israeli territory. As has been widely documented, the wall has cut thousands of people off from essential services such as hospitals, schools and other urban resources.[2] It has cut a swathe through East Jerusalem and has separated many Palestinians from their lands and neighbors. The wall creates yet another level of military and bureaucratic obstacles for an already besieged population; not least of these is the establishment of new restrictive categories of residency to control the large number of Palestinians trapped between the route of the wall and the 1967 borders of Israel. Israel seeks to justify the construction of the wall as a means of preventing Palestinian attacks, but many suspect that the wall is a crude attempt by Israel to seize *de facto* control over Palestinian territory in advance of any future agreements.

In September 2003, the report of a United Nations Special Rapporteur expressed grave concern about the effect of the wall on the living conditions of the Palestinian population.[3] On 14 October 2003, the United Nations Security Council considered a resolution calling on Israel to cease construction of the wall, but this was vetoed by the United States.[4] The United Nations, in an emergency special session of the General Assembly, passed a resolution calling on Israel to "stop and reverse the construction of the wall in the occupied territory."[5] In a subsequent session, the General Assembly noted that "Israel, the occupying power continues to refuse to comply with international law vis-à-vis the construction [of the wall]."[6] The General Assembly also requested an advisory opinion from the ICJ on the matter. Article 96.1 of the United Nations Charter allows the General Assembly or the Security Council power to request the ICJ to "give an advisory opinion on any legal question."[7] The Court was enabled to act under Article 65.1 of its Statute, according to which the Court:

> May give an advisory opinion on any legal question at the request of whatever body may be authorized by or in accordance with the Charter of the United Nations to make such a request.

It is worth noting that the request for an advisory opinion did not fundamentally concern the legality of the wall. The General Assembly had already decided that the wall was contrary to international law, and the purpose of the advisory opinion was to guide the General Assembly in its future conduct on this matter (although Israel contested this conclusion in its written submission).[8] Furthermore, as the ICJ was providing an advisory opinion, rather than a decision in a contentious dispute, Israel's lack of consent to the Advisory Opinion was not regarded by the Court as an automatic prior bar to the proceedings.

United Nations member states and a number of international organizations were invited to make submissions to the ICJ on the matter; these national submissions will provide much of the focus of this chapter. The submissions varied from highly detailed and legalistic texts, (such as that of the United States) to short statements of position (such as that of the European Union).[9] Israel though it did not consent to the Court's jurisdiction and did not allow itself to be represented in the hearings, did submit a written statement to the Court. Israel's submission focused almost entirely on questions of jurisdiction and propriety, rather than examining the substantive issues of legality raised by the case. Among Israel's jurisdictional arguments was a claim that the request of an Advisory Opinion had been beyond the competence of the session of the General Assembly as convened. More significantly, the Israeli submission claimed that the request was not one which referred a "legal question" to the Court for the purposes of Article 65.1 of the Court's statute and Article 96.1 of the Charter.[10] Israel's submission noted a previous statement of the ICJ which said:

> In accordance with Article 65 of its statute, the Court can give an advisory opinion only on a legal question. If a question is not a legal one, the Court has no discretion on the matter; it must decline to give the opinion requested.[11]

Israel argued that the terms of the question before the Court were too uncertain to constitute a legal question; consequently the Court had no jurisdiction to hear the case.

Israel also raised several arguments based on judicial discretion and propriety, arguing that even if the Court had jurisdiction, it should exercise its discretion under Article 65.1 of the Court's statute not to use it (Article 65.1 states that "The Court *may* give an Advisory Opinion..."). The main reasons presented for this were: Israel's lack of consent to the proceedings; the possibility that an Advisory Opinion judgment might complicate ongoing political negotiations; the lack of requisite facts at the Court's disposal; the view that the Advisory Opinion would serve no useful purpose and, more generally, the argument that the issuing of an Advisory Opinion would offend principles of judicial propriety.

The view that the ICJ should exercise its discretion not to intervene was not unique to Israel's submission, but was also put forward by a number of states who had nonetheless expressed concern about the humanitarian consequences of the wall, including the United Kingdom, Netherlands, Germany and the United States. Most of these objections to the involvement of the ICJ in the matter argued that the building of the separation wall was an issue better dealt with by political means rather than by a legal forum. The United States, in the United Nations General Assembly, said that that "referring the case to the Court risks politicization of the matter and does not help with peace efforts." The United Kingdom, having voted in favor of ES-10/13, also argued in its submission that the ICJ should not consider the matter, and should exercise its discretion under Article 65.1 not to issue an Advisory Opinion. The submission of the United Kingdom went on to quote with approval Uganda's General Assembly statement that "we should avoid politicizing the court, as this would undermine its impartiality and credibility."[12] The United Kingdom also made reference to Singapore's General Assembly declaration that "we rely on the integrity of international law, of which the ICJ is one of the most important pillars. …We do not consider it appropriate to involve the ICJ in this dispute in this way."[13] Finally, the United Kingdom made reference to the statement given by the Switzerland in the General Assembly: "We do not think it appropriate in the current circumstances to bring before a legal body a subject in which highly political implications predominate."[14]

Other national submissions offered little legal argumentation at all and merely stated their view that involvement of the ICJ in the issue would be politically undesirable or inappropriate. The Submission of the European Union did this most dramatically, particularly given its earlier sponsorship of Resolution ES/10-13. The brief European Union statement did not even engage with the legal issues of jurisdiction or propriety raised by the case, but simply declared that "the proposed request for an advisory opinion from the ICJ is inappropriate. It will not help the efforts of the two parties to re-launch a peace political dialogue."[15] A similar pattern is to be seen in a number of other submissions. Japan, for example, declared, in its submission to the ICJ, that "the information at its disposal [does not] definitively justify the construction of the barrier."[16] Nevertheless, Japan explained its abstention in the vote to refer the matter to the ICJ on the grounds that the issue was "political in nature."[17] The Spanish submission expressed the view that the construction of the wall was a violation of international law; notwithstanding this, the request for an advisory opinion was "inappropriate."[18] The Cameroonian submission expressed a similar view, that "rendering an opinion on this question should be avoided… …in order to escape the risk of politicization of the International Court of Justice."[19] France, while giving very detailed legal response to substantive questions of international humanitarian law raised by the case, was particularly vague as to the question of jurisdiction, merely stating that the request for an advisory opinion "is not conducive to re-launching the necessary political dialogue between the two parties," [20], and emphasizing that:"This request for an advisory opinion could set a dangerous precedent, inciting states to seek a vote by the General Assembly to refer to the Court disputes over which the Court would not have contentious jurisdiction."[21]

Israel's submission to the ICJ, as well as making extensive jurisdictional arguments, also made reference to other more general political considerations, such as the "broader dimension" to the request, asking whether

> Palestine, armed with an advisory opinion...[will] proceed to reconvene the Tenth Emergency Special Session for purposes of requesting further opinions? Is the Middle East dispute to come for resolutions piecemeal to the Court by way of expedited requests for advisory opinions at six month intervals? And what of other conflicts?[22]

The subtle rhetoric of this statement should not be overlooked; international law is depicted here as a means of "arming" an ever-demanding "Palestine."

The Israeli submission also uses individual accounts of the horrific deaths of civilian victims of Palestinian attacks to supplement its legal argument. These emotive and sometimes lurid accounts are liberally peppered throughout its submission:

> ...That evening, girls were allowed in free of charge. Many were teenagers. Twenty-one people died that night when the bomb exploded. Most were under 18 years of age. One of the victims was Anya Kazachkov. She was a newcomer from Russia.... She was 16. Her drawings decorate the walls of her school...[23]

Comparable personalized accounts of Palestinian civilian suffering are unsurprisingly absent from the Israeli submission, but it is also significant that the negation of the Palestinian experience extends to an attempt to deny the legal personality of "Palestine" itself in the proceedings. Israel argued that as Palestine was not a state, it should not be allowed to participate in the proceedings.

> The presence of "Palestine" before the Court clearly signals the contentious nature of the proceedings...it is neither a state entitled to appear before the Court nor an international organization.[24]

Curiously, this argument was included in Israel's submission notwithstanding the fact that Palestine, which has special observer status at the United Nations, had already been given special permission by the Court to participate in the proceedings.[25] It is worth noting that throughout the

Israeli submission, "Palestine" is consistently referred to in inverted commas.

"Law" or "Politics" at the ICJ?

These various objections to the Court's jurisdiction and propriety might have been expected to have posed some significant difficulties for the judges of the ICJ, particularly given the weight of international opinion that they represented. This, however, was not to be the case: the Court unanimously dismissed the argument that it had no jurisdiction to issue an Advisory Opinion![26] The argument that the Court should exercise its discretion under Article 65.1 of the Statute of the Court not to issue an Advisory Opinion was also rejected by fourteen votes to one.

The issue of whether the request was too "political" to be a "legal" question (for the purposes of both Article 96.1 of the United Nations Charter and Article 65.1) was dispatched by the Court with remarkable ease. Rejecting claims that the request for an advisory opinion lacked the clarity to constitute a "legal" question, the Court stated that the question submitted by the General Assembly has been:

> framed in terms of law and raise[s] problems of international law. It is by its very nature susceptible of a reply based on law; indeed it is barely susceptible of a reply otherwise than on the basis of law. In the view of the Court, it is indeed a question of a legal character.[27]

Later in its judgment, the Court declared that

> It cannot accept the view, which has been advanced in the present proceedings, that it has no jurisdiction because of the "political" nature of the matter posed.[28]

The Court also quoted with approval an earlier statement:

> [the fact that a legal question has political as well as legal aspects] ... is in the nature of things, is the case in so many questions of international life, does not suffice to deprive it of its character as a legal question and to deprive the Court of a competence expressly conferred upon it by statute.[29]

The Court also relied on its most unambiguous previous statement on the matter, from the *Advisory Opinion on the Legality or Threat of Use of Nuclear Weapons*:

> The political nature of the motives which may have been said to have inspired the request and the political implications that the opinion given might have are of no relevance in the establishment of [the court's] jurisdiction to give such an opinion...[30]

Finally, the Court relied on a 1980 statement that:

> Indeed, in situations in which political considerations are prominent it may be particularly necessary for International Organizations to obtain an advisory opinion from the Court as to the legal principles applicable with respect to the matter under debate.[31]

As to the question of whether the ICJ should exercise its discretionary power to decline to exercise its jurisdiction, the Court was equally unambiguous. The Court noted that it had never, in the exercise of its discretionary power, refused to give an opinion on grounds of judicial propriety, and stated that:

> Given its responsibilities as the "principal judicial organ of the United Nations" (Article 92 of the United Nations Charter), the Court should in principle not decline to give an advisory opinion. In accordance with its consistent jurisprudence, only "compelling reasons" should lead the Court to refuse its opinion.[32]

The Court then considered all of the reasons submitted to it for exercising its discretion not to issue an Advisory Opinion (as listed above: lack of consent; the effect of an Advisory Opinion on political negotiations; lack of requisite facts; lack of useful purpose and judicial propriety). None of these were considered by the Court to constitute a "compelling reason" to refuse an Advisory Opinion.

Given the clarity and ease with which the Court dealt with these arguments, it is impossible to avoid the sense that the arguments submitted by most Western states against the Court's intervention were primarily of a political rather than a legal nature. Indeed, even those national submissions which are framed in more legalistic terms rely as much on political considerations about the undesirability of judicial involvement in a contentious international dispute rather than on international legal precedent. It is surely paradoxical that the objections to the Court's involvement in a "political" issue carried such little weight as legal arguments. As Scobbie has noted:

> It is not the request for an opinion in the instant proceedings [the request for an advisory opinion] that is diversionary, but the claims of those states that the political implications of the request should cause the court to refuse to entertain the case. Such a claim contradicts the settled jurisprudence of the court is irrelevant as an objection to the Court's exercise of its competence.[33]

Nevertheless, the fact that the "political" objection to the Court's exercise of jurisdiction was so central to so many national submissions, despite its legal flimsiness (as the unanimity of the ICJ on the topic indicates) is interesting in itself. There are good reasons why Western states may have wished to keep the issue of the separation wall within the realm of politics as much as possible, rather than submitting it for legal consideration. It is possible, for example, that the European Union, by opposing the jurisdiction of the ICJ in relation to the separation wall, may have wished to use its submission as an opportunity to counter Israeli accusations of Europe's pro-Palestinian bias.

It is also worth noting that most states which opposed the intervention of the ICJ in the issue also made extensive positive reference in their submissions to the predominance of the "Middle East road-map" in any future peace strategy. Canada, for example considered that "these issues would be more effectively addressed in a broader negotiation context than within the procedural limitations of a judicial hearing."[34] Australia, likewise, considered that "...the giving of an advisory opinion could have "a harmful effect on current initiatives aimed at achieving a settlement..."[35] Responses such as these, which were widely expressed in the national submissions, do more than express a vague commitment to the value of peace negotiations; they also reveal assumptions about law as a regime of closure and certainty as opposed to an "open-ended" domain of politics as the "art of the possible."

However, what is fascinating about such arguments is not simply their political motivations, but their paradoxical relation to legal discourse. On the one hand, these arguments claim that the question before the Court is not sufficiently "legal" to justify the involvement of the court and is better suited to political negotiation. On the other hand, as we have seen, this objection carries little weight as a legal impediment to the Court's jurisdiction and thus operates mainly as political discourse. These arguments presuppose that the distinction between the legal and the political needs to be rigidly maintained, but are not themselves framed in sufficiently "legal" terms to affect the outcome of the Court's deliberations. By expecting the Court to accommodate political arguments in order to delineate international law as distinct from international politics, these submissions unwittingly collapse the possibility of making a categorical distinction between the legal and the political.

This insistence on the limitation of the Court's jurisdiction to the domain of the legal appears particularly curious given the way in which international law has always been so obviously enmeshed in international politics (or, as Rosalyn Higgins might more elegantly put it; in "process"). To call for a categorical split between the legal and the political seems even more out of place considering the past willingness of the ICJ to entertain explicitly "political" cases. In this context, it seems worthwhile to explore some aspects of the positivist ancestry of this expectation that law and politics are categorically separable and distinct fields of knowledge.

International Law: A Heritage of Positivism

The drawing of a strict boundary between the legal and the political reflects what Higgins describes as the "classical" view of International Law. This was expressed most definitively by Judges Fitzmaurice and Spender in a joint dissenting opinion in the *South-West Africa Cases*:

> We are not unmindful of, nor are we insensible to, the various considerations of a non-judicial character, social, humanitarian and other...but these are matters for the political rather than for the legal arena. They cannot be allowed to deflect us from our duty of reaching a conclusion strictly on the basis of what we believe to be the correct legal view.[36]

Such an understanding also recalls a positivist jurisprudential tradition in which legal decisions are considered to be of a categorically different order from political or moral judgments. Austin's positivism, for example, conceived of law as a set of commands which flow from the sovereign will: if a command does not originate in the sovereign will, then it is not law.[37]

For positivism, any conflation of the legal with the political would undermine the possibility of autonomous, self-contained, knowable legal rules with a clear provenance in the sovereign will. Significantly the inter-mixing of law and politics would undermine the possibility of genuine legal judgment: if the boundary between law and politics is muddied, then how can it be possible to know whether a judicial decision represents the instantiation of the law as opposed to the mere political opinion of a judge? However, in order for this autonomy of law to be maintained, how can the dangerous boundary between the legal and the political be policed? The drawing of a categorical distinction between the legal and the political presupposes a third position: that of the sovereign, which belongs neither entirely to the domain of the legal nor to that of the political. Positivist legal theory presupposes the sovereign not only as the locus of "legal" authority but as the ultimate guarantee of a coherent distinction between the legal and the political. Unsurprisingly, Austin did not consider international law to be law at all, but "positive morality," which was observed by states either due to a sense of moral obligation or fear of retribution.

The more sophisticated positivism of H.L.A. Hart, while rejecting Austin's reduction of law to the coercive commands of an unlimited sovereign, nevertheless also insisted on a the necessity of a clear categorical distinction between the legal and the political. Hart argued that Austin's understanding of law failed to take account of the way in which legal authority also relies on the habitual obedience of legal rules and through the legal subject's feeling of being "bound" by legal duties.[38] Hart conceived of law as a system of rules: Some rules (primary rules) impose obligations on individuals, while others (secondary rules) delegate legal power, thereby providing the means by which primary rules can be correctly created, interpreted and altered. The most important of these secondary rules is the "rule of recognition," which is the foundational legal rule by which the validity of other rules can be determined. Hart described the rule of recognition as "a remedy for the uncertainty of the regime of primary rules"[39]; and as "a rule for conclusive identification of the rules of obligation."[40] The rule of recognition is more than just a rule of interpretation: it is the rule by which law can be identified as law and distinguished from non-law.

Hart famously considered that "international law," while sharing many of the substantive moral and social qualities of national (or "municipal") law, could not properly be described as "law," but as resembling formally a "simple regime of primary and secondary rules."[41] Crucially, for Hart, international law lacked the most important precondition of legally binding rules; a "rule of recognition": a basic rule whose application can determine whether the other primary and secondary rules indeed qualify as valid law. As Hart says,

> ...We have not something which we have in municipal law: namely a way of demonstrating the validity of individual rules by reference to some ultimate rule of the system.[42]

More importantly, international law is not "binding" for Hart, because it is not supported by organized sanctions. He notes that "all speculation about the existence of law begins from the assumption that its existence at least makes certain conduct obligatory."[43] The problem that international law poses for positivism, as Hart has articulated, is that in the absence of a rule of recognition or, indeed, a global (sovereign) regime of enforcement, international law becomes difficult to distinguish from an statement of political or moral values.[44] There is, as Hart notes, no international legislature or police force. Hart's positivism still presupposes the existence of a sovereign power underpinning the legal order, albeit one whose legal capacity is constituted by a habitually obeyed rule of recognition. Ultimately, for Hart, the physical capacity of the sovereign power to impose sanctions (to "organize repression and to punish crime"[45]) operates as a necessary guarantee of the coherency of municipal law, and enables a coherent formal distinction to be made between the legal and the non-legal.

In contrast to the "dualism" of Hart and Austin, who consider international law and national law to have entirely distinct sources of legitimacy, there is also a different positivist tradition which considers the international legal system not only to be inseparable from national law, but superior to it. This "monist" view of international law finds its foundations in the work of Hans Kelsen. Kelsen's "pure theory of law" conceived of law as a normative system governed by its own inner "scientific" logic: "Law is not, as it is sometimes said, a rule. It is a set of rules having the kind of unity we understand by a system."[46] For Kelsen, sovereignty was not a legal or political fact, but a normative construct; "a concept created by law and concerned only with law."[47] Kelsen described sovereignty as "the presupposed assumption of a system of norms... ...whose validity is not to be derived from a superior order." For Kelsen, the unity of a legal system does not flow from its relation to a sovereign authority, but from the linkage of laws to a chain of legal authority; the validity of a legal norm is always tested in relation to another legal norm. This chain of legal authority leads ultimately to the Kantian guarantee which, for Kelsen, underpins the coherency of the legal system: the *grundnorm*. The *grundnorm* is the basic norm of the legal system; the originary principle that must be presupposed in order for the validity of laws to be determined and for law to be ("scientifically") distinguished from non-law.

Kelsen saw international law not simply as a set of agreements between sovereign states, but as a universal legal system in itself; a sovereign legal order based on global legal norms, from which national political authority could be derived. In the first edition of *The Pure Theory of Law*, Kelsen described international law as a positing a basic norm by which the validity of the *grundnorms* of municipal legal systems can be recognized.[48] The value of such an approach is clear: if international law is the normative basis for recognizing that state sovereignty is based on control over territory, then changes to state sovereignty (such as those that result from a revolution or decolonization) can also be given a legal justification.[49] Roger Cotterrell notes that "Kelsen's rejection of state sovereignty entails not only a rejection of the claim that the state is above the law, but also of the claim that there can be no higher allegiance and legal obligation than to the nation state." For Kelsen, international law is the ultimate legal system, the key to assessing the legitimacy of state sovereignty and the validity of national laws.[50] Moreover, Kelsen's normative solution avoids the problem of the "location" of sovereignty in international law, because it treats the international legal order as a sovereign entity in itself. As Carl Schmidt has said *apropos* of normative legal theory, "The sovereign......the engineer of the great [legal] machine has been radically pushed aside. The machine now runs by itself."[51]

A contemporary attempt to re-conceptualize a monistic account of international law can be found in legal cosmopolitanism. Adherents of legal cosmopolitanism typically argue that the emerging global political system relies on complex networks of interconnectedness between states, officials and international institutions, a reliance that renders obsolete traditional notions of sovereignty. Consequently, for legal cosmopolitanism, it becomes necessary to re-conceptualize law in non-formalist terms, which do not involve the creation or enforcement of law by the sovereign.[52] Instead, from the perspective of some writers, concept such "civilian inviolability" offers an alternative basic norm for an international legal order in a time of globalization, providing a normative foundation in the place of obsolete discourses of sovereignty.[53]

In between the dualism of Hart and the monism of Kelsen, there are also various pragmatic shades of thought that seek to maintain the normative integrity (if not the autonomy) of an international legal order.[54] The British ICJ judge, Rosalyn Higgins, for example, describes international law as a set of normative obligations which constitute a legal process notwithstanding the absence of effective sanctions. For Higgins, the state's obligation to submit to international law is drawn from a combination of normative consensus and reciprocal self-interest.[55] In opposition to a rules-based notion of international law, she sees the international legal order as a "process" in which decision-makers have to make difficult choices that necessarily involve a political as well as a legal dimension.

Policy Considerations, although they differ from "rules" are an integral part of the decision-making process which we call international law; the assessment of so-called extra-legal considerations as *part of the legal process*, just as is reference to the accumulation of past decisions and norms. A refusal to acknowledge political and social factors cannot keep law "neutral." for even such a refusal is not without political and social consequence. There is no avoiding the essential relationship between law and politics.[56]

The brief account given above of the jurisprudence of sovereignty in international law allows us to examine some of the theoretical assumptions that were made by the "international community" in their submissions to the ICJ in *Legal Consequences of the Construction of a Wall in Occupied Palestinian Territory*. To begin with, their insistence on the categorical distinction between law and politics means that pragmatic approaches to international law as "process" are of limited value in understanding the national submissions. Moreover, the desire by states to exclude "political" matters from the scope of the ICJ runs entirely contrary to a monistic conception of international law, which situates the international legal order as the touchstone by which the legitimacy of all political authority is evaluated. If anything, the national submissions to the ICJ, which echo the "classical" version of international law, broadly reflect a positivist conception of the demarcation of law from the political realm. This, of course, raises the obvious jurisprudential problems endemic to the positivist project, particularly where international law is concerned; how can the porous border between international law and "the political" be sustained? Is there a "third" sovereign position unwittingly presupposed by these submissions (i.e.: a sovereign position capable of delineating the scope of "positive" international law)? If it is possible to speak of such a sovereign position in the international legal order, just where, or what might that presupposed sovereign position be?

International Law and the "Empty Place" of Sovereignty

In any attempt to articulate the location of a presupposed sovereign position in relation to international law, the obvious temptation would be to imagine this position to be occupied by the world's only superpower: the United States. On first examination, this would appear to be consistent with the insistence by so many states in their submissions to the ICJ that the "road-map" is the most appropriate forum for criticism of Israel's wall. The United States, as Israel's greatest ally (and also, incidentally, as a significant sponsor of the Palestinian National Authority) is also the main sponsor of the "road-map".[57]

Additionally, such an interpretation of the United States as playing the role of a "global" sovereign fits with the United States' ambivalent attitude to international law. On the one hand, the United States claims to embody the values of international law (principles of constitutionalism, democracy, etc.) However, the United States is famously resistant to the application of international law to its own affairs, as evidenced by its vigorous rejection of the jurisdiction of the International Criminal Court, for example.[58] Such ambivalence about the relationship to an international legal order resonates with a paradoxical aspect of sovereignty: While the legal sovereign is the embodiment of the legal order (i.e.: the sovereign is the "most legal" thing), sovereign power is also never entirely contained by legal justifications; there is always some element of sovereignty eludes legality, that is extraneous to the legal order.

To reduce the presupposed location of sovereignty in international law to the foreign policy of the United States, however, would fail to do justice to the complexity of the relationship between the legal and the political. Moreover, it would ignore a crucial feature of the international legal order (and indeed, of the democratic tradition)—that the location of sovereignty is an empty space! This is perhaps best illustrated by Claude Lefort's account of the French revolution, of which the crucial "democratic invention" was the requirement that the political system maintain the "emptiness" of the sovereign position. The political system must ensure that the occupier does not become "glued" to the position: "Power is and

remains democratic [only] when it proves to belong to no one."[59] In Slavoj
Zizek's words, Lefort has described the locus of sovereignty in the age of
liberal democracy as a "purely symbolic empty space of Power that no real
subject can ever fill out."[60] This account of sovereignty is relevant not only
to municipal law, but also to the operation of any sovereign position
presupposed in relation to the international legal order. Lefort's description
of modern sovereignty as "empty" is consistent with the principle of formal
legal equality between sovereign states[61] and it also helps to describe the
special position of the United Nations in international law. The exercise of
power by the "international community" under the auspices of the United
Nations (formally at least) is exercised irrespective of which precisely
which particular states constitute the will of the "international community"
at a particular moment in time.[62]

Despite this, one could argue that the United States has indeed become
"glued" to a position of sovereignty in relation to the international legal
order, particularly since the end of the cold war. For example, the decision
to invade Iraq without clear support from the United Nations might be
taken as an example of this. Indeed, the principle upon which the United
States abrogates to itself the sovereign position is often that it acts to
defend the normative foundations of an international legal order (democracy, human rights, etc.), rather than submitting to the expectation that it
too should be bound by the judgment of an "international community".
Nonetheless, this analysis would surely overstate the omnipotence of the
United States (as events in Iraq forcefully demonstrate), however grandiose
the United States' own view of its own role in spreading "democracy". It
should be recalled that "unilateral" military action without United Nations
backing is neither unique to the United States nor is it an especially recent
phenomenon. Indeed, it has been the norm, rather than the exception of the
modern period, with the notable exceptions of the Korean War and the
invasion of Kuwait.

How, then, can one conceive of the exceptional role the United States
claims for itself or, indeed, which much of the "international community"
presupposes for the United States? Lefort's account of the French
revolution becomes relevant again here. Lefort explores the way in which
the Jacobins saw their role as one of ensuring that the sovereign position
remained empty (by beheading all those who appeared to come too close
to it!): "...the terror is revolutionary in that it forbids anyone to occupy the
place of power. In this sense, it has a democratic character."[63] However,
Zizek neatly supplements Lefort's account with the following observation:

On the level of the enunciated, the Jacobin safeguards the emptiness of the
locus of power; he prevents anybody from occupying this place—but does
he not function as a kind of King-in-reverse—that is to say, is not the very
position of enunciation from which he acts and speaks the position of
absolute power? Is not safeguarding the empty locus of power the most
cunning and at the same time the most brutal, unconditional way of
occupying it?[64]

Does this not describe the "sovereign" role that the United States
presupposes for itself in, for example, its legal and political response to the
West Bank wall? Not so much as actually representing global sovereignty
in an international legal order, but as the agency that abrogates to itself the
right to maintain the universality and emptiness of the locus of sovereignty
in the international sphere? Is this not also what is most unconvincing about
the claim that the "war on terrorism" is fought in the name of the universal
values (democracy, human rights etc.) that characterize international law?[65]

This perspective also throws a different light on the other national
submissions to the ICJ that we have examined. The submissions undoubtedly presuppose a special role for Western powers (and for the United
States in particular) in the determination of the future of the Middle East,
not least through their almost universal endorsement of the "road-map" as
opposed to the involvement of the ICJ. Ironically, this special role is framed
not only as a means of "resolving" the issue of Palestinian self-determination, but also as a means of protecting the universalism of the international
legal order from an entanglement in the political; This is reflected back in
the predominance of procedural arguments about jurisdiction and judicial
propriety among the national submissions to the ICJ.

However, the insistence in those submissions on a distinction between
law and politics does not so much presuppose that there actually *is* a
sovereign actor in international law capable of maintaining the division
between law and politics, but more accurately presupposes that the
sovereign position in the international legal order always *remains empty*,
even when this is obviously not the case. The apparent paradox of Western
states presenting to the Court an essentially political argument for
separating the legal from the political in *Legal Consequences of the
Construction of a Wall in Occupied Palestinian Territory* can now be seen
in a different light in the context of Zizek's reading of Lefort because these
states are not so much attempting to engage in a "legal" defense of the
construction of the Israeli wall, but are themselves seeking to occupy the

insidious position of the protector of the emptiness of the sovereign position. By speaking *for* the universalism of international law, while denying the possibility of its application in a case where its relevance is undeniable, Western states, in their submissions to the ICJ, have sought to claim for themselves the mantle of the "sovereign-in-reverse": By doing so, they have sought to act as the power behind the international community's empty throne.

Notes

1. See "Legal Consequences of the Construction of a Wall in the Occupied Palestinian Territory, Advisory Opinion," ICJ REP. (9 July 2004) available at <http://www.icj-cij.org/icjwww/idocket/imwp/imwpframe.htm> (checked 20 August 2005).
2. For more information on the impact of the separation barrier on the Palestinian population, see United Nations Relief and Works Agency for Palestinian Refugees in the Near East (UNRWA), "Special Report on the West Bank Barrier" (2003) <www.un.org/unrwa/emergency/barrier> (checked 20 August 2005).; United Nations Office for the Co-ordination of Humanitarian Affairs (OCHA), UPDATE—Humanitarian Impact of the West Bank Barrier on Palestinian Community (March 2005), http://www.reliefweb. int/hic-opt/ > (checked 20 August 2005).
3. See, "Report of the Special Rapporteur of the Commission on Human Rights, John Dugard, on the Situation of Human Rights in the Palestinian Territories Occupied by Israel since 1967," UN ESCOR, 60th Sess., UN Doc. E/CN.4/2004/6 (8 September 2003).
4. See "Guinea, Malaysia, Pakistan and Syrian Arab Republic: Draft Resolution," UN SCOR, UN Doc. S/2003/980 (14 October 2003).
5. See UN GA Res. 10/13, (27 October 2003). This session of the General Assembly was a resumption of the tenth Emergency Special Session. *See also* Report of the Secretary-General Prepared Pursuant to General Assembly Resolution ES-10/13, UN GAOR, Doc. No. A/ES-10/248 (24 November 2003)
6. See UN GA Res 10/14, (12 December 2003).
7. See also "Interpretation of Peace Treaties with Bulgaria, Hungary and Romania, Advisory Opinion," 1950 ICJ REP. 70 (March 30); "Legality of the Threat or Use of Nuclear Weapons, Advisory Opinion," 19961 ICJ REP. 226(8 July), at 232-233.
8. See "Written Statement of Israel on Jurisdiction and Propriety (Legal Consequences arising from the Construction of the Wall being built by Israel: Request for Advisory Opinion)," (30 January 2004), at 116, para.9.9.

9. Written statements were submitted (in order of submission) by Guinea, Saudi Arabia, the Arab League, Egypt, Cameroon, Russian Federation, Australia, Palestine, United Nations, Kuwait, Lebanon, Canada, Syria, Switzerland, Israel, Yemen, United States of America, Morocco, Indonesia, Organisation of the Islamic Conference, France, Italy, Sudan, South Africa, Germany, Japan, Norway, United Kingdom, Pakistan, Czech Republic, Greece, Ireland (on behalf of the European Union), Ireland (on its own behalf), Cyprus, Brazil, Namibia, Malta, Malaysia, Netherlands, Cuba, Sweden, Spain, Belgium, Palau, Federated States of Micronesia, Marshall Islands, Senegal; and Democratic People's Republic of Korea.

10. *Supra* note 8, at 57-88.

11. See "Certain Expenses of the United Nations (Article 17, para.2 of the Charter), Advisory Opinion," 1962 ICJ REP. 151 (20 July), at 155.

12. See "Written Statement of the United Kingdom of Great Britain and Northern Ireland (Legal Consequences of the Construction of a Wall in the Occupied Palestinian Territory, Request for Advisory Opinion)," (30 January 2004), at 8, para.2.17.

13. *Id.*

14. *Id.*, para.2.18.

15. See "Written Statement of the Minister of Foreign Affairs of the Republic of Ireland on behalf of the European Union (Legal Consequences of the Construction of a Wall in the Occupied Palestinian Territory, Request for Advisory Opinion)," (30 January 2004).

16. See "Written Statement of the Government of Japan (Legal Consequences of the Construction of a Wall in the Occupied Palestinian Territory, Request for Advisory Opinion)," (30 January 2004), at 2, para.3.

17. *Id.*, at 1, para.1.

18. See "Written Statement of the Kingdom of Spain (Legal Consequences of the Construction of a Wall in the Occupied Palestinian Territory, Request for Advisory Opinion)," (30 January 2004).

19. See "Note Verbale from the Republic of Cameroon (Legal Consequences of the Construction of a Wall in the Occupied Palestinian Territory, Request for Advisory Opinion)," (28 January 2004).

20. See "Written Statement of the French Republic (Legal Consequences of the Construction of a Wall in the Occupied Palestinian Territory, Request for Advisory Opinion)," (30 January 2004), at para.3.

21. *Ibid.*, at para.6.

22. *Supra* note 8, para. 1.18.

23. *Id.*, at 48, para. 3.69.

24. *Id.*, at 13, paras. 2.14 - 2.15.

25. For details of the legal status of Palestine and the Palestine Liberation Organisation, *see* UN GA Res 29/3237 (22 November 1974); UN GA Res 43/160 (9 December 1988); UN GA Res 43/177, (15 December 1988); UN GA Res 52/250 (7 July 1998).

26. The issue of the Court's competence to deal with the matter was not the only jurisdictional question at stake in the case. A number of other procedural objections were raised as to the capacity of the General Assembly to refer such a case to the ICJ (under Article 96.1) and as to the procedural propriety of the Emergency Session of the General Assembly. All of these arguments were also rejected by the majority judgement of the ICJ.

27. See *supra* note 1, at para.37. See also *"Western Sahara, Advisory Opinion,"* ICJ REP. 12 (16 October 1975), at 18, para. 15.

28. See *supra* note 1, at para.41.

29. *Id.* See also "Application for Review of Judgement No.158 of the United Nations, Advisory Opinion," ICJ REP 172 (12 July 1973).

30. See "Legality of the Threat or Use of Nuclear Weapons, Advisory Opinion," 1 1996 ICJ REP. 226(8 July), at 234, para. 13; *See also supra* note 1, para. 41.

31. See "Interpretation of the Agreement of 25 March 1951 between the WHO and Egypt," 1980 ICJ REP. 73 (20 Dec.), at 87, para.33. *See also supra* note 1, at para.41.

32. See *supra* note 1, para.44. Examples of the "consistent" jurisprudence to which the Court refers can be found in: "Interpretation of Peace Treaties with Bulgaria, Hungary and Romania, First Phase, Advisory Opinion," 1950 ICJ REP. 71 (March 30), "Difference Relating to Immunity from Legal Process of a Special Rapporteur of the Commission of Human Rights, Advisory Opinion," 1999 1 ICJ REP. 62 (29 April), at 78-79, para.29; *supra* note 11, *at* 155; *supra* note 30, *at* 235-236.

33. See Ian Scobbie, "Legal Consequences of the Construction of a Wall in the Occupied Palestinian Territory, Request for Advisory Opinion—An Analysis of issues concerning competence and Procedure," HOTUNG PROJECT—LAW, HUMAN RIGHTS AND PEACE BUILDING IN THE MIDDLE EAST—Paper No.1, p.19 www.soas.ac.uk/lawpeacemideast. See also Ian Scobbie, "Words My Mother Never Taught Me—In Defense of the International Court," 99 AMERICAN. J. INT'L LAW 76 (2005); Geoffrey Watson, "The 'Wall' Decisions in Legal and Political Context," 99 AMERICAN. J. INT'L LAW 6 (2005); Michla Pomerance, "The ICJ's Advisory Jurisdiction and the Crumbling Wall Between the Political and the Judicial," 99 AMERICAN. J. INT'L LAW 26 (2005).

34. See "Written Statement of the Government of Canada" (Legal Consequences of the Construction of a Wall in the Occupied Palestinian Territory, Request for Advisory Opinion), (30 January 2004).

35. See "Written statement of the Government of Australia" (Legal Consequences of the Construction of a Wall in the Occupied Palestinian Territory, Request for Advisory Opinion), (29 January 2004), at 5.

36. See "South West Africa Cases, Preliminary Objections" 1962 ICJ REP 319 (21 December), at 466, also quoted in ROSALYN HIGGINS, PROBLEMS AND PROCESS—INTERNATIONAL LAW AND HOW WE U.S.E IT 4 (2001), . See also "South West Africa Cases" 1966 ICJ REP. 4 (18 July), at 6, para.49.

37. "...Every positive law, or every law strictly so called, is a direct or circuitous command of a monarch or sovereign number in the character of a political superior... ...And being a *command* (and therefore flowing from a determinate source), every positive law is a law proper, or a law properly so called." John Austin, *The Province Of Jurisprudence Determined* 134, 193-195 (1954).

38. See H.L.A HART, THE CONCEPT OF LAW 96 (1982).

39. *Id.*, at 92.

40. *Id.*

41. *Id.*, at 232.

42. *Id.*, at .234.

43. *Id.*, at 212.

44. A current debate explores whether it may be possible to derive a notion of "international legal sovereignty" from the mutuality of obligations created by states' recognition of each other. However, such a notion of sovereignty is subject to the relative strengths of the states involved; the "mutuality" of such recognition invariably takes place in an environment of unequal power between parties. See Stephen Krasner, *Sovereignty: Organized Hypocrisy* 43-72 (1999).

45. See *supra* note 38, at 214.

46. See HANS KELSEN, GENERAL THEORY OF LAW AND STATE 3 (1961).

47. See MARTIN LOUGHLIN, SWORD AND SCALES; AN EXAMINATION OF THE RELATIONSHIP BETWEEN LAW AND POLITICS 126 (2000).

48. See HANS KELSEN, INTRODUCTION TO THE PROBLEMS OF LEGAL THEORY 61-62 (2002).

49. See ROGER COTTERRELL, THE POLITICS OF JURISPRUDENCE 115 (1992)

50. However, this approach, which was outlined in the first edition of Kelsen's *Pure Theory of Law*, was also problematic for Kelsen, as it effectively treated public international law as the *grundnorm* of all municipal legal systems. Notably, Kelsen's "solution" neglects the fact that the expansive system of modern public international law is a fairly recent arrival on the legal scene. Indeed, in the second edition of *The Pure Theory of Law*, there is evidence

that Kelsen retreated from this earlier position. See HANS KELSEN, PURE THEORY OF LAW 214-215 (1967).

51. *Id.,* at 112, quoting CARL SCHMIDT, POLITICAL THEOLOGY: FOUR CHAPTERS ON THE CONCEPT OF SOVEREIGNTY (George Schwab trans., 1985). See also Andy Olson, "most of the papers were originally delivered at the 7th conference of the International Centre for Contemporary Middle Eastern Studies held at Eastern Mediterranean University in Northern Cyprus, April 29th to May 1, 2004; and then revised and updated for your book. Perhaps you could mention the two Haifa's and Dhair's were from the conference of the International Association of Contemporary Iraqi Studies held at East London University the 1st and 2nd of September 2005. "An Empire of the Scholars: Transnational Lawyers and the Rule of Opinion Juris," 29 *Perspectives on Political Science* 23 (2000).

52. See Kenneth W. Abbott, Robert. O. Keohane, Andrew Moravcsik, Anne-Marie Slaughter & Duncan Snidal, "The Concept of Legalisation," *in* POWER AND GOVERNANCE IN A PARTIALLY GLOBALISED WORLD 132-152 (Robert. O. Keohane ed., 2002).

53. See Anne-Marie Slaughter & William Burke-White, "An International Constitutional Moment," 43 HARVARD INT'L LAW REV. 1 (2002). For a critique of Legal Cosmopolitanism, *see* Jean Cohen, "Whose Sovereignty? Empire versus International Law," 18 ETHICS AND INTERNATIONAL AFFAIRS 1 (2004).

54. Denis Lloyd, for example, argues in "dualistic" terms that international law, though not properly "legal." can still give rise to obligations which can be incorporated into municipal law without undermining the notion of state sovereignty. See DENIS LLOYD, THE IDEA OF LAW 190 (1983).

55. See Higgins, *supra* note 36, ch.1. The opening words of Higgins' book are: "International law is not law. It is a normative system." For a discussion of the role of consent as a moral basis for obligation in international law, *see* ALLEN BUCHANAN, JU.S.TICE, LEGITIMACY AND SELF-DETERMINATION: MORAL FOUNDATIONS FOR INTERNATIONAL LAW 301-313 (2004).

56. Rosalyn Higins, "Integrations of Authority and Control: Trends in the Literature of International Law and International Relations," in TOWARD WORLD ORDER AND HUMAN DIGNITY: ESSAYS IN HONOR OF MYRES S. MCDOUGAL 79-94 , at 85 (Myres Smith McDougal, William Michael Reisman, Burns H. Weston eds., 1976). See also Anthony Carty, "Review Essay: Higgins, Rosalyn, Problems and Process: International Law and How We Use It." 8 EURO. J. OF INT'L LAW 181 (1997).

57. See <http://www.state.gov/r/pa/prs/ps/2003/20062.htm> (checked 20 August 2005).

58. See further UNITED STATES HEGEMONY AND THE FOUNDATIONS OF INTERNATIONAL LAW (Michael Byers & George Nolte, eds., 2003).
59. See CLAUDE LEFORT, DEMOCRACY AND POLITICAL THEORY 27 (1988), See also SLAVOJ ZIZEK, FOR THEY KNOW NOT WHAT THEY DO 267 (1991).
60. Slavoj Zizek, "The Spectre of Ideology," in MAPPING IDEOLOGY 29 (Slavoj Zizek ed., 1997).
61. United Nations Charter, 1945, Article 2.1.
62. The allocation of the "big five" permanent seats on the Security Council (China, France, Russia, UK, U.S.A) is of course a notable exception to this principle.
63. *Supra* Lefort note 59, at 86.
64. *Supra* Zizek, note 59, at 268.
65. This point is illustrated by the United Kingdom's interpretation of United Nations Security Council Resolution 1441 (UN S/Res/1441 (6 November 2002), which authorized United Nations member states to uphold previous Security Council resolutions against Iraq. Although the United States and United Kingdom were unable to secure an unambiguous endorsement by the Security Council of their invasion of Iraq, British politicians argued that under Resolution 1441, the United Kingdom and United States were authorized to act *in the place of* the United Nations, and indeed to "defend" the values of international law. In this sense, the United Kingdom sought to justify its role as a protector of the "empty place" of international sovereignty, even if this same international legal order had failed to recognize the legality of the United Kingdom's action.

11

ENEMIES OF PEACE
The Tripartite American Alliance to Prevent a Resolution to the Palestine-Israel Conflict

ഇന്ദ്ര

William W. Haddad

Why Palestine? For almost sixty years, politicians, students, academics, and common citizens have asked this question. What is there about the Palestinian-Israeli conflict that galvanizes people and their opinions? Of course there are many answers. For some it is the issue of colonization; that the answer to the question of Palestine is that it is the last vestige of an imperial era when one country, Britain, determined the fate of a darwinianly inferior people. For those who see the Israeli-Palestinian issue through this lens, the analogy is Ethiopia. During the late nineteenth century, all of Africa was colonized and no one seemed to care. But the fall of Ethiopia to the Italians in 1928 raised a storm of anger throughout Africa and the remainder of the world. The same can be said of the Arab world. Thoroughly colonized or subjugated after World War I, no one seemed to mind until the formation of the state of Israel. Supporters of Israel maintain that those who focus solely on the issue of Palestine, arguing that it is unique, are mistaken and therefore probably anti-Semitic.[1] This bloc believes that Palestine was part of a general pattern of re-organization of the Middle East and the world, and that to argue for the singularity of this conflict hides an anti-Jewish agenda. The response should be that the anti-Semitic canard is absurd. Had Palestine been colonized by Swedes, the response of the Palestinians and Arabs would have been the same: Wherever colonization included demographic change, the response was violent: south Africa, the Americas, northern Ireland, and Algeria, are good examples.

Others, for example Edward Said, have said that the Palestine issue is unique and has garnered support because it is a question of justice. Having sympathy for and an understanding of the victims of the Holocaust is imperative. But transforming that injustice into a grant to allow the Jewish people to in turn destroy the Palestinians and their national identity is intolerable. The Holocaust and the transformation of Palestine are both injustices and need to be condemned.[2]

For the supporters of Israel, the overriding issue is the Holocaust. Had there been no Hitler or no anti-Semitism, there would have been no need for a Jewish state as a refuge. If some have to suffer minimally, this is not too large a price to pay for the safety of the world's most hated people. This line of argument continues that historic Palestine comprises less than one percent of the total land mass of the Arab world. For the Arabs to demand this small parcel was greedy, while the survivors of the Holocaust were starving.

Sixty years of fighting for the same land has created a legacy of mistrust on both sides. U.S. support for Israel has alienated the former from much of the world, especially the Islamic one and Europe. From whence did these barriers to reconciliation emanate? And what is the solution?

To answer this question simply is to state that the Jewish state, with the overwhelming support of the U.S., has, for the present, won the Palestinian-Israeli conflict. What we are witnessing today is no more than the attempt of the victors to impose their will, and the Palestinians struggling to prevent an unfair "peace" to be forced upon them. Will the victors choose to make a peace so generous that the losers have no desire for revenge? Or will the peace be so Draconian that the defeated will not be able to inflict revenge. It is the latter path that the Sharon government has chosen. The current situation brings to an end the forty years of conflict between the two antagonists that began in the mid-1960s. Whatever the final result of the "negotiations" between the two sides, it is doubtful that this peace will be the last one. An historian can be forgiven for imagining that all of the borders of geographic Syria are artificial and as such will not stand the test of time. What is occurring in this first decade of the twenty-first century is therefore likely ephemeral, though important.

Since the peace process envisioned by the Oslo Accord of 1992-93 involved negotiation and compromise (that is, to make a peace that was generous from the victor's point-of-view), what is curious about the current discussions over the terms of surrender is that they have powerful enemies. Since the beginning of Oslo, there has emerged strong cabals who are bitterly opposed to any negotiated settlement between Palestinians and Israelis, and desire only a complete and final destruction of any Palestinian claim to rights and statehood. It is common to think that the most important of these groups as Neoconservatives, dominated by American Jews with a strong attachment to Israel.

But to think of the movement to stop a negotiated settlement between Israelis and Palestinians as only American Jewish supporters of Israel is to not understand the Neocon movement. More correct is to identify the opposition as at least three-pronged: American imperialists, Christian fundamentalists, and the Neoconservative supporters of Israel.

The first of these three, those who long for an American Empire, is focused on the Project for a New American Century (PNAC) founded in 1997. It has been arguing since its inception for the war against Iraq. Marginalized during the presidency of Bill Clinton, it has since January 2001 been one of the three legs that has supported Bush Jr. in his attempt to remake the Middle East and institute a "Crusade," to use one of Bush Jr.'s terms, to reform Islam. The American Imperialists have close ties to American businesses and view the world as something that must be managed for profit. The Bush family ties to the Carlyle Group, an investment firm with plans to exploit the natural gas and oil of Iraq and Central Asia, is a good example of the connection between power and money. Dick Cheney's bond as the former head of the contracting firm Halliburton, is another prime example. What this group wishes to accomplish is the pacification, by force if necessary, of those who question American imperial dominance, or who threaten their desire to impose a *pax Americana* in the Middle East. One of the many reasons for invading Iraq was to remove from the scene a strong supporter of the Palestinian people. Equally important was the American imperialist[3] belief that the world would be a better place to live if everyone followed the model of American democracy. In public they do not speak openly of the benefits of empire, but strongly imply that an American-led world would be a better place for all. They also speak in terms of educating and guiding, not of conquering, dominating, and exploiting. Still there is the occasional slip-up by the Imperialists. Ron Suskind wrote of an unnamed senior adviser to Bush Jr. who said of Suskind that he was "in the reality based community... That's not how the world works anymore. We're an empire now, and when we act we create our own reality."[4]

Among the leaders of the PNAC who have thoroughly embedded themselves in the Bush Jr. administration are Vice President Dick Cheney, one of the PNAC's founders; Secretary of Defense Donald Rumsfield, also one of its founders; World Bank president and former deputy Secretary of Defense Paul Wolfowitz; Eliot Abrams, a member of Bush's National Security Council and son-in-law of Norman Podhoretz, editor *emeritus* of *Commentary*, the Bible of the Neoconservatives; John Bolton, Undersecretary of Defense for Arms Control; Richard Pearle, an administrator during the Reagan presidency; Bruce Jackson, former VP at Lockheed-Martin and member of the Republican Party Platform committee; and William Kristol, writer for the pro-Israel *Weekly Standard*—about whom more later. What characterizes all of these men is: their belief in the efficacy of American military power, their view of Israel as a bastion of capitalist democracy in the Middle East, their generally assiduous avoidance of serving in the military, and their belief in unfettered capitalism. Besides being well placed in the Bush Jr. administration, they are in command positions in the Defense Department, Pentagon, and in the Congress of the U.S. They are not generally enamored of the rule of law, view with disdain Old Europe, international relations, and the need to compromise with allies. As for the United Nations, it is their favorite bogeyman more harmful than useful. The UN's resolutions are, generally, archaic, contentious, and outmoded, to paraphrase former Secretary of State Madeleine Albright. The Geneva Conventions on warfare, according to Bush's Attorney General Alberto Gonzales, can be set aside in times of war.

With the reins of power firmly in their grasp, an intellectual spokesman of this group, Norman Podhoretz, wrote in *Commentary* in September 2002, that any number of regimes needed to be overthrown. Those candidates who could benefit from American tutelage should not be limited to the three mentioned as the Axis of Evil (North Korea, Iran and Iraq), but should include "Syria and Lebanon and Libya, as well as 'friends' of America like the Saudi royal family and Egypt's Hosni Mubarak, along with the Palestinian Authority, whether headed by Arafat of one of his henchmen."[5]

The second leg of the troika that is a barrier to peace between Palestinians and Israelis is the Christian Right, sometimes known as the Evangelicals or Christian Zionists. What makes them unique is their belief that the Old and New Testaments are the literal words of God. As literalists, they can be compared to Muslim Fundamentalists, in the sense that both do not believe that their divine books were *inspired* by God and written by men, but that the Qur'an and the Bible are the exact words of God.

The Evangelical movement was born in nineteenth century England, and its rise is chronicled in Fuad Shaban's chapter. What is important for us is to understand that prior to the Protestant Reformation, the official, Augustinian, view of the Bible was not so rigorous. Especially with the rise of *la recherche de la vérité,* the Roman Catholic Church was willing to accept that many of the stories of the Bible were apocryphal, not real. For example, as science advanced, intellectuals no longer believed that the age of the Earth could be determined by adding up the ages of the prophets. Jerusalem and Zion had two locations, a corporal one and a spiritual one. It was the latter that was most important for Christians to achieve.[6]

Nonetheless, the Protestant Reformation also brought unexpected changes to the religious marketplace. Martin Luther's translation of the Bible into the German vernacular popularized religion as literacy spread through the European continent. People became more free to interpret the Bible according to their own needs. As a result, and over time, many whom we now call Christian Zionists began to view the Old Testament as a veritable history text and as a result to take a greater interest in ancient Israel and the Jewish people.[7]

Today, the literalist interpretation of the Bible is mainstream American. What was once a relatively small movement in American Christianity now dominates both the religious and political discourse. The names Billy Graham, Jerry Falwell, and Pat Robertson are commonly recognized. They and their followers argue that a close relationship between Israel, the world's Jews, and the Christian Right is necessary for the fulfillment of Biblical prophecy—thus the term Christian Zionists.

An alliance denotes, at the very least, a bilateral position in which one gives support and the other returns that support or at least accepts to be supported. However, this twenty-first century alliance was not always welcomed by American Jews. Because of the Christian Right's uncompromising view of how history will unfold, American Jews and supporters of Israel were early on reluctant to accept a Christian alliance. In 1994 the

Anti-Defamation League (ADL) of Bnai Brith published a report titled, "The Religious Right: The Assault on Tolerance and Pluralism in America." In it, the ADL argued that because of their bigotry and desire to convert Jews, the Christian Right and American Jews were on a collision course.

Perhaps as Israel became more isolated in the 1980s and 1990s, especially in Europe, and the Palestinian cause more popular, this wariness on the part of Israel's supporters largely disappeared. Nowhere is this one-hundred-and-eighty degree turn more apparent than within the ADL itself. In 2002, the ADL sponsored an ad which featured Ralph Reed, a leading Christian Zionist, former director of the Christian Coalition and the head of the Republican Party in Georgia. Since "Israel" is where Jesus lived and preached, he argued, there must be a close tie between Christianity and the modern Jewish state.[8] Though as stunning as the ADL's turnaround appears, we should note that at least for the last quarter century, Israel has courted Christian Zionists. In 1978 Falwell traveled to Israel at the latter's expense, a trip he replicated the following year. In 1980 in New York City, then Prime Minister Menachem Begin bestowed the Vladimir Jabotinsky Award on Falwell for his unwavering support of the Jewish state. Israel's consuls throughout the United States routinely thank fundamentalist Christians for their support of Israel.

Besides the fact that Jesus lived and preached in the Holy Land, what is there in the Christian Right's belief system that engenders such blind devotion to Israel? The best explanation for this phenomenon remains Grace Halsell's *Prophecy and Politics*. Her book is based on interviews and observations gained by joining two of Falwell's Holy Land tours. According to the theme of the tours, the world will soon end in a fiery cataclysm. Consistent with this world-view, there will shortly be the prophesied battle of Armageddon in which nuclear weapons will destroy life on Earth and there will be rivers of blood. Born-again Christians will be saved, but all others will perish. In order to hasten this cataclysm, which will proceed the second coming of Christ, Jews must be gathered in Israel. And they should claim all of the territory allegedly promised to them in Genesis, from the Nile to the Euphrates. No compromise is possible because this is what God has promised.[9]

Thus, those who support aiding Israel at all costs, for example former House Majority Leader Tom DeLay, while denying any right accruing to the Palestinians, are not doing it from a love of Jews. Nor do they wish peace in the Middle East, but just the opposite: The expansion of Israel to its Biblically ordained borders will hasten the violent end of the world and the return of Christ. Of course what is left unsaid in this scenario is that the Jews living in Israel will need to be converted to Christianity in order to be lifted to Heaven. What of those Jews who do not convert? And those Christians who are not born again? And the world's Buddhists, Muslims, Hindus, Shintoists, Zoroastrians, and whatever? As explained by John Walvoord, a professor at the Southwestern School of Bible in Dallas, Texas, "God does not look on all His children in the same manner. God has one plan for the born-again Christians, and a different one for everyone else."[10]

In Halsell's book, she interviews someone named Owen. According to his vision, it will be necessary to wage a nuclear war against the forces of evil, and also someone will have to blow up the Aqsa Mosque and the Dome of the Rock on the Muslim's Noble Sanctuary.[11] The Temple Mount, as the Sanctuary is known to Christians and Jews, must be cleared so that a Third Temple can be constructed. In the Evangelical Christian viewpoint, the Third Temple is one of three requirements for Jesus' return to Earth; along with the restoration of Israel and Jerusalem must be a Jewish city.[12] Therefor compromise is unacceptable.

There is a group called the Christians' Israel Public Action Committee. It lobbies Congress to oppose the Road Map. Founded over a decade ago, it pushes a fundamentalist agenda, or to use its own terms:

> CIPAC lobbies on Capitol Hill every day. We work with the Senate and the House of Representatives, and with officials in the executive branch, as well. Then we communicate the information that we learn to the grassroots, and Christians from across America contact their elected Senators and Representatives. This way, we have an impact for solid policies that support Israel on biblical grounds.[13]

Among those who adhere closely to its message are Congressmen DeLay and Inhofe.

The result of this growing Christian Zionist influence has been a major change in American foreign policy since 2001. George W. Bush, as a born-again Christian who once declared that only those who accept Jesus as their Savior go to heaven, has adhered almost literally to the Christian Zionist position. One only needs to be reminded of the Bush Administration's support of Ariel Sharon and his policies that have included, for example, "extra-judicial assassinations," building of the "Security Wall" in the West

Bank, and the isolation and non-recognition of Yasser Arafat or his prime ministers. As expounded by the *Wall Street Journal,* the evangelical position more than any other factor explains the Administration's position in which the Palestinian Authority is a pariah, and Sharon is presented as a "man of peace."[14]

Rabbi Yechiel Eckstein, founder of "Stand for Israel" and co-chair of the International Fellowship of Christians and Jews put the Christian Zionist support for Israel and how it operates succinctly: "When you have a situation, for example, where someone in Washington is pressuring the prime minister of Israel to hold back in the fight against terrorism, then that's where we press the button and mobilize the troops. We will provide them with a tangible and meaningful way to do something."[15] In a full-page advertisement in the *Washington Post,* Stand for Israel wrote: "For decades, Jews have viewed Christians with a mixture of suspicion and fear. Some have even accused them of being intolerant or dangerous. But the crisis facing Israel has demonstrated yet again the simple truth that evangelical Christians are among the strongest supporters of Israel in the world today."[16]

There has been some tension between the Christian Right and the Bush administration, especially when Bush Jr. introduced his Road Map on 25 June 2002. In this major policy speech, the president called for the creation of a Palestinian state.

The final borders, the capital and other aspects of this state's sovereignty will be negotiated between the parties, as part of a final settlement... Israel needs to withdraw fully to positions they held prior to September 28, 2000, and consistent with the recommendations of the Mitchell Committee, Israeli settlement activity in the occupied territories must stop.[17]

Pat Robertson responded:

...if the United States takes a role in ripping half of Jerusalem away from Israel and giving it to Yasser Arafat and a group of terrorists, we are going to see the wrath of God fall on this nation that will make a tornado look like a Sunday school picnic... If we ally ourselves with the enemies of Israel, we will be standing against God Almighty. And that's a place I don't want to be.[18]

The third leg of those whom we may call the peace obstructionists are the American Neoconservatives. What motivates them is a belief in the ability of American power to shape the world. A second, equally important motivation is their support of Israel. In these views, they are sharply at odds with traditional conservatives like Brent Scowcroft, David Eagleburger, James Baker, and Pat Buchanan who preferred to deal with rulers as they were instead of provoking regime change, and discounted the view that two nations always had the same interests.[19] In the Neoconservative view establishing a new Middle East with countries friendly toward Israel involved, first, the elimination of Saddam Hussein. Taking out a principal supporter of the Palestinians would make it easier for Israel to establish peace on its own terms without the need to negotiate or compromise over the borders of the state. Further, in the Neoconservative analysis moving first against the Baath Party in Iraq, unable to defend itself after twelve years of disastrous sanctions, would be an easy victory and send shock waves throughout the remainder of the Arab world. What would result, in this vision, would be a pro-American, pro-Israel Middle East. Avi Shlaim, the Israeli academic at Oxford, responded:

> This is one of the great contradictions in the neocon outlook on the Middle East: the belief that democracy would lead to pro-Western and pro-Israeli governments in the Arab world. In fact the reverse is true. The Arab ruling elites are much more pro-American in their attitude to Israel than the Arab street. The rulers are better informed and more pragmatic. The Arabs and the wider Muslim world are bitterly hostile to Israel because of the oppression of the Palestinians; therefore this is a misconception of the neoconservatives, that the Arab democracies would be friendlier toward the West and Israel.[20]

Even mentioning this third leg of the troika opens up oneself to the charge of anti-Semitism, because most of the identifiable Neoconservatives are American Jews.[21] So it is best when discussing their political attachments to use an Israeli source: Ari Shavit of *Haaretz* wrote, "In the course of the past year [2003], a new belief has emerged in the town [of Washington]...disseminated by a small group of 25 or 30 neoconservatives, almost all of them Jewish, almost all of them intellectuals (a partial list: Richard Perle, Paul Wolfowitz, Douglas Feith, William Kristol, Eliot Abrams, Charles Krauthammer), people who are mutual friends and cultivate one another and are convinced that political ideas are a major driving force of history."[22]

Irving Kristol is perhaps the godfather of the Neoconservative movement operating as the editor of the pro-Israeli journal, *The Weekly Standard*. His son, William, carries on the Neoconservative banner as a journalist and editor of the same paper. Irving's best known protégé is Richard Perle who served in the Reagan Administration and now writes extensively about the Middle East and its evils. His Neoconservative colleague is Paul Wolfowitz—the two were students together at the University of Chicago. Wolfowitz was Deputy Secretary of Defense under Donald Rumsfeld. Perle mentored Douglas J. Feith who was an undersecretary in the Department of Defense, and generally regarded as the intellectual architect of the invasion of Iraq.

Others in the Neoconservative movement include Richard Pipes who battled the "Evil Empire" for Ronald Reagan and Pipes' son Daniel who now fights a new evil, Islam. The younger Pipes sees Muslims in America as fifth columnists, and thus advocates their surveillance, and includes Arab-Americans in the same category of suspicion. When confronted by Japanese-Americans about the notion of profiling based on ethnicity, and asked what he thought of the internment of Japanese-Americans, he stated that it was justifiable.[23] Also to be mentioned in the group is David Wurmser. He is Perle's friend and political ally. Perle wrote the introduction to Wurmser's book *Tyranny's Ally: America's Failure to Defeat Saddam Hussein.*

When the Oslo Declaration of Principles was signed on the White House lawn in September 1993, featuring the famous handshake between Yitzhak Rabin and Yasser Arafat, the Neoconservatives were in the forefront of those who opposed a negotiated peace. Despite the fact that in Oslo, Arafat agreed to the loss of seventy-eight percent of historic Palestine to the Israelis, Rightwing Israelis like Ariel Sharon and Benjamin Netanyahu, opposed the settlement and sought to scuttle it. In this endeavor they were aided by the Neoconservatives. Wurmser co-authored with Perle and Feith a 1996 paper titled, "A Clean Break: A New Strategy for Securing the Realm." The essay was written for incoming Israeli Prime Minister Binyamin Netanyahu who was about to embark on his first official trip to the United States. The article suggested ways in which the new prime minister could ingratiate himself with House Speaker Newt Gingrich by, for example, privatizing or selling-off public holdings. However, its most important parts were recommendations that would scuttle Oslo and end the process of Israel trading "land for peace." Rather the article urged the initiating of a policy of hot pursuit against Palestinians, and their "uncondi-tional acceptance...of our rights, *especially* in their territorial dimension."

The article called on Israel to form a new alliance with Turkey and Jordan, to oust Saddam Hussein, "an important Israeli strategic objective," and resurrect the failed Hashemite monarchy in Iraq. After this was achieved, Syria would become the focus of Israeli wrath with the aim of bringing Damascus to heal and lessening its influence in Lebanon by using "Israeli proxy forces" [Phalangists?] based in Lebanon and "striking Syrian military targets in Lebanon, and should that prove insufficient, striking at select targets in Syria proper."[24]

When Netanyahu did not entirely abandon Oslo, as the Neocon-servatives wished, Feith in 1997 wrote a second piece titled "A Strategy for Israel." In it, Feith argued that "land for peace" was not a solution to the Palestinian conflict, and in fact made Israel weaker. Oslo had given the Palestinians too much hope and no reason to reform Therefore the only solution was to abandon Oslo and reoccupy the West Bank and Gaza. The price in human life would be high but was necessary because of the toxic Oslo Accord.

Though the Neoconservatives were in the political wilderness in the 1990s, they came dramatically to power in November 2000 when Dick Cheney was named head of the transition team for President-elect Bush Jr. Cheney discovered that he was the best candidate for vice president. Given this unexpected *entree* to the highest levels of the U.S. government, prominent Neoconservatives quickly joined Cheney; for example, Wolfo-witz was designated as deputy Secretary of Defense, and Feith as undersec-retary for policy, also in the Department of Defense.

The war with Iraq, as the first step in remaking the Middle East, now moved from the realm of fantasy to that of reality. Though Netanyahu fell from grace in Israel, and there was a short interregnum with Ehud Barak and a failed attempt to revive Oslo in 2000, those opposed to a negotiated peace were buoyed by Ariel Sharon's rehabilitation and election to the prime ministership. The Likud Party was in control, not interested in a negotiated settlement, and all three legs of the American tripod were now firmly locked on target: The American Imperialists' dream of imposing American hegemony on the world, beginning in the Middle East, and accessing oil at the same time; the Christian Zionists under the protection of American arms within reach of the violent Rapture of which they dreamed; and the Neoconservatives able to secure the Israeli realm without having to worry about mollifying the Palestinians or any Arabs. The zeal with which the Neoconservatives, in particular, advanced their pro-Israeli agenda led to a split within the conservative ranks. Though rarely articulated in polite circles, the issue was the propriety of a group of largely American Jews pushing through a pro-Israeli policy disguised as an American one. Pat Buchanan wondered about those with "a passionate attachment" to a country not their own.[25]

Buchanan quotes Harvard Professor Stanley Hoffman:

> ...there is a loose collection of friends of Israel, who believe in the identity of interests between the Jewish state and the United States. ... These analysts look on foreign policy through the lens of one dominant concern: Is it good or bad for Israel? Since that nation's founding in 1948, these thinkers have never been in very good odor at the State Department, but now they are well ensconced in the Pentagon, around such strategists as Paul Wolfowitz, Richard Perle and Douglas Feith.[26]

Echoing Buchanan was a 2003 article in the *Washington Post.* In it, Robert Kaiser quoted a senior U.S. official as saying, "the Likudniks are really in charge now." The article went on to name Richard Perle, Douglas J. Feith, Elliott Abrams and David Wurmser as members of a pro-Israel network inside the administration. Noting that Ariel Sharon repeatedly claimed a pecial closeness to the Bush Administration, Kaiser wrote, "for the first time, a U.S. administration and a Likud government in Israel are pursuing nearly identical policies." [27]

In assessing the barriers to peace and reconciliation in the Palestinian-Israeli conflict, it is often too easy to blame outsiders: The British, the U.S. government, the Christian Right, the Neoconservatives, and so on. What of the principles—specifically those on the Israeli and Palestinian sides who have opposed a negotiated settlement?

The recent political history of Israel has been dominated by Ariel Sharon. Though one may credit Shimon Peres and Yitshak Rabin for attempting to bring about a negotiated settlement to the conflict, it has been Sharon, virtually alone (with the aid of Rabin's assassin), who has derailed the peace process. Netanyahu and Barak held office for too short a period to make a difference. It has been Ariel Sharon, capped by his election in February 2001, that has defined the Middle East peace process.

Known as "the Bulldozer" he has used real ones to tear apart the Middle East for the last fifty years. A list of his exploits is stunning. Some of the highlights: commander of Unit 101, a clandestine unit of the Israel

Defense forces, in 1953 it attacked El Bureig refugee camp in Gaza. Grenades were thrown into refugee huts and as people fled they were attacked with automatic weapons. Later the same year, forces under his command attacked the Jordanian village of Qibya, where forty-five homes were destroyed and sixty-nine civilians killed. In the summer of 1971, troops under Sharon's command blow up 2,000 homes leaving 16,000 people homeless.

As Menachem Begin's Minister of Agriculture between 1977 and 1981, and later as Minister of Housing in the 1990s, he became known as the father of the settlement movement for allowing the building of numerous illegal outposts in the West Bank.

Most notorious was the attack in 1982 on the Sabra and Shatilla refugee campus outside Beirut when Sharon was Defense Minister. After the Lebanon war, the Israeli Kahan commission, named after Yitzhak Kahan, head of Israel's Supreme Court, released its findings about the attacks and found Sharon indirectly responsible for the slaughter. Similar to the Indian fighter, General George Crook, who "pacified" the Apache and defeated Geronimo after the American Civil War, Sharon is an Arab fighter. In his view, the Palestinians are ignorant, must be defeated and put on the equivalent of reservations. One Israeli has called Sharon's actions "politicide" and defined it as the process by which the Palestinian people would cease to exist as a legitimate social, political, and economic entity.[28]

As a member of the Knesset, Sharon voted no for peace with Egypt, no against the withdrawal of Israeli troops from Lebanon, was against the Madrid Conference, and voted no on the Oslo Accords.

Perhaps worried about his place in history, since coming to power in 2001 he has tried to portray himself as a statesman, not necessarily the old bulldozer. Bush Jr. called him "a man of peace." Arguably his most lasting legacy as prime minister has been the building of the "Security [Apartheid?] Wall" ostensibly to separate the West Bank from Israel, and thereby make terrorism more difficult. His unilateral call for an Israeli withdrawal from Gaza lost him as much support as the building of the Wall had garnered. The abandonment of settlements [colonies] in Gaza caught the Diaspora off guard. For decades, Sharon had been known as the greatest supporter of settlements, and had argued that none should ever be abandoned. Literally millions of dollars had been donated by overseas Zionists to support the building of new settlements and the "thickening" of old. In 2005, Sharon was viewed as a traitor by many Israeli supporters.

But seen as a bit of *real politik*, Sharon's moves made excellent sense. The Gaza Strip is one of the world's poorest territories. It is teeming with Israeli enemies. Why not cut loose and focus one's attention on the more important West Bank? Though some see in his move to disengage from Gaza, a leopard who has changed his spots,[29] it is no coincidence that as Sharon removes himself from Gaza, he issues building permits that will complete the encirclement of Jerusalem and enable the Likud government to implement a modified version of the "Sharon Plan" for the West Bank.[30] The 1992 Plan came into being in response to the Oslo Agreement. At that time, the Israeli establishment put forward several different views of what a final settlement would look like between the Palestinians and Israelis. According to the Sharon version, two-thirds of the West Bank would become part of Israel, leaving only Arab villages and towns in Palestinian control. Sharon's vision would result in what has been called the Bantustanization of the Palestinian nation.[31] Opposition to the unilateral departure of Israel from Gaza, voiced by Brent Scowcroft and Edward Said, among others, sees the withdrawal as freeing the Likud government to concentrate its attention on the unfinished business of the West Bank and the implementation of the Sharon Plan.

According to the Oslo Agreement and the subsequent Declaration of Principles, Israel was to redeploy not withdraw from the West Bank, except for Jericho. The issues of Jerusalem, borders, sovereignty, settlements and the return of the refugees were to be negotiated later. From the Israeli point of view, Why not preempt all of these issues by implementing a unilateral *fait accompli.* By annexing large parts of West Bank, without those portions with large Arab populations, Israel could proclaim that the longest foreign occupation of any territory in the twentieth century had come to an end. Israel might never see another conjunction of opportunity as that which it now has with Bush Jr. firmly under Sharon's spell and the world preoccupied with the Iraq war.

One cannot end an essay by castigating Ariel Sharon and not mentioning Yasir Arafat. As one can imagine, there are at least three major schools of thought on the former Palestinian leader. One holds that even though he failed to bring about an independent Palestinian state, he should be remembered for raising the world consciousness concerning their cause.

In the eyes of his people, Arafat's enduring legacy is that he firmly implanted the Palestinian issue at the top of the international political agenda and transferred the axis of their struggle from the diaspora to the homeland. [32]

William Safire, the now-retired columnist of the *New York Times*, and Likud's spokesman in the West, had a different view of the deceased Arafat:

> Israelis should remember Arafat's one "good deed": four years ago [2000], a soon-to-be ousted Israeli prime minister and a Nobel-hungry U.S. president made the Palestinian Authority an incredibly generous and dangerous offer: dividing Jerusalem, handing over almost all of the West Bank, and even partially establishing a "right of return" for some Palestinians who fled an Arab invasion of the new Jewish state a half-century ago.
>
> Arafat's "good deed" was to reject this sweeping offer and to launch another wave of suicidal homicide. In a macabre diplomatic sense, his refusal to take "yes" for an answer was a lucky thing for Israel's image: if those huge concessions had later been presented to Israelis in a promised referendum, Jewish voters would surely have turned down the Clinton-brokered deal. Proof of that was in the avalanche that then ousted the desperate Ehud Barak and elected the determined Ariel Sharon.[33]

The third view holds that Arafat compromised what was once a superior moral position in order to stay in favor with one or another U.S. Administration or the European powers. These powers used Arafat to further their own Middle East agendas, and when they achieved their ends, they jettisoned him: "Yasir Arafat and his small coterie of supporters can furnish little resistance to the Israeli-American juggernaut…"[34]

If Arafat is to be condemned because he was used, what this author cannot understand is why did Arafat not understand that he was being used? Put another way, If the Israeli public was going to reject the 2000 Barak offer, why did Arafat not accept it and let Israel face the blame for a failed peace process? One is reminded of Abba Eban's famous dictum that the Palestinians never missed a chance to miss a chance. I would be even more harsh: In the Arab-Israeli conflict, the Palestinians and Arabs have always been one war or one event behind. What was unacceptable before a war becomes the goal after the war. In 1947, partition was unacceptable. After 1948, it became the goal. Before 1967, it was the rejection of the state of Israel; after 1967 it became recognition of the Jewish state if it would withdraw to its pre-June '67 borders. Before 2000 it was a demand for return, Jerusalem and restoring the pre-1967 borders. In 2004, the demand for return and Jerusalem have disappeared from the political discussion. Israel's security fence has once again imposed new realities. Hanan al-Ashrawi admits the validity of this view of Arab failings when she comments that it was a mistake not to accept the Partition Resolution of 1947.

Granted that it has become increasingly difficult to compromise as each side demonizes the other, and introduced God as a major player. With Bush Junior talking to a "higher Father," Shas saying that God gave the Holy Land to the Jewish people, and Hamas saying Palestine was promised to the Muslims as a *waqf*, there is less chance for compromise where everyone claims God is on his side. In the present climate, to compromise is to go against God's specific injunction.

But compromise and the establishment of a Palestinian state on whatever land can be garnered is, in today's climate, not a failure but finally a small victory. From a small victory, larger gains can accrue. Supporters of Palestinian statehood should consider abandoning the fear that the most recent agreement is the last agreement, since it has prevented the Palestinians, their supporters, and their leaders from taking small steps toward larger goals. We should remember that Chaim Weizmann said he would take a Jewish state the size of a tablecloth as a beginning. If the Palestinians, and we who support their call for statehood, would adopt this strategy, perhaps this would lead eventually to the one-state solution envisioned by Glenn Perry in his chapter. Or ultimately, may one dare to say, to a Greater Syria.

Notes

1. There is an entire industry attempting to tarnish reputations by charging that those who are anti-Israeli are without exception anti-Semitic. See Alexander Cockburn and Jeffrey St. Clair's most recent effort to diagnose the issue: *The Politics of Anti-Semitism.* Another important chronicler is Norman G. Finkelstein. See his *The Holocaust Industry*, Second Edition, p. 33 *passem.* At the same time, anti-Arab diatribes are often accepted without question— witness Alan Dorshowitz's mythological tale of good versus evil in *The Case for Israel.*
2. This can be a dangerous analogy to make: witness the Israeli government's angry reaction when Justice Minister Yosef (Tommy) Lapid said that a picture of a Palestinian woman sifting through the rubble of her home after the bulldozing of the Rafah refugee camp in Gaza reminded him of his grandmother during the Holocaust. *Jerusalem Post,* 24 May 2004.

3. Avi Shlaim, an Israeli academic at Oxford, calls the American Imperialists, the Nationalist Neocons. See the web version of *The Nation*, 28 June 2004, where the web-only interview with Shlaim is published.
4. Sunday Magazine, *New York Times,* 17 October 2004.
5. *Commentary*, September 2002, page 28.
6. "Zion shall be redeemed with justice and those that return to her with righteousness." (Isaiah 1:27). This notion of a divine Jerusalem is also reflected in the Talmud where Jewish worshippers are warned that Jerusalem will not be gained by climbing its walls.
7. For a more detailed account of the transformation over time of the Bible amongst Evangelicals, please see Allan C. Brownfeld's article, "Strange Bedfellows: The Jewish Establishment and the Christian Right," *Washington Report on Middle East Affairs,* August 2002, pp. 71-72. I am indebted to Brownfeld, Editor of *Issues*, the quarterly journal of the American Council for Judaism, for many of the ideas that are found in this article.
8. *New York Times*, 2 May 2002.
9. James M. Inhofe, Republican of Oklahoma on the Senate floor: "I believe very strongly that we should support Israel—because God said so—look it up in the Book of Genesis. This is not a political battle at all. It is a contest over whether or not the word of God is true." His entire outlook on this issue is contained in the *Congressional Record.* 4 March 2002, pp. S1427-1430.
10. Brownfeld, op cit
11. Halsell, *Prophecy and Politics,* Lawrence Hill Publishers (Westport, Connecticut) pp. 90-95. A group called "Faithful of the Temple Mount" was prevented in 2003 from alying the "cornerstone" of the Third Temple. *London Times,* 9 August 2003. An American who ran for the U.S. Senate in South Carolina, Orly Benny-Davis, is a fervent believer in the need to build the Third Temple, and attended a convention in Jerusalem whose attendees were of the same belief. *Jerusalem Post,* 25 January 2005.
12. This sounds simple enough. But according to some readings of the Old Testament, in order for the Temple to be rebuilt, Jews must be blessed with the ashes of a red heifer (Numbers 19). There is in Israel an organization called the Temple Institute which has a small museum and office in Jerusalem, and is planning to raise some of its male children to be priests in the rebuilt Temple. The Institute is also looking for red heifers. The bizarre tale of cattle, Temple, priests, and Evangelical Christians is told by Lawrence Wright, "Forcing the End," *New Yorker Magazine,* 20 July 1998.
13. From its web page, cipaconline.org.
14. "How Israel Won the Support of the Christian Right," *Wall Street Journal,* 23 May 2002.

15. As quoted in Allan C. Brownfeld, "Strange Bedfellows: The Jewish Establishment and the Christian Right," *Washington Review of Middle East Affairs,* August 2002, p. 71.

16. 11 June 2002.

17. See among others, *New York Times,* 26 June 2002.

18. Quoted at www.patrobertson.com/teaching

19. Scowcroft, in a fit of lese majesty, said that Bush Jr. was "mesmerized" by Ariel Sharon. *Washington Post,* 16 October 2004. Thomas Friedman wrote that, worse, Sharon had Bush Jr. under house arrest. *New York Time,* 5 February 2004.

20. Shlaim, *The Nation,* 28 June 2004, op cit.

21. See the lower left home page of "Stand for Israel" (www.standforisrael.org) which has "Anti-Israel=Anti-Zionism=Anti-Semitism." A thoughtful article on the topic appeared in the weekly international edition of *Haaretz,* 28 January 2005. In that article Eliahu Salpeter writes about signs of anti-Semitism disguised as criticism of Israel; for example, alternating "Jews" and "Israel" in one's writings, indicating that there is no difference between them. He remarks, however, that "when Israel notes that the overwhelming majority of the Jewish people stands behind it, it is creating the equation between itself and the Jews." The attempt to condemn those who criticize Israel as anti-Semites stumbles when one notes that most Jews until 1948 opposed the creation of a Jewish state. Neturei Karta, a small ultra-Orthodox group, still does.

22. *Haaretz,* 2 September 2003.

23. The idea of possible incarceration is ludicrous. Can one imagine a jail cell with Ralph Nader, Muhammad Ali, Doug Flutie, Casey Kassem, Paula Abdul, Michael Debakey, and George Mitchell?

24. The document can be found at: www.israeleconomy.org/strat1.htm

25. The words in quote are taken from George Washington's *Farewell Address* in which he warns his fellow citizens to avoid "a passionate attachment of one nation for another..." *American Daily Advertiser,* 19 September 1796. "So likewise, a passionate attachment of one Nation for another produces a variety of evils. Sympathy for the favourite nation, facilitating the illusion of an imaginary common interest, in cases where no real common interest exists, and infusing into one the enmities of the other, betrays the former into a participation in the quarrels & Wars of the latter, without adequate inducement or justification: It leads also to concessions to the favourite Nation of privileges denied to others, which is apt doubly to injure the Nation making the concessions—by unnecessarily parting with what ought to have been retained—& by exciting jealousy, ill will, and a disposition to retaliate, in the parties from whom equal privileges are withheld: And it gives to ambitious, corrupted, or deluded citizens (who devote themselves to the

favourite Nation) facility to betray, or sacrifice the interests of their own country, without odium, sometimes even with popularity; gilding with the appearances of a virtuous sense of obligation a commendable deference for public opinion, or a laudable zeal for public good, the base or foolish compliances of ambition corruption or infatuation." The complete Address is at: http://gwpapers.virginia.edu/education/life/quest9.html

26. Pat Buchanan, "Whose War," *The American Conservative,* 24 March 2003. The entire article is vintage Pat Buchanan. Charged with anti-Semitism, he fires back, all guns blazing. The article is available on-line at: http://www.amconmag.com/2003/03_24_03/cover.html.

27. 9 February 2003.

28. Baruch Kimmerling, *Politicide: Ariel Sharon's War Against the Palestinians.* Verso Press, London, 2003.

29. Thomas Friedman argues that Sharon is now the leader of a "New Israeli Center." According to Friedman's view, Sharon has realized that Israel cannot indefinitely occupy the West Bank and Gaza without losing its "Jewish majority and democratic character." Therefore, he has determined that for the survival of the Jewish state, the territories must be abandoned. Sharon's opponents, according to Friedman, do not recognize the state's sovereignty over the "Land of Israel," i.e., the state has no right to give away what God has bequeathed to the Jewish people. *New York Times,* 13 July 2005.

30. Published in *Yediot Aharanot,* 7 August 1992.

31. For a more complete discussion of the Sharon Plan, see Elaine C. Hagopian's "Is the Peace Process a Process for Peace?" in Haddad, Talhami and Terry, eds., *The June 1967 War After Three Decades,* pp. 51-78.

32. Majd Al Zeer, Director of the Palestinian Return Centre, London. URL: palestinianrefugee.com. 12 November 2004.

33. *New York Times,* 10 November 2004.

34. Edward Said, *The End of the Peace Process,* (Pantheon Books, New York, 2000), p. xi.

12

IMAGINING PEACE IN THE
MIDDLE EAST

℘℧

Kamel S. Abu Jaber

In imagining peace, we have to make some attempt at defining it. Is it merely the absence of violence? Or does it have some positive components so that people can wish for it and hope for its arrival? This is especially true in the Middle East which, historically speaking, has rarely enjoyed long periods of peace while even those moments when violence was absent, its expectation was enough to keep the people in a state of agitation. Peace, meaning a state of peace of mind where individuals or groups can become free of fear or need, never, from ancient times until the present, visited the area. On the contrary, its people were always alerting themselves to expect the worst.

Responsible for this unstable condition of fear was the ever present real or imagined external threat which, when combined with the mostly abusive and tyrannical states within, made life merely a constant struggle for physical survival.

The sudden arrival of modernity and the Western intrusions and eventual penetration and control either actual or remote by an aggressive and often hostile Western civilization added further violence and instability to the lives of the people. Never having experienced it, most Middle

Easterners, perhaps including even the Israelis, wonder what is peace, who is at peace and what does peace mean or entail?

What determines peace has never been a problem in the hands of the people of the area but subject to an interplay of forces external and internal beyond their reach to control or influence. Such a condition has never been more true than at this present historical moment and, perhaps, will remain so well into the future. Can the fear of the Palestinians or the Jews or the minorities ever be removed and how? Or, to look at it differently, can there be peace without justice?

For peace to break out in the same way that violence breaks out, certain criteria and conditions must prevail. Neither now nor well into the future is it likely that such conditions will be met. The skill divide that separates the North from the South and the economic disparities and exploitation only promise to deepen and widen. The West, from whence relief and hope for a peaceful and better future may be offered, seems to be only interested in keeping the area and its peoples at bay while the governments of the area, with the exception of Israel, continue to stumble and falter in their pursuit of modernization.

The dream of peace has to be defined against the present and the historical background of the area. For this is an area where the lamb has never been able to co-exist with the wolf, and while the West continues in the case of the Arab-Israeli conflict to equate the aggressor with the victim, neither the Arabs nor any of the peoples of the area accept Western premises.

Of course, peace can be imposed for a while, but then only for a while, for one must ask if that is truly peace or merely the containment of violence. The Western double standards in dealing with the area's major problems over the past several decades has only resulted in cooperating with mostly tyrannical regimes in containing violence not resolving problems. In this sense the West has, ironically, come to behave like most Arab, indeed Middle Eastern governments believing that if you ignore a problem long enough it will go away. The problem with this approach ignores the terribly long memory of the peoples of the area. For neither Arab, Jew, Turk, Iranian, Kurd, or the multiplicity of minorities seem to ever forget or indeed forgive. It is here where ideas do not seem to change or indeed develop. And, once an idea is planted and collects adherents, it tends to endure, confining its followers to its tight box of premises. It was after all from the deserts of Sinai, the wild hills of Palestine, and the deserts of Arabia that the three great monotheistic religions grew. Around these, other mysterious offshoots have arisen in fantastic combinations that lie somewhere between myth and reality. Each group has its own symbols to which it clings for dear life and around which its identity revolves. None of the major groups of the area have been trained to compromise when it comes to principles; a statement that is exceedingly curious when all have been traditionally middle men and merchants.

Compounding the inability to compromise are certain cultural factors chief among them is the characteristic of "other" directedness. Religion and ideology not the rational experimental approach are what ultimately determine thought and action. The extreme of such a condition is the attitude that if the facts do not support the prejudice then they can, and in most cases, must be ignored.

Israel

One of the most important factors that will continue to influence the future of the Middle East is the establishment of the state of Israel in 1948. Until the advent of the twentieth century, the Middle East housed four major groups: Arabs, Turks, Iranians, and Kurds. Though the language of these major groups was different they all shared, participated in and lived the civilization of Islam. The mosaic culture of the area with its communal *millet system* also housed a great number of ethnic and religious minorities each living under their own personal code socially, while their political allegiance and loyalty was to the Islamic state in which they lived. The Jews, like the various Christian denominations, the Sunnis, the Shia, the Druze, the Zaidis, the Bahais, etc. were part and parcel of that mosaic.

Modern Zionism not only changed the picture, but tipped the balance in ways that have colored and affected the internal and external politics of every country in the region and promises to do so for the future as well. Between Israel and its Western external supporters on the one hand, and the confused and convoluted attempts at internal socio-economic development on the other, the politics and the economic fortunes or misfortunes of the area will continue to be influenced.

For the Arabs, the Turks, the Iranians, the Kurds, and others in the area, certain major factors have affected their politics and promise to continue to do so well into the future.

In contemplating the future of the area, one must remember that the internal dynamics of the area cannot but be highly influenced by the Western external interference. Today, especially after the collapse of the

Soviet Union, the previous remote control by the West has been replaced by direct military intervention. The American-Israeli strategic alliance has been strengthened with the ascendancy of the right wing control of the neo-conservatives in the United States and the right wing control of the political spectrum of Israel. The move towards the right in both countries has accelerated since the 1967 war, with the American support politically and militarily far exceeding the bounds of maintaining the qualitative military superiority of Israel over the Arabs. Israel today as well as into the future will remain as the regional super-power not only in conventional weaponry but those of mass destruction: nuclear, biological and chemical.

It should be recalled that one of the most important developments in the field of international relations in the last century was the historic reconciliation between Western Christianity and Judaism leading to the great influence of international Zionism on Western nations' politics especially towards the Middle East. From a Western vantage point, all Middle Eastern countries' behavior, whether internal or external, is measured against the yardstick of how they view and behave towards Israel. The historic hostility and hatred of the Jews in the West, which culminated in the barbaric Fascist and Nazi holocaust was transformed within a generation to a strong sympathy and support for Israel and its international depth, the Zionist movement.

This development promises to continue and increase, for the Arabs in particular. It is also true of all other groups in the Middle East: they must understand, and take into account that the Zionist factor in the politics of all Western nations promises not only to be maintained on the high level it enjoys now, but will, no doubt, increase. Partly because of Arab miscalculation and partly because of a right wing Zionist vision, the reconciliation that occurred between Christianity and Judaism in the twentieth century, and which could have paved the way for a tripartite reconciliation between the three great Abrahamic monotheistic religions—Judaism, Christianity, and Islam—never took place. On the contrary while the term Judeo has come to precede that of Christianity, the breach with Islam has widened. From the heart of the capitalist city of Boston, Samuel Huntington spoke with the certitude of Marxist historical determinism about the inevitable clash of civilizations. His theme about "Islam's bloody borders" provided the intellectual fig leaf to the neo-conservatives and their Islamophobic inclinations.

Now that Israel has emerged as the regional superpower, all the major nations and groups in the area must consider their politics while keeping the Israeli factor in mind. This is true not only of the Arabs, but of the Turks, the Iranians and the Kurds as well. Along with oil, Israel and its Zionist depth in the West will continue to influence the future.

The Turks

Indeed it takes a lot of imagination to hope for a condition of peace in the Middle East. For, of all the major regions of the world, this area remains the most troubled, confused, violent and unstable. It is an area that has generated some of the most important ideas in the history of man and once was a beacon of knowledge and a storehouse of civilization for the rest of humanity. Today, and for the past few centuries, its conditions, indeed, its fortunes have changed and it continues to struggle to extricate itself from that condition of transitionality between what it once was and its confused and muddled attempts to modernize and build a better future. Resistance to change remains powerful internally: a resistance that has since 1967 and the collapse of Arab nationalism, Pan Arabism, socialism, and liberalism left the field wide open for a call to hark back to the familiar: Islamism.

The étatic state of Kemalist Turkey is still fiercely holding onto an ever thinning secular ideology that is continually being challenged, indeed eroded by the Anatolian Islamist heartland. The forces trying to pull Turkey away from its history and geography towards the West were forced to share power with the Islamist government of Regib Tayyib Erdughan. The dynamics of the unseen struggle between these two strange bed fellows have not yet resolved themselves promising further developments, perhaps surprises. Complicating Turkey's situation is not only its very close alliance with the West, once more defensible while a threat from the Soviet Union was present, but also its close alliance with the State of Israel. To many Middle Easterners, the Turkish-Israeli relationship is indeed a very strange one.

Turkey after all, whether ruled by secularists or Islamists or any other party, is an Islamic country. The Ottoman Caliph was for centuries the defender of Islam, indeed the personification of the legitimacy of the Islamic system. His banner fluttered over the entire area of the Middle East, with the exception of Iran, dispensing equal injustice to all. That an alliance with the West may be understandable in view of Turkey's modern circumstances, the close relationship with Israel is at best questionable. To most Middle Easterners, Turkey is in the Middle East, part of it, and is indeed, but for Israel, the largest and most powerful country in it. They, like many Europeans, hope that Turkey's attempts to join the European Union will fail and that Turkey will once again resume its role in its natural Middle Eastern milieu and participate in the rebuilding of its future.

Iran

The ongoing struggle over the soul of Iran and its place in the Middle East will no doubt continue to reverberate for a long time into the future. The Islamic Republic established by Ayatullah Khomeini does not seem to be the final answer. Since the advent of the Safavids, Iran too has witnessed several life orientations. The failure of the Shah, while supported by the United States and Israel to extricate Iran from its medievalism, resulted in the establishment of a unique theocratic state unlike any in the contemporary world or in history. Here too this does not seem to be the final answer with forces within Iran already seething to bring about a change. If anything, the election of President Mohammad Khatemi is indicative of the Iranian people's wish for change. And yet this election has not quieted the desire for change; partly due to the fierce Mullah right wing opposition, and partly because Khatemi himself has been too feeble in his reformist efforts.

The internal struggle between the traditionalist Islamists and the modernist reformers will no doubt continue to throw its shadow over the fortunes of Iran leading to the question as to who truly rules Iran: the Supreme Ayatullah Khamanie, or now Mahmoud Ahmadinejad, or the President of the Republic Khatemi?

Complicating Iran's situation, of course, is its nuclear program which has gained the attention of the United States as well as the enmity of Israel which threatens to destroy its nuclear facilities. Iran's support of the Palestinian struggle and of Hizbullah of Lebanon will no doubt continue to be factors in how the United States and Israel deal with it. More importantly, the Anglo-American destruction of Iraq has left Iran as the main Middle East power conceived as an enemy and a potential threat to Israel and other Western interests in the region.

The Kurds

Today, more than ever before, the unresolved Kurdish question promises to become more complicated. The Anglo-American military occupation of Iraq in 2003 not only upset whatever imbalance existed in Iraq itself but opened a regional Pandora's Box of infinite proportions. During World War One, the Kurds, unlike the Arabs, remained loyal to the Ottoman Empire and it was only in the wake of that war that they began seeking autonomy. In fact, the Treaty of Sèvre, which was not implemented, allowed for Kurdish independence from Turkey. In the years and decades of the twentieth century, the Kurdish agitation for a special status never abated. Their uprisings in 1925, 1929, and 1930 were suppressed and soon their question became a pawn to be used by external powers especially between Britain and the Soviet Union.

Spread in various percentages among the populations of Turkey, Iran, Iraq and Syria, their destiny was never in their own hands. During the Second World War, the Soviets supported Kurdish aspirations for autonomy which culminated in the short-lived Republic of Mahakad. In the remaining decades of the twentieth century, the Kurdish question and agitation never subsided. Following the ouster of Iraq from its occupation of Kuwait in 1991, and the practical division of Iraq into its three major regions of the North, Center and the South, corresponding to the three ethnic and sectarian identities of Kurdish, Sunni and Shia, a defacto autonomous Kurdish government was established in the North. Under the supervision of the Untied States, this autonomous region quietly and efficiently set up the needed administrative, security and socio-economic machinery necessary for a modern state. The occupation and subsequent collapse of Iraq in 2003, in spite of Western protestations to the contrary, brought closer the possibility of the creation of an independent Kurdistan sometime in the future.

This awakening of Kurdish nationalism remains a major bone of contention between Turkey, Iran and Syria on the one hand and the Anglo-American covert support and approval of the Kurds on the other. Turkey in particular, which houses the largest percentage of Kurds within its south-eastern borders with Iraq, on several occasions warned of its readiness to go to war not only to prevent an independent Republic of Mahabad, but even a federal system in Iraq that may institutionalize an autonomous region for the Kurds.

The defeat of Iraq will for decades to come continue to be a major cause for regional instability and violence: among its many consequences, the complete security exposure of every Arab country in the Mashreq between Israel, Turkey and Iran, all powerful and all having their own ideas regarding the region and its future.

How the reduction and the marginalization of the Arabs will impact the future is a question that does not seem to greatly worry the Western capitals. In turn, how this will impact on Israel in the long run is yet another question. This entire situation is quite new with perhaps very few observers aware of it, or indeed of its future implications. As far as the center of the Arab Mashreq, major decisions dealing with the course of events, indeed perhaps the destiny of the area, are no longer in the hands of its own peoples. Such decisions are now made elsewhere in Western capitals on one level and in the regional capitals of Ankara, Tehran and Tel Aviv on the other.

Nineteenth century European capitals were once pondering the so-called Jewish question. That question today has been resolved, and now, and it seems well into the future, the question will remain - what to do with the Arabs.

Concluding Remarks

The collapse of the Soviet Union and the emergence of the United States as the only superpower also impacts on the politics and the future of the area. The United States now, in addition to its close alliance with Israel, is physically militarily in the region. It is a neighbor, physically, to every state in the region which is a fact that all countries must take into consideration. Since its establishment in 1948, every group in the area is only too aware of Israel's ability to influence.

The entire area of the Middle East is too important to be left alone and, therefore, the interaction between the internal and the external factors affecting its future are inseparable. Complicating this situation are three important factors: first, the weakness and fragility of the regimes with the exception of Israel; second, the fact that the major decisions dealing with the future destiny of the area are no longer made in its own capitals. These two factors remain more important in light of the third factor, the inability of all these countries to extricate themselves from the morass of their ongoing bewildering and lengthy transition period. Again, Israel is the exception. For the Arabs, the long-running conflict with Israel, and the failure to reach a settlement cast further dark shadows over the picture. No-one can measure the enduring effects of the intractable Arab-Israeli conflict on the socio-economic and political destiny of the area or on their psyche. One of the most devastating byproducts, however, is the impact of the ever present violence on every aspect of their lives. Since 11 September 2001 and the Western war on terror, the people have come to expect violence as well as the possibility of personal abuse everywhere.

Imagining Peace

In imagining peace, one should project oneself a few centuries forward in time and then attempt a look back at the new atmosphere of peace in an area that since the dawn of history has never tasted it. This quantum leap in time is an absolute necessity in describing a possibility promising a new style of life for the peoples of the area. The process of change that will lead to the creation of this condition of positive peace, that is more than the absence of violence, and which some may describe as Utopia, will require several generations of cooperative efforts within the socio-political forces of the region as well as the world at large.

The traditional rhythms of life of individuals, communities and states within the region will have to be dramatically replaced by a new style of life alien to the region and its inhabitants. Peace will come unto the major groups of the area, Arabs, Turks, Iranians, Kurds, and Jews as the result of a slow, careful transformation: The mindsets of each one of these major groups and the many ethnic and sectarian communities will begin to soften as a result of a slow but deliberate erosion of the old exclusivist cultures of the area..

While culture, any culture, has its own attractive features, it, however, binds the body and the soul of the individuals and the communities within an almost iron-clad shroud impossible to escape. The deterioration of the more or less hostile cultures will come as the result of consistent efforts to modernize from within as well as through the penetration of new ideas from without. The once abhorred so-called cultural invasion will at last be seen in its proper perspective as no more than a healthy process of cultural give and take: a rational eclectic process allowing for the survival of the fittest while at the same time enriching diversity.

Fear of change and resistance to it must finally be recognized as not only futile but also harmful. The virus of change first brought to the area in modern times by the Napoleonic invasion and much later enforced by mass media, television, and the internet will finally take route along with the recognition that ideas, especially good ones can never be stopped at the borders of any state or culture and that once they touch any culture they soon become internalized, developing a momentum of their own.

The inner processes of thought of the vast majority of the peoples of the area must change from an "other directed," fatalistic, submissive and generally irrational approach in order to release the human mind from the web of tethers of the patterned traditions of thought and behavior. Change and attempting it in the pursuit of progress will then become an important value replacing the quietist acceptance of one's lot in life unquestioningly. A man-centered culture not only not anathema to spiritual values but in fact a realization of God's scheme for man on this earth will emerge.

Slowly, the different and hitherto separate and exclusivist pieces of the cultural mosaic will begin to overcome their time-honored traditional separateness. The walls of self-enclosure in which each *millet*, community, housed itself must break down and a new atmosphere of neighborliness, physical and mental must be developed. The apprehension, indeed, the fear of each other will be replaced by the mutual discovery of the basic humanity of each other: the dramatic change of these mental attitudes leading to the discovery of new sources of knowledge and the development of a new ethos based on the empirical rational approach that shared experiences and values not only make for social peace but encourage it and also encourage experimentation and innovation.

Mutual hostility that once dissipated great mental and natural energies will be discovered to be the brain child of polluted, contaminated processes of the false logic of each community dehumanizing the others. Thus, Arabs, Turks, Iranians, Kurds, Jews, and others that once shared the same terrain but lived in mentally different time zones will learn to enjoy their new-found mode of positive co-existence. The historical echoes of hatred will recede into the hearts of small die-hard minorities that somehow continue to cling to an ugly vanished world. The unevenness that remains both on the socioeconomic and cultural levels will be on the fringe fighting a losing battle, for the millennial mentality based on competitive struggle will have spent itself.

Religions and ideologies that once got in the way of rational living that harmonizes the spiritual and the secular and that were once the public concern of the states of the area will become the private beliefs of individuals. And the strong even tyrannical systems of governments based mainly on charismatic leaders and their whims, even whimsies, will be replaced by the more stable counter veiling democratic systems based on popularly elected institutions of constitutional decision making processes.

The mosaic groups of the area will come to recognize and accept each other, the theme of unity in diversity, finally emerging. Each subculture will settle down to a dynamic mode of life in the area. Perhaps for the first time in history, the pluralism of the area, based on a more equitable division of labor, social justice, health and educational standards and a rational tempo of life will become cause for beauty and harmony rather than strife. And it is thus that reason and belief in the rational approach; harmonized by the rich cultures already deep-rooted in the area will be at the root of the new Middle East. One of the most important traits of an enduring civilization is the ability to resolve issues and disputes without recourse to violence. Though it may take a long time in developing, after many bloody and tragic clashes, this characteristic will become one of the hallmarks of the new Middle East.

Factors That Will Lead to Peace

It is at this juncture that we need to consider the historical factors that may lead to this historic regional turnaround making peace possible.

Perhaps the most important factor will be the positive atmosphere that has to develop between the two great civilizations of Islam and Judeo-Christianity from their earlier intrinsically hostile demeanors to a gradual and mutual acceptance of the basic premises of each other. The erosion of fundamentalism, xenophobic on the one hand and islamophobic on the other will come with the gradual realization that neither can annihilate the other and that indeed there is beauty in diversity. Of course, pockets of malcontents will remain on the fringe but these will lose not only their luster but also their credibility.

The change of atmospherics and attitudes will come as the result of sustained international efforts spearheaded by the more effective United Nations Organization and its component institutions. These efforts must include the frequent convening of social summits not only of political leaders but of religious and intellectual leaders too. Gradually the resolutions of these summits will be implemented by incorporation into the educational curricula emphasizing the theme that acceptance must replace tolerance. Accepting diversity brings with it a certain peace of mind for both parties in addition to its contributing to the enrichment of both civilizations. For mere tolerance may at best be a compromise with a situation that one really dislikes, like tolerating a bad odor, an ugly sight or a condition that one cannot change.

Such an arduous process of replacing an earlier ethos with another will be a slow process that must be aided by modern technology in mass communication and transportation. The spread of ideas speeded up by an accelerated computerized life will be vital to breaking down the walls of exclusivist nationalisms and ideologies. The realization that a global culture based on humanism need not negate spiritual values but will, in fact, in privatize them, liberate them from use as tools in the hands of governments. Such an atmosphere will provide for the flourishing of a global civilization, housing hundreds of component cultures.

The ascendant Western civilization that once thrived on adversity and competition will benefit from the harmonious tones adopted from certain Middle Eastern philosophies and thoughts. Now that cooperation replaces adversity the redirection of resources from the military to civil developmental efforts will begin to bear fruit. Such redirection will make possible the adoption of regional Marshall Plans for socio-economic and political development. The proper combination of human and natural resources in a rational fashion will eventually replace the politics and economics of despair with those of prosperity and hope.

Hope in the future and strategically planning for its betterment will replace the once grim and fatalistic patterns of life. It is now that everything is possible if only man can place nature in his service as God originally intended.

Middle Eastern emphasis on justice as the supreme value will eventually combine with the Western emphasis on freedom. The combination of freedom and justice will again be the result of sustained efforts by external and internal forces: these efforts making possible the gradual replacement of the hitherto largely tyrannical regimes in the Middle East by a colorful array of participatory systems linking freedom with justice and meritocracy.

A Final Note

Culture, any culture, is indeed a wondrous phenomenon, for once it is imprinted on the psyche and the processes of thought of a people, it becomes that people. It is an accumulated process that eventually makes it impossible for individuals to escape its web. It becomes the more difficult to escape, erode or change if it does not, somehow, develop a capacity for a rational approach to life: future not past oriented. If the ideal remains in the past whence all fundamental truths have been discovered and reside, little or only superficial change can take place. It is thus that the future is turned around so that it can imitate the ideal past, and where the notion arises that there is no need for further independent thought. This conservative, rather than innovating atmosphere, by definition values social peace and stability as superior to freedom of thought and expression. And it is in such circumstances that society declined not because it did not pursue forward looking progress but because it deviated from the pursuit of the ideal perfection of the past. This in part explains not only fatalism but more importantly the emphasis on the patterned ritual and the interplay between myth and reality: myth by definition always looking backward.

In imagining peace we have to consider how and if this largely conservative Middle Eastern culture can live at peace in the modern world, resting as it does on the Western values of rational thought and constant innovation and progress. It was in 1882 that Frederick Nietzsche declared the death of God in Western society which has since then become man centered. These philosophical underpinnings of the oriental and occidental societies will continue, no doubt, to influence the present as well as the future.

Peace needs stability and security not only internally but externally too. Neither of the two civilizations across the Mediterranean seems, at this historical moment, to be able to rise to the occasion.

ABOUT THE CONTRIBUTORS

Kamel Abu Jaber received his Ph.D from Syracuse University. Following an academic career in the United States, he returned to Jordan becoming Minister of National Economy, in 1973, and in 1991 Minister of Foreign Affairs, heading the joint Jordanian-Palestinian delegation to the Madrid Peace Conference. Abu Jaber writes on socio-economic and political developments in Jordan and the Middle East.

Barry Collins is a senior lecturer in the School of Law at the University of East London. He writes on constitutionalism and the Irish peace process. His research draws on contemporary legal and psychoanalytical theory and has been published in journals including Law and Critique, the Penn State Review of International Law and the International Journal for the Semiotics of Law.

Richard Falk is Milbank Professor of International Law Emeritus, Princeton University, and since 2002, Visiting Professor, Global Sudies, University of California, Santa Barbara. He is the Chair of the Nuclear Age Peace Foundation. His most recent books are *The Declining World Order: America's Neo-imperial Foreign Policy*, with Howard Friel; *The Record Of the Paper: How The New York Times Misrepresents American Foreign Policy*, and *The Great Terror War*.

William W. Haddad is Professor and Chair of the Department of History at California State University, Fullerton. For over a decade he was closely associated with *Arab Studies Quarterly*, serving as Editor from 1995-1998. He has published extensively on the Arab-Israeli conflict, and his works have appeared in Arabic and Japanese, as well as in English. His most recent publications are "Jordan's Alliance with Israel" in *Israel, the Hashemites, and the Palestinians* and *Iraq: The Human Cost of History* with Tareq Ismael.

Tareq Y. Ismael is Professor of Political Science at the University of Calgary, Canada, President of the International Centre for Contemporary Middle East Studies at Eastern Mediterranean University, North Cyprus, and the Secretary General of the International Association of Middle Eastern Studies. He is the author and editor of over twenty books on the Middle East, Iraq and international studies, as well as four books on various Communist and leftist movements throughout the Arab world, including a forthcoming volume on the Iraqi Communist Party. His most recent work, with Jacqueline S. Ismael, is *The Communist Movement in the Arab World* (2004).

Jacqueline S. Ismael is Professor of Social Work at the University of Calgary. She has published extensively on Canadian social policy and international social welfare, including *The Canadian Welfare State: Evolution and Transition (1989)* and *International Social Welfare in a Changing World (1996).* She has also written articles and monographs on social change in the Middle East and co-authored a number of works with Tareq Y. Ismael, including *The Communist Movement in Syria and Lebanon (1998), The Iraqi Predicament* (2004).

Dahr Jamail is presently in Iraq reporting accurately on the realities of war for the Iraqi people and U.S. soldiers, something the U.S. media has failed to do. He reports for *The Nation,* the *Guardian* and the *Sunday Herald,* to name a few. His war dispatches have been translated into every major world language. He is also special correspondent for the BBC. Jamail uses his mailing list <http://www.dahrjamailiraq.com/email_list/index.php> to disseminate his dispatches.

Norton Mezvinsky is a professor of history at Central Connecticut State University. He has been honored as a designated University Professor statewide by the Board of Trustees of the Connecticut State University System. He has published numerous books and articles on Judaism, various aspects of the Arab-Israeli conflict and American policy in the Middle East. His most recent book, written in conjunction with the late Israeli scholar,

Israel Shahak, is: *Jewish Fundamentalism in Israel*. He is currently completing a book on Christian Zionism.

Glenn E. Perry is Professor of Political Science at Indiana State University. He is the author of many books, articles, and chapters on Middle Eastern politics and history, including *The Middle East: Fourteen Islamic Centuries*, 3rd ed. (Prentice Hall, 1997) and *The History of Egypt* (Greenwood Histories of the Modern Nations, 2004).

Fuad Sha'ban is Dean of theCollege of Arts and Sciences at the University of Petra, Jordan. Sha'ban received his Ph.D. in English from Duke University, and held many senior academic posts and taught at the Universities of Damascus, Riyadh, Duke,the UAE and Jordan. Shaban has written extensively on English Literature and American Orientalism.

John Strawson works in the area of law and post-colonialism. He teaches international law and Middle East studies at the University of East London where he directs the LLM programs and the Encountering Legal Cultures research group. His publications include: (eds. with Roshan de Silva Wijyeratne) *Tracking the Postcolonial in Law* (2003) and (ed) *Law after Ground Zero* (2002).

Haifa Zangana is an Iraqi who, for political reasons, left in 1975and has lived in London since 1976. As a painter and writer she has participated in various European and American publications and exhibitions, with one-woman shows in London and Iceland. *Through the Vast Halls of Memory*, her biographical novel, was published in 1990; followed by three collections of short stories and two novels. She edited and published *Halabja,* an Iraqi and Arab writers and artists homage to that Kurdish town. Zangana is a contributor to the *Guardian, Al Ahram* weekly and *Al Quds.*

INDEX

A

Abbas, Muhamad on reconstruction of Iraqi medical services, 104

Abbas, Nedhal, poem on tragedy of Iraq war, 81–82

Abood, Sheikh Munthr, 40–41

Abrams, Eliot, 278, 286

Abt Associates and reconstruction of Iraqi medical services, 104

Abu Ghraib Field Hospital, 105–06

Abul Rahman, Dr. Thamiz Aziz on medical supplies in Iraq, 86, 90, 91

Act Together: Women's Action for Iraq, 67, 68

Action Aid on military action in Iraq, 68

Afghanistan, 31, 32, 164–65

Agence Franca-Presse, 86

Ahtisaari, Martti report on destruction of Iraq, 167

Akiva, Rabbi, 181

Alattar, Mara, 66

Albright, Madeleine
  on deaths of Iraqi children as acceptable, 155–56, 168, 176n16
  on effectiveness of U.N. resolutions, 278
  National Democratic Institute (NDI) and, 72

Alexander, Justin on legality of Iraq constitution, 50–51

Ali, Dr. Abdul on U.S. military treatment of Iraqi patients, 95

Against All Enemies, Richard Clarke, 30

Allawi, Iyad, 46, 49

Alliance for a Democratic Iraq (WAFDI), 70, 75

Al-Qaida, 31, 164, 171

American Enterprise Institute, 38, 39–40, 54

American imperialism, 277–78

American Islamic Congress (AIC), 70–71

American Jews alliance with the Christian Right, 279–80

American militarism
  Bush (George W.) Administration and, 22, 25, 26
  globalism and, 24
  historical overview of, 21–22
  indicators of, 22
  mechanisms for continuation of, 22–23
  the Vietnam war and, 22, 23–24

American military bases and Iraq, 53–54

American neoconservatives
  advocating elimination of Saddam Hussein, 283
  Jewishness of, 283
  motivation of, 282–83
  opposition to Oslo Declaration of Principles, 284–85
  Palestine-Israel conflict and, 282–86
  Shlaim, Avi on, 283
  war with Iraq and, 285

American neo-liberalization of Iraq, 43–47
  Bremer, Paul and, 43–44, 45
  its effect on China, 44

J